I AM NOT STUPID

I AM NOT STUPID

Ingram Spark

I

I am not STUPID

Bruce A. Brown, PhD

2

"The best way to predict the future
is to create it"
Abraham Lincoln

3

❧

The old cliche "we don't get to pick our parents" is in many cases the ugly truth. Problem is, we often don't know how bad it is until much later in life. We grow in that world with often the thoughts that where you are and who you are with is normal. When I found out my young life was not normal I wasn't young anymore. I had a choice to either live the verbally abusive life I was to believe normal or to rise above it. The problem with that is not knowing how to soar.

I did soar to heights nobody expected of me. My driving force was vindictive, I wanted to maliciously prove I was not a stupid person and I believe it came with a price. And the reality is I did rise and I did create a means and method for success. And now I am truly bothered that others in similar environments didn't have the opportunities and conviction I had. This is my message to them. I hope my story opens some minds and shows what can happen. And in the same light I need to say my achievement left a life often lonely and often questioning my existence.

Usually when you hear a statement about a person whose mother regularly called him/her "Stupid" there was either a reason or the person was on a one-way trip to really destructive self awareness or a self professing failing mode.

Oh, I was there many times but I still had this insatiable drive to prove her wrong, and it consumed me. Thoughts of suicide, no one would miss me, and all that garbage in your head. I remember visiting Plymouth Rock and telling anybody that could hear me that I never would see the next Anniversary in 2020 because I didn't expect I would be alive.

I didn't go to the Anniversary, we had the Pandemic, but I was alive, the weight my mother put on my mind and shoulders was not heavier than the drive I had to prove her wrong!

Lucky for me, in 1967 I saw this young lady across the dance floor at a bar in Denver, Colorado and I was so attracted to her beautiful blue eyes I had to talk and be with her. That was in October and the following May she became my wife, my love, my partner, and my life saver.

My story is not unique, far from it. I have been with people around the world that never see beyond the place they are. Their dreams, goals and visions rarely go outside the world they live it, and probably some will die in.

My jail key was to not be like my mother. I saw things she did and I said I was going to do the opposite! But like so many, you can wish and never have the means or ability to make those changes. Soon you lose sight of your dreams. The military was my opening.

I could easily hate my mother, she readily opened the door and invited my hatred in. But at the same time hatred was ruling my life and actions. Buddha was an educator, not a God, and he said to know hate you must know love. I didn't have much love.

I guess I thought I would kill myself in some spectacular way, nothing simple for me. But I guess there was that little light out there that beckoned me to discover, so I didn't kill myself. But I also didn't fear death as most people, especially Americans, fear. I have saved nine lives, often putting myself in danger to do so. Why? Guess my lack of fear of death took those barriers away, those "possibility of injury or death" scenarios from my consideration. Ironically, I did some small time motorcycle racing. I was very good at it but never won a major event because I could never pass that point of no return.

One very good friend said I was a tricky person to be around. Things just happened around me, so not a good thing. Yet, when things happened I was there to save the day, a good thing.

At a time when the military recruiter said never to volunteer, I volunteered. I wanted to see what was behind that curtain and then see if I could make it better, all the time saying I am not stupid!

So it doesn't come off as I was a useless kid being called stupid and then blossomed into a cape wearing super hero, there is not a day I don't feel pain. I covered up the worst visible scars by growing a mustache and hair style, but could not do the same for those internal scars. There is not a day I am not worried about falling back into the darkness of depression. I take pills nightly to prevent me from remembering my nightmares. All the consequences of stepping forward while others stood there.

It is my hope you, the reader, sees some of the roadblocks you are facing and can see ways to go over, under, or around those roadblocks. It is a common belief men do not ask for directions, I do. I have had three tremendous mentors. I do talk to God. And I live with my savior, my wife.

I love you Peggy.

4

There is only one person I can dedicate this book to. Two years after I graduated High School I was just married and was on the ground in Vietnam. I came home a year later to this woman I hardly knew and I was not the same person I was a year prior. She stuck with me through all my hurt and anger, my PTSD, Clinical Depression, and lasting effects of Agent Orange.

Peggy, I owe my life and ability to love to you.

Chapter 1

In the beginning

Mom graduated early from High School in Portland, Maine and traveled to Boston to attend Bryant and Stratton Business School on State Street. Her name was Lucille Mae Jones.

Dad was born in Glasgow, Scotland and immigrated to the US, landing in Boston at the old age of 13 1/2 months. His name was Gavin (NMI) Brown. That becomes very important later that he had No Middle Initial and was born in Glasgow.

Mom was 17, Dad 16 when they first met. There isn't a lot to reveal about their relationship then but they were apparently close as they corresponded throughout the years and when World War II started Dad enlisted in the Army Air Corp and trained in Florida and Illinois as a Radar Navigator to be assigned aboard B-17 Bombers.

Although Dad said that during a night involving substantial amounts of alcohol while in Florida, he woke up next to a "Big Busted Blonde" that he had married the night before! I don't think he even remembered her name and the marriage was dissolved.

Dad was now corresponding with both my mother and another woman, Henrietta. It was 20 years after Mom and Dad had met. Dad saw the terrors of the War and was suffering much what we now call Post Traumatic Stress Disorder (PTSD) and to simplify things for him he decided to marry which lady met him on the docks as he came off the Troop Ship.

My mother was there, Henrietta was waiting for him in her parlor. Mom and Dad got married. Both liked to drink and if it was anything like my sister and I grew up into, the relationship was an alcohol assisted volatile relationship.

Dad, then 36, told Mom before they married that he knew he had problems from the War and didn't want to have children. Mom agreed, however, she had my sister at age 38 and me at 39. Like her mother, my sister had dark hair and dark eyes whereas I was a spitting image of my father, light skin and hair. The Scotch bloodline came through hard on me.

And it started early. We lived in Roslindale, south of Boston, and Dad worked for John Hancock Insurance. His boss, Joe, and Joe's wife Mary liked to drink a lot, so booze was always there. Yes, I would classify them all as alcoholics.

My mother got my sister a dog, I got nothing. Dad's boss, Joe apparently saw what was happening so when he could he would take me to places like the Franklin Park Zoo. I believe there is where I got my love for animals started.

I was going to a Parochial school, nice little uniforms and all.

At the age of 7 my Grandmother Carrie was living in Union, Maine and was in late stages of Cancer. We packed up and moved to Maine, at least my sister and Mom did, after Dad and I dropped them off we went back to Roslindale and our house down the end of the block and put it up for sale. By now I started seeing the reality I was not a favored child to my mother. Again, not knowing anything different I accepted this as normal.

6

The First Near Death

The house on Meyer Street sat down at the end of the dead end road. The road sloped down off the main road and was next to an undeveloped area. In 1954 we had a terrible hurricane and our house was flooded past the cellar and inches above the first floor. All the undeveloped land behind us and the overflow of some of the sewer systems made the water in our house terrible. It was just my father and me as my mother and sister were still up in Maine.

Something bit me, I felt it, and soon I started swelling, all over. Joe parked up the main street and wadded/swam down, too much alcohol for anything to happen to him, and with Dad in tow, Joe carried me up to his car and we went to the hospital.

I was swelling more and more and the doctors who could see me, they were very busy, could not determine what had bitten me! I got a little amount of meds and then told the swelling had to go down. If we could get the swelling down then I had a better chance of survival and still unknown what the long term effects might be.

By direction of the doctors I ended up on a couch in the house, on my back with cushions raising my arms and legs, hoping the swelling would go down. Thought that was it, dead at age 7.

Mom didn't drive so she and my sister stayed in Maine with me near death in Massachusetts I was already feeling the rejection and hurt, so her lack of action made me basically give up and die where I was on the couch. My father did what he could but it was stressed nothing could be done until the swelling went down.

The swelling slowly went down, doctors still didn't know what caused it. When the house sold we moved up to Maine. While Dad was finishing up, Joe and Mary drove me up to Maine in their Nash.

Joe drove with a box of uncooked hot dogs next to his seat. Mary had magnetic glasses that stuck to the glove compartment open swing down door. She would mix the drinks and keep Joe's full. So for 200 miles Joe drank steady and ate raw hot dogs!

When we got up there, Joe and Mary stayed for a while and while Joe was well into it, drink in hand, he wanted to cross over the barbed wire fence and pet some of the neighbors cows! It was all good until he caught his crotch on the top barb and then realized the fence was electrified! It pulsed every few seconds and you could see Joe spasm when the pulse hit and when it stopped he smiled. Took us a long time to get him off the fence, mostly because the adults were drunk and all of us laughing too loud.

I still have some unexplained illnesses, possibly from the unexplained bite, and exposure to Agent Orange from Vietnam. Can't blame my expended girth on it now. My mother never talked about the swelling incident and I wondered if she cared. I had beat the unknown odds and survived.

I don't know the origin of my learning disability, I was a stutterer. I also had two large teeth in front, normally called "buck" teeth, so between the stuttering and the buck teeth I fit more into the victim role. Many people thought my teeth were cute! It didn't feel cute from my perspective. Later, due to two accidents, I lost all my teeth. So now I was even more reclusive and self pitied. I didn't smile much and I thought I was really stupid and was letting that be my self professing prophesy.

I guess I had suicidal thoughts even at a very young age. Unfortunately I also thought that everyone had those thoughts.

Chapter 2

Welcome to Maine

The first day of school was almost enough for me to take my life! Mom insisted I wear my Parochial uniform to first day of school. I didn't want to but was forced and the word "Stupid" was part of her dialogue to me. I was really starting to see her pattern of use of the word.

If I thought that was bad, hang on. In a farming town where many boys walk from milking cows and right to the schoolhouse, cow shit and all, I show up in blue shorts, white shirt, bowtie and blue jacket with big emblem on the front! It was terrible! Then add the big front teeth and the stuttering!

I was shunned, called "City Boy" and an outcast. Fortunately I found another outcast, a boy my age born with a tiny penis and a mother who incessantly held him, checked his penis and his stools, etc. So he was as pathetic as me, and we hung out together. The two pathetic misfits. I heard "Stupid" often now from the kids along with my mother.

8

Dad left

Dad had gone from a respectable job in Boston to now working in a chicken house in Maine just so we could move there to watch my grandmother die of cancer. I believe he lost a lot of his manhood and was extremely unhappy. They both drank a lot and their fights often resulted in my mother throwing things at my father. The things she threw were mostly her shoes and I was ordered to pick them up and give them back to her. The way she did it and tormented Dad and I with her bare feet scarred me for life, I don't think I can touch anyone's feet, ever.

Her abusive language got worse toward me, not much if any toward my sister. I can't recall what my sister was doing during these fights, maybe in her room so she didn't get involved. I know I was ordered to get everything my mother threw and often when they got drunk I would sneak behind their chairs and drink some from their drinks. I liked the taste.

My Dad went back down to Winchester, Massachusetts to pick up his mother, Mary, and bring her up for a visit. Mary was proper British and besides looking down her nose at everyone in the family but her son, she was outspoken and nasty. She and Mom argued endlessly. I was now just turning 9 years old.

As I said, my sister had dark eyes and hair, but also her hair was very curly, tight curls. She and I looked totally different since I was definitely my father's son, even with the slight red tint to my hair.

During one of their fights, my grandmother told my mother to her face that she knew my sister was not from her son, accusing my mother with having an affair with a Negro! My mother kicked her out of the house and my Dad took her back to Winchester and didn't come back. I was left in the care of my mother and I can say she became the nastiest woman I have ever met! Mind you, she didn't treat my sister the same way.

Hardly a day went by that I wasn't told that I was stupid and was blamed for my Mother's hair being straight and her teeth falling out because of her giving birth to me. My mother took all her anger with my father out on me and I rebelled.

The only thing good happening for me was one of my teachers took me to her house twice a week and we were able to break my stuttering! Simply, the mind thinks 300 times faster than the mouth moves, so the theory that if I could think in my mind what I was going to say before I said it then I could cure myself of stuttering. It worked but didn't slow the use of "stupid" at our house.

I smile. The teacher, Ida Hughes, was a large woman who believed in corporal punishment and many a student was pulled up by an ear and led to the front of the room for the apparent well deserved wooden ruler across the knuckles! She kept a disciplined classroom and no student wanted to get on her bad side. But! I saw the side of her that really cared and saw I needed help. I believe she also knew the unpleasant situation I was in at home and that added to her caring about me. I don't even know if the other teachers knew how caring she was.

9

Not a good boy

And then that day we missed the bus and had to walk home. The school was about a mile from the town center and since the town was very small, so was the Center. We walked to and through the town center, past the Gazebo at the center of what was called the Town Common. A couple minutes later we went down the hill, still another 3 miles to my house. We walked across the bridge over the river and over the next small hill where we heard and soon saw the lone house by the quarry where the three brothers were firing guns.

The brothers, one already a graduate of Reform School, were nasty were bullies. I knew that going by their house would be uncomfortable and we would be harassed.

As we got closer, my friend started crying and moved across to the other side of the road to avoid them. Yes, they were that bad. I kept on walking and since my self esteem was low already, why not face the problem head on. As i got closer, two of the three came out to the road and basically pulled me into their yard. I looked across toward the quarry and on a tree near the end of their property they had hung a crabapple on a string from a protruding limb..

"Hey City Boy! You ever shot a gun before?" I lied. I had played with toy guns and watched Westerns, but never fired a real gun. A rifle was put in my hands and I was told it was already cocked and ready to fire. I was pointed toward the tree and the crabapple and told to shoot the crabapple.

The meanest brother laughed and went to the limb and started the crabapple to swing. I held the gun like I did my toy gun and aimed. I believe I was holding my breath and when the shot rang out I know I closed my eyes.

"God damn, son of a bitch! Holy shit" was said all around me and I felt a slap on my shoulder and back! I opened my eyes and the crabapple, and part of the string was missing! Through their explanative language I realized I had missed the crabapple but not the string it was attached to! I had shot the string holding the crabapple!

Word got around school in a couple days and I was accepted finally! I was no longer the "City Boy" and that was the last time I hung out with my former friend with the tiny penis.

I was also mad all the time, and believed I had a right to be bad and angry. I remember a year earlier going to the store with my mother and sister, my Grandfather had driven us, Mom still never got a driver's license. At the store I was having some stomach problems and knew I had to go to the bathroom. Mom was just standing there with her arm on my sister's shoulder, telling this woman how smart my sister was and some of the things she was doing. I tried to tell my mother I was about ready to mess in my pants and all she would say was for me not to bother her, couldn't I see she was talking to someone! The woman could see I was having problems and she asked my mother who I was? My mother simply responds I was her son and we were pulled out of the store. I never made it to the bathroom and ended up messing in my pants.

We had just moved to a rental property and my mother made a big deal out of my stupidity and the mess I made and in front of her, my sister and grandfather I was forced to strip down naked and step into a big metal tub used for clothes washing. I was the hosed down to clean the mess on me. I was humiliated and demeaned beyond belief and more than a year later I was still angry.

Not only did my sister get treated better but I didn't believe my sister really understood. The school and my mother were the enemy, not my sister, but because of her I had a lot of problems. She was a

"Straight A" student, I had a couple "B" grades. My mother talked about how great my sister was, but didn't go to her events.

I started talking back to my mother and when she took a belt or other object across my ass to discipline me I would not shed a tear but just look up at her, "Do you feel better now?" and it would cause her to beat me even harder. I actually felt like I deserved it and was glad it hurt.

My rebellion took the form of me doing bad things. My neighbor who was a year older, stole a pack of Old Gold Filtered cigarettes from his mother and we snuck out behind the barn to learn how to smoke. There were four of us, me and two brothers who had never smoked before.

I liked the taste and was able to keep from coughing on it, something the others were not able to do. They choked and coughed for a long time and I did neither. I guess I just wanted to prove something. With that, word got around and I again was elevated in social status. I was thought to be cool and started smoking at age 9.

When I was 11 a friend of my mother told her she had seem me smoking! My mother confronted me with fury, "You embarrassed me! If you want to smoke, you smoke in the house and not where you can embarrass me!" "Okay" I said as I pulled out a pack of Camel cigarettes, "Do you want one?" From that day forward I smoked in the house as did many of my friends.

At 11 I had already started working the hay fields and the blueberry fields. I could drive a tractor and was cleaning out chicken houses, possibly the nastiest job there is. I started damaging things when I got angry. One day while riding in the truck from a hay field, the driver, another alcoholic, gave me my first beer, a Pabst Blue Ribbon. Up until then I had snuck some of the booze my mother had but this was my first beer. I liked it and soon found ways to get it often.

I still was active in just about every sport and activity except Student Council, etc. My sister was two years ahead of me and often told her friends unkind things about her little brother. I also felt the school had it in for me. When I decided to do a Science Project for the Science Fair I submitted my topic and Mr. Black, the science teacher, said I could not do it because I would cheat! My sister had done her project on "Reflection" and I was planning on doing mine on "Reflection versus Refraction" but Mr. Black said I would just copy my sister's paper.

I can't remember what made me think about it. I submitted my topic of "Soap Bubbles and the forces that mold them". Both Mr. Black and Mr. Rochon, the principle, said I should do a real science project, anything I would do they didn't think I could do as well as my sister.

Two things happened; I wrote my paper and had a display, and I won first place in the Science Fair! It sure wasn't recognized very much, nor was it said my sister didn't win two years earlier. The biggest thing I got was a nickname from my fellow classmates, "Bubbles"!

I also was driving my grandfather's 1950 Chevy since he had gotten very ill from a hernia operation gone wrong and could not drive himself. If I had been stopped by any police then, they would probably find at least a 6-pack of beer in the trunk.

When I turned 13 I was hanging out with different crowds and often going to parties on one of the many lakes in the area.. During one of these lake parties I was taken advantage of by one of the older girls. I also had some friends who had a summer cottage in Union and their family had a dance studio west of Boston. I learned how to dance from them and often would go to adult places and dance with older women who loved to show me how to dance things like the Old Fashion Waltz. I also drank a lot and got drunk often.

One of those nights I was involved in an incident I actually do not remember. The Sheriff's Patrol brought me home drunk and disorderly that night. The next morning my mother gave me the same speech, telling me she did not want me embarrassing her and if I had to drink, drink in the house! This time I went out to the Chevy and came back in with a 6-pack and said, "Well, it should stay a hell of a lot cooler in here!" and put it in the refrigerator. I think my mother was a little happy, it was hard for her to get alcoholic beverages and I helped supply some. It also meant she had someone to drink with. A few of my friends, or maybe not friends, used to come over and smoke and drink at my house.

An old friend of my mother would show up occasionally, especially after my father left. He used to take my sister and me out fishing for white and yellow perch. One day he invited me to go bear hunting, I had become very good with guns and already had shot deer, rabbit, raccoon, and other game so I said "Yes" immediately. We headed north, his dog with us. Ever since his wife died his dog was always with him.

The small group of us went up to northern Maine and the second day out we came across our first bear. I shot him first, but didn't drop him, so he was lumbering toward us and the second shot from the guy behind me finished him. I got my first bear at age 13! A few months later the guys dog died of apparent old age and he didn't take it well. He committed suicide. That made me think a lot more about my condition, I truly thought about stuff like that whenever I heard my mother calling me "Stupid".

I actually cleaned up my act as I got more involved with sports. I felt many sports were individual efforts and sometimes even with team sports I was always so competitive I felt it was me against everyone else.

IO

Jock and more!

Sports were my savior. I could gain self respect and do something I loved. I was into all school sports, cross-country, track, baseball, basketball. I was the fastest sprinter in the school and placed second in Regionals for cross-country. I was first string basketball. I was pitcher for the baseball team.

I was a volunteer fire fighter where if there was a fire the school would let us trained guys assist the volunteer Fire Department and let us leave the school. I went twice to the Regional Spelling Bee, placing second one time. I was a member of the National Thespian Society and acted in many plays, also directing and staging others. I had many awards.

And then a couple things slowed me down, we were playing a "pick up" baseball game and one of the guys asked if he could join us, but he didn't have a glove. I said the pitcher doesn't need one that often and loaned mine to him. A few minutes later I pitched to home plate and the batter drilled it right back to me and since I didn't have a glove I turned. The ball hit my right knee and damaged it badly. Although I continued to play, I could not pitch anymore so I played mostly left field and still was about the only player who could single throw to home plate from the outfield.

Unfortunately the damaged knee also messed up my track success, but I could still play basketball. I was at my neighbors big driveway where a basketball rim was on the side of the building and we were playing some challenge game. One of the guys tried to run a couple steps up the wall and try to dunk the basketball. He lost balance and fell back! He was waving his arms to catch his balance when his wrist bone struck my mouth hard and knocked out my two big front teeth and a couple more! I no longer had buck teeth and in a couple weeks had a partial plate with new front teeth attached to other teeth by wires.

I joined the Band and soon was second seat playing the trumpet. Now I didn't have buck teeth so I could now play the trumpet. Between work when I wasn't in school and the extra activities I was very busy and felt the doom and gloom lift. I had also loved to cook, I believe out of necessity, and even won First Place for my cookies at the Fair!

The truly sad part is that my mother never attended a single event I was playing or involved with. That made all the accolades I got to be like affirmations that I did something to gain distance from the mother I seemed to hate. I found more things to do to be away from the house as much as possible. I was cooking my own meals.

One time I was in stocking feet in front of the stove and was boiling water to cook something for my sister and me. My sister said something that set me off and we had a fight. She grabbed the boiling water off the stove and dumped it on my feet! Of course the thick wool socks absorbed the water and kept the burn going, so I jumped around trying to keep my feet off the floor as I was struggling to get the socks off and that resulted in moderate burns to my feet and water all the way into my bedroom where I was able to sit on my bed and get my socks off.

When mom got home from the bank or grocery store where she was working then, she saw the mess and the trail of water into my room. I tried to tell her that my sister had thrown boiling water of my feet, she simply told me I had a hell of a mess to clean up! She never worried about my burned feet and she never did anything to my sister beyond that she shouldn't do that. Of course I was stupid for having a pan of water on the stove and starting a fight with my sister.

I also followed my sister's footsteps when I started acting in school plays. I was always a little risky and I auditioned for a stupid part in a play. Hank was a large kid and he got the part of the father that was having problems with his son. I played the son and when Hank said he wished he had a daughter instead of a son, I appeared in a wig and a skirt as his son turned daughter! All I had to do is be the worst daughter, bad enough he wished for his son back. So I entered the next scene as his son again! I got rave reviews for that and my mother never saw it.

I later played the Jailor in the Sir Thomas Moore play "The Common Man". As it was written and the way I played the part, I was the key person in the play. Again, rave reviews and not any effort for my mother to see it. I became a member of the National Thespian Society.

I had a thing with animals. It was as though they knew I would not hurt them so I could hold my ground and they would come to me. There were exceptions, like the time I was pulling some weeds around a rhubarb bush and a garter snake coiled around my arm! I was then officially not a snake enthusiast. Besides the snake, a cow with long horns and a moose you meet in an open blueberry field, there were few animals I didn't like. One day I was sitting on the end of a metal culvert that ran under my neighbors driveway just at the end of our property when my mother came running out of the house yelling at me. I heard a man's voice that basically told her to shut up or she would scare the animal. He had stopped his car and was standing by the open door and looking over the top of the car where he could see me and yell at my mother. I wasn't interested in either of them as I was sitting there petting a skunk! I never got sprayed on but soon the skunk seemed a little bothered and just walked away.

One of the guys had some lake front property his parents didn't mind if we camped out there. He also had Charlie, a raccoon that he had kind of adopted. Charlie would join us at the lake shore when we slept under the stars and if we didn't hang our food from a tree or put it in plastic and stow it inside our sleeping bags, Charlie would feast. He wasn't too friendly with people, more like tolerating them and only a couple of us could pet him. I wake up in the middle of the night with Charlie in my sleeping bag trying to get my food! He normally didn't do that because he was still cautious of people, however, he apparently liked me so he felt comfortable to crawl in my bag with me. I liked Charlie and he liked me. At least he never bit me!

I worked hard, starting very early mornings helping my neighbor with milking cows and after school I would change tires at a local garage or drive a tractor in the hay fields. I even stocked shelves at a local grocery store. And did one of the nastiest jobs in the world, cleaning out chicken houses!

At the garage I learned to change tires and did some non-mechanical work. I had a very trustworthy relationship with the owner, even once he took me and a couple other guys up to the near top of Maine to get a performance engine from a car. He bought a car engine that was still in a car that was located a stone's throw from the Canadian border and we went up to remove the engine and bring it down to Union.

Did I mention the car was as far north as you could go and still be in the continental United States, and it was dead of winter! So cold, the four of us worked off a schedule and diagram. Take the engine bolt, for example. One would dress heavy with the wrench in his gloved hand and go out to turn the bolt a couple turns and then back in before his hands were too cold. He would mark the progress and the next would do the same until the bolt was out. I think it took us three days to remove the engine and put it in the back of his truck. I worked well with him.

One time I had just finished a big truck tire and the truck owner was trying to muscle it up onto his load of high stacked logs. He had parked the truck next to the island separating the highway from the garage. We helped him flop the tire up the front bumper, onto the hood, up the windshield and cab. We were trying to figure how to get it on top the load. An old beat up truck pulled into the garage area and Tiny stepped out! Don't know why they called him "Tiny" because he was the bigger of the three brothers. The smallest brother was all muscle and stood probably 6' 3" and looked up to his little brother!

Tiny saw we had a problem so he asked my boss if he put the tire on top the load, could he get a Coke? I was sent into the office to get the soft drink and came out just as Tiny reached up, placed his huge hands on the center of the truck tire. He gave a big yank and pulled the tire off the roof as though it was light and in a single rocking motion threw to tire up on top the load! He drank his soda, talked a little while, and then drove off. The driver was so grateful, until he walked around and onto the island to get into his truck and found the tire sitting on the island! Tiny had tossed it all the way over! It took the better part of an hour to get it on top.

We did a couple things in Summer. I went to work for a guy who cut, raked and bailed hay. In Maine you didn't need to have a license to drive a John Deere tractor with "tricycle" front wheels. He had a Ford tractor with wide set front tires like a car that I could not legally drive. That job ended when he put the Deere in his lift bed truck to take it to another field. He had been drinking so when he went to move the long arm shifter on the floor, he pulled the release arm instead and dumped the Deere on the pavement going down the road!

I also cleaned chicken houses. Not what you might think, we used dung forks and shovels to dig through all the many feet of chicken shit built up while thousand of chickens roosted and produced eggs. Places it was six feet deep and quite often we had rats the size of small dogs living in the dung. When we got a new member of the crew we would initiate him. When he least expected it, usually while we were riding in the truck at the end of day, we would take a couple of the very rotten eggs we had dug up and grabbed the guys hat and replaced it with the eggs! The slime all through his hair and dripping down on his head smelled the worst! That is why we waited until the end of the day so we wouldn't have to work with that smell around.

In the summer we had blueberry raking. A blueberry rake is a box with multiple prongs protruding out the bottom of the wooden box and a handle mounted on top the box open in the direction of the prongs. You basically grabbed the handle and swung the long prongs through the blueberry bushes so the blueberries would be stripped off the vines and scooped into the box. When the box got full you would pour the blueberries into a large wooden box. Tedious work for $1 an hour.

Then when the blueberry season was over, the farmer would burn the fields. We would use what we called "Indian Tanks" filled with water and by sliding the long nozzle you could send a stream of water quite a distance. We would wear that on our back so we could control the burn. The reason we burned it was after the first year the harvest were smaller and less tasty blueberries so by burning the fields you knew the following year there would be no blueberries and the year after there would be a new growth of top quality berries that sold very well.

I took on more work and on September 23, 1963 I had finished helping burn the blueberry fields so we could get "first growth" the following year. I went home, cleaned up and went with two friends who were in the grade ahead of me to get ice cream at a favorite spot in a city 11 miles away. I was in the center of the front bench seat when it happened . . .

11

Chapter 3

Death's Door Again

8:05 PM, State Route 17 east of South Hope and next to Grassy Pond on our right, posted speed and our speed both 40 mph. There was a slight right curve in the road. Gary at the wheel, me in the center and Harold on the right. I saw it first and yelled. Harold was leaning forward to look around me and talk to Gary. I instinctively took my left arm and across my body as I pushed Harold back and hoped I could lessen the impact to his head with my arm. It didn't.

There, 40 feet in front of the 1955 Ford we were in was a large truck in our lane, dark except the little reflector I has seen and yelled. There was a 1953 Buick with high beams coming east and a deep pond on the right, along with the trees in front of the Pond. Gary managed to get his foot on the brake before we impacted the abandoned truck.

The driver of the truck had been drunk at the time. The truck ran out of gas and he ran the battery down attempting to start it. The truck was carrying a full load of "Pulp" wood, trees cut to four foot lengths and stacked high and fully loaded. He had abandoned the truck in the middle of the lane.

We hit the truck at near 40 mph and as the car stopped, we were thrown forward against the windshield. Lucky for us the Pulp wood toppled off the open back of the truck and onto the windshield as our heads struck it. I say lucky because if our heads had hit and went through the windshield before the wood hit we would have been decapitated.

The first person on the scene was the man I had been working alongside all day while burning blueberry fields. He didn't recognize me.

I remember reacting to someone yelling and something in my throat, but I could not move or say anything. I later found out that the partial plate I had in my mouth following the basketball accident that knocked out my front teeth had been pushed down my throat, along with all but 10 of my teeth! As the Emergency Room doctor was starting to cut a hole in my throat so I could breathe, one of the nurses yelled at him to stop as she saw a piece of plastic in my throat. She pulled out all of the partial plate in one large piece and many smaller pieces.

For the next two weeks I saw people coming and going but I still could not talk or move, I was in a coma. I guess I was in a "transit" state as afterwards I talked to friends and classmates who came to see me and we validated what happened while I was in a comatose state. For example; one friend brought me some car magazines and I recalled another friend take about half of them! He confirmed it a couple months later. I did not tell people I could see them as if I was staring down at them from a window, a foggy window. I thought people would say I was crazy. However, I did talk later to many of the people who came in and their stories of what they did in the room validated that. Mind you, I seemed to be able to see them but could not hear anything. I didn't see either my mother or my sister in my room.

Not saying I was in bad shape, my classmates had a Wake for me, I was supposed to die. Obviously, I didn't. However when I came out of the coma I was told Gary had serious injuries to his stomach from the steering wheel and major injury to his foot/ankle from the brake pedal pushing back. Harold, despite my pushing his head back, had sustained a severe head injury from hitting the door/windshield post and he had been sent home with his nurse mother to die at home. He didn't.

I was told they estimated I had less than a 15% chance of living! I don't really know or remember if I cared, I believe I was getting good treatment in the hospital. They would not let me look into a mirror or let me get up and go to the bathroom, mainly because there was a mirror in there. I could see some of the facial reactions from friends so I was pretty sure my face was a mess. I made friends with one of the Candy Stripers and tricked her into helping me go to the bathroom. When I saw my face in the mirror I vomited all over the mirror and sink and floor. You see, I had more than 400 stitches in my face alone!

The Candy Striper felt so bad about it and I convinced the nurse it was me who tricked the girl into letting me go to the bathroom. The Candy Striper was allowed to stay and she often came in to see me and talk with me. I still had all the stitches in my face and bandages on my broken nose. Later when the nose bandages came off and I could breathe better, she would come in and we would talk. This day we sat by the window and were warmed by the radiator right in front of us. We kind of had a cute bit of flirting and I tickled her. She squealed and went to tickle me back but hit one of my injured areas. I doubled over forward and hit my nose on the radiator! Yes, I broke my nose again and she was not allowed back in my room!

My left elbow was destroyed. When I pushed Harold back with my left arm my left elbow went into the dashboard through the round radio in front of me. My whole body hurt and I had also lost 45 pounds during my hospital stay. When I was released I was too weak to climb a flight of ten steps without stopping once or twice.

My sister had started her Freshman year at University of Maine. I really don't know if she came home to see me while I was in the hospital, I have heard conflicting stories and during my coma I was not totally sure who visited me. My mother said she told my sister not to come, there was nothing she could do, but later my sister said she had come down to see me.

My mother had many excuses, of course the big one was she didn't drive. Whether she came to visit me was questionable. I do know that Harold did not die and Gary's insurance covered both him and me. My mother settled my claim almost immediately for the sum of $1,000. Guess she needed the money.

Of course I had to find out the hard way that she had settled.

Remember the 400+ stitches in my face, most were to sew things back where they belonged, like my lower lip, my nose, my eyebrow, part of my ear, you get the idea. The largest scar came down from my nose and through my upper lip. It not only looked bad, it messed up my ability to play the trumpet. I was good at the trumpet, as was attested by playing echo Taps to my friend playing from the Common. I stood up on a hill overlooking the Common and when John played the base notes I would do the same as if it were an echo. It sounded so professional. Well, the doctors said they might be able to do surgery to get my lip back. That never happened because my mother had settled and there was no money to do that.

Similar was my elbow that went through the Ford radio and was literally an open wound where I had to put dressing on it daily to close it up. Boston Medical Center was going to graft skin from probably my hip to close up the wound. There was no money or insurance for that! I was just lucky I was at the good age for growth and in a few months they were able to pull the skin together and close the open wound. It also helped that I had lost the 45 pounds and that left some loose skin for them to work with.

Then there was the issue with my teeth. I was to have massive Orthodontic work because not only had the teeth been ripped out, now the nerves were heavily damaged and stopped any chance of recovering the existing teeth, they were simply dying.

When I contacted the clinics/doctors who were going to fix me up, the doors quickly closed in my face. One said they would help some as a kindly thing to do, but all the rest had their hands tied because the claim with insurance had been settled!

So instead of what should be done with my face, elbow and teeth, my mother chose $1,000 settlement. I wanted to run away, or even better would be to end the existence of the monster I saw every time I looked in the mirror. I thought that maybe there was something I could do to end all the pain and the way I looked. I didn't want to commit suicide, I remember the old guy that did that when his dog died, and another who was shamed because he was queer. No, I wanted to go out in some way that was somewhat glorified, as in a car accident or shooting incident that didn't look like suicide. I even cursed the fact I had survived the car accident. Only 10 teeth left, a gaping hole in my left elbow, a face full of scars, and this face is not what I grew up with! I was always called a pretty little boy by people other than my mother. I hated it then, not very masculine, but now I would have loved to have that funny little face with the buck teeth.

It was 7 months before I could return to school. Some of my classmates helped me get assignments but when I did return to school I was told I would be held back a year. I fought that and won, with the full knowledge I was a fool, and stupid, and my A and B grades were now failing grades.

Since I could not do any of the activities and sports I did before, I learned how to wrap ankles and stuff like that and assisted the team that way. I did get to play basketball my Senior year and because of what I had done and making it back to playing, I was to receive my "Letter" jacket. However, my mother was working at the General Store where the Coach ordered new balls and equipment and she let him know I was still smoking! The Coach kicked me off the team and withdrew my Letter Jacket. I hated her.

I got serious about getting back in shape so I spent a lot of time with a friend who had a shed he converted to a weight room. When I started I could only lift a little and at that nothing much over my head as my left elbow would lock up on me and not extend fully. Months of lifting and healing I was able to "Clean and Jerk" 305 pounds fully over my head! Couldn't figure why the big deal until one of the guys asked me how much I weighed and I said "147 pounds" and he told me that many world class lifters cannot lift more than twice their body weight! Guess I got good, but where did it get me? I was just a stronger pathetic and ugly person.

12

Bad got worse . .

Destructive, angry, pathetic, out of control, juvenile delinquent, and stupid was used by many as time went by that year. Everything I had done with sports, theater, academics, music, and often friendship was taken away from me. Whether bored or pissed off I acted very poorly.

I broke things and stole things. If I had a really bad day, and it didn't take much, I might go through a parking lot and smash windshields with the heal of my clenched fist. I loved watching them shatter. A few times I took a bright flashlight fitted with a blue front cover and drove up on people I didn't like and flash the light like a Cop car! Usually when they pulled over and saw it was me they wanted to fight. I never threw the first punch but again I never failed to throw the last and don't remember ever losing a fight.

I came up with some really bad stuff to do for fun. I had an old station wagon and Thanksgiving was almost upon us. I went to a pumpkin field and filled the back of the wagon with pumpkins. Then a few of us started racing around town to get the cops involved When we saw some lights I laid down on my horn and started up the hill from the Common in the wagon with the tailgate open. Half way up the hill we could see the cop car with lights flashing turn onto the road behind me. I didn't worry, the tailgate was down so they could not see the license plate. As they got closer, one of the guys started pushing the pumpkins out and the cop car slammed on the brakes just before the front of his car was struck by close to 20 pumpkins He never caught us.

My friend planned this and got most of the firecrackers. We all had a handful when we all entered the little town of Camden, Maine. A quaint town where the movie "Peyton Place" was filmed. Like Union the center of town was like the body of a spider with streets running up hills away from the center. At a specific time a single firecracker was set off near the edge of town. Cop cars soon moved toward the sound and just then another firecracker was set off across town! We had them screeching around town, at least three police cars! They stopped one of us and as the police was getting out of his car, one of us who had wired a spark plug to his exhaust pipe, slowed down, hit the switch on his dash, and flames flew out of the exhaust on his car as he raced by! The cop threw his stuff into his car and took chase! My friend that was stopped just drove home.

Don't know why we picked on the police, but I believe it had something to do with us being harassed by them. Four of us drove hot cars. I mean, I got retread BF Goodrich tires through the owner of the gas station I worked at changing tires. When I got the Pontiac Star Chief I put on the retreads on the back and took on the "Rubber Hill" in South Hope. A very steep rise up to Route 17 made this section of road perfect for making donuts. You would put your car in first gear and let it roll backwards down the steep grade. Then you would hit the gas and pop the clutch so the rear tires would be burning rubber down the hill until the car started moving forward up the rise. The best "rubber" was in the shape of a teardrop. My heavy Pontiac with the big engine laid the longest teardrop of rubber marks on the road!

Probably the worst thing we ever did was suggested by one of the guys. It was near Halloween and all the trees were turning colors and shedding leaves. We always did something mean around this time, so State Cops would come onto the Common and back in against the stone wall in front of the old Sanitarium. We knew what was going to happen as one guy said he heard about this and wanted to try it. We took out one of the lower rocks and fed through a logging chain. We wrapped one end in old towels and covered it up with leaves and the other around the base of a tree. The State Cop pulled in near perfect to the chain. One of the guys ran across on the other side of the Common so to distract the Cop. Another guy crawled under the rear of the police car and wrapped the toweled end of the chain around the cars rear axle and hooked it together. After he crawled out and we had moved away and to near the center of the Common, another guy did a donut in the middle of the far street and sped off up the hill. The cop hit his lights, threw his car in gear and hit the gas! The chain strung out tight and not only did it take out a section of the stone wall, it tore out the rear axle of the Cop car!

The old adage that girls are attracted to bad boys is sometimes true. I'll just say my sister would have had a fit if she knew I was seeing two of her classmates! My sister was two grades ahead of me in school, a couple years older.

Growing up in rural Maine with a mother who took some odd jobs sometimes it embarrassed me. Why would a woman who attended a business school in Boston take a job doing laundry at a summer camp? And I had to help her! Even more embarrassing is who owned and operated the camp, Retired Colonel Goderre. He was a disciplinarian and ordered his kids and others as though they were in his command. His son, John, tried his best to make his father proud of him. He worked out and always sucked his gut in. He was in such good shape that one day one of my classmates got into a scrap with him and threw a punch into John's abdomen. He broke his wrist! Anyway, I felt totally demeaned helping my mother doing laundry for the Colonel. John and I remained friends.

John was tall and stood rigid. He was ahead of me in school so I was still in school when he enlisted in the Marines. Next thing we heard was he left Basic Training and was sent immediately to Vietnam. It just seemed that John was destined to be the best he could be and we all knew he was the man for the job. It was like he was in the Marines even when he was still in high school. Then I heard John had died in action in Vietnam and his body was being sent home with a fellow Marine accompanying him.

I went to the funeral, it was closed casket. I talked to the accompanying Marine and found out he had been there when John died. He said the entire unit at the front where he was shot were amazed at John's will to live. He said John took a round in the head that literally blew off the top of his head and John lived like that for three hours!

After hearing all this and also listening to his friend about Vietnam I withdrew and thought this was a great argument against suicide. John had died a hero and the people I knew that committed suicide were basically shunned and thought to be lesser people. I guess it strengthened my will to live.

I was still a dedicated worker and many saw that side of me. When Vietnam took all the older boys, guys like me, now 16, could take on rolls meant for the older boys. For instance; at the Union Blueberry Plant we produced the little cans of blueberries that were put into the Betty Crocker pancake mix. The cans needed to be transported by tractor trailer 84 miles to the Distribution Center in Portland, Maine. I drove the truck and I was never stopped by the Police. I did this for a couple months.

Then management had a proposal for me. Our main plant was 45 miles north in Liberty and they were hurting for men to run the plant, as we were, because of Vietnam. I was to pick the team and manage it, Basically my team started at the local Union plant at 7am and we punch out at 12 noon. We would punch back in the Union plant at 5pm and get on a bus for the 45 mile trip. We would get to the Liberty plant around 6pm and punch in there. We would do odd jobs until 10pm when we would take over the management of most of the plant and run the night shift until relieved at 6am. Take the bus back to Union and punch out at 7am and then punch back in.

That program lasted about three months and succeeded in two things: I didn't have time to be a delinquent, and secondly I was giving my mother half of what I was making to help my sister in college.

I remember going to one of the lakeside cottages for a party and I spent a lot of time with Charley, the friendly raccoon. Back to the cottage I told my good friend, Elaine, about my continued problem with the law and some of the bad things I had been doing. By then my face had cleared up some. I knew it would be just a matter of time before I took self action to end my suffering. That is when Elaine turned to me and professed she wanted to help.

<h1 style="text-align:center">13</h1>

Here Comes the Navy!

Elaine told her father and he shared it with his twin brother, both in the Navy.

A couple weeks later I was invited to meet Elaine's father and uncle at a family gathering to be held near Augusta. We agreed, and the night before the meeting Elaine and I got drunk and decided to hit the beach before the afternoon gathering. We both passed out and both got the worst sunburn ever! I had to drive without my shirt or skin on my back touching the seat at all!

I met with the twins, both had their Navy uniforms on as they had been on weekend Reserve duty. They definitely looked sharp in their uniforms and were serious and reasonable about what they wanted me to do. I wonder if maybe they believed Elaine and I were getting serious and the thought of me being with her needed some serious intervention. What they didn't know was we were just great friends, nothing more.

I was still in High School and still questionable if I was going to graduate because of the time lost and my grades were in the cellar, but we still moved forward. They pulled in some favors and if I could pass the physical I would join the Navy Active Reserves until such time I could go Active Duty.

I surprisingly passed the physical and signed the commitment paperwork, I was now in the US Navy Reserves! I swore to Elaine and myself that I could get my stuff together. I actually attended Navy

Basic Training at the Great Lakes facility outside Chicago during the two weeks at Christmas. I often wondered if the twins or the Vietnam Conflict allowed them to lower their standards because I had improved greatly but felt I should never had passed the physical.

Finishing school still a factor. I was still going to school and working three part-time jobs that sort of took precedence over school because school was lost to me and working allowed me to give my mother about 50% of what I made as I believed her when she said that it was going to help my sister in college.

My sister even invited me up to Orono to attend the Homecoming, she had set up a date for me! Got there and met the date! She was so boring and didn't even drink, didn't like me smoking, and after a couple hours I dumped her. Shortly after that my sister got word to me how disappointed she was in me and that, here it goes again, "You embarrassed me"! She now sounds like and sometimes acts like my mother, and yes, she has been known to call me stupid and what I do was being stupid. That word again.

When my sister quit school to get married, I was devastated! I was pissed! And that night i got really drunk and was going to be arrested but the local Sheriff gave me a break, he knew what was going on. But he did warn me if I didn't straighten up the next encounter would not be good.

It was getting near graduation and I was being called into Bill Rochon's office, he being the principal. Many of the staff was there to help with the process for those of us who had problems and needed help to graduate. I was 1/2 point short of graduating and would not graduate with my class.. The options were something like Summer school or staying back a grade, either way I would graduate with the Juniors graduating the following year.

I was upset! One of the teachers stuck up for me and tried to calm me down. The music teacher stepped forward, smiled at me, and told Bill he had completely forgotten the Memorial Day Taps Echo I did, most likely because of the car accident, and took the form in front of Bill and gave me 1/2 point for Music! I was going to be able to graduate with my class. Ironically some of the school records show me as graduating a year later than I did.

My next door neighbor who I often thought more of a mother to me than my own mother, also a substitute teacher, had a very deep meeting with me. She knew I saw myself as a failure and acted out on that. She has done a project for the school and it involved access to IQ scores. She had a copy of mine, knowing that was against school policy, but believing it would help me believe in myself and what I was capable of doing. Won't say what my IQ is but I know people with a lower IQ that got accepted into Mensa! Her message got to me and I tried to change for the better.

Now committed to the Navy and soon to be a High School Graduate, even though I was ranked the lowest scholastically in the class and highest ranking of those unlikely to succeed, it just went to further my self-professing uselessness and stupidity. But I was going to do better.

I was going to Reserve meeting every month, training to be an Electronic Technician and waiting for when I could deploy on Active Duty and get the hell out of town and away from my mother! I went to Great Lakes Training Center for Basic Training with the Navy. Christmas time outside Chicago was no fun and the Navy prepared you for cramped quarters aboard ships and submarines. We had 100 people living so close that if you were sleeping in one of the stacked three high bunks and put your arm out, you would most likely hit another bunk! In the chow line we had to be up against the guy in front of you and same with the guy behind! The DI would walk up the chow line saying, "Nuts to butts, make the guy in front of you smile! If I can get a hand between you I will run you back to the end of the line!" And he would.

We ate very fast. One day we ate lunch and then went to the "Gas Chamber" where you were taught how to protect yourself from tear gas. We did as instructed and most of us who were fighting the effects of the gas inside were released out the door to an area that just about everybody vomited. We had corn as our vegetable at the chow hall before the gas chamber and the ground was now covered with kernels of corn! Corn does not digest well.

While there we split the 100 guys into two groups and each group got a day off to see Chicago. The group I was in went en mass to Chicago and most of us found places to see that were inside. The cold weather was bad around Christmas but the wind off the lake made it near unbearable. One of the guys met a girl and they got intimate in the back of a movie theater!

Back in Augusta we met up with many of the guys for our monthly duty. The guy who did his thing in the movie theater said he had caught something from the girl! A couple of us told him to get it treated. He did not. The following Reserve meeting we had was interrupted by the DI bursting in the room and telling our theater friend to report to the front of the room! He did, and as he was standing there at attention, a uniformed Marine crashed into the room! Loudly the Marine asked the DI if this sniveling little piece of crap was the one who didn't understand? They quickly explained that failure to get treated for a self imposed disease was called "Destruction Of Military Property". The DI explained the marines are part of the Navy Department and the Marines said now the sailor was his and he was going to make a man out of him or kill him! He literally pushed our little guy ahead of him and kicked his ass so hard he was thrown head first through the door! We never saw him again.

My mother was still trying to get money from me to help pay for my sister's college, even though my sister had quit school to get married! Instead I had traded in my 1957 Ford for the 1961 Pontiac with the big engine. I bought the used car and while still changing tires at the Service Station/Garage I worked on the car. I drank too much, forgot about anybody who was now trying to help me and got worse. I thought when I went active duty I would get my stuff together. Lucky I was dating Glenda, she lived about 40 miles away. Because now not a single local girls would have much to do with me. I was bad news.

I started working full-time at a Chicken farm called Union Egg Producers where two of us took care of thousands of chickens, laying hens, in two large chicken houses. The manager was the father of one of my dear friends and fellow classmate and I enjoyed working with him, I respected him, we worked well together.

Then it happened . . .

After recovering from the car accident I actively sought to find out the name of the driver who abandoned the Pulp Truck in the middle of the street. I chose the high road, I would not go hunting for him but if I ever met him I was going to kill him. Then Rockland Egg Producers bought us out and I was to meet the new owners in the office in chicken house 1. The management staff walked in and was being introduced to my manager and his wife and then to me. Before the new manager could get to me I recognized his name and at that moment had a choice, kill him or quit. I walked out the door and never looked back. I believe if I had met him alone he would have been dead.

I got really drunk.

14

The Sheriff's Ultimatum

Union Fair was in full swing and I went there still a little drunk. I had helped one of the "Carnies" with setup for a few tents and was told then that I was too young to see the "Girly Show" but he would let me in through the side flap. I needed to get my mind back in shape so I took him up on the offer.

I found myself standing in a tight crowd of men looking up on the stage above us when all of a sudden this guy pushes up against me. I don't push easily so I stood there hoping he would move on. Instead I feel his hand reach over and grab my genitals! I hit his arm at the wrist so hard you could hear him groan, I felt like I might have broken it. I left the tent and when I glanced back I saw he was also coming out holding his wrist and was follow me. I saw my neighbor and asked where his older brother was, I knew the brother would have a gang around him and they would be drinking heavily. I also knew he had a hatred for queers. I asked my friend to go ahead and tell his brother I was being followed by a queer and would come out to where he was.

The older brother was sitting on the hood of his car with his foot on the bumper. I immediately noticed the bottle he appeared to be drinking from still had the top on it, he was pretending to drink. He gave me a slight nod as his friends started talking to me. When I got closer and the guy following me apparently was not aware of what he was walking into, the older brother tossed the bottle to me and basically dove over me at a full run and hit the guy so hard he dropped like a rag doll.

I leaned against the car and drank while they finished up with the queer. I wondered if he was still alive when the brother said "Let's move, this place stinks like shit and trash" pointing at the queer. I hopped on the fender and we moved the gang to another parking area. I got increasingly drunk and one of the guys challenged me to do something. I was drunk enough to take the challenge and the ten dollars I would win if I could do it.

The challenge: I was driving a beat up Ford Station Wagon and someone put a full case of glass beer bottles on the back floor of the station wagon. It was not secured, just sitting there. I was to take a witness along and I was supposed to take Hilt's Hill at 70 mph and return with at least half of the full bottles of beer unbroken! Hilt's Hill was on one of the roads spread out from the town where the owner, Mr. Hilt had a steep entrance onto his driveway. It was so steep that in winter he could not get up it because of the ice. He built an extension to his driveway to make it a less angle to help him in icy conditions but the extension stuck out into the road and if you didn't't know it was there and going a little fast your car might go slightly airborne. We figured 70 mph would take all four wheels off the roadway.

When we were driving up the road and were near the bump, I sped up to 70, laughed that it wasn't good enough and sped up more. When we hit the Hill we were doing close to 110 mph and the car went very airborne! The road dipped down after the Hill and I could look down at the top of two vehicles, a car and a blue pickup truck! We hit the pavement so hard the right front shock exploded and the result was the car bouncing up and over the cattle fence to the right and landed in the pasture!

The blue pickup truck appeared on the shoulder as me and my witness were counting the number of full beer bottles that hadn't broken. I was going to get my $10! Unfortunately, the driver of the pickup was just straddling the fence and I realized it was Bliss Fuller, the Sheriff. We were at his office a while later after we had arranged for the fence to be cut and the car towed out, the fence repaired and my promise to pay for the services rendered. Bliss was reasonable, to a degree. My witness was let go and it was just Bliss and me.

"Bruce, you did it this time, I can't keep giving you breaks. Here's how it will be" and he told me I had 30 days to go Active Navy and get out of town or I would be thrown in jail! He got my attention.

Through the Twins I got into the Navy system and requested I be deployed immediately to Active Duty and get out of town. It was late July/early August and I was told the closest date they could deploy me was September 16. I pleaded that was too late, I would be incarcerated by then! They didn't budge, so I sought different solutions.

15

⚜

Chapter 4

Off We Go Into the Wild Blue

Bangor, Maine was 60 miles north and the military recruiters were all in one building. I went to the Air Force Recruiter first and played the son of a war hero that flew in the same formation over France with Jimmy Stewart! It piked interest and the Recruiter finally said he would see what he could do. He said I would have to pass the physical again. I sat with him discussing options. He said since it was a civil action and I was in the Reserves, he believed they could do an inter service transfer and while I was taking my physical he had been working hard on it.

Finally I was told the Navy had agreed to it, with some things I had to do. I had to return all my Navy uniforms, including the socks. I would get an Honorable Discharge but could not take any rank or time in service forward. I would be starting in the Air Force as though I had no military experience or rank. Then the Air Force must find a slot for me, hoping they could do so before the 30 days were up. I wasn't out of the woods yet.

On August 3rd I got the call. August 8 there were Recruits being sworn in and headed for Basic Training in San Antonio, Texas. One of the recruits had Scarlet Fever as a child so they were watching him and apparently they detected a heart murmur. Instead of moving the next recruit up, I was slid in his place! Five days notice was good enough.

I was seriously dating Glenda and we had talked about marriage so I had to square it with her. My mother was upset, she had already talked about Glenda as a daughter in law. Glenda took it hard and when I left, she went up to Bangor and tried to enlist so she could be with me. She was anemic and could not pass the physical. She did meet a guy returning from Germany with his two small girls. His wife had been killed in a car accident on the Autobahn and he was getting a Hardship Discharge. Glenda and I had discussed her possible inability to have children due to her anemia, so I believe she may have seen the two young girls as needing her. Apparently she started dating the guy shortly after their meeting.

I talked with the owner of the garage I worked at and he agreed as soon as I left he would take my car from my mother and sell it for me, getting a nice commission of course. He would give some of the proceeds to my mother and send me a portion of the money. I told a few friends I was leaving town and then went on a three day drunk!

When I took the bus up to Bangor, got sworn in, and got on another bus to the airport and on the plane to San Antonio, Texas. I was still a little inebriated. I slept on the airplane.

Basic Training in the Air Force was diametrically different than the Navy. First of all the Navy Basic was in the dead of Winter at the Great Lakes Training Center outside Chicago, and to simulate condition we would encounter aboard ship we were crammed into a small space with no room or privacy. The Air Force Basic Training was in the heat of Summer in South Texas and we were not anywhere as near crammed together.

I was starting out as though I had no military experience, I was the same as all the other new recruits as I had not been able to carry anything forward from the Navy, except experience. I took the same placement exams, etc. and knew there was not much of a chance to become an officer or especially a pilot that I always wanted to be. In the Air Force, anybody with a record of head injury could not fly their aircraft and two weeks in a coma definitely wiped out that dream.

I met the Sergeant who was responsible for job placement. I had my results and it was color coded. A chart on the wall showed the jobs open and the associated color coding. It was easy for some guys, the color on their test results matched with a color associated with a job and they were assigned that career choice. Some guys had more than one color and if available, they had a choice. I was pulled from the group and basically asked what I wanted to do. I asked what was available and was told I had a choice of any one I wanted, I had qualified across the board! I looked at the job titles and was drawn to Weapons Mechanic since I had become exceptionally good at shooting/marksmanship. Little did I know the Title really meant a Bomb Loader! Too late, I was assigned.

I made some friends there and during a day off we got a few of us went to Breckenridge Park. We had about 10 of us so we paired up and rented two person paddle boats to paddle around the waterway circling the Park. I was paired with a good friend, a tall black guy from Louisiana. We were passing by some bushes and high grasses when a Coke can was thrown at us from behind the bushes! I didn't understand why someone would do that. Later, my black friend sat me down and explained the can was thrown because he was black. I didn't understand and soon got my first education about prejudice. I understood what he and a couple others with us were saying, but I just didn't think that way. Nothing got in the way of our friendship.

I finished Basic and was assigned to Lowry Air Force Base in Denver, Colorado for my Technical Training, simply called Tech School. I also received my Draft Card because the Navy showed me as no longer a service member and the Army tried to draft me.

16

Denver, Colorado

Situated at the base of the majestic Rocky Mountains, Lowry Air Force Base was a beautiful place, and it was way beyond the attitude at Basic Training. We didn't just follow directions and procedures, we were competitive amongst ourselves and even more so against other training units. I have never been in a more competitive organization. The different classes going on were in competition at all levels with other units, ranging from inspections for compliance in the dormitory, physical fitness, appearance, and just about everything else. We were pushed to be perfect!

That all added to the strain but at least we were allowed to get off base often if we did well. A few of the guys from Basic were there with me and we remained friends so it was almost like being back in school with classmates. We worked as a team in the classes and in the Unit but also during times we left the base together to discover Denver.

I was having a lot of problems with my teeth, thanks Mom for settling, so I went to the Base Dental Clinic and was seen by a young Captain. He wanted to see if he could save my remaining teeth, I had formally requested they be extracted and I be set up with dentures. The nerves dead in my gums were allowing my teeth to basically die. I was working with the Clinic and had weekly appointments.

At that time my class was moving forward in training and I believe I was in the top tier of the class, I was good at being a Weapons Mechanic, so I was surprised when I was held back from continuing training which now was going into the "Black Hangar". That was where we started working on classified programs. I was told my security clearance had not come through. My classmates went forward and I did menial tasks around the barracks and areas around the Base. I was no longer with my friends and was told when my clearance came through I would join the next class going into the Black Hangar.

It was the first week in October. I was dating a girl from a Catholic college. She was good at a lot of things but was death against drinking so we didn't join any of my friends going out drinking. This put a further wedge between my friends.

Then our unit won an award, something my idle time had helped greatly with, so en mass we went to the Airman's Club on the Base and started celebrating. I got a little too much alcohol in me, enough that I tried to call the girl I was dating and fake I was sick or something, knowing it would be much worse if I met her after drinking as much as I had. I could not reach her and the guys wanted to go to a bar down-town called the Baja even though it was on the second floor. Baja is Spanish for bottom or lower but the bar was up on the second floor.

We got there off the bus and as we walked toward where we thought we were going. Just up from the area the bar was thought to be, we were confronted by a small group of Hispanics who wanted to push us around, us being the Air Force guys. A fight ensued, leaving us with mostly minor cuts and bruises to a couple of us and them running off with the loss. One of us was wearing glasses and he got punched in the face. His nose and one cheek was bleeding but he said he wanted to go to the bar. We were cocky then, we were bad dudes!

We entered the bar and was met by the very large Samoan Bouncer who warned us ahead of time he would throw us down the stairs if we started any problems. He apparently saw the blood on our guy's face. Each of us ordered a pitcher of 3.2 beer. That is beer of a lower alcohol content and was served to people 18 years or older. You had to be 21 to drink normal beer. The Bouncer immediately came to our tables and informed us only one pitcher per table, or we would be tossed out! Immediately a couple open tables were found and we split up with our pitchers. Only one table left so two of us shared it and I put my pitcher on the floor. The Bouncer was there immediately and said one of us was going to forcibly leave right now! I stood up with my pitcher and walked toward the dance floor and the large support posts from floor to ceiling that were around the dance floor. Pitcher in one hand, glass in the other, I was drinking straight from the pitcher and apparently drawing a lot of attention. People were pointing and others craning or turning toward me.

A table with a group of people were doing the same pointing and turning. I saw this very young looking girl turned toward me at the urging of others at the table. They may have seen a drunk but from my end I saw the most beautiful blue eyes. I headed straight to her and some at the table tried to get her attention from me. As you recall, I was pretty beefed up at that time from my lifting regiment following the accident. The girl looked maybe a 100 pounds so I reached for her shoulders and arms and lifted her straight up, turned her to face me and stated, "You're dancing with me!".

We talked and danced until late night when the girl she came with said it was time to leave. I walked her out to their car and leaned forward and kissed her. She slapped my face out of reaction but I could tell and kissed her again without any more physical damage. I went back in and later the guys all walked back to the Base.

The next morning I was fighting a real hangover when I found a piece of pink paper in my pocket with a phone number on it. I later called the number and the girl I had met the night before was on the line talking as we had done at the bar. I invited her to meet me again and we agreed to meet in front of the Capital building the following weekend.

Then, during the week I had a very bad toothache and went to the dental clinic requesting a tooth extraction. The Captain I was seeing was not there and this huge Black Major came in and questioned the fact I had asked for a tooth extraction. He was looking at my charts and looked inside my mouth. He asked if I really wanted them all out? I said yes and he asked me if I could wait a few minutes, he agreed they were beyond saving. A few minutes later he came in with multiple needles and injected the pain killer nine times throughout my gums to numb them. A few minutes later he came back in with his tools and pushed the chair back even further. I glanced at my watch as I used to wear it with the face on the inner side of my wrist and noted the time. He asked if I was ready and leaned over, once putting his knee up on me and the chair to get leverage, If they didn't pull straight out he would twist and break the tooth and pull it out in pieces!

I waited a day and called up this girl, Peggy, and told her I wasn't sure she wanted to meet me as I had just had all my teeth removed? She said she was actually happy because her biggest problem with me was the terrible sight of my teeth! Nothing now standing in the way of our dating so we met the weekend at the Capital building and before she got there I got a Tamale from a street vendor, my first Tamale ever, and the following day I had my first ever food poisoning!

A couple good things that week, I was cleared to go into the Black Hangar and Peggy and I were officially dating! I found the problem with my security clearance getting a Secret Clearance was because of my father. As stated before, he was born in Glasgow, Scotland, he entered the US through Boston, not Ellis Island. He had no middle name or initial, just Gavin Brown, and I could not tell them anything about what he had been doing the last 8 years since he left us. They had to do a more in-depth background check for my security clearance.

Peggy and I met each weekend and in a few weeks I was fitted for dentures. My good friend from New York owned a Barber Shop. His dad owned many and gave ownership of one each to his sons so they could run a business and have some spending money. He knew I was getting serious with Peggy so he offered to give me some money and he and his new girlfriend, along with Peggy and me could go to an expensive restaurant.

I told him I didn't want to be in debt, but when I got the money from the sale of my car, we could do it then. We ended up at a local bar just getting a drink when this lady came in I thought I might have recognized her. She hugged all the staff and the owner, plus a couple people she knew at the bar. You could hear her protesting and saying she didn't have her guitar. The owner went toward the back and soon came out with a guitar. The lady sang and I realized I was listening to a free concert of sorts by Judy Collins, the famous folk singer! This was the bar she started singing in at the start of her career!

17

The Relationship and New Mexico

Peggy and I were getting serious. We talked all the time and met on weekends. I met her mother and her mother's husband, not her step father. Her mother finally said I should spend the weekends in their guest bedroom, no hanky panky allowed. No problem, Peggy saving herself for our wedding. We discussed our family problems and her childhood was troubling but different than mine, however we could easily see all the bad stuff we suffered getting to this point.

Her mother let us take her car occasionally so we could do things, neither of us had much money. Even though I didn't bring forward any of my Navy rank or experience, I could see my Navy time gave me an edge and I was treated differently as others saw that edge also. On top of that I was excelling as a Weapons Mechanic. So I found it fairly easy to work with the Tech School managers and was rewarded with a slight more freedom to see Peggy every weekend and stay at her house without having to report to the Unit on the weekends.

During one of the calls shortly before Christmas I asked Peggy what she would say if I asked her to marry me? Yes, I guess I really did propose over the phone but honestly I was still so troubled with myself I thought I would have real trouble with face to face rejection. She said yes!

I didn't have a lot of money and didn't know how I was going to afford a diamond ring although one of my buddies who owned a couple barber shops in New York offered to loan me the money. I was about to agree when we were told about a program at the Base Exchange where young Airmen could get as much as 50% off items including fine jewelry. And they announced a special three hours one afternoon where single young Airmen could meet with an Exchange representative for further discounts and assistance with Christmas gifts, etc. I was able to get the 50% off and another near 50% off during the special shopping hours and purchased her diamond ring for $47!

We told her mother of our engagement on Christmas day and called my mother to tell her the same. Marie, Peggy's mother, expected it, but not so soon. We told her not to worry, we planned on getting married in October, a full year from when we met. My mother had a different take on it, somewhat upset that I was not going to marry Glenda. It was as usual, I was stupid at all levels as far as she was concerned. She was quite vocal of how stupid I was.

Peggy and I were driving her mother's car. As we approached the left turn onto the road toward Peggy's house an older couple in a station wagon with an older couple in it starting to cross the two lanes to turn left. In the opposite lanes we suddenly saw a new "muscle car" come speeding over the hill and broadside into the turning station wagon! Parts of the car landed on our car!

The woman on the passenger side died almost immediately but the man driving was still alive. I jumped out of the car and ran to the wreck. It was obvious she was dead. He had severe head trauma and a wheezing sound from his chest. I know we aren't supposed to move people with a possible neck injury, but if I didn't I knew he was going to die. I got clothing and towels from bystanders and turned him on his side until the wheezing sound lessened and his pulse was stronger. When the Ambulance got there I briefed the medic on what had happened and that I had moved him and made attempts to stop the bleeding. The Medic soon told me the actions I took probably saved his life.

I was told after I came out of the coma following the near death accident I was in that my actions to push Harold's head back most likely saved his life. Now I was up to two lives saved!

I knew I was going to get an assignment very soon so we hoped it was going to be some Base near Denver. When it came, it was for Cannon Air Force Base in Clovis, New Mexico, only 458 miles from Denver. We went to Peggy's Priest, the Father who she had known for years, Paster Van Suise. The Air Force had a say in it and before they would allow me to get married, I was only 19, I had to attend marriage counseling. I was to have three sessions with a Clergy signing off on all three. Plus I had to have a letter from my mother stating she gave permission for me to marry. Barbaric and old fashioned, but in the long run it saved many young Airmen from situations they were not mature enough to handle.

Her Pastor started stating facts about our chances of a successful marriage based on the fact Peggy was from a broken home, her father had left the marriage similar to my Dad but when she was just a very young girl For that reason he said he felt uncomfortable about performing the ceremony. He was sure our marriage was doomed to failure and divorce. I was getting a little angry about his attitude and words, so I asked him what he was going to do when I told him I was from a broken family also. He shuddered and got up, turning back to us saying he could not perform the ceremony, the statistics stating our marriage would be doomed in a year and a half!

Peggy was crying.

I got up and followed him while I called his name. I told him how much I respected Peggy and she really wanting him to perform the ceremony and wed us. However if he refused we would find another Clergy to do it because we were getting married. It would hurt Peggy and diminish her long time respect for him. We talked a little more, reasonable arguments, and finally he agreed he would. When I told him I also had paperwork where I had to meet three times with Clergy on marriage counseling, he asked if I had the papers with me. I handed them to him and he signed all three and passed them back saying he would do this for Peggy but counseling with me would be a lost effort.

My mother also signed while writing something on the permission letter that made the AF representative smile and shake his head. He asked me if I had to twist her arm as the response read like she was forced to sign it. We laughed while I knew she was still pissed I was not marrying Glenda.

We spent a lot of available time with Marie on the planning, she would have to pay for most of it since we didn't have the money to do what she wanted for us. One thing kept coming up was a feeling we needed to get married earlier, for which we assured her we would not get pregnant, if that was her concern. It wasn't, she just had a feeling, a premonition.

When I got the orders for Cannon AFB I chose not to take any leave between assignment so I could save the leave for a honeymoon. I was catching rides with guys going up to Denver for things similar as I was doing so I could see Peggy as much as possible. Marie kept insisting the date needed to be closer and we moved it to August, after all she was paying for it. I was still waiting on the money from the sale of my car back home.

I had made a name for myself. I had learned how to drive most of the equipment and especially what we called a MJ-1 "Jammer" that was used to load bombs on the F-100 aircraft. One late morning the horns around the Base started sounding off. We were told to get inside one of the hangars, the sirens were for tornado warning. Crews were getting aircraft in hangars, tying them down, or flying them away. All the support equipment was being brought in but very sporadically. I ducked away from the others and ran out to the flight line and starter driving equipment into the hangars. Not many people knew how to drive Jammers so I concentrated on driving them in. As a matter of fact, the remaining Jammer was on the line when the tornado touched down just a couple blocks from us. I got to it and raced toward the hangar! I slipped into the small opening as the hangar door was shut behind me. I shut it down and turned to look out the slight opening between the hangar doors as the tornado swept through less than 50 feet from the door!

They thought I was crazy, especially since all the other guys with me had gone into reinforced areas in the hangar and I had run out and brought in all of the Jammers! I hate to say it, but it went through my mind that would have been a cool way to perish.

Then I was called into the First Sergeant's office where he asked me if I was happy being there or would I like to go to Louisiana? Reason being is apparently the Air Force thought I had taken leave and had sent new orders to my home in Maine directing me to report to England AFB in Louisiana! I told him I didn't want to leave since we were close enough to Denver and I was getting married. We talked about that and I guess he approved because he told me to go out in the waiting area and tell my "little brother" to come in? The little brother happened to be young officer that was about to go up against a tough Chief Master Sergeant. It wasn't a fair fight, the little brother left and I stayed in New Mexico, plus the Chief was interested in the success of my long distance romance.

My roommate in the dorm was a Cajun named Dennis and he stood tall and skinny, but with a prominent beer gut. Dennie would buy two cases of Falstaff beer for the weekend. He would start Friday night with a true Cajun song, sing about half of it and stop! He would almost yell, "Time for a Falstaff" and would drink half of a bottle of Falstaff. Another song, song stopped, and half a bottle of Falstaff gone! He would do that all weekend and I don't remember him sleeping too much and never repeating a Cajun song! His favorite joke was to ask if anyone knew the highest point of land in New Orleans? He claimed it was the trash dump!

Still listening to Peggy's Mom and her premonitions. Our dates were changed another three times before we settled in on May 20, 1967. Marie had gotten almost psychotic with this feeling and we accommodated.

18

May 20, 1967

Peggy was like a little kid one minute and near crying the next, but always gleaming happiness in those beautiful blue eyes. My Best Man and two others flew up in a small airplane while others drove up from New Mexico. The wedding was going to be bigger than we expected but nobody from my family was there. I never got a phone call or anything from my mother congratulating me. I was glad she didn't, there would have been an argument about me not marrying Glenda.

Our wedding was truly beautiful. Someone asked me if I was tickling Peggy because she had a little laugh on her face most of the time. She was so happy. We had the "dull" reception at the church. The long tables were set out and right at the head of the table was the lift up doors the ladies would use to serve food for church functions. The cake sat right in front of doors. We didn't know the ladies were on the other side of the doors when we went to cut our cake! Mom was red faced when she asked what we had said while cutting the cake? The ladies heard me tell Peggy, "Lets finish cutting this shit and get out of here and go to bed!"

At the party at Mom's house we had alcoholic drinks. Peggy's brother was there in his

Navy uniform. He is 6'5" tall and my buddies were having fun, Air Force against the Navy. When Bob would set his glass down, one of my friends would fill it up without him realizing it. As the night went on the refill was probably much more alcoholic than intended. Bob got smashed! When the Uncle was getting ready to leave he looked for Bob.

It took a minute or two but it was quietly announced Bob thought he was where he wasn't! He was tall enough that he could rest his head on the wall above their little sister's closet and he could lean forward against the wall and urinate all over Kathy's shoes! He thought he was in another room of the house.

We spent our first night in a Denver hotel and caught a ride back to Clovis where I had rented a second floor studio apartment where the bed folded down from the wall. I had a history with motorcycles so it was cheap to buy a Sears 50cc motorcycle, we could not afford a car.

We were HAPPY!!! Maybe drank and partied a little too much but we were happy. I took Peggy over to Muleshoe, Texas and a ride with a crop-duster! This was her first time in an airplane and with him flying like he was making a dusting run, diving down onto the field over the power lines and only feet off the ground before coming straight up as he would with more power lines, and going up until the plane started stalling and then back for another run at the field! It was crazier than a giant rollercoaster!

We buzzed around the town on our little motorcycle and partied some more. We were young kids. I was only 19 and she was 21 so we, well she, could buy booze. We were planning on nothing, just being in the moment and acting like young newlyweds in love. We didn't worry or get very serious about the future.

June 14 a truck pulled up to where I was at the end of the runway arming aircraft guns on F100 fighter jets. This Black Staff Sergeant, Wayne, got out and said he was there for me. He took me to the Personnel Office for my "Special" Orders to Phu Cat Air Base, Vietnam. I had been married 24 days and now I would be gone for a year. The Personnel guy asked me how many days leave I wanted before going to Vietnam? I said I wanted 30 days. His response, "okay, then you were relieved from Duty last week." And gave me orders and directions for vaccinations and processing out.

The Staff Sergeant took me where I needed to go and said he knew what I was about to be thrown into, he had just returned from Vietnam. So after the meeting he took me to the Bowling Alley where we could get a cup of coffee and talk about what to expect. He bought two cups and I said I would get cream and sugar. He said NO! He told me I had to be man going over there and the first step was for me to drink my coffee like he likes his women, "Hot and Black"!

When I got to the apartment that afternoon and told Peggy, the smiles disappeared and one of the first things she said after she was cried out was that she didn't want to go back to live with her mother in Denver. That caused us to look at many options and basically we could afford only one, ask my sister who was now living in Virginia at an Air Force Base because her husband had enlisted. We asked if she could live with them for the time I was gone. She would have family, which she had not met yet, and the Base was right there for her medical, etc. And then the question of how were we going to get there?

We had a shaky plan that was to take the train up to Denver, stay there a few days, then standby discount flight to Boston where a family I knew well in Melrose/Malden would take us up to Maine as they had a summer home there. We would meet my mother and stay a few days and then take a bus down to Virginia. We hoped that would work and started planning from there. I also had to return the motorcycle back to Sears. I started making calls and the basic plan was starting to come together.

I saw the First Sergeant the next day and he was rather angry at the way the Air Force was messing with me. First the problem with the wrong assignment and now with less that a month with my wife they were sending me to Vietnam. He told me he had found out from Wayne right after we had left Personnel and he had been trying to see if he could get it dropped or delayed, but it apparently was a "Special Assignment" and he could not help. However, he wrote my leave before deployment as if it was "Emergency" Leave so I would get Standby priority on the air leg of our trip.

We got everything together and took the train to Denver. Peggy's mother was very upset and angry. She tried to talk Peggy into staying in Denver with her but we stuck to our plan.

We went out to Stapleton Airport in Denver. We went to the

departure gate. Peggy was flying on a standby discount program called the 12 to 21 Club and was assigned Priority 7. With my paperwork I was assigned Priority 1. I tried talking with the Gate Attendant and she was somewhat nasty about following the rules. I even played the "I'm going to Vietnam" game and she seemed even nastier. I told her that was fine, I would wait until Priority 7 was called and would go then, I was not going without Peggy!

She was now near yelling that by law she had to put me on first and my wife would not get on with me! She was almost at the yelling stage when the Flight Crew arrived at the Gate. The Pilot put down his case and stepped up to the Gate counter and asked what was going on? The Attendant was still talking loud when she explained her side of the story and then he turned to me and first asked if I was on my way to Vietnam? Yes Sir! And then I explained our situation. He thought for a few seconds and turned to the Attendant.

He read her name tag so he directed his comments to her, by name. "Do you understand there are basically two parts to every flight, the Ground side and the Air side? You may believe you control both, but you don't. Once through that gate and ramp you will enter the Air side and since I am flying the airplane, I own that part, you don't!"! He then told her he controlled who got on his airplane and she was to board both of us first and together! And she would assign us good seats together and if there was room in First Class to put us there!

We got good seats although not First Class. The Captain came back during the flight and talked to us, making sure we had some complimentary drinks, etc. In Boston my friends picked us up and the next morning we drove up to Maine.

I was surprised to see my car in the driveway and Mom said she didn't give it to the guy from the garage, she wanted it there for me. Actually I talked to my friend and it appears she didn't want to give it to him since he would be getting some of the money from the sale, so she planned to sell it herself but had no idea how to. My friend told me he would still honor our agreement after I left. I told him not to worry about me, just give the money to my mother.

My mother seemed to make excuses and said she wanted the car there when I came back home, but even then I questioned how long she intended to keep it? She had no idea I would get immediate orders to Vietnam, so was she just letting it sit there? I told her to give it to the guy who owned the garage, because if she left it there the car tires would rot and the engine clog up.

Also, my mother made it very clear that I had married the wrong girl! She said this right in front of Peggy! She kept saying that I should have married Glenda! She didn't care when I told her Glenda had tried to follow me by going into the Air Force but she was anemic and could not pass the medical exam. While there she met a guy coming home from Germany on a bereavement leave because his wife died in a car accident on the Autobahn and left him and his two little girls. Glenda actually started dating him and got married about two weeks before Peggy and I got married. Mom still insisted I married the wrong girl. Peggy shed some tears over that.

I called my father. I now was married and heading to Vietnam so I thought it only right to reach out to him after nine years. We took the bus to Boston and stayed with Dad for a day or two. The woman that waited at home for him instead of at the docks as my mother did when he came home from World War II was now his wife, Henrietta. Her only living relative, her sister Helen, lived with them. We readily accepted her as Dad's wife and liked her a lot. I just could not call him "Dad" yet.

We took the bus from Boston on down through New York City and down to Virginia. I let it be known that we knew it wasn't the best thing for my sister to have my wife dropped in her lap, but she realized the situation and said they would try to work through it.

I took a flight to Chicago and another flight to Seattle/Tacoma Airport where the next day I processed in with the Military Terminal and the following day I was west bound through Tokyo Japan and on to Cam Ran Bay, Republic of Vietnam. 48 days after I had married the wonderful girl with the beautiful blue eyes I was in a war zone.

19

Chapter 5

Phu Cat Vietnam

The runway was still PSP, basically large metal plates laid down as a runway. The barracks I was assigned to wasn't even completed and I finished building my own locker. I immediately ran into a guy I had gone through Basic Training with so I at least knew somebody.

The barracks had a wood wall built about half way down the first floor that had a door in it. It separated the NCOs (Non Commissioned Officers) from us Airmen. You had to have a rank of E5 or higher to bunk on the other side of the wall. I had met a couple NCOs when I processed in and word got to a couple of them that I was doing some "Special" work. The ranking NCO was Rodney and before I was really settled in he directed me to a bunk right next to the wall and I understood I would have a liaison between him and the Airmen. Rod and I got along well and he helped make my year tolerable.

I processed into the MMS (Munitions Maintenance Squadron) and was assigned to the Weapons Release section. We were responsible for maintaining the ordinance system on the F100 aircraft. If a bomb failed to drop, a gun failed to shoot, or a missile got stuck in the launch tube, we fixed it. We also were responsible for the aircraft weapons components such as the flap in the intake that would open when the guns were fired to allow air in to cool the guns, and such things like the Bomb Sequence Control units that tied into the armament system. I was good at schematics and troubleshooting so I went to work immediately in somewhat of a training position.

Air Force standards state there will be two Weapons Release specialists for every 6 aircraft. We had eight people in the section, of which only six of us were Specialists with one supervisor and one Admin. We had 84 aircraft! I never worked so hard in my life, and I still had to spend some time on the "Special" assignment. It was classified so not many people knew about it. It caused some problems because people without the right to know thought I was being nasty when they asked what I was doing. I told them I could not talk about it.

The Base was shaped like an upside down "U" with Base Headquarters, the Hospital, aircraft revetments, runway and support hangars on the North side of the arch and barracks and some facilities on the Southwest of the arch. Later the Clubs and the dining families would be off the top and Northwest of the arch.

It was very humid and when the monsoons came it was deep mud. We had to lay wooden boards across many of the shortcuts when the rains came down because if you stepped off the boards your foot would sink in the mud and chances are you would have your boot sucked off your foot trying to pull it out. A real problem if you were returning from the Club and had too much to drink!

There was a constant odor. Some came from the aircraft, some from vehicles and work facilities. And there was always an odor I cannot describe, but all Veterans remember, the smell of death.

There was activity 24/7 and especially with the very small crew we had and very large number of aircraft, many of us worked more than 24 hours straight and I can remember at least three times I worked three days straight with only short naps in the service trucks we used. We had old International Step Vans to work out of and carry aircraft gun, pylons, etc. I took two days off the entire year and one Temporary Duty training in the Philippines. The two days off were to see the Bob Hope show with Raquel Welch and when Ann Francis toured.

When Bob Hope came I got very near the front with two of my good friends, Andy and Alberto. Just before he came on, the Army guys were flying in troops on their twin rotor helicopters to see the show. As one came in to land behind us, the rear rotor fell off and dumped the Army guys out the back. All were sent for medical treatment and right before the show started we had gurneys and wheel chairs with injured soldiers put up front and we were made to move back for them. I was walking by the side of the stage only feet from where Raquel stepped out. She was chewing out one of the stage hands and I could not believe the amount of foul language she yelled at him!

When Ann Francis came the weather was very bad so she was put on a very small stage in an area of a hangar. She was there to talk to the guys and sing some. I was right in the front of the circular stage because I helped set it up. We got hit hard that evening by enemy mortar shells and she came down and in the middle of four of us. We stood directly against her and many more behind us to protect her. She was a very nice lady and it was such a pleasure to meet her. But mostly it was nice to see her stop shaking from the noise and realize we were there to protect her. I got a personally signed picture from her.

I was only 19 when I got there so I could not buy booze, only beer, because I could not get a Ration Card. Older guys could go to the store where they could buy bottles of booze and beer. So I worked out a deal where the guys were smoking some frowned upon stuff and I would stand on the second floor balcony as a lookout for them. For payment, the guys who didn't drink booze would give me the rations for their booze.

I also would go outside where the cleaning ladies would meet for lunch and I would squat next to them and try to learn Vietnamese, often eating some of their fish heads and rice. Since the Vietnamese often refer to their friends like they were family, the first thing I learned was what I thought to be one ladies name and later when I got better I found it wasn't her name, I was calling her Great Aunt! Since I usually worked a later shift I often had time to stop and talk with them. Some military members looked down at them but I have never done that. I respected them as people living in their country where we were the visitors.

One of the house ladies told me one day that she would not be coming in the next day. Okay? Well the next day we got hit by mortar. It wasn't until it happened another time that I realized she was warning me. I talked to the Office of Special Investigations (OSI) stating I didn't want to get her in trouble, but? They said not to worry, that happened with a few others. They just asked if I would let them know when it happened and that nothing would happen to her. I did that for most of the remaining months I was there.

Some very unpleasant things happened that I will discuss but not in detail, there are things we just don't share. I will share as much as I can.

I worked a lot of nights and those days when I had time I tried to catch up on my sleep. Often a couple of us would take Army cots and go outside in front of the barracks and sleep. It was away from the human odors and if there was a little breeze it was great. One of those times I was awakened by a familiar voice. First you could tell by the Maine accent and then I knew the voice. I sat up and there in an Army vehicle was Donny, one of my friends from back home! He was asking directions. We talked. He was taking a fellow Army guy to the Base Operations Terminal. His friend had caught an incurable disease and was being sent to the Philippines to meet his wife to say goodbye. He could not enter the US as a possible carrier.

Not more than a week later I was contacted and asked to go to the Terminal again. Donny had asked for me. He was being sent back to the US in chained restraints. He was under arrest! From what I could gather, while Donny was there a week previous the Lieutenant over him had led his troop into an ambush and 14 of his troop were killed! The Lieutenant didn't even have a scratch on him. Donny lost it and tried to kill the Lieutenant! I only had a minute or so with him.

Andy, Alberto and I did a lot of things together, Alberto was in Basic Training with me. One evening before I went to work, Andy and I decided to catch a movie at the outdoor theater. The theater doubled as a stage and the stage was about four feet high, made of wood. We took some incoming mortar that night and Andy and I dove for the base of the stage for protection. Andy was facing away from me, my feet by his head, his feet by mine. He was against the wood and me outside of him.

We could hear all the explosions across the Base. They often stair stepped the mortar as though they fired one and mover the launcher up a little and fired again so we could hear the mortar coming closer. There seemed to be some gaps in the sequence when Andy said loudly, "Yeah, what do you want?" I told him I didn't want anything, why? And he said I had just slapped or hit his foot, I don't remember the exact wording, but I turned my head to look at the end of a mortar round that had crashed into the wood above his foot! It was a little less than a foot from my head. We found out that about 4 mortars had hit the hospital, all duds, and five other duds hit but didn't explode. My response involved adequate amounts of alcoholic beverages.

One mid morning Rod was standing by my bunk. I looked up at him (I was in the lower of two bunks) and he asked if I had seen the new guy, a skinny older NCO that we heard more than saw, he was crying. Rod asked me to find him a bunk as far away from the wall as possible as he was not going to let the new NCO back in their area because if he had to listen to that crying he would probably kill him! I told the crying NCO that the area for NCOs was full right now but I would place him in a more private area with us Airmen. It was right by the showers at the end of the building so he would not have another person across the hall from him because it was the wall separating the shower. You could either enter the building through the shower or the entrance door.

Rod basically told me the NCO was my responsibility.

He started really crying harder and I went up to where he was and found he had stepped by the open shower and saw one of the house girls taking a shower! She was partially naked! I assured him it was okay, they did it often and we didn't bother them nor them us. Besides, all the house cleaning girls were noticeably older than us. I left him still crying, it was hard to take.

It was getting close for me to go to work, I started work mostly at night. I had on my jungle fatigues and knowing a single shift could turn into a day or two, I had at least one five pack of White Owl Ranger cigars and at least two packs of Camel cigarettes in my pockets. The sound of explosions and sirens filled the air so we all flooded out and into the bunker right next to the barracks. Andy, Alberto and I sat on the floor with our legs out and we smoked heavy. Neither had any cigarettes on them so we smoked mine.

Apparently the crying Sergeant had decided to take a shower and didn't know what to do in response to the noise, other than cry harder. He ran out of the shower with a towel around his middle, which he lost on the way to the bunker! He exploded through the entrance and landed naked across our outstretched legs! We were not kind to him, we literally kicked him off us and he found a corner to crouch and cry. I was extremely pissed off at him and went almost directly to work after the "All Clear".

A couple hours later we had a slow minute on the flight line so I took the guy I was working with and we drove over to the barracks, I had not picked up more cigarettes after the three of us smoked most of mine so I was going back to get a couple packs. I walked in first and I immediately saw the NCO hanging from the wood rafters with his belt around his neck! I yelled and the guy with me cut him down while I was holding him up. The medics came and took him away, too late to save him. Rod had passed the responsibility to me to take care of this guy. Nothing was ever mentioned that I should have known he was unstable, should have known he was a nut case, and should have been there. Quite the opposite, no one blamed me but myself. Some even said they knew the guy was still alive when we handed him off to the medics and proclaimed I had saved his life! If I accept that, then he would be number 3 of people I have saved their lives.

There is a major problem with that. When someone does something like that and I was the one Rod asked to take care of him, I hold some responsibility. And that means the scene will visit my nightmares.

That same bunker where he ran naked into and on our legs was just outside the East wall of the barracks, The top bunk on that side down one row from us could look through the ventilation wire area between the top of the side wall and the roof hangover for the second floor you could see the top of the bunker through the screen. The wood walls were up to about four feet from the overhand separating the first and second floor. The rest up to the second floor was covered with a screen for air and bug control. The guy who had the top bunk was a loner, I didn't hardly know him. He had strung an electrical wire and a single light bulb down to where he could lean against the head railings and bring his knees up to rest a book on and spend hours reading.

I heard the sound and looked up and over just as the lightbulb exploded and he was blown off the bunk. The mortar shell hit the top of the bunker and blast directly at the wall and him. It was a mess, he didn't survive. I saw just like many books I have read that use the term of a red mist spraying where his head was. Much of that is true in reality, that is what I saw.

But nothing can be as bad as what was to follow.

Let me set this up for you. Whenever there was a lull and the right people thought we could leave the base for a couple hours, a group of us would go to one or both the Orphanages we supported. Since I worked a lot at night I often had time to go. And I usually switched driving with another guy, him usually driving if I was tired from working the night before.

One of the orphanages was Buddhist and the kids were likely not the same ones we saw there before, so we built them things you would see on a playground. The other Orphanage was Catholic and was like day and night in comparison. This one was a very nice almost castle looking enclosed area. We even had a locked closet we could store our M16 rifles, Flak vests, and helmets. The kids were usually the same ones we saw every time and one especially would walk with his hand hanging on my big fatigue pants pocket. Although maybe 6 years old, on occasion he would shimmy up one of the smaller coconut trees and bring me down a coconut. It took you away from the war around us and the boy and I had a wonderful relationship. I talked with the Father and asked if anyone had ever talked about adoption.

Early December we got in a new First Sergeant and immediately I was on his bad side, my handlebar mustache was better than his and people told him that. I was told to trim mine. Then he asked what special assignment I was doing. First he asked me that when people were around so to make him look better, and secondly you don't discuss classified projects with people who don't have a clearance or a need to know. He was pissed and actually threatened me, telling me that he was in my chain of command and that I was to tell him what I was doing! He didn't like it when he wasn't the top dog and when I explained he wasn't privy to what I was doing, I would be in deep shit if I told him! He replied I would be in deep shit if I didn't. I didn't and was officially on his wrong side.

The end of January 1968 we were planning on the down time during Vietnam's "Tet" and their expected cease fire to celebrate their religious holiday. I had planned to visit my hometown neighbor who was stationed at Cam Ran Bay but I had some work to do on my project. I decided to join a group going to the Catholic Orphanage. I come out to the truck that day and the First Sergeant has borrowed an M60 Machine gun from the Army and had mounted it on sand bags on the cab of the truck! There were many more sand bags on the floor so he can stand on them to shoot the M60. He's yelling like a battle cry, "Lets go get us some Gooks!" There were a good dozen of us in the back of the truck, many from other squadrons. One guy even asked me what was it with the "First Shirt", especially the way he was talking down to me, singling me out? I can't remember my response. I was tired so the other guy drove.

We got to the Orphanage without a problem. Often hard to find because of all the side roads through the rice paddies unless you knew what to look for. In the distance from the road you could see some trees and high grasses that told you that was where you went through and took the back road to the Orphanage which set out on a large plot of land. There was enough land we could set up a small baseball field and teach them the American sport. Which we did shortly after having a drink similar to tea with the Priest. As usual, this young guy held onto my fatigue pants pocket and leaned against me where I was sitting.

We had locked up our weapons, flak vests and helmets so we went out in the field. The Priest had four of the older boys placed outside the perimeter as an early warning should something happen. This was normal procedure. The bases were set up and we brought out the bats, balls and gloves. It was very informal, more for easy fun than competition because we didn't want the kids to get hurt trying to run in makeshift sandals or barefooted.

One of the boys started speaking loudly and we were told we had to leave because there were people in the rice paddies with guns and if we were to be caught it would harm the Orphanage. We started rushing back in and the little guy still wanted to hang onto me and told the Father he had to get me a coconut. We didn't have time so he was asked to help the boys bring in the bases, bats and balls from the field.

We gathered our vests, guns and helmets and jumped on the truck which had been turned around facing back the way we came. We went toward the trees and grasses, slowing to make the tight turn. I was standing up holding onto the side boards.

We heard it before we saw it. There were sounds of weapons being fired and it appeared we were the target. I placed my left arm over the top side board and looked out. I saw a face pop up from the grass area and watched him raise his weapon toward the truck! Having grown up with weapons it became a reaction and I slung the weapon over the top board, glanced at the sights, and pulled the trigger. As he was pointing the rifle at us it exposed the left side of his face and I watched the explosion as the bullet I fired entered his left cheek and took a lot of his face with it! There were others that I fired at but all was a blur as I could only see his face, my first kill.

My clip was empty about 20 seconds before we hit the clearing and the paved main road ahead. All shooting had stopped from the truck and I had a chance to look around inside the truck. I expected to see the macho First Sergeant manning the M60 but he was trying to rearrange the sand bags he had placed on the bed, he was trying to protect himself. All the other guys had also hit the floor and I was the only one standing! No one else fired a single round. The shooting maybe lasted 30 seconds.

I was in shock and barely heard a couple guys ribbing the Sergeant because of his cowering instead of what he said he was going to do. I wasn't watching him, I was dazed and not really focused on anything. I looked out in the field and saw a Water Buffalo with a plow behind him. The Vietnamese farmer had dropped the reins and ducked down into the protection of the banks of the rice paddy.

I found myself being grabbed and basically backed into the corner and told by the Sergeant that I had an empty clip and when we got back to the base I would be questioned about it. I was told I would not say what happened and would say I had shot a Water Buffalo instead! If I didn't, he would make my life a living hell! I realized the truth would make him look weak, and he couldn't let that happen. The truth should have got out because of the guys, but I never heard anything, the Sergeant must have talked to them too, I don't know. Maybe they hadn't seen. I don't know.

I was still basically disoriented when I told the Security Police I shot a Water Buffalo and emptied my clip on it. The First Sergeant talked with the Police and my Commander and I was placed on a restricted duty. I was pulled off the Flight Line and was made to clean aircraft guns using a vat of chemicals. I was now cleaning the aircraft guns instead of my duties as Weapons Release. Between Sergeant Murray, head of Weapons Release, and the boss on the "Special " project I was working on, they got me back at my regular job. I did the cleaning in the nasty chemicals for almost two weeks before I was allowed to go back to my job. A small cut I had on my finger became infected from the chemicals.

The First Sergeant must have spread some story about me because I was being watched by other Sergeants that would step up and tell me how to do my job. I remember we got in this new Technical Sergeant who had been a cook at Barksdale AFB in Louisiana for 14 years and since his rank said he should be a manger he was sent to Vietnam with no experience with munitions, but he was a manager with MMS. He was determined to do the First Sergeants dirty work and even he started asking me what I was doing with the Secret project.

One day he climbed up the cockpit ladder and looked at me hunched down against the right cockpit fuselage replacing a Bomb Sequence Control Unit and started telling me how to do it and I was taking too long, etc. What he didn't realize is that I had designed and made a special tool just for removing and replacing the unit. Prior to my designed tool it would take as much as three hours for a weapons mechanic to take out all four corner bolts and put a new unit in, hook it up, and put the bolts back in. A very hard job because of the location against the sloping inward cockpit and the unit rested right up against it. Most guys only put back two or three bolts. The tool I designed would allow me to remove and replace all four bolts in half the time, barely taking more than 90 minutes to complete, yet here was this really ignorant shit head telling me what to do!

A follow on to that was I was in the process of submitting the new tool design to Headquarters. I didn't know how to do it so Sergeant Murray was helping me. I believed him when he said it was taking a long time through the bureaucracy but he assured me he was working it, he would help me.

We got hit hard one late afternoon and there was extensive damage to about 1/3 of our hangar. After we came out of the bunker I was given a flashlight and a pad of paper to document the damage. All power was off. There were about four or five of us doing it and I climbed up on a pylon rack so I could see the damage. The lights came on as i was looking down and writing. Someone yelled at me and suddenly something hit the top of my head and threw my head back and then something stuck in my forehead right over my right eye! I don't know what it was, and I don't remember how I got down. For one thing I had blood flowing into my right eye and what I could see was a lot of blood and then an Army Medic was closing and stitching my head wound. One of the guys said it might have been a ceiling fan that came on when the power came back on. I don't know, one minute I was standing there looking down and the next I was being treated by an Army Field Medic.

I was asked by our squadron Admin if I wanted to put in for a Purple Heart as it happened during the time around destruction of our hangar from enemy action? I said I didn't know what hit me, and did I need to do anything or would Admin take care of it? I later said I wanted the Purple Heart and I was assured Admin would take care of it. I followed up twice and the first time I was told it was still being reviewed by the First Sergeant and the second time I was informed the paperwork had been lost. I went back to work and basically let it slip.

I never received the Purple Heart. Later I tried in vain to follow up again only to find out there was no record. I believe the First Sergeant screwed me again. Later I followed up again but someone put the entry in as a time, no mention of the enemy action, and simply stated "Individual walked into a fan"! It was totally a lie like the Water Buffalo story I was forced to say, I was not walking and something struck me! The First Sergeant totally messed with my career.

The next chance we had to visit the Orphanage I went. Very tired but knew I had to see my little friend. I believe I was driving this time. We got there and while everyone got out I turned the truck around and stepped out of the truck. I was met by the Priest. We talked, I cried. The last visit I made and we sent my little friend out to help the older boys, the Viet Cong shot all five of the boys! The little guy died immediately. That last visit I had not only killed people but I let this precious little boy die. I was serious about adopting him. Now my mind was severely fucked up.

Through all the mortars and serious times we had in Vietnam, there were some events of possible humor, a couple I got in trouble for.

I often ate only one meal a day and it was breakfast, It usually consisted of a plate of bacon, plate of eggs, and plate of potatoes with some toast in there somewhere. It was early morning and I had just worked basically 36 hours and I was dragging. I had dropped off my helmet, flak vest and weapon and caught the bus to the Chow Hall. I got off the bus and standing there on the top landing of the few steps was a Colonel in clean uniform along with a Senior Master Sergeant. They were "inspecting" the troops and when I headed up the stairs and before I could salute, if I was going to, the Sergeant asked gruffly, "Airman, where is your hat?" Tired and worn out mentally and physically,

I simply responded, "Sir, it is in my back pocket but I don't make a habit of loaning it to anybody, Sir" I found myself in front of the Base Commander for that comment.

Part of the "Special" program I was doing was kept in a secure area at the Bomb Dump. That is where bombs are being stored and built before being taken to the aircraft. Also Explosive Ordinance Disposal (EOD) is located out there and I knew quite a few of them. One time, a few of us took a break out there to watch some of the aircraft that were either shooting at apparently Viet Cong or were spraying "Agent Orange" that was used as a defoliant on the trees and bushes to kill them so the enemy couldn't hide. Twice, on two separate occasions, we got sprayed by the poison. I remember watching the tracer bullets like it was fireworks and later a flight very close to the perimeter of the Bomb Dump was spraying the defoliant and we all got a heavy overspray on us.

One time I was at a gathering in the Bomb Dump, a few of us having beers, when a Captain in fatigues came up behind me, I was the only "guest" there. He reached up and grabbed the back of my hair in a fist and started shaking it back and forth, "Airman, you need a haircut!". Yes sir, I know that but haven't had time, sir. He did it again and this time actually hurt my neck! He repeated I needed a haircut!

I turned around to look at him and asked him if I could say something to him "Off The Record"? Of course he said no and I said I wouldn't tell him then. He argued that he knew my kind and I would say it anyway. We bantered and I said I wouldn't unless it was "off the record". He finally agreed, he wanted to see what I was going to say. I affirmed with all the guys around and with the Captain that anything I was going to say was off the record, they all affirmed. I looked at the Captain, "Captain Montgomery, what is your first name?" and he responded "John" so I responded, "Fuck you John!" Luckily the guys backed me up or the Captain would have had my butt.

I was called out to one of the F100s with a report one of the missiles had stuck in the pod and was about 1/3 way out when it stuck. You could see the front warhead and part of the body hanging out at an angle. It had to be de-armed before I could take it down and troubleshoot the pod and the system. The Tech Sergeant former cook was there trying to supervise, again having no idea what he was doing but now he had been promoted to Master Sergeant. The F100 was in the high metal revetment facing forward as we did with all fighters to allow fast response.

Soon the green six passenger pickup EOD used screeched to a halt slightly off to the side and three doors opened and three EOD guys jumped out to assess the problem. About a half minute later the fourth door of the EOD truck opened and a fourth EOD guy emerged and we could see he was still intoxicated! He staggered over to the protruding missile we were being real careful of because we haven't determined yet if it was armed! He stepped closer stating, "The son of a bitch is stuck" and kicked it! I dove behind the main wheel and others scrambled in all directions in case it exploded! It didn't but the guy was by himself by the missile. As we gathered again we heard a loud groan and after looking on the opposing revetment we found the new Master Sergeant laying on his side! He had climbed up the revetment, what looked to be a near impossible task, and then had fallen on the other side of the wall! The impact had separated his shoulder! Hate the say it, but I was glad he was temporarily out of my way.

I said earlier that I got my booze by being a look out while a few of the guys got high on something they smoked. I never participated but one evening the sound from inside was so much laughter I had to duck in to see what was going on? One of my coworkers was a huge former football player that had gained a few extra pounds. Still probably the strongest guy in our unit, he looked heavy. He had gotten real high and a couple guys shaved his head, pierced his ear, and made an earring out of safety wire! He had on only his undershorts and was sitting on the floor with his legs crossed close in to his body. He looked just like the Buddha statue at Kamakura! Pictures were taken and his name now was "Buddha"!

I went to Qui Nhon a few times, usually when we had a real lull in action. A few of us would go to drink a beer. Every time we would be surrounded by "Bar Girls". I just drank beer. This one trip Buddha was with us and a new guy came along. The new guy was short and looked very small standing next to Buddha. He made the mistake sometime earlier of letting it be known he had never been "with" a woman! So when this very pretty Vietnamese Bar Girl came out and sat on his knee, Buddha talked to her and soon the new guy and the young lady disappeared with Buddha behind them to make sure it happened!

A couple days later I heard someone say I had to come upstairs to see something. He was laughing. I went upstairs and here was Buddha standing there with his head back a little and his chest thrown out. And there, pounding on his chest, was the new guy! Come to find out the little guy had just got back from the hospital. He apparently got a an infection from his first encounter with a woman! Buddha was just standing there with his deep laugh!

It was also a place to learn real life lessens. I was good at training and when a new guy came in I took him out with me on the Flight Line to troubleshoot a reported problem. I was very impressed with his knowledge of schematics so I laid out the aircraft schematic and we traced the problem to a unit in a panel a short distance behind the nose gear. I pointed out the panel on the underside of the F100 where we had to gain access to fix the electronic problem. I sent him out with a Zoos screwdriver to take off the panel. I was working on another problem when I realized he hadn't returned. I went under the F100 and he was still there staring at the screwdriver and the panel. He said he didn't know how to use the Zoos screwdriver and I questioned why he would say something so dumb? It was just like a regular screwdriver but had a rounded end to fit into the recessed latch. He told me he had grown up in a big city apartment building in Pennsylvania where all maintenance was taken care of by the building maintenance so he had only recently learned how to use a screwdriver, but not one like this! I changed my outlook on people because of that, understanding my common sense was not always common sense to others. It helped me become a better trainer.

We flew into Tan San Knut to catch another flight to the Philippines. As we entered the Passenger Terminal I heard someone yelling "Short"!

Only he was not pronouncing the "R" like people from Maine don't. He was a tall guy and was leaning against a round support beam. He had a Samsonite suitcase between his legs, protecting it like he might have some souvenirs in the bag. I could tell the brand of suitcase by the metal band around it. We talked. He was from Lewiston Maine, 24 miles from my town of Union. Every minute or so he would turn his head and yell "Short" and laugh because he was going home!

I left with my group and we boarded a C130 cargo plane. We taxied out to the runway and the pilot turned the plane onto the runway. Just then you could hear and see where a rocket had hit the terminal! There were more landing so the pilot threw the throttles forward and we raced down the runway and lifted off! A couple days later the incident was reported in the military Times newspaper. The first rocket hit the terminal, exploding when it hit one of the support beams. It commented about all the people sitting around or leaning on that beam, noting the approximate 3 inches of a metal band from a suitcase was all there was left of the people there where the missile hit.

Getting close to rotating back to the States, most guys would yell "Short". I never did. Some said I didn't respect the tradition. Then one day I had just left the barracks and this guy said, "So, I guess you must be Short? Where are you being stationed?" It didn't take long to figure out someone had painted the word "Short" on the back of my fatigue shirt! I still never said "short".

I had proposed that Peggy meet me in Hawaii, that since I didn't take an "R&R" (Rest and Relaxation) while in Vietnam, I should be able to meet her in Hawaii. She gave me this excuse that she had heard Hawaii wasn't worth it and was too expensive. Later she said it was simple, we could not afford it.

Quite a bit more happened, some good though mostly bad. I'm hoping what I have talked about has given a realistic glimmer at some of the life of a person fighting in Vietnam at 19 years old during 1967-68.

20

Chapter 6

Returning Home

Arriving at Seattle/Tacoma most of us kissed the ground! We had left Cam Ran Bay with a stop again in Tokyo at Yokota Air Base. As approaching Yokota the pilot told us we had minor mechanical problems so we were coming straight to the Base runway. We landed and as the pilot reversed the engines to slow down, one sputtered and stopped, out of fuel! He turned onto a taxiway and stopped, shutting down the engines. We were informed a seal within the fuel system had failed and we were losing fuel rapidly. We would be there until they could located another seal.

We were there for quite a while and when we boarded we were told they found one and the seal had just being replaced. We then headed for the US and Seattle/Tacoma Airport. When we got close to the US the airplane started to descend somewhat rapidly and the pilot said apparently the new seal was having problems and we were losing fuel fast. We were braced for possible crash impact when the pilot touched down. No dramatics like Tokyo but many still kissed the US soil.

The delay in Tokyo and the fact someone had slashed open my suitcase in baggage caused me to miss my direct flight to Denver. The airline would get me there but the non stop flight now was two stops in between.

I was standing in line at the counter to get my new tickets when an elderly woman walked up to me, I was in uniform, and she asked me if I was going to Vietnam? I kindly stated I was just getting back from Vietnam when I had to turn my head to the left. Her spit landed on my cheek and neck, not in my face as she had intended.

I walked around waiting for my flight and saw a lot had happened since I was gone. I was called over by one couple behind a table asking me to sign a paper against the War in Vietnam. I told them I was in uniform which prevented me from signing, and then I walked on. Another guy had a similar but much flashier presentation for the same reason. I gave the same answer and he said if I did sign he would give me a poster! He pulled it up and held it so I could see it. It was a full colored picture of Jane Fonda in her Barbarella outfit, one breast exposed, and the cation read, "What spreads faster than peanut butter?"

I got on the airplane later without the poster. My suitcase heavily taped. We stopped first in Boise Idaho and another small town I basically ignored to catch a little needed sleep.

I met Peggy in Denver. She had bought a new Opal and we were so glad I made it home. Only problem is, we both had changed. She had been with my sister and her husband, which was not easy for her. I was definitely not the same person at all. I had lost my youth, killed another human being, seen horrors beyond anything ever seen to me before. I could not get rid of that smell of death.

I had been gone for a year and my sister's husband had been sent to Vietnam for six months while assigned to a military cargo aircraft. He got back the same day I did.

There was something I realized right then. If her mother hadn't forced us to marry when we did before I went to Vietnam I probably would not have married and possibly would have died during the next few years. I realized Peggy was a beautiful person I had committed to by marriage and I would honor that commitment. We had to learn to love each other again and I had to cope with my underlying problems. I was hoping I could. All I could see was me as a person returning from doing things and seeing things nobody should do in their moral mind, and here was this innocent, naive, wonderful young lady that would have to put up with me. I didn't know if it was anything but bad for her.

One of the guys I was stationed with in Vietnam had suggested I put in for a Base in northern California, Mather Air Force Base in Sacramento. I had, and now had orders for there. My friend was stationed in Denver and I called him shortly after we got to Peggy's old house. We agreed to meet and have drinks and dinner.

Not as easy as we thought. Although Peggy was 22 she looked much younger. So every place where we tried to get a drink automatically checked her ID. While at it, why not check the guy with her! I was only 20. We were turned away. I told the three we could go somewhere nice and I would not drink. My friend said hell no, I earned the right to have a drink! The sixth place we went to did not check my ID and we had a great night.

Now on to Mather Air Force Base. We packed the car and drove.

21

California

Mather Air Force Base outside Sacramento was my next duty station.

We got there and I was assigned to a loading crew on B52 Bombers. I was the team leader, Number 1 Man and the "supervisor" was responsible for the team. He had the final say but I managed the team of four people. Each Member having a specific duty in the Team. For example, the Number 3 Man was responsible for connecting aircraft power and Number 4 Man drove the Bomb Loader.

The supervisor was a practicing alcoholic and that left me with more responsibility and more problems. For example, we were loading Special Weapons that we would check out of secure storage facilities. When we did that he would be at one end of the storage facility, out of sight from me at the other end. We each had to pick up a secure phone and give a constantly changing Password before we could check out the weapon. He often forgot or gave the wrong password and I remember at least four times we were both forced to the ground spread eagle and taken to a secure facility because he screwed up!

Another thing is I was now assigned to SAC (Strategic Air Command) and the other guys told me I was now "SACumsized" meaning once in SAC people did not leave! I was told that I would be going between Guam and Mather, no where else. I was told I would probably do the rotation every six months! I wasn't sure I liked that but was told repeatedly that once in SAC always in SAC, so I made the best of it.

A couple months later I read in the Air Force Times that Sergeant

Murray had been awarded $300 for his invention of a special tool to remove and replace the Bomb Sequence Control units on F100 fighter jets! $300 was a lot of money in 1968 and I was screwed out of it.

I was called into the Colonel's office and there was an awards ceremony, for me. Seems that even though I didn't receive the Purple Heart I was awarded a couple awards, notably a Commendation Award for what I had done in Vietnam. I was now a Decorated Veteran.

Our team moved up in status and when the MEI (Management Effective Inspection) and the ORI (Operational Readiness Inspection) came down upon us, my team was selected to demonstrate procedures and be judged and rated by the inspection teams. When we were selected to do the CCMC (Critical Circuits Maintenance Check) I knew we were being taken seriously. This was performed by only the four team members, no supervision, and I was the key player.

Before any special weapon can be loaded a CCMC has to be performed to validate the critical circuits were functioning as necessary. This was the hardest task to be tested on, especially the Number 1 Man. I had to read the checklist and all of the team members responded through headsets as they checked off the function. I would state an action and the Team Member responsible for that item would respond by stating the task was completed. We could not move forward until a positive response was answered back to me. The best time ever recorded was right at seven minutes from start to finish with no discrepancies. It was a real competition.

We started with all four of us at Attention in a straight line in front of the B52. When the clock started we all rushed to our stations, mine in the cockpit. My #2 guy went in the back, #3 guy grabbed the large power cables and ran between the nose wheels to hook up power, and #4 man was in the bomb bay area. We all had headsets and when all members called in I started the checklist. I gave the action and each man responded with the component and that it was good. We finished and time stopped when we formed up in front of the aircraft just as we started. The inspection team had been listening and watching.

The Inspection Team met and we could hear their comments. One of them wanted to site my #3 man for tossing his hat on the front landing gear wheels instead of placing it there. He tossed it from less than 3 inches so we knew it was that inspection team member not wanting us to have a clean CCMC. The rest of the Inspection Team agreed it was such a minor discrepancy they were not going to mark us down for it. All smiles and then very rigorous thanks to me and my team for a job well done. In about an hour our Colonel came to us with the leader of the Inspection Team and we were told we had completed the CCM with no errors in 6 mutes and 57 seconds! That was a new record! We all received recognition and I was put in for another award because it truly was on the #1 Man's shoulders.

Later I was doing another special task I cannot talk about and during another Ceremony I received the prestigious Missile Man Award! Those were few and far between. We moved up to be the top team in the unit.

Peggy was pregnant with our first daughter and was seeing the Base medical people. She got her due date. We were both scared and overjoyed, we were going to be parents. Many of our friends were happy for us and we had people over often. Our neighbors Jackie and Harriet were becoming good friends. He was African American, somewhat slender and had a high voice. His wife Harriet was white and larger all around than Jackie. They were the first Interracial couple we had ever met. He was in the Air Force and she worked on the Base, but the marriage caused her father, the owner of the majority of warehouses in Los Angeles and very rich, to sever all ties with her. We got along well with them.

It seemed as though I was always on Standby. One Saturday afternoon I was called out to the end of the runway. One of the pilots called in a problem. The aircraft was sitting there with engines running. The pilot had reported a security problem with one of our weapons controls. I contacted one of my guys that was on standby that weekend day and told him to meet me with his tool bag at the aircraft. When he did I took it up to the cockpit and talked to the pilot. One of the weapons control switches that had to be wired and sealed so it could not be inadvertently activated had a seal that was questionable. I reached into the bag for one of the seals we are supposed to carry in the tool bags, I already had my crimping tool out and had already checked the system. There were no seals in the bag and my team member was still at the arming area while we had moved out to the runway. I got permission from the pilot to repair the old seal and crimp it. He said I could use the old one since he could see me safe the control. Which is what I was doing when he leaned over and asked me if I had my "High altitude" card. I did and soon was airborne for near three hour flight in the B52!

I got called in to Personnel and was told I had orders for Torrejon Air Base, Spain. It was for three years and I had less than that left on this enlistment. That meant I needed more time to accept the assignment. I could extend my current four year commitment with enough to accept the assignment. Or I could take a "Short" reenlistment that would mean I would serve an additional four years from then. If i didn't do either then I would complete my four year service at Mather and leave the Air Force.

Peggy and I discussed it. We had talked earlier about wanting to go to Europe but had pushed that thought back since I was told I would never leave SAC. This assignment would put me in USAFE (US Air Forces Europe), basically a TAC (Tactical Air Command) Base. We decided to accept it and I would take a short reenlistment. I went to Personnel and signed the papers and my Colonel did the honors to reenlist me.

We hadn't thought about it, after all I was only 21 and excited, but when I got the orders I had to report to Spain too close to Peggy's due date. I tried to change it but I guess I was "by name" requested for the position because of the work on the special project in Vietnam and they actually wanted me there earlier. Because we had already talked about Peggy having her mother come out for the birth we decided she would have the baby in Colorado. That meant she would be able to travel after six weeks from birth and they could join me in Spain. We definitely would not get any of my relatives involved, the year with my sister was not the best and my mother was still calling me stupid for marrying

Peggy and for having a baby. Then I got "stupid" repeatedly from my mother for going overseas, especially for leaving Peggy behind. I think I was stupid in their eyes for breathing.

We drove to Denver. We were both going to fly to the East Coast to see both Mom and Dad and friends who had never met Peggy. Her mother had a fit! We got a written note from the doctor that said Peggy was healthy enough to fly. While he was doing that he checked her due date and discovered the Base had messed up on the date! Peggy could have flown over with me and had our daughter in Spain! I could not change the orders. We also knew that would make it impossible to have her mother there, so we left it alone. Now I could get a car and apartment set up for them when they joined me.

We saw some of Peggy's old friends and when they noticed Peggy was pregnant they didn't realize we had been married more than 18 months and assumed we had to get married because she was pregnant! I honestly think she was such a shy girl they didn't expect her to be married, pregnant, and soon to be living in Spain!

When we got to Maine we saw friends and I got a chance to introduce Peggy to my neighbor. I soon became surprised and shocked when my neighbor started crying and held Peggy's hands and told her how proud she was of us both and that she had never expected to ever see me again! She alluding to what she saw and the way I was treated by my mother and all the trouble that had caused and the trouble I was in. We got very uncomfortable and told Tina we had to meet one of my old friends. We hugged her for what seemed a long time and left. Peggy commented that it must have been worse than what I had told her. We agreed not to discuss it then.

We saw my relatives and visited with Dad again. I put Peggy on a flight to Denver and I headed to Spain.

22

Chapter 7
Spain, Turkey, Greece, Italy and beyond

We landed on Torrejon Air Base and I was met at the airplane by none other than Wayne, the guy who brought me in from the end of the runway for my orders to Vietnam! It was like seeing an old friend and one of the first things out of his mouth after happy greetings was to Congratulate me! For what? For making Staff Sergeant ahead of anybody else! When he realized I didn't know he asked why Personnel at Mather had not told me? If they had I would have taken an extension and then reenlisted for the $6,000 bonus! Well, I got screwed again, and in 1969 $6,000 was a lot of money.

Oh, and I told Wayne I had nothing but black coffee since our first meeting!

I quickly fit in and was soon trained as a #1 man again on a four man team. We started to rise to the top, as usual.

The squadron had a mission change and was faced with major problems. We had to reconfigure about a dozen F4 Fighter Jets for the new mission. For us it meant downloading practice bombs and installing real bombs. If we followed the strict procedures we could never do the reconfiguration. I talked to my crew and then I went to the Officer in Charge. I told him we could do it, if we were left alone. He asked for specifics and I gave him just enough for him to mutter "Yes"!

The practice bombs are placed in a clamshell pod. Each carried six and were placed in a cradle that when released would be pushed out the open clamshell with a plunger being pushed by 300 pounds of pressure! It may sound crazy, but I positioned the crew so one guy would crank open the clamshell and then step back a couple feet. I would hold the small bomb in place, allowing no movement. Another guy would put the safety clamps on the bombs so they would not go "Boom" if we dropped one. Then he would take a tool similar to a screwdriver and when I told him to release the bomb I was holding he would use the tool to release it!

Knowing the laws of physics, I knew that is there was any movement before the bomb was released into my hands, I would never be able to stop it. But if I held up the bomb so it could not have any inertia, I could lower it slowly down with my arms and hands. I would then pas it to the guy behind me and he would roll it a few feet to my last crew member where he would put it in the storage rack on the trailer. The standard procedure uses a crank on an attachment that you have to mount under each bomb. You would have to crank the brace up to rest on the bomb, release the bomb, and then crank it down. Then remove the bomb and put it in the trailer rack. Then you would have to attach the rack to the next bomb, repeating the procedure for each bomb. And each aircraft had two dispensers, meaning 12 bombs for each aircraft. That way took over 30 minutes per aircraft.

The way we did it, we downloaded four aircraft, 48 bombs, in less than 40 minutes! I caught some crap for it, but we saved the mission and nobody was injured! Basically, my team saved the mission! We were recognized quietly.

My squadron had a commitment in Turkey and every second or third month we went as a squadron Temporary Duty to Turkey for 30-45 days. Our mission there was much different than Spain, mainly because we were about 10 flying minutes from Russia! We were always on alert!

The Turkish culture was hard to take in many ways, so we had to learn a few things to survive. If you disrespected Ataturk, the great father of the Turks, you would be harmed! That included such things as one American dropped a Turkish coin on the ground at a market and the coin started to roll. He stepped on it to stop it and he found a knife stuck deep in his foot! The Leader's face was on the coin so by stepping on it he stepped on the Leader's face and was immediately punished! He had to be sent back to Spain for treatment, and so there would be no further action by the Turks against him!

In between our Turkey trips I had to go Temporary Duty to Aviano, Italy, just northwest of Venice. And I had to do a special project with my team to Athens, Greece. I traveled a lot, as a matter of fact the week after Peggy and Susan arrived six weeks to the day after Susan was born I had to travel to Turkey.

I was promoted to Staff Sergeant and was told I was 21 days short of breaking the record for achieving that rank in our career field! That did help with me now being an NCO I had better quarters and privileges. I also had more money. We lived in an apartment building in a town named Alcala de Henares. It is a small town 7 miles north of Torrejon Air Base and 21 miles north of Madrid. Had I known of my promotion before I got there I could have applied for housing at the Base Housing Area, Royal Oaks, which was located right outside the back entrance into Cuidad Madrid.

I had bought a car from a dealership on the Base. The salesman, Alberto, did that only part time. We became friends immediately and he basically became Susan's Godfather. Susan was our first baby and my mother found another reason to call me stupid and remind Peggy that I should have married Glenda! All because the name Susan was not a family name!

Alberto's family lived along the southern coast in a town called Alicante. We were invited for our first Christmas in Spain there. We spent it with his family at their place. So many great memories of that. We were also later invited to his brother, Rafael's wedding to the daughter of the owner of Iberian Airlines! We were the only American couple there and went to both the wedding and reception.

While Peggy was still in the States awaiting her trip to join me, I went to a show at the NCO Club. I met a trumpeter from the band. Since I played Trumpet before my lip was damaged in the car accident,

I was drawn to the sound and Michael was very good, a natural artist and musician. We did a few things together, became best of friends and he went back to England.

In Spain we traveled a lot and visited Madrid as often as we could. Alberto introduced us to a Countess friend of his that actually owned a diamond mine and designed jewelry. The first meeting with her we immediately liked her and she said something about Peggy's diamond having a cracked setting! She saw it and showed us under her magnifier, it was cracked. This is the same diamond I paid $47 for when we became engaged. She said the diamond was very nice and offered to design and make a setting for it. We agreed and she designed a beautiful six point star setting for $160! It was so unique and beautiful.

During one of my trips to Turkey I was in the Base Exchange and heard my name being called in a somewhat high voice! I knew immediately it was Jackie! He and Harriet were stationed in Turkey and were of course invited to visit us in Spain. We met often when I came to Turkey.

So remember Harriet's father has disowned her. Jackie said her mother was trying to meet with her and they talked about meeting in Madrid, were we game for that? So every so often her mother would arrange a trip to Spain, often without her husband and Harriet would come to stay with us and meet with her mother! That went great until she came over especially to see her mom because she was pregnant. Unfortunately she had a miscarriage at our apartment. I believe her embarrassment was such she didn't attempt to come again and I also believe her mother laid down the law with her husband and he agreed to see her, at least that was the way Jackie explained it to me during one of my trips.

The only one to visit us was my aunt while on a woman's club trip. We had plenty of friends there, both American and Spanish One was a Personnel guy and we were very close and later he saved my career. I took classes and spoke often to the Portero at our apartment building and soon was speaking fluent Castilian Spanish.

Back at work I was recommended for the Lead Crew which are the trainers for all crew members. You had trainers specifically for specific positions, nobody trained for all positions, that is until I came along. Guess I was still trying to prove I am not stupid! I trained in all positions and could train others in those positions. I was a rarity, I was the only person ever to do that. Unfortunately, one of the duties of the Lead Crew was to maintain team integrity if for some reason a crew member could not perform his duties, then the option was to either decertify the team or the training member of the Lead Crew in that position could step in and keep the team certified. So like when a Team Leader, #1 Man, got food poisoning I filled in for him until he could resume his duty. Another time a #3 Man while boar hunting in Turkey fell and broke his leg, I filled in for him, etc. The main problem is most of the time the person was in Turkey so I had to fly over and fill in. I spent more time in Turkey with both scheduled rotation and member fill ins than anyone.

I also traveled to Italy and Greece. One Greece trip one of my crew and I were walking back to the Americana Hotel in Athens when we saw a group of people on the beach. As we got closer you could see the crowd was panicking and pointing out toward a girl swimming. She was in definite trouble and everybody was just standing there sucking air and pointing toward her! I don't ask why, I just do. I took off my boots and emptied my pockets, wallet included, into one of the boots. I gave my boots to my crew member and ran toward the water! Mind you, Athens beaches are not sand, they are small rocks! So my running until I got to the water was painful.

I dove in and swam to her. I was thinking how to tell her not to fight me, just lay on me while I swam in. That was a lot easier when I realized she was British and we could communicate. She fought a little but I was bigger and she soon gave in and we made it to shore. A couple people grabbed her and took her to a bench. I crowded in so I could see if she was alright. I guessed by her size and shape that she was probably 20 years old. She was calming down and explained she had a bad cramp and didn't know what to do until I swam out.

We were sitting on the bench and I was checking her pulse. She had been leaning on my shoulder exhausted and crying when I was physically yanked away from her! I was caught by a couple people who prevented me from falling onto the rocky beach! The girl saw that and almost at a scream told the man, "No Daddy, He saved my life"! The mother arrived and the father got a little information but quickly wrapped the blanket around her tighter and got her off the beach!

We left amid the cheers and back slaps, and I think a couple proposals. We got back to the hotel. I showered and cleaned up. My four person grew were going to get a drink first, a "Fix" which is the name of the local beer. Then to dinner and back for some more drinking. After all, I had just saved another life!

There was a knock on the door. We thought it was the two crew members in the other room so we said to come in. A hotel uniformed man entered. He informed me that my limousine was waiting for me downstairs! I asked and was told it was just for me. I had no idea what was happening and told my guys to stay out of trouble. I went down to the lobby and here was the man who grabbed me earlier. In a British accent he apologized for the earlier problem. He stated he saw his little girl and went a little crazy. He now realized I saved her life and if I would be so kind to allow him to take me to dinner?

His mother and daughter were in the limo. I don't know which vied for my attention more, but I soon found out the daughter was a very well developed 14 year old! Soon we were getting used to each other. He took us to a very nice restaurant. I found they were living in Southern England and were upper middle class, he owned his own company. Food was great and after dinner they dropped me off at the hotel!

I remembered where my crew said they were going, so I headed out to have a drink with my crew. When I found them I quickly realized they were having a lot more fun without me there! Something about me being the boss!

We went to work the next morning and finished early. A couple of us went shopping and then back to the hotel. I was given a note at the front desk with a time. I guess something might have been said the last night and I was prepared. Just in case I took the scarf I had bought my boss' wife along with me. Sure enough, the same limo driver came in and I went back out to the limo! A gift for the girl and her mother to fight over. And another great traditional Greek dinner to die for. I didn't have much money but told him I would pay for some of this. He refused. We did that three nights. I was invited to their house in England and hinted the young lady wanted to see me again.

I talked with her away from her parents until her mother found us. She repeated the offer and it sounded a little more involved than I cared for. I told them about my wife and daughter that I loved dearly. I assured her she would find a great young man she would want to marry and have kids. I told her if she did meet that man she was to tell him that her dear American friend would personally seek him out if he did anything bad to her! A little scatter brained in youth but there was a beautiful woman there just waiting to blossom.

Back at the shop in Spain I was becoming a "manager". I had achieved a higher level of proficiency that carried more responsibility. But there was something getting in my way of moving up. That was my boss. Fred was a Master Sergeant and he ran the weapons shop. He had the rank but his writing and management skills were very poor. That meant he was now writing my Performance Report and the written summary did not match the higher rating.

I can't remember how we got on the subject, but we did. He knew he was not a great writer and we worked out a deal. I wrote the Performance Reports he was supposed to do and then he put his form of expression to it and he did the rating. We kept it quiet, but I truly believe had I not done the writing there would be many Non Commissioned Officers (NCO) that would not see the promotions they did.

Fred also turned over most of the Career Counseling duties to me. We get a new Airman in and the Career Counselor is to help them move to the next proficiency level and ultimately persuade them to stay in the Air Force. I looked at it a little differently. All of us with higher proficiency levels were the ones going to Turkey and busting our collective asses working there. It was much more work at a much more rapid pace. If I could get these Airmen to the next proficiency level it would allow them to rotate to Turkey with us and reduce some of our work.

I tackled that by working with all of them and setting short term goals. I will never forget the three Airmen I took on. All about the same age but one of them was a stutterer! Gee, years before, so was I. The other two guys made fun of him, even calling him "stupid"! I did everything I could to keep from lashing out at them! All I could see is my mother calling me that! So I did get very stern and told the two that I didn't want to hear that word again! They laughed! So I told them they had better be prepared because I expected soon they would be working for the one they think is stupid! They laughed again and said that would never happen. I told them it would, because I was going to make sure of it!

I worked with all three but spent a lot of time with the one Airman. I helped him like Ida Hughes had helped me get over stuttering. We weren't able to get him to where I am but he was talking much better when he took a pause every now and then. During one of our training sessions I was talking about short term goals. He asked me what my goals were? I told him I had ridiculously high, long term goals. My biggest goal was to someday achieve getting a PhD! I told him if I got more than half way toward the PhD I would be a hell of a lot further than where I am now. But I am not going to accept half way as a goal, I would get my PhD!

When the testing came up for the next level, all three were ready. Their testing would be scheduled by their supervisors. I came back from a Turkey trip and the Airman I worked with on his stuttering had tested extremely high and would get his Proficiency upgrade ahead of the others who showed a need for more training in a couple areas.

When Fred asked me to get a couple Airmen together for a detail. I chose those three. And then told them the guy they called "Stupid" was the team leader for the detail, so he was in charge! They protested until

I told them he had passed the testing and they hadn't, so I was right, they would be working for him!

The story has an even better ending. He had taken my instruction so well he was promoted three months ahead of the other two! I was invited to his promotion party. I took Peggy. I knew he had married a girl from the Philippines but I had never met her. At the party, Peggy and I were the only Anglo couple there, all the other couples were anglo men and Philippine wives. And they split up; women cooking and preparing and men away from them talking and smoking and drinking. Soon Peggy came up to me with a spoonful of a green substance, "Here, try this". She was followed by at least two ladies telling her that it was too hot for me! They had chopped a Papaya with a machete into a pulp and then added peppers! It was HOT, but I could handle it!

After that party I could be walking on the Base and one of the ladies at the party would see me and loudly tell her friends, "There he is! The American who can eat hot food!"

As if he knew we were starting to get ready to return to the States, the President directed all overseas tours to be extended to save money or relocating military members. My three year tour was now a four year tour.

Not saying I was doing much more than expected and more than most anybody else, one of my pilot friends, Fred, a different Fred, let it slip that I was being rewarded for what I was doing. He would not say anything else. So the next trip to Turkey I was fitted for a G-suit, the flight suit like outfit that squeezes you when you exceed gravitational or G forces on your body so the blood doesn't leave your head and you pass out. And sure enough I went into the pilot flight briefing as the guy getting the incentive ride! I had won 7 awards but the incentive rides were few and far between. I was lucky, and I was assigned to fly with Captain Jack Frazier! He was probably the best along with Major Bonner that we had in the squadron. And it was "free air" in Turkey so there were no flight restrictions. In the US you had restrictions and had to follow flight paths. In Turkey we could do what we wanted, within reason. So it was destined to be a great ride!

We teamed up with Fred in another F4 and after strapped in we had a hell of an exciting 2 hours in the air! I got to fly it from the back seat, we did "dogfights" and went well past 5 Gs one time. I only got sick twice and was able to use the barf bags so I left nothing I would have to clean up later. It was the most thrilling thing I have ever done. Unfortunately three months later Captain Frazer had mechanical problems with the jet. He was able to keep it under control long enough to eject his back seater but he crashed and died.

Fred seemed like a quiet country boy from Oklahoma or Texas. He became a fighter pilot but getting to know him was hard because he was an officer and I was not. The fraternization rules were pretty stiff. We talked quite a bit on the flight line as if it was business. The flight with Captain Frazer and him in the other F4 brought us together.

One day we had a new configuration on the F4 jet. I was out near the end of the runway with a group of people. The aircraft was sitting there with engines running. A crew chief was doing final checks and removing the wheel chocks. It was a cold day and the crew chief had on a winter parka with a hood. The hood was resting back over his back and shoulders.

When anybody is working under the aircraft, the pilot must put his hands up where all can see. This is to ensure he is not working any controls. At that moment the crew chief came out from under the aircraft. His loose hood caught the jet intake and he was pulled into the engine tube! A couple of us made the sign of a finger across the throat for the pilot to shut down the engine! No response! I looked at the cockpit and the pilot's head was down along with one of his hands!

As usual, I was the first to react. I pulled a 14 inch screwdriver from my belt and threw it at the cockpit! I then went to the crew chief and grabbed his legs and started pulling! Two things were in our favor; the parka had pulled up and as he was being sucked in the fat over his belt and his belt got caught on the air speed indicator. The indicator stuck out a few inches and stopped him from being pulled in fully. Secondly, the pilot came fully aware when my screwdriver hit his canopy and he shut down the engine.

I had pulled him out unconscious and barely breathing. I monitored his vitals and directed someone control the bleeding from the gash on his side. Medics showed up and took him away. He survived. I was told I had saved his life. What, is that number three or four lives saved?

One of the guys I worked with was in a severe car accident and there was a call for people to donate blood. The first guy to take my blood was an old black man with very gentle touch. The process was simple, so I started giving blood regularly. Soon the old guy was replaced by a younger guy and that hurt! I had seen the benefit of giving blood so I continued.

The Commander came over to Turkey and announced to me that the Air Force was not going to pay me for unused leave again and ordered me to go back to Spain as the only passenger on a C5 heading that way! I was to take leave or else!

You get 30 days leave a year and if for operational reasons you can't take leave you can carry it over some next year but you get to a point with 60 days accrued where they have to pay you for the days over 60 not taken. I had been given a few days off after each long trip to Turkey or Italy and we would travel through Spain and maybe Portugal but I hadn't been able to take any leave for almost the entire time there. The Air Force had to pay me for that and the Commander caught hell for it, so he said I had to take leave and sent me back to Spain.

While I was back waiting for some paperwork to get into some restricted countries during the trip we were going to drive around Europe, Fred had come back for some reason and had just picked up a new Porsche Targa! He saw me at the squadron. He whipped in and told me to hop in and we headed for Madrid. In Spain there are no speed limits so we headed down the road very fast. I had raced cars and motorcycles so speed did not bother me.

We turned around just outside Madrid and when we did he stopped the car, got out and told me to get behind the wheel! Wow, what a car! As we were getting close to the turnoff to the base the exit to the right I took my foot off the gas. The exit to the right went up and crossed over the highway. Then another 3/4 mile to the Base. I slowed down for the exit and Fred asked why? I said the week previous a sporty Opel had crashed doing 70 around that curve. He let me know in no uncertain terms that this was not an Opel and as long as I didn't "Red Line" the Porsche, step on it! I drove the Porsche around the curve at 115 mph! Wow!

While waiting on the Flag Pass for travel into Communist Block countries, I decided to grow a beard, there was nobody there but one admin, everybody else was in Turkey. So with three weeks growth and not looking like a military person, Peggy, Susan and I took 34 days to drive throughout Europe. We drove up through Spain and onto the French Riviera. Then over to Italy where we spent time in Florence and spent a few days in Venice. We drove up near Aviano where I did a lot of Temporary Duty and then on up the mountains to Austria and Switzerland. At one sweater store in Switzerland we attempted to communicate with the woman store owner. We did remarkably well in spite of her only speaking Swiss and German while I spoke Spanish and English. I believe she said her brother was in Germany and owner a cuckoo clock shop in the Black Forest area.

We crested the Alps and down to Germany. We stopped to eat and went into a couple shops, one being a cuckoo clock shop. We talked to the owner and happen to mention we bought a sweater in Switzerland. As we were telling him, he asked what the woman we talked to looked like? He described her to near perfection and when we said that was her, he laughed and said that was his sister! We had some finger food with him and when we were going to leave he pulled down a clock from the wall and gave it to us! He would not let me pay anything!

Next was a couple days camping in Munich. It was Oktoberfest and I learned real quick that the Oktoberfest beer was very strong! I had one big bottle and felt the effects! One bottle of Lowenbrau beer and I was tipsy! It was crazy and everyone was having a great time.

We went to Amsterdam and stayed at a famous hotel overlooking the Gran Canal. We took a nice walk and as we were passing the Diamond Sector I was on the curbside with Susan in between us holding our hands. Admiral Zumwalt had just relaxed the facial hair standard for the Navy and coming up from the opposite direction was about four Sailors with beards! The lead guy stepped up to me and leaned over to say in my ear, "Hey Lifer! Ain't it a bummer that you had to pick up a bitch with a kid!" I didn't tell Peggy what he said.

On to Belgium and Luxembourg before we dropped back into France and to the ferry to England. We docked under the White Cliffs of Dover and set off to Canterbury for the hotel. Big problem was me driving a Volvo Station Wagon with steering on the left and we had to drive on the left! I did it but arrived with a massive headache! Then on to London.

First we met with my trumpet player friend, Michael, and stayed there a couple days before heading up to Scotland. We stayed in a Bed and Breakfast on the shores of Lock Loman. That evening we sat in their little bar area and were talking to this elderly man with two beautiful Irish Setters laying on the floor on each side of his chair. He asked many questions and then asked me, "Might your grandfather be named John?" Yes! And might your grandmother be a British lady named Mary?" Yes! "And might your father have been born on the first day of the year?" Yes! He went on to tell me he was a very small lad and was outside playing when they brought my father home from the hospital. He lived two "flats" down from them in Glasgow! What a night. What a trip! When the evening was coming to a close, the man and I argued who was going to pay for the drinks. The hostess/owner said nobody was going to pay, she hadn't had a night like this ever! The drinks were on the house.

In the morning she knocked on our door and asked if she could "borrow" Susan? I asked if I could go and we left Peggy to sleep more. We walked up the street to a farm where the woman who owned the farm had six Highland cattle that were actually friendly. The Highland cow is known for the long hair, and for a nasty disposition. However, she had kept the six in the lower pasture so we could see and actually pet a couple of the cattle!

We went to the Edinburg Castle. Quite historic and allegedly some of my relatives names are on the castle walls. Apparently my Grandfather fought is the wars. We went across the street to a Tartan Shop.

Since my father and I had just started seeing each other, still not calling him "Dad" yet, I didn't know what Clan I was associated with. The Brown Family Clan wasn't established until 1957 so I knew that was not it. I learned later that the surname Brown was most likely a misspelling. The scribe who was documenting the Clan names and sub-clans probably misspelled "Braun" and wrote down "Brown". I bought a nice Tartan gift for my father and we got a tartan skirt the same for Susan. Scottish women wear skirts, Scottish men wear kilts!

We drove down to Blackpool and then to London again. This time Michael took me to where the Tottenham Hot Spurs hung out. He used to be with the team. Well, they play hard and drink equally as hard. I have drank Vodka with the Russians, the Finnish and Germans with beer, and now with a Premier Soccer Team! They acted pretty normal until a conflict at the dart board. These guys are competitive at everything and when one guy won the game, his opponent sitting in a chair picked up a dart and threw it at the board, just missing the guy's ear as he was retrieving his darts. No words spoken, just the guy at the board turned toward the guy sitting with one knee over the other and he sidearmed the dart right into the middle of the knee! The dart was stuck straight in the knee as though it was a dart board! The guy slowly looked down at the dart, raised his head back up to look at the thrower. "Ow" was all that was said and all the team looking on just cheered and more drinking!

Back across the English Chanel to France. We got on the outskirts of Paris and I had a problem seeing the direction signs as they are down the road a little. Just then a grey Peugeot whipped in front of me and stopped. I didn't. My Volvo tapped his left side bumper hard enough the rubber made a mark on his car! He jumps out while tearing off his driving gloves and throwing them on the roof of his car. "Assurance, Assurance" he yelled at me while looking at both cars. I had American Insurance that I knew not to show to him. So I gave him my Spanish additional insurance we were required to have if crossing borders. I was hoping he was either mad enough or could not read enough Spanish to know it was supplemental insurance. We were in luck. He read what he could and then basically threw the Spanish Insurance papers at me and "You cannot get anything out of a damned Spaniard!" He jumped in his car and raced off with his driving gloves blowing off the roof where he had thrown them!

We continued back down France and back to Madrid and our apartment in Alcala de Henares. It didn't take long before I was back at work and school again. I had learned to speak Spanish through my Portero who ran the apartment building. However, I had started going to the University of Maryland classes taught on Torrejon Air Base. Besides taking normal classes I took Spanish 1 and 2 to get credit. Luckily we were taught the traditional Castilian Spanish where the pronunciation was different than what you would speak in countries like Mexico or states like Texas so I could more easily learn more by talking with the locals.

The locals had a name for me, "Rubio", which means light red as in reference to my Scotch heritage of light auburn/brown hair. I had so many friends, both Spanish and American. One Spaniard literally scared my American friends. He was large for a Spaniard, over 6 feet tall and very bulky. He didn't have all his teeth and his face was pocked and combined with his size, he was scary! Early on I had met him at the bar right outside our apartment building and I don't know why but we became friends! I think a lot had to do with me realizing what it was like to be missing teeth and having problems with my face. Mine was scars but I still knew what he must be going through.

I remember one day I was asked to sponsor a couple new guys that had just been assigned to Torrejon. I brought them down to my apartment to meet my family and some friends before we went to the bar. I had become very good friends with the owner/bartender Louis. We had just had a big laugh because I was speaking Spanish ordering beer for us. A Cana is a standard glass whereas a Corto is a short glass of beer. I had joked around and one of the guys said he didn't drink that much beer so I told Louis "Dos Cana y uno Corto" so he brought two big glasses and a short glass of beer for the one guy.

Pretty soon one of the guys said he would like to order. He looked over at Louis and tried to order three glasses of beer for us. Only problem is he mispronounced Cana and said a very bad word! The entire bar was laughing at this when my big friend came in! He walked up behind me and wrapped his massive arms around my shoulders in like a bear hug! I acted afraid and joked with him in Spanish and he roughly called me Rubio and rubbed the top of my head! I looked at the two guys and there was fright on both their faces! I told my big friend what he had done to them, but of course they didn't know what we were saying. My friend played it a little rough and as Louis brought our three drinks he acted like he was breaking it up. You should have heard the stories at the shop the next day about this crazy guy who attacked me at the bar!

Another day I was walking out the front of the apartment with an empty bottle of wine. I could take the empty bottle to the store around the corner and get a full one for 3 pesetas, we used the wine for cooking. As I came out the door to where a lot of bar tables were set up as usual on good days, two teenager Spaniards were harassing the Americans by asking, "Tu es Maricon?" and many Americans thought they were asking if they were America so they would say yes or Si. Maricon means queer or gay. When they asked me that I replied no and stated in Spanish that I was an American and they were Maricon! They got pissed and started to block me from passing! I told them to move and they got nasty so I flipped the bottle around so I was holding it by the neck and I lifted it up as if I was going to swing it. "Ben aqui, Pendejo"! I had learned some Spanish while stationed in Texas and New Mexico and in that Spanish it meant "Come here Stupid".

They started laughing, as did many Spaniards, enough so I could walk around them and get my wine. I finally asked one of my Spanish friends why they had laughed, and he started laughing also. He told me that Pendejo in Castilian Spanish did not mean stupid or ill of wit as it does in "Tex/Mex" it means "Pubic Hair" in Castilian!

I was back in Turkey again and our mission then was to load some ordinance on the centerline pylon on the belly of an F4 Fighter Jet. I moved the ordinance into position and duck walking under an F4 fighter. My knee collapsed and I fell face first onto the pavement. It was possibly due to the damage from the car accident. I was pulled out from under the aircraft and taken to the hospital I had what is called Chondromalacia, where the cartilage under my kneecap was damaged. The problem with my right knee resulted in temporarily removing me from my duties as a Weapons Mechanic. I refused surgery because then the possibility of full use was very poor. I had learned during my recovery from the accident about muscle groups and knew I had better odds getting full use back without surgery.

Another of my pilot friends said he had bad headaches but due to flying he could not take medications, he practiced Transcendental Meditation. He started teaching me that and after I got good at I could control the pain in my knee.

My tour had been extended like everybody's overseas from a three year to four year tour to help save relocation expenses. So I had close to two more years there and could not do my job. Unfortunately we had just gotten a new Lieutenant who thought he was as good as his father, an Admiral in the Navy, and the first thing he did was claim I was faking the injury! He knew I was the best in the squadron and now losing me was against his ego and his record. So he made sure I went on all scheduled rotations to Turkey and he gave me jobs like cleaning bathrooms. He directed me to do so many it was impossible to do all of them. He documented everything and threatened that he would destroy my career if I didn't withdraw the removal from the Career Field.

This went on for months until I was called into the Commander's staff room and met with some people who handled Classified materials for the Base. They needed a person knowledgable of the Weapons Operations and one that had a Top Secret Security Clearance. I told the Commander I only had a Secret Clearance and he laughed. He thought it was funny nobody told me that the problems with getting my initial security clearance in Denver was because they had to do much more in-depth investigation, equal to that of a Top Secret background investigation. He said any of my commanders could have just signed the paperwork if they needed a Top Secret asset and I would be assigned the security level! He signed it and then I kind of figured what was behind much of the treatment I got through the years. Command knew and I didn't, so they probably treated me different than the others. Anyway, I moved into an office and handled Top Secret paperwork for the Base. I was now able to work more diligently on getting my college degree.

Since I no longer had a career I had to test for assignment to another job where my knee didn't get in the way. I tested and then again they asked me what I wanted to do? I chose becoming a Computer Programmer so I would go to Programming school when we went back to the US.

We also had our second daughter, Carrie. She was born in Spain but we were due to go back to the States when she was about four months old.

Unfortunately I worked for the Lieutenant long enough he had to write my Performance Report and sure enough he dragged me through the mud with such low ratings my career was ended. Where 9 was the best you could be rated he gave me between 2 and five on every performance. He had screwed me and my career was soon to be over. I told my friend at Personnel. He was going back to the States about the same time I was so he masterminded a plan. I was to write my own Performance Report, rating myself near perfect of course, and sign it similar to the Lieutenant's signature. I was to drop it off at a specific office on a specific day just prior to flying back to the US. I did. I took my new and improved Performance Report to the office he had directed. The contact person had my records. He removed the bad report, stamped the good report and placed my records in an "out" basket. Within a minute or two the record was picked up and placed with a stack of records on a cart going to all the offices and picking up outgoing records. That was it.

We left Spain a couple days later and seated not to far from us was the guy who had altered my records. We acknowledged each other with a simple nod and never spoke. And damn, the Lieutenant had written one of the best Performance reports I have ever seen!

23

Chapter 8

South Florida

Homestead Air Force Base is where I was assigned but as soon as we got on Base I went to Shepard AFB Texas for Computer Programming training. I was the second to graduate so I left the school early and went back to Homestead.

We lived off base for nearly a year before I got on-base housing. It was very expensive, my motorcycle insurance was the highest in the nation and I later started working nights for the Miami Herald to make ends meet.

We found a small house in the town of Homestead while waiting to get on-base housing. Homestead had a nice statistic, it was the town most likely to get shot at in the United States! Luckily we got on-base housing.

I went to work at Data Automation as a Computer Programmer and soon found I was the second highest ranking NCO but the least experienced. I was tested from day one mostly to see if I fit in. The Lieutenant was prior Enlisted and had no right to manage anything, he was in love with himself and chose to treat NCOs like there was no way we could become Commissioned as he did. He made me feel like I was back with my mother and was being told I was stupid all over again.

The Burroughs 3500 system computers we worked on had the large disks and were fed information by use of IBM punch cards. He assigned me the largest customers, basically every one the other NCOs didn't want, I'm the new guy. And it so happens that if the customer has a very large, often 12,000 cards to run, chances are certain you would get called out to correct an error with the cards while they run the cards at night. I spent a lot of evenings back at Data Automation.

As I said, I was new to a very lax and somewhat unprofessional office culture. The first week I went around by myself and met and talked to everybody, I'm like that. Along one wall we had low filing cabinet, low enough you could pull a file and work on it on the top of the cabinet like a low desk. I came up to three Airman, two guys and one girl. She was sitting on the trop of the cabinet with a guy standing along each side of her. They had been in school together and they were the young click.

I introduced myself and each guy said his name and in unison each guy grabber the leg next to him and spread her legs wide, she had on a skirt, and then together they said her name and told her to take a picture of me! She was laughing and slapped them playfully. I stood there without any emotions at all and asked her if she wanted to press charges? She got a little serious and defended them by saying they were only kidding, playing around. I told her she could press charges any-time and if I ever saw them do that to her again I would start taking stripes. One guy had two stripes, the other had one. I pointed at each one and told each what charges could be levied and I told them legally how many stripes I would take from each. The word got around fast and I was on the Lieutenant's shit list.

I also didn't help my situation when I asked how come we don't program, only process? He snapped back and said there were three programs I could write, and then laughed after he went and got the program problems. One other NCO apparently had fallen into the same trap. He said the programs were basically unsolvable. Apparently the programs were something organizations on the Base had asked if it was possible to write? These programs would help their product? He added the Lieutenant had tried to do all three and could not! We concluded the Lieutenant just wanted to prove I was his underling and again how stupid I was.

A few days later I walked up to the Lieutenant and waited until there were some people around us. I handed him three folders and announced the program was written for the first two but we didn't have the available data base or memory to solve the third program. He was pissed and I was secretly told he would make it hard for me. I laughed, I had been through a lot harder than he could imagine.

Every three months we had a small group of guys from Puerto Rico that would bring their products and we ran their programs for them. The Lieutenant gave me that project also. That meant amongst three programmers I had more than half the programs and now the Puerto Rican account. The contingency came in very formal, almost Stoic. The Lieutenant was very businesslike and he spoke at a higher pitch like some people do when speaking to someone whose second language is English, he spoke as if they were hard of hearing. He introduced me and I stepped forward.

I was getting the Lieutenant angry at me often but what I did then really pissed him off! I introduced myself in Spanish and spoke only Spanish to them for about three minutes. Then I said to them in Spanish that I thought we should speak English now or the boss will think we are talking about him! Big laughs and the meeting was much more relaxed. And if that didn't piss him off, when the Puerto Ricans came in to Data the next morning we talked openly about our visit to a local restaurant and club after work the night before! They brought in two bottles of Don Q rum for me. I asked if I could give one of the bottles to the office and they said sure, they brought enough with them. So I handed it to one of the other NCOs and not the Lieutenant. I enjoyed pissing him off, he basically asked for it.

We had moved on Base housing and I was the Vice President of the Motorcycle Club we had on Base. I had traded up to a new Kawasaki 500cc triple. Fast and fun.

A neighbor of ours was a very quiet man. He was nice and he asked what I did for a job? I told him and he seemed to know it. His son was trying to get into motorcycles. He had bought an old Harley Davidson that didn't have an electric start. One day he had done some work on the engine and could not get it started with the foot kick starter. I heard it and went across the street to their house. I had on my motorcycle boots. I told him I could hear the engine firing but not getting enough boost. I flooded the carburetor with more fuel. I then stood with my left foot on the peg and right foot on the kick start. I basically jumped up and with all my weight slammed down on the kick starter. The engine fired but didn't catch.

I did it again with maybe even more jump and slammed down on the crank, holding it down. You had to do that or the engine might cough and throw the foot crank and rider up! I had seen broken legs from that. The engine sputtered and this time actually started running! It was then that I felt the sharp pain in my right leg, the calf muscle. I looked down and saw the corner of the battery protruding from the side right next to the kick start. I also saw the blood. I had torn my calf muscle on the corner of the battery! My right boot was filling up with blood. A few stitches and time to heal took care of it. There was a lot of blood.

The father came over to see how I was doing and we got a chance to talk. He asked me if I was interested in a different assignment? At that time with all the problems I readily said I would talk about it. I was right, he knew a lot about me. He confirmed I had a Top Secret Clearance. He said he would get back to me soon.

A couple weeks later he asked me to take a walk with him. We walked down to an open area by one of the holes for the golf course. We sat on a bench and he made sure there was nobody around. He asked me if I wanted a "Special" job? He would not tell me which Federal Team he was on. I guessed either CIA or FBI. He said my name had popped up and would I like to go to Washington DC and work on some special projects as a Computer Programmer? He said I could not talk about this conversation to anyone, Peggy included.

I told him I was honored. However, I had spent time in DC and had taken Peggy there. I knew she would not want to live there, and me neither. He understood. We never talked again.

I received a call from a General with 9th Air Force, our Major Command. He calmly told me the 9th was developing a Motorcycle Safety Training Program, the first of any military command. The reason being there were 40 times as many cars registered on bases than motorcycles but there were equal numbers of motorcycle and car fatal accidents! He noted the bike accidents always involved greater injury or death. He added he had asked the President of The Club but he was soon to retires and recommended his VP, me, for the position. There were to be 12 charter members led by a guy down on Shaw AFB, South Carolina and our first gathering was, and gave me a date. He said orders would come from HQ for the meeting. The plan was for people to dedicate a portion of their day developing the program and training while still working normally assigned jobs. He would have Base Commanders and 9th Air Force Command work with unit supervisors to make sure a portion of each day/week would be dedicated to this program and it not be additional work to a full day. I told the Lieutenant. He was already mad, saying some Colonel had contacted him and he had told the Colonel he could not spare me, but he was outranked and was told by the Colonel he would support the program!

I started moving work around to the other NCOs and had orders in hand for the first meeting at Shaw AFB. When I got back the Lieutenant told me I was scheduled to go to a Data training program in Chicago and I had better forget about the "motorcycle thing" because I was being assigned this new program and would/could not have time for the "fun thing" I thought I was going to do. The Colonel and General had expected something like this from managers so when I contacted the lead person of our Charter group my boss was contacted again and outranked again. I remember the General telling me later that my boss was a real ass.

While I was doing the training my boss threw in assignments as though he was daring the General to step in again. I did trips and training for both groups and was set up in the Base Safety Office with a desk and supplies. I started writing the motorcycle safety program. As usual, I spent many evenings at Data. I spent most afternoons at Safety, and still got the nightly calls to correct the program inputs from our customers. A day for me was in excess of 12 hours, easily.

When fully trained and the program developed, the Charter members would establish programs on respective Bases where Motorcycle operators had to go through our programs and pass the test to get authorization for bringing the two-wheeler on the Base. So half days were getting hard and I saw the good the people at the Safety Office were doing. I went to Personnel and put in for a change of career to Safety. I worked with the Personnel papers for a couple weeks because I hadn't been in Computer Career Field for 18 months yet. We were working on that, possibly getting the General involved. Then I had to travel for Data Automation again.

When I returned I went to Personnel to check the change status and was told nothing could be done for another 18 months because I was now Code 51! What the hell is Code 51? It was explained that I had put in as a volunteer to be an Augmentee Driver for the new USAF Conference Center! The present Air Force Conference Center was in Ramey Air Force Base Puerto Rico but was being moved to a new Center being built on Homestead. I told them I hadn't volunteered! I believed my boss had volunteered me. Personnel could only go with the official documents. I was stuck. This may have backfired on the Lieutenant because this would take even more time away from Data.

I went to the office set up at the Motor Pool and met with Staff Sergeant Howard Hoffman and said I was reporting for duty. He said I could not work for him as I outranked him! I was stuck and he was saying he didn't have time, he was writing and implementing the program. I suggested we work together. I would learn all there was and help develop the program. I think I also wanted to be more of a pain for the Lieutenant! We did build the program. We worked well together and the program was looking good. He had permanent party people assigned to the Motor Pool that would drive higher ranking, usually Generals or above. The Augmentees would shuttle around the lower rank attendees.

One day a group of VIPs from Canada landed and Howard was supposed to take care of them but he was swamped. I had learned enough so I grabbed a Staff Car and went out to the Flight Line Operation to take care of them. I did so and did it extremely well but the immediate boss, Major Arbuthnot came down hard on us both! I was not assigned to the Motor Pool, I was an Augmentee so I should never have done that! Later he talked with Howard. Since I had probably handled it better than anyone else could, I was allowed to help at that level with the Major's authorization. My Code 51 covered his butt enough to allow me to assist in the daily operations. Soon I was doing so much the Major gave blanket approval for me to step in when needed. I was getting a lot of favorable comments about my problem solving and professionalism.

I was still part day at Safety and teaching classes, still having to do more than my share at Data, and working with Howard. Howard said he was working a second job at the Miami Herald. He would go down late evening with a truck and pick up bundles of news papers and drop them off at specific areas for paper boys to distribute within the neighborhood. I rode with him and was immediately hired!

The first night I arrived at the Herald by myself I backed the truck into a slot. I watched the truck being loaded. I took a minute to go to the bathroom and when I rounded the corner coming back I saw another driver stealing some of my bundles! The boss sat up a flight of stairs in a glass fronted office looking down on the trucks. I walked up and I banged on his door! He acted like his English was poor, he was Cuban, he told me he couldn't help me! I guess they did it to new guys, especially white boys like me.

I started cussing him in Spanish and he smiled, opened the door and we talked. He spoke English very well and in about a minute he got on the speaker and told all the drivers who took my bundles to return them! A few nasty words were used to say what he would do if they didn't! We had coffee and from that night on we sat and talked in his office and never again was a bundle removed from my truck. I was surviving with about three and a half hours sleep a night, but the money really helped.

On weekends I worked at the Kawasaki shop in Homestead often training new riders in motorcycle safety. Soon Bird Honda on 40th Street in Miami contacted me to teach new riders classes there also. After a few months and both dealers were truly pleased with the great results, I was contacted by Bird Honda to come down to their Dealership. They wanted me to drive a new motorcycle they had. It was the first Gold Wing, number 14 off the assembly line! Since I was teaching the Base Motorcycle Safety class and was responsible for motorcycles being approved for Base entrance. And now I was President of the Motorcycle Club, they wanted me to be driving their new Gold Wing. I didn't like it. The switch to a drive shaft from chain driven was new and the drive shaft shook bad when full power was applied.

When I saw Al at Kawasaki he was not happy about Honda doing that. About a half hour after telling him he walked up and handed me a piece of paper. It had the cost, not retail, but his cost of the new Z1 900cc sitting in the crate on the floor. The price was actually $62 over cost. The servicing and setup by the mechanics cost $62. I now owned the fastest production made motorcycle in the world!

Meanwhile another General from the Pentagon contacted me and said he had heard great things about me! Apparently it was recommended he contact me to drive for Dr. John L. McLucas at the upcoming Commanders Conference! He asked if I knew who McLucas was? No Sir, I don't. He was the Secretary of the Air Force, the highest ranking person in the Air Force!

I first met briefly with The Secretary's Aid, Colonel Gene Farrington. He was a professional person and we planned the Secretary's first day. The following morning I realized Gene had done an extensive security check on me! We worked well together and even though the Secretary was not an easy person to work with. The Base Commander, Colonel Dudley Foster, stopped by and talked to me at least once a day, usually while I was waiting for the Secretary in the morning. Colonel Foster talked about all the outstanding comments he had received about me and my professionalism!

That was tested one night at a gathering of top brass at the Golf Course Club House located right outside one of the gates to the Base. We were to keep all Staff Cars inside the Base, and one of the coordinators could basically hide in the bushes with a radio for a staff car to pick up the attendees. Dr. McLucas wanted his car right there in the parking lot by the front door. After all, he was the ranking person at the Conference. So I sat alone in the best Staff Car by the front door of the Clubhouse.

While sitting there, the Chairman of the Joint Chiefs of Staff, General Jones, came out and I immediately signaled for a staff car and I stood at Attention next to mine. He said he wanted a ride back to his quarters and I told him I could not, Sir! He laid into me and asked me if I knew he was? Yes Sir! And that he was the highest ranking General in Active Service! He stepped back from me a little, he had been right in my face. He said something about he forgot there was a civilian at the Conference that outranked him and asked if I was with the Secretary? Yes Sir, but I had called a staff car, and just about then the car pulled in.

General Jones talked with me for a short time and just before he got in the car he said, "Since I have had a Star on my shoulder I have never had an Enlisted man tell me 'No' and get away with it. Well, you are the first!" Along with him being a very nice man for being in his position, I truly respected the fact that this was the first time during the Conference that he rode in a staff car, he normally took the bus with everyone else.

The last day I was at Dr. McLucas' quarters and Colonel Foster stopped by, pulling his staff car up to mine where driver window was to driver window. I had not only taken care of the Secretary but had done a lot of stuff while everybody was in the Conference and Colonel Foster thanked me for that and how great and professional a job I had done. He asked if there was anything he could do for me?

Yes, I told the Colonel about my attempt to retrain into the Safety field. He asked if I had gone through Personnel? Yes, and I have a large folder with all the paperwork. He asked if after I finished taking the Secretary to his flight, could I drop that folder off with his secretary. I did just that. Later his secretary called me and asked me to come to Headquarters at 3:30 pm by request of the Colonel? I was there at 3:30 and was sent into the inner office. The Colonel's secretary told me the Colonel wanted to be there but had to leave to take care of a problem. She handed my a yellow piece of paper that had the date April 15 on it. I looked at it and before I could ask, she told me that was my Class Date for training to be a Safety person!

My boss at Data was livid and I know he tried to get that retracted, but he couldn't. When we told family, especially Peggy's mother since the school was in Denver, most all were happy for us. Not all, as my mother didn't understand what "Safety" was and again said I was stupid for doing some of these things! And of course she got in again the fact I hadn't married Glenda, even asking if I was still married to Peggy.

The school went well, I had learned a lot from working next to Safety guys while doing the Motorcycle Safety Program so it seemed to come easy for me. My new boss at Safety and the Chief of Safety had welcomed me to the office before I had gone to school. Where other new Safety trainees in my class where wondering about their new bases they would be stationed at, I already had a desk and knew what I would be doing. When I left school it was just a natural transition, I went back to my office.

When I got back I was told the Chief was putting on a barbecue that Sunday at his house welcoming me to the Safety family. I immediately contacted David, one of the Motorcycle Club members and asked him if he would take my place that weekend at a charity race for a fallen Homestead Police Office? We were supposed to lead the opening possession at the race track and carry the flags and colors. David had come up to me much earlier and said he wanted to buy a motorcycle like mine. I told him it was too much for him to handle but he came from money and said he was going to buy it anyway! I trained him and he was pretty good, not an expert. I contacted him at the barracks and told him to come by Saturday and pick up my President's jacket and he could lead the parade. He was ecstatic!

Saturday he never showed up so I thought he was busy and would come by Sunday morning. I had checked the barracks and his friends said they saw him outside Saturday polishing his bike, so he must have a date, etc.

Sunday morning I was frantically calling around to find Dave. I was using the wall phone and had just hung it up when it basically rang in my hand. It was Dave Varnes, my new Safety supervisor, "Do you know a David A. Winchester?" Yes, I told him, I've been looking for him all morning. "He's dead, I will pick you up in a couple minutes."

My first Fatality Investigation as a Safety person. At the scene we could tell Dave was coming down the road where it "T"d onto another road. He was probably going too fast, could not stop for the Stop sign and went straight across the cross road and into the ditch. He was thrown forward and slid through the small trees and bushes until he struck his head on an old discarded cement traffic stop like what you see in parking lots. He hit it so hard it damaged the helmet but it also allowed his brain to slam forward and he died from that. It is called a brain contusion. And here he laid, looking like nothing happened! In the bushes lay a motorcycle that looked almost exactly like mine. My first Fatality Investigation, and my first week as a Safety person. And I was about to bury one of my best friends.

I took it hard! Peggy and I discussed what I could do to get out of Safety. We both knew I still had problems from Vietnam and asked if this would send me over the edge? I didn't leave but did make sure my investigation was beyond question. Later one of the Command Safety people contacted me and said by protocol any fatality report had to be reviewed all the way up our top headquarters and every level in between. All who reviewed it said the report was the best and most thorough report they had ever seen. I was still too depressed to get excited over it. I didn't tell a single one of them about my association with David. I put my personal self away and displayed my professional self. All the time the tears were just under the surface. My anxiety attacks got worse and now I was using Transcendental Meditation to keep my cool.

I was also asked by one of the State Police to teach Motorcycle Safety to some specific groups. The Coast Guard being one. We taught groups of organizations and new riders sponsored by volunteer Police. I got noticed by the Police Force and when I was investigating a drowning of an Air Force member and working with the State and City Police I got noticed again. I was asked to assist in more motorcycle fatality investigations and soon I was able to turn off all emotions and became known for my expertise and the ability to do it without emotions getting in the way. Granted, sometimes I would leave the scene and find a place to pull over and I would barf along the side of the road, I am human after all.

About that time there was a racial issue aboard a ship in the Navy so all branches had to have special "Human Relations" training. I was scheduled and I made it to the training almost too late and rushed to find a seat along the wall. There was one empty seat next to me and very soon the seat was filled. I didn't see who it was, I was still writing something when the training began. I then noticed the guy next to me had on a Flight Suit, he was a pilot.

The instructor said we were going to introduce the person next us and counted by ones and twos around the room. I was to introduce the pilot and him me. I don't know how he got anything about me to tell the group because when he told me he was a 6 1/2 year Prisoner of War in Vietnam and was held at the Hoa Lo prison all that time! We called it the Hanoi Hilton. Wow! And he was the first POW I had ever talked to. He was also the first Vietnam Veteran who talked about his POW experiences! Most of us Veterans did not talk, but Mel went on the premise if he could tell one person who could stop us from doing it again, he would talk!

We talked a lot and I was very surprised when Mel came to the Safety Office. He was assigned to the Flight Safety Office and I was in the next office in the Ground (Industrial) Safety Office. Our Wing

Commander was Colonel Guy who was famous for trying to press charges against some of the enlisted POWs based on them getting along with the captors. He also claimed he was beaten more than any other POW, etc. Mel talked only truth and we smiled when Colonel Guy had to present Mel with an Award higher than what he received himself.

When Mel was shot down he had broken his back from the ejection. He did not get medical treatment. He exercised and his back fused to where he could do just about everything. I imagined he got the desk assignment because of that. He did learn fluent Russian while in captivity. He invented the tapping communication against the walls so POWs could talk with each other through his created code. Mel and I talked a lot.

Each POW brought back was assigned a military escort to help them get settled and a few other things. One of the things was that Chevrolet was giving medium range cars to each POW. The young officer escort and Mell were at a Chevy dealership and the son of the owner was showing them stuff like the Impala series they had on the lot. Mel looked across at a bright Yellow Corvette and said he wanted that! The son apologized and said they could only talk Malibu or Impala models. The sponsor talked to the kid briefly and the kid agreed to talk to his father, the owner. The two appeared in the second story glass and you could see there was a lot of heavy discussion. Finally, you could see the Manager take something passed to him, hold it up, drop it in his son's hand. And then he turned toward Mel and presented a near perfect hand salute to Mel. The kid was there in a hurry and told Mel he had to fill out some paperwork and then handed Mel the keys to that Yellow Corvette!

The office was made up of mostly people retraining into Safety. It was said the Chief of Safety got his job because he had backed his truck into the Commander's car and was assigned to the Safety position to 'prove a point'. I noticed one of the new sergeants did not do the standard "On Call" rotation where one of us had to be close to a phone if our beeper went off and would respond to whatever it was, usually an accident. During a time a couple of us were together, the subject came us and caught our interest. We soon found out the Sergeant was doing the schedule and purposely omitting himself from the duty.

I had heard a rumor. Then I reflected back to when his wife joined Peggy, me and the girls on a short trip to catch some beach time on Miami Beach. It was a very uneasy venture. First of all, his wife was attractive, stood a good three inches taller than him, and had a very full figure. The part of the beach we went to didn't officially allow nude sunbathing, there were a few naked bodies laying around. And the bikini she wore left nothing to the imagination, her large breast were held up by very little cloth. Her bikini bottom was small but not as revealing as the top. She did make a comment that she had sometimes came to that section of the beach without anything on. It was obvious by the lack of tan lines. We were uncomfortable being there and trying to answer our daughter's questions about her body.

Back to the schedule and the rumor. Apparently, her husband, the Sergeant, walked in on our boss making love to his wife! And the payment was him being able to set the schedule and his work hours. We observed them at the office and what appeared as circumstantial evidence, the rumor may have been the truth.

I had now become one of the top Accident Investigator and possibly the top Motorcycle accident investigator in Command. Because of my ability to basically shut off emotions I often went into the hospital while they were working on the victim. A couple times I helped them with procedures like X-rays where they needed someone to hold a near severed limb so they could take the pictures. I was training new guys and taking on some management duties.

We got a new civilian supervisor Chief of Ground Safety. He was at Nasa before and really didn't want to leave but did because he thought he was as far as he could go there. Frank was a great guy and we all liked him. One day he came in and said NASA had contacted him and he was invited to view a launch. He could bring two cars full and get as close to the launch as the VIPs. So we piled in and drove up the Cape Canaveral and right up front for the Apollo/Soyuz launch! I climbed up a support tower for the "Crawler" and with my telephoto lens I got some great pictures. When we got back I took the film to the Base Photo Lab. They said they would develop the pictures.

One picture in particular was of the rocket blasting up in the sky and I caught a Seagull in the foreground that was very clear. It was a phenomenal shot! When I went to get the pictures I was told by the Lab that all the pictures in that roll looked like they had slight exposure and didn't come out. The negatives looked like something had been rubbed across them. I was quite upset.

My father came to visit! When we were in Spain my Aunt visited us while she was on a tour but Dad hadn't visited yet. We had a great time and although he was trying so hard to make our relationship right, he often went too far. We agreed he was a pain in the ass when he apologized and tried too hard. We talked some and that was when I found out he had wished he had stayed in the military. He envied our travel and wished he had the opportunity to travel. He said that often. We invited him to come to wherever we were stationed.

The Weather Office was in our building. This is where many units, especially flying units, got the official weather forecasts. I was talking with one of the Weather guys and he said the Base was trying to come up with a way to fight the costs of Air Conditioning during the summer. I thought heavy on this and put together a suggestion. I researched weather patterns, sometimes with a little help from my friend. I looked at times of day that were the hottest, etc. I was thinking along the line of the Spaniards taking a Siesta during the heat of the day. Hours were changed to accommodate that.

I submitted my official Suggestion. I knew that people got a share of money saved due to their suggestions, if the suggestion was through official channels. Mine was. I suggested the Base change the operating hours by one hour during the summer, similar to Daylight Savings. I had calculated the savings and I was looking at a good amount of money! I should have realized with everything that had been stolen from me, the Purple Heart and the tool design, I should not plan on anything.

My Suggestion came back declined! I asked why and they had no answer. I found out my suggestion was the only Official Suggestion for changing hours. I asked again, especially now there was talk of adjusting work hours! Finally the official word was that a Colonel had mentioned doing this in a meeting! What meeting? Was it Official? Was the cost savings defined? All the answers were unknown, only that a Colonel suggested it so my suggestion was not valid. End of story, screwed again!

Sitting in my office, I had been there about a year, loving it that Safety was exempt from any additional duties so I could work with little interruption. My Chief of Safety Colonel buzzed me on the intercom. He told me to get on the extension, he had someone who wanted me to join in on the call. It was a two-star General! I was asked if I would do the General and Command a favor? He acknowledged I was exempt but wanted to see if I would help them. He stated the new Secretary of The Air Force, the Honorable Thomas Moore, was coming for the Commander's Conference and all levels of command involved with last years Conference applauded what I did! It would be an honor for me to do it again.

He told the Colonel he would get off the line for a couple minutes so the Colonel and I could talk. Basically I was not sure I wanted to do it again but the Colonel said I would be stupid or foolish to turn down this request! He said there are people who dream of meeting some of these people, knowing they never will, and I am asked to work with them! He said he was jealous and maybe I could introduce some to him?

The General came back one the line and I agreed and told him I would get with Howard and see what has changed? Maybe do a practice run. He was so thankful. The office was stunned when they heard it from the Colonel almost immediately. By the way, my practice run was the Prime Minister of Japan!

I met Tom Moore and his aid. He had a slight cold and I ended up doing more than required for him. I didn't mind, mainly because he was one of the nicest people I have ever met. I pictured him like the CEO of a successful company and all employees were treated well and really liked him. So much different from Dr. McLucas the year before. I remember he asked me if I could take him and the General who headed up the Recruiting Command to the Recruiting Office in downtown Miami? Not a problem, I did not tell him my association with Bird Honda and the Miami Herald. I figured that helped me to negotiate Miami quite well.

They were in the back and Secretary Moore had a newspaper, the General writing some notes. I had a sticky squeeze open coin purse on the dash as I knew the road had a toll. As I approached it I took out the coin for the toll and rolled down my window to drop the coin in the hopper. My hand hit the window that I hadn't totally rolled down and the money fell to the ground. Without missing a beat i squeezed the coin purse and took out another coin and tossed it in the hopper! It took maybe five seconds before we were getting back up to speed. I looked in the rear view mirror and saw the Secretary looking over the newspaper at what I had just done. Our eyes met, he smiled and nodded his head in approval. He was kind like that.

We had a busy yet relaxing good time, I spent much more time with him than with McLucas. The day before he was to leave he asked me to take him to the Officer's Club right across from the Convention Center. He mentioned the complaints about the long hedge fronting the Club and the long stairway up to the landing and entrance. He mentioned he wanted to talk to the Club manager. Many complaints came from people going in the club and looking down from the stairway or landing at the area behind the hedges and the building. The area was laden with trash

He also set down the ground rules for me. He said he did not want to see me standing by the car waiting for him. I could get out about the time he was descending the stairs and then give the proper salute, open his door and we would be off. If, for some reason I had to wait for him outside the car, he did not want to see me standing at attention and salute every officer going by. He said to stand at "Parade Rest" and if the officer coming by was Captain or below I was just supposed to give them a military greeting, professionally, and only snap to and salute Majors or above. Okay. He went up the steps and was met on the landing by the Club Manager and a couple senior officers. I sat in the Staff Car.

The Secretary spent some time inside and soon came out with the Club Manager. He stood there just a few seconds before he walked to the top of the stairs and descended maybe two steps and stopped. I was already out of the car standing by the back door when he stopped and was talking to the manager while pointing at stuff behind the hedge. He looked my way but stepped back up a step and pointed at more trash.

I was standing there with my hands clasped behind my back and feet spread in what is called "Parade Rest". A lot of officers came by as I was stoically looking straight at the Secretary. Captains and Lieutenants I would turn my head slightly and say something like "Good Afternoon Sir". When a Major or above came by I would slam feet together, arms at my side and execute a perfect salute and recognize them. All is going well until . . .

Here comes my old boss from Data. He had been promoted to Captain and when I remained at Parade Rest he jumped up in front of me and started yelling! He was shorter than me so I could see the Secretary by looking over the Captain's head. I was ordered to stand at attention and show due respect! I was to salute him! The Captain was loudly berating me! He was making a big scene and told me he was not going to return the salute until I learned how to respect the rank, and him! You can't drop your salute until the officer returns it, so I was in full brace.

Secretary Moore looks puzzled and realized this was wrong. He started slowly down the stairs appearing to listen to the abuse the Captain was putting me through. He said sternly, "Captain". The Captain didn't respond and when I started to tell him the Secretary was calling him, he shouted at me that I was not supposed to speak unless spoken to! He was now demanding I would report to him for punishment for not respecting an officer! I looked over his head and Secretary Moore was down about two steps from the bottom. He put his arms out as to ask what was going on. He was still calling the Captain with no response.

I made a motion with my head and eyebrows toward the Secretary and the Captain asked what the hell I was doing? I simply said, "Captain, I believe the Secretary of The Air Force wants to talk to you"!

The Captain turned around and then quickly faced the Secretary and came to full attention and saluted. The Club Manager was still up on the landing. Secretary Moore told me to relax. I went back to Parade Rest. The Secretary informed the Captain that he would not be returning the salute for quite some time. He then spoke to the Captain and asked why he was harassing me? He said he would not let the Captain talk to his Aid like that! He said the Captain was acting like a spoiled brat instead of a professional officer in the Air Force! He looked up at the manager and said he now had the team to do what they discussed.

He turned back to the Captain and told him he was to put together a team of officers. The Captain would be in charge to form the team and they were going to "Police" (Clean up) the area behind the bushes. He told the Captain that he was responsible and would keep going until it met the Club Manager's acceptable scrutiny! It is your responsibility and you will report to the Manager until it is done, "Do you understand me Captain?" He said if the Captain could not do the job to the approval of the Manager, the Secretary would come to him personally and remove one of those bars from his shoulder!

The Secretary walked around him, never returning his salute. I opened the door, let the Secretary in the back seat and I got in behind the driver's seat. While I was buckling my seat belt I heard a real low type giggle. He had leaned ahead and asked, "Well how did I do?" I could not help but laugh. He asked me the story about the Captain and it made his laugh even more. I received a wonderful personal note of appreciation from the Secretary. Great man.

I did not do any more work with Howard or for the Conference Center. I was asked a couple times but before the next annual Commander's Conference I had an assignment to North Carolina.

Then there was Ken, a very handsome African American. He was unique because Safety had very few African Americans at that time. I was tasked to train him for field work and we soon became best of friends. His wife was one of the most beautiful woman I had ever seen and had the great personality to match. Ken worked well with me and often I would get a call to respond to an accident and Ken would come along. I had an extra helmet for him as we often took my motorcycle, especially if it was easier than a car to get there. For example, we had a dirt track just outside the base fence line and one day an inexperienced rider was on the track, lost control and scraped his unprotected knee along the perimeter fence, resulting in the kneecap being torn off the knee! We used to bike to get to the scene.

One Valentines Day we both planned on getting our wives flowers and we took my motorcycle down to the flower shop in the City of Homestead. I gave Ken the amount of cash for mine and he jumped off the back seat and went into the florist. I didn't want to leave my bike unattended in the City due to a high crime rate. A few minutes after Ken went in, a group of four African Americans approached me and started talking about how nice my motorcycle looked and started to tell me I was going to give it to them! Just about then, Ken came out of the florist with the flowers and got on the back of my bike as I started it up. A couple of the guys questioned why he was riding with me Ken simply replied, "What, you jealous you don't have a 'Honky' chauffeur?. He then tapped the top of my helmet and said, "Home James!" and we drove off without incident.

The incident with the perimeter fence was the catalyst for Ken leaving the Safety field. When the ambulance got to the scene the guy was transported to the emergency Room. We were there when the ambulance got there. I knew a lot of the Med Techs and it was a Sunday, so the Tech asked if I could help him with X-rays? As I did, Ken was watching and the sight of the gory mess that used to be the guy's knee got to Ken. He told me later he had nightmares from that sight and honestly didn't know if he could take all the blood and guts he saw. He and his wife talked and soon he let me know it had been great working with me, but he had taken a position as a Recruiter.

One of my jobs was to come up with cute Safety sayings to put on a couple billboards. We changed the sayings often, especially if there was an event or holiday. A lot of emphasis was being placed on seat belt use as it was very low. Ken and I came up with a plan and the boss said it was okay, he would take the heat.

We bought a bunch of lollipops and put them in a large plastic bag so anyone could see what they were. Then Ken and I went to the gate by the school and stood there while parents had picked up their kids from school and bringing them back on Base. We were standing there with all this candy and the kids were going wild, all smiles! That is, until we looked to see if the driver was wearing seat belts. If they were, the kids all got candy. If not, the kids were told they could not have any candy because the driver was not wearing a seat belt! The boss pulled the plug on that after about a week because of all the parent's complaints, but we found seat belt use increased dramatically!

I had a suggestion for a seat belt slogan and my boss laughed but said he would back it until the pressure got too bad. The slogan did not last a day! The picture was the two ends of a seat belt about to be connected. The slogan under it read, "Save A Life, Belt Your Wife"!

24

North Carolina

Seymour Johnson AFB, North Carolina. I believe it was a "by name" request for the assignment. Goldsboro, North Carolina was a nice community, however we moved directly into Base Housing without any wait. I think they said I was "Key Personnel".

We went up to Maine for a Class Reunion. My mother said my sister had been upstairs and had gone through all the stuff mom had. My mother said my sister had separated all of the stuff into two equal piles/stacks. Politely, Bullshit! She had taken all my mother's jewelry! We were upset because she had two sons and we had two daughters! We believed most of that stuff should pass down to girls in the family. My sister had taken everything of value, either sentimental or monetary. She had it all neatly stacked along the wall. My "half" was crap with no value in a heap in the middle of the floor. Not only was I pissed off, I was hurt. I don't know why, it was normal. Mom was moving to a new rental. I looked at the junk and I wanted to leave everything, so I did. The pile was still there. The only thing I took from the stack was a bible, a true antique that was priceless.

My mother still insisted I married the wrong girl!

The guy I was replacing was going downtown Goldsboro to get a bed for his son and asked if I wanted to come along, he would show me the city. We left the Main Gate and then took the first left toward the city. On the right was a gas station that was shut down then to replace one of the pumps. An old black man was there swinging a pick axe breaking up the concrete base the pumps were set on. We drove into the gas station and the driver pulled up to the pump and addressed the black man, "Leroy, how are you all doing?" He talked to the old man some more and the manner of speech and attitude bothered me. When we drove out I asked him if he knew the old guy? No, he didn't. So why did you call him Leroy? "I call all the old black boys that."

I made some excuse and got him to drop me back at the base. I didn't really talk to him again and didn't go to his going away party. I just am not like that and don't want to be.

I was still fighting the "stupid" thing. One of the first things I did when we got back was to enroll in the local college. I was more than half way toward my Bachelor's Degree and wanted to keep the thing moving forward. I had seen more than my share of death and severe injury, so I started improving my CPR and First Aid techniques. I got very good and soon started teaching mostly CPR. I got very proficient and soon became the second Instructor Trainer in Southern Virginia/ Northern North Carolina. I volunteered to teach at the Base Hospital and was soon teaching a 16 hour CPR training class there.

I got to know many of the medical people. One night at the Hospital I was co-teaching with Larry. He and I thought of a good exercise to determine the level of competency of our graduating students. We called it the Hysterical Bystander test. At near the end of class on the last night I would take one student at a time and walk down the empty hall by the training room and all at once throw open the door to a room where our CPR dummy was on the floor. "I am not here" I would say until the student realized the exercise was to assess and perform CPR as trained. When a rhythm was started I would let one of the volunteers I got to come in and start screaming something like, "What are you doing to my sister?' and then start pushing or bothering the student!

Our training had covered what to do, most likely to keep the bystander busy by having them call 911 or something like that. If the student did something like push the bystander I would stop the exercise and inform the student that he/she just broke the law by using physical force. I would tell them that because of the problems it caused at the moment, most likely the patient, our dummy, died! The exercise got the highest rating of the entire class and often a lot of humor since my prize volunteer was a Black Doctor! When Winnie came in and asked what the person was doing to her sister, the student was often really taken back. Mainly because the CPR dummy was white.

Since I trained under the Charter of the American Red Cross and American Heart Association I was granted permission as a Red Cross Volunteer to work in the hospital. I helped out in the Emergency Room under the watchful eye of Mike Hartford. Mike is probably one of the best medical technicians there is. He had no hair on the front of his head because as a Fireman and Medic he had run into a burning house and saved two kids. The fire was so hot his helmet burned to his forehead and when removed off his head it removed about a third of his hair.

I had attended the Accident Investigation Training for Security Police. The training held at Lackland AFB in San Antonio, Texas was as good as City and State Police Officers get, and each class had a slot open for a Safety Professional recommended by major command. I was the one selected and found there was another unique thing with me attending, I was the ranking person in the class!

I got along well with all the Security Police in the class. I had driven my Ford Econoline van that I had customized. So often I had a van full of people from the class. One day, with seven Cops with me, we went to the Base Exchange area to grab a quick lunch at one of the vendors. I was slowed to near stop as a car was backing out of a parking slot in front. All at once a Security Police operating a radar speed gun waved us over to stop! I was doing maybe 5 mph as I was waiting for the car to exit the parking space.

I pulled over and the Cop came up to my driver's window and instructed me to shut off my vehicle and pull out my license and regis-tration. I had high-backed king seats in the van and tinted windows so he could not see anybody in back. I asked the Cop what he was stop-ping me for and he replied I was speeding well over the posted speed limit! He stated a number and I knew he was full of it! So did the Cops in the back of my van. I heard one whisper just behind the seat, telling me to act normal!

I saw the back door to my van open as I glanced in the rear view mirror. All my passengers had their uniforms on so there was no doubt who they were when they appeared on either side of the young Cop! They all outranked him by a lot! He looked stunned as the guys actually picked him up and put him in the van. I was given directions to the Police Headquarters.

When we got there I parked right in front and accompanied the entourage of Cops literally carrying the young Cop into the building and toward the Command First Sergeant's office. Nobody bothered us, they stepped aside, including the security at the entrance. The secretary stood open mouthed and one of the Cops told her we were there for the "First Shirt". She made a motion and apparently more than one knew the office and the man because I heard a couple voices directed at the man by name and rank. We entered in and the guys holding up the young Airman planted in front of the Shirt's desk!

First they introduced me as the Class Leader and the Shirt asked what the hell was going on? One of the top guys with us told him the entire story. The Shirt asked if this was true, to which all of the Cops said yes, they were eye witnesses to that! The Shirt shook his head, asked where the radar gun was and had it been tested? Again, the lead Cop said he had turned it in with the clerk downstairs and he had verified it was in correct operation.

The First Sergeant came around the desk, the young Airman still at full Attention. The Shirt reached over and took the Airman's Badge from his uniform and told the Airman that he was now back in the first class on new Security Police and if he didn't stay in the top 10% of the class he would be reassigned to either Cook or Motor Pool! He looked at the badge and said he knew he could not do it, but he wanted to give me the badge! Instead we had a strong grip handshake and an apology.

Back at Seymour Johnson I continued volunteering at the hospital and the Chief of Security Police often asked me to come down to see him and often asked if I could help with an investigation. I worked with most of the Security Police and I was accepted. I was also given right-fully the control of an accident scene during my safety investigation.

I got a call and responded to a severe vehicle accident where a guy in a Ford Falcon station wagon was drunk behind the wheel and speeding on Base. Right before you get to a "T" intersection where the Fuel Farm was located and protected by high metal fencing, the road had a huge dip where it dropped to where we had railroad tracks, then straight to the "T". The Falcon cleared the ridge and the front end bottomed out at the tracks. It caused the Falcon to flip end-for-end four times before coming to rest just shy of the intersection. There were car parts all over the place and although the driver survived and was transported, he left a lot of blood and some body parts.

I asked if the Base Photographer had been called and was told she was on the way. She? I knew most of the photographers and I didn't know a 'she'. When she showed up I found she was new to the job and had just been assigned to the Base. I told her how I wanted the scene photographed, starting from the direction the vehicle was traveling and then the path and marks up to the wreck. Then do a 360 degree of the wreck at the same distance from the wreck, making sure she had adequate signs or similar so we can relatively estimate distance and measurements.

When I told her then to come in closer to get some specific shots, like his bloody ear laying just inside the car, she got hostile! "I am not going to take that picture!" I talked, she shouted. I was told she would get sick if she had to see all the blood and parts, and she wanted to see the on-scene Commander to complain about me! In a relaxed tone I told her I was at that moment the on-scene Commander and if she had to get sick, don't do it in my accident scene and don't barf on the camera in her hands, it belonged to the Government. She was now crying and said she would not take the pictures. I calmly said if she didn't and I had to take the camera and the pictures, she would never work as a photographer in the Air Force again! She cursed me, said I was not a human being, I had no compassion, I was an asshole, and a lot worse names! She ended up taking the pictures, barfed a few times, cried a lot and extended her middle finger as she left!

The next morning bright and early, I got a call from my friend, her boss! He asked me what the hell had I done to his new photographer, adding he didn't know guys who talked as bad as she did. I am now the scum of the world in her eyes! So I asked what he said in response? "That was easy. I told her you were the best and she could learn a lot from you."

Probably three month later I was investigating another crash and she was the photographer they sent. She was smiling and I asked her if she was ready to be a photographer for me? "Yes sir, I know about you!" I asked but she would not tell me. We did the shots and when I was supposed to release her, I wouldn't until she told me what she knew about me. She said she was appalled by my lack of any emotion, I was not a human being. Then she found out that sometimes after I did my job as a professional that I might stop along the road and vomit in the ditch! I was apparently human after all. We had many professional meetings at accident scenes and we became friends.

I was still giving blood. They had a blood drive at a tent outside the hospital because of a need somewhere, so I went there instead of the usual Blood Bank. I happened to be lucky enough to have one of the doctors, a female red haired Major who was lucky enough to get me! She knew it all, just ask her, which I could not because I was Enlisted and she was a Commissioned Officer, a Doctor at that! She was a terrible stick with the needle.

When she came to me on the donor's chair I told her I had given a lot of blood so she will see scar tissue on the right inside elbow and my left inside elbow the veins crossed at an angle and were harder to stick. She didn't care. She put the tourniquet on my upper arm, cleaned the area with alcohol, and then roughly jabbed the needle in my left arm! The problem was, she pushed the needle through the vein and the end struck my muscle! As can sometimes happen, the body will react and mine started to go into the fetal position! I quickly grabbed the needle and pulled back slightly until I could not feel the needle and then guided it into the vein! "Please put some tape on it".

From my work in the hospital and my training I knew veins do not have nerves, so if I could not feel the needle it was most likely in the vein. Of course she didn't see it that way and soon I was greeted by two Security Police at my side. She had reported that if someone can do what I did to myself, he was a drug user! I told the guys not to waste my time, there was plenty of blood I had just given that could be tested, I am clean. They still had to take me to their boss, whom I knew fairly well. When I met with him he was laughing and asked who I pissed off now? He was still laughing when his guys took me back to get my motorcycle.

I was often the Safety who was asked to go to the hospital following an accident. I knew the hospital staff and they would talk with me. I had also become the alleged expert on Motorcycle Fatalities. One night I was awakened by my phone and told by the Duty Officer, "Under the verbal orders of the Commander, you are to go to Danville, Virginia and investigate a motorcycle fatality". He gave me some specifics. I got up, cleaned up, and drove to Virginia.

I met with the Sheriff and was immediately told that our, he used the N word, caused a fatal accident. On his motorcycle he had come around a corner and ran head on into a car. There were five teens in the car and all 7, including the (N word) girl on the back of the motorcycle had died. He made it clear our Air Force, N word again, was at fault and the Air Force would pay heavily! Our Airman had just got out of Basic Training and was home on leave, the rider was his girlfriend.

I checked into a Motel 6 type hotel and started reviewing the records I had received from the Sheriff. The elderly lady at the motel counter was very impressed with my manners and we kind of formed an friendship. I would stop and talk with her when I came in or went out She and her husband owned the motel and he had passed a couple years before. She went out of her way to tell me the best places to eat, etc. She happened to tell me the driver of the car was the Sheriff's nephew!

I went to the scene and started looking at tire striations and marks on the pavement. I did measurements and took photos. I walked the entire site, including down the hill where the car, a Chevy Camaro, had gone through the guard rails and down the embankment. I came to a definite conclusion, one I could prove with my investigation. The Camaro had come around the corner at a high rate of speed, cut the corner and impacted head on into the motorcycle. Our driver had been thrown through the windshield and into the driver of the car. His girlfriend on the back was ejected into the air and landed on her neck in the middle of the road, dying instantly. With a dead body on the lap of the car driver, the driver lost control. The speeding car crashed through the guard rail and all the people inside died from the crash. Not a single one of the five in the car was wearing a seat belt.

I went back to the motel and started writing my report. I contacted the Sheriff's office on the availability of the Sheriff to brief my findings. The meeting was scheduled for the following afternoon.

When I briefed the Sheriff he became visibly angered! He was shouting that I was full of shit! He said I didn't know what I was talking about! He asked why the Air Force sent such a stupid person, etc. He was threatening me, leaning over his desk and screaming at me! Two deputies moved in closer to see what was going on and intervene if necessary! I left as he was throwing my report at me and saying he was going to get my ass!

I went back to the motel after I gassed up my van. I told the lady I would be checking out early in the morning and paid my bill. I gave her my information in case there was something I owed. We talked a while. She told me, "Why Mr. Brown, you are such a gentleman I am sure the Air Force must be proud of you!" I went out to eat, came back and packed my bag. I watched TV for a bit and around 11 o'clock I went out to my van and drove off. Two days later I got a call from the lady at the motel. "Mr. Brown, I guess you are right smart too." She said at about 2 or 3 in the morning three pickup trucks, she recognized one as belonging to the Sheriff, pulled up in front of the motel. Many men jumped out of the trucks and busted down the door to the room I had been in! I was a couple hundred miles away by then.

I continued Motorcycle Safety training and started off-road safety training. I believed that a novice rider could practice and fall with a lot less consequences on dirt than if he was learning on the highway in traffic. There was a large sand area with nothing around it right after the end of the last houses on my street. I got permission to use it. When it was seen as a success, the base motorcycle club was authorized to use it and build a "safe" dirt track. I designed the track and the Club built it. It include a jump that was way past beginner level and made for advanced riders like me. When someone from the Base came to look at it he was not happy with the jump! I showed him by walking to it and by riding my dirt bike that I built in a straight track so this was not a part of the track unless you were very experienced. I did both the by-pass and the jump and even though just seeing it scared him, we were allowed to use it with people signing a waiver.

I also kept cooking. I started as a kid out of need because my mother was not always there and then spending all the years overseas I learned to cook foods of the different cultures and styles. For instance; five of us got together for Monday Night Football at a different house every week. The week it was to be at my house I made Philippine Lumpia. However we had an Exercise that night and all of us had to go to work. The following week I brought the frozen Lumpia to my friend's house. He was married to a woman from the Philippines. I had forgotten, and she first asked me was why I brought them. I told her. She basically said I would probably be taking them back home, she had made her own! However, later she snuck in to the TV room and asked if she could talk to me? I followed her into the kitchen and she said I didn't tell her that my wife was Philippine! I said she wasn't. Then she asked who taught her to cook like that? I told her I cooked them and she did not believe me! After a short time I was able to convince her that I did. I went back to the TV room. A while later she again asked me to come to the kitchen. She asked for my recipe! She had never had them like the way I cooked them. Basically, there are 39 different dialects of Tagalog and each different region cooked differently. I showed her how I had learned to use raisons as a natural sweetener and she was elated!

One thing turns into another and apparently she had talked to all her friends and others at work. I was approached by the Adult Education person on the Base and after we talked I started teaching an adult cooking class! And that was the first time I wrote the Spice Section of a published cook book! Spices were my strength, even cooking a meatless casserole that one of the other teachers could not tell it didn't have meat! I loved to cook, and was very good at it.

Peggy and I took the girls and drove to a lot of places. We had seen most of Europe and decided we needed to see more of the United States. We actually drove to Yellowstone National Park! We stopped and saw many things along the way there and back. Peggy and I went to New Orleans. We also drove up the coast. We lived close enough to the Atlantic Ocean we did a lot of day trips.

Peggy had surprised me earlier by contacting my boss for a surprise. He had authorized leave without me asking so Peggy could take me on a trip to Cozumel Mexico. We went to an all inclusive hotel, rented a scooter, toured the island, ate a lot of seafood, and decided we needed to continue traveling like we did when stationed overseas. So we planned to travel every year for our anniversary.

I was reading the Air Force Times one afternoon and I saw my picture of the Apollo rocket lifting off with the seagull in the picture! That was the one the Homestead Base Photo shop said was destroyed, but there it was in the paper! The caption read the same as what I had called it! The guy who submitted it was not known to me but it said he was from Homestead Air Force Base! The picture was submitted and the photographer said he shot it at Cape Canaveral on the same day that I did! The picture won second place in the World Contest and his prize money was in the thousands! I got screwed again!

During one of my inspections I met a guy who was a professional painter. He was a painter by trade and liked to paint characters as a hobby. I showed him some safety comics I had been writing. He loved them and took a couple of the crazy stories I had written and drew comic book style characters to match the story. While researching what the typical military member reads first in a newspaper, I found most read the cartoons first. So I created the crazy antics of the "Safetyman"! I went through my boss and sold him on the idea. Then I met with the Base Commander and pitched it. He loved it and brought in the guy who edited the Base newspaper, and he loved it. The Commander asked how long I was planning to run this? I told him I had quite a few stories written that covered topics like Seat Belts, Bicycle Safety, Fire Safety, etc. All with this crazy Safetyman that told the story through humor. He asked what would be the thing that would stop me from writing the articles every week? I said nothing, except if someone tried to rewrite what I wrote. He agreed and I wrote a weekly article about Safetyman with cartoons from my painter friend.

I was also on the radio once a week! A local station had me come in and talk about the Base Safety Programs. Peggy listened every week and would report to me the number of times I said "Um". I would walk in from the radio station and the first thing she would say is maybe "7" or another number. Besides Ida Hughes breaking me of stuttering as a kid, Peggy helped break me of saying "Um" during pauses of sentences. I now count the number of "Um" other speakers say because I don't say it at all any more. I told a group of Safety people during an invite for me to talk about my writings and talks/speeches, that saying "um" was like a man with a pipe! "A pipe gives a wise man time to think and a fool something to stick in his mouth!" Meaning you can use "um" if you need to think but should not be used without thought.

Soon my immediate supervisor, Verne, started taking the credit for my Safetyman series. I walked into the office and caught him twice doing it. Others told me he was doing it also. One day when I sent my article to our secretary I got it back different than what I wrote. I asked her and she said Verne had made some changes to it. I took the article and tore it up and threw it in the trash! Two weeks passed without the Safetyman article when the Base Commander came to my office! I could hear the people in the offices he passed telling people to come to attention, so I knew some one was coming. He came in and told everyone to stand down and came directly to my desk. He asked what had happened and I simply pointed toward my supervisor without saying a word. He turned to Verne and asked if he had done something to my article? Verne said he was trying to help me by editing. The Colonel tore him a new one and said one of his people heard he was also trying to take credit! Verne was told that the Safetyman articles were mine and if he touched the articles again he would have to answer to him! I wrote the article for another couple years. I had a blue Ford van with a blue spare tire cover on the back. My cartoonist friend painted Safetyman on the cover. So many people honked their horns and waved or talked to me when they could, it was a huge success.

The Flight Safety office was down the hall. We were on the second floor with the access a narrow flight of steps. I heard a lot of yelling and went to see. One of the Weapons guys was bringing up a 304 pound four drawer document safe using a dolly! It was too much for him to pull the dolly up and the stairwell was too narrow for two people to pull, The Flight Safety Officer was entering the building and saw he could maybe help by awkwardly pushing up from the bottom. The guy at the top, pulling the dolly lost his footing just about the time he was near clearing the floor landing. One hand slipped and it was certain he could not hold it! If he let go the Flight Safety Officer was going to get hurt badly! I stepped around the guy on the landing and grabbed the upper side of the dolly just as it slipped from his hands. With lifting experience I stepped down one step and grabbed the dolly to stop it's slide. Once secure, the guy could grab it again but he could only get hold of the top corner. Together we raised it and my back was nearly touching the wall of the landing. I lifted it straight up and swung it onto the landing! Since I twisted with over 300 pounds, I messed up my back! I could not stand straight for 3 1/2 weeks! The Captain pushing the safe did considerable damage to his wrists and pulled a muscle in his arm. He said if I had not done that he was sure the safe would have ended up falling on his head. He said I probably saved his life!

Then it was the Weapons Safety office. It was run by a young Lieutenant that took credit for everything the three guys under him did. It was so bad. He also treated them like crap, no respect at all. The guys started doing things to him. The Lieutenant might come in first thing in the morning and find his desk stacked on top of two other desks! He might have Vaseline all over the hand piece of his telephone, etc. all to send a message to the Lieutenant what he was doing was not right. He didn't get the hint and I think he thought it was like a game. Then he got orders to Greece.

The guys told him to come talk to me since I had been there. He ignored them. He finally did come see me. He looked down on me as he did his guys. I told him a couple things which I believe wasted my time. However when I told him they had a special program where he could sell his American car to one of the Greeks after 18 months and make a bucket of money, it got his attention He didn't believe me and apparently asked someone else who verified that. He came back to see me, this time very interested.

I told him that since he was authorized to take a car over, he should buy a very large and very black American car. After he drove it 18 months he could go through one of the Greek agencies and sell the car. Most likely a Greek businessman would buy it for possibly twice what he paid for it! He bought a Ford LTD, solid black of course, and shipped it over to Greece!

I was still involved with the hospital. The head doctor asked if I would like to attend the hospital classes to become an Emergency Medical Technician (EMT). I had already helped at accident scenes so when the head of Surgery, asked if I would like to take the training, I jumped on it. Luckily the classes were in the evening and weekends so I could work and attend the classes. Mike had taken me under his wing along with Jan, a new med tech that really was going places, she just had "it". We trained and worked well together. We made a great team. When it was time for the class to take the EMT test for the State of North Carolina, the instructor suggested we team up on the Team tasks. On individual tasks we were on our own.

We went to the State testing facility and took our written test first. Jan and I both scored 100 on it. We did our personal physical testing and both of us scored high. When it came to the Extrication testing, Jan and I were teamed up with another two person team from a local hospital for the four person testing exercise. Jan told the other two that I was exceptionally at this so I was pronounced the Team Leader! We did the entire testing and when we were finished the head examiner asked who our trainer was? We told him Henry. He stated if Jan and I showed how well we did it, he was going to bring the rest of Henry's class in to retest! Jan and I had the highest score to date with the State! I was now a State Certified EMT!

Back at the hospital the ER Surgeon heard and soon made a proposal to me. I had kind of hinted earlier that I wanted to do it. He said up to that time the only thing I had done associated with the ER was not with any patients. He continued. For a Red Cross Volunteer to work in the hospital it had to be under the supervision of a Registered Nurse. There were no Registered Nurses working ER after hours. He said he was willing to stick his neck out and he allowed me to work in the ER! I eventually could do everything except Sterile procedures and prescribe medications!

I could not begin to tell you all the things we did. We had heart attacks, burns, illnesses, etc. but I don't think I can go on without mentioning a couple incidents.

We would get guys in who had caught a VD. They would come in and Mike would administer the drugs through a large plunger and very long needle into one of the butt checks. Mike would tell them he did not want to see them back in for more VD treatment for at least three months! If we got someone in and I checked the records and found they had been in to see us less than three months previous, Mike would get the tube of penicillin out of the freezer! He would roll it in his hands until the fluid was barely able to flow. He would attach the needle and then tell the military member that apparently the member had not heeded his advice. He told them the problem with shots so close together the second one usually hurt much worse! When he squeezed the cold meds in their cheek, there was usually a guttural scream!

I was taking Psychology classes and was concentrating on Educational Psychology and Child Abuse and Neglect. One night a couple brought in this really cute little blond girl maybe five or six years old.

She had a big bruise on her left temple. Her right eye was rolling back into her head. Many doctors and the police showed up. I was pushed out of the way. All the additional doctors on the scene were trying to stabilize her. We were readying the Ambulance so we could take her to one of the big trauma hospitals in the Raleigh/Durham area.

The cops measured the man's fist and saw it matched the bruise and put handcuffs on him.

I watched the interaction between the three people, mother, father and daughter. I noted the man was thin and his wife significantly larger. The Head Surgeon was there with a half dozen doctors when I spoke up, "He didn't do it, his wife did"! A couple of the doctors came unglued and even said I should leave the ER! The Head Doc stepped up and raised his hand to quiet them. He turned to me and asked why I said that. A couple doctors were quick to their opinion of me and loudly voiced them. The Doc asked again while telling them to shut up.

"An abused child will most likely try to please the abuser in hopes the abuse will stop. The child went to her mother almost in a servant like sense. The mother is the abuser".

Another uproar but the Head Doc went to the Police and asked them if they had measured the mother's fist. Of course not, his fit. To please the Doc they did the measurement and found her beefier fist also matched the impression on the girl's temple! When they turned their attention to her, the Father started to cry and babbled, "I kept telling her she would have to control what she did when the baby cried! I told her to stop hitting her!" She confessed to it and was taken to jail. The little girl died in the ambulance two miles from the Raleigh Trauma Center.

Doctors don't apologize. However the ER Doc did thank me. Not long after he came to me and told me I was doing as good as anyone in the ER. He said I had a talent, and proved it with the little girl incident. He put a piece of paper down in front of me and told me to sign it. It was a fast track toward being a doctor. I would be a Physician's Assistant for about two years before I would be sent to medical school to become a doctor. I refused to sign it and he intently asked why I would pass this up? I explained that in the ER everything was intensive and fast. In a less active setting I would get anxiety attacks, set off by things I had no control over. So I had to say no. That was my first time refusing to become a Commissioned Officer.

Last one for ER. I was doing Patient Surveys which are checking people in at the front desk and then getting their records so we could know medical history, etc. I was sitting there at the small counter. I was in my Red Cross shirt. A large man reached in and grabbed me by the shirt and pulling me over the desk and counter! Someone rushed to help and we subdued the man. My shirt was pretty torn.

The problem was his wife was terminal, expected to die soon. At the hospital we had changed some drug suppliers and in doing so some of the meds were in a different color. He thought we were giving her different meds so to kill her and lessen the strain on the system. We assured him that was incorrect. By then the police were on scene. They were satisfied they had taken care of the problem. The cops walked the patient out. The top Doc saw my shirt and commented it was wrong, I was a volunteer, and I should go home for the night. The hospital would pay for the damage to my shirt.

As I had just crossed the main road and toward my house I heard a siren! I immediately thought it didn't should like an ambulance. I did a "U" turn but was stopped from entering the parking lot by a police car. I went home and later heard about the shooting. The same guy apparently didn't believe us or was in a very bad state. He went to his car, pulled out a shotgun and came back in through the ambulance entrance. He apparently shot nine people of which two died. These were people I was working with less than 15 minutes earlier. That was my first Workplace Violence.

I got orders for Kunsan Air Base in South Korea. A couple things happened; I got approval for my family to stay on base while I had this unaccompanied year tour. I put in for a later report date to report for duty there. I got a call from Rich. He and I knew each other for years, we had been together during training. He loved himself, always doing things better than others and ready to rub it in when he did. We talked.

He said he had orders for Kunsan also! He then asked my if I had a line number for the next rank, he said he was sewing his new stripes the following month? I told him I didn't because I was promoted already! He started stammering and then asked when I was going? I told him I was trying for the end of the reporting month. He rambled on that even though I outranked him, he was going over early and set up the office like he wants to run it! When I got there the Chief of Safety would see he should run it and I would work for him!

My family stayed on Base and the Air Force said they wanted me there at the first day of the month, something about another "by name" request.

25

Chapter 9

Kunsan Air Base South Korea

Rich arrived on the third day of the month, I met him when he stepped off the bus He was very surprised. He still insisted he could run the office better than me! He did some things for the first three months trying to undermine me. I finally had a heart to heart with him and basically said if he didn't get on board, he was gone. We worked together well after that, often making it a challenge. For instance; we had a fire in one of the dorms that resulted in a fatality. A fire science expert was sent in from Alaska to determine the origin of the fire and help us investigate it. Rich and I had been through the scene and while waiting for the expert we each had a theory where it started. We wrote that theory down and kept each theory from the other. When the expert came in we had a bet on which of our theories was correct. I nailed it! I won.

I ran the Ground Safety Program at Kunsan. I had directional responsibility over the Safety people at Kwang Ju, Kim He, Taegu, and Sachon. They reported to me even though a couple outranked me. I traveled to all these sites regularly, making 101 trips that year. My Safety Program won the best under the Pacific Command. I also had my own assigned truck. I had one of only 7 issued passes allowing the bearer to be out during the nightly curfew. The area three miles outside the Base was "off limits" and there was a midnight curfew for travel off the Base. So we called my exempt from that rule my "Get out of Jail Free" card. Command said I shouldn't be restricted if I was responding or investigating an accident.

I had four people working for me at my office. There was a Korean National, Rich, my Admin and David. Mr. Nam was the third ranking Korean National on the Base. That made me "Special" since he worked for me. Rich came around and was a great help. David was always doing what he wanted, he didn't follow orders well. I shared my Admin with the Chief of Safety.

Mr. Nam had a welcome dinner for me that doubled as a going away dinner for the guy I replaced. He had a very attractive lady with him. He introduced her as his fiancé. He said he had to fix things at home first before he came back to get her. He asked me to help her until he got back. I was to check in on her occasionally and make sure she was okay. She mildly protested and when we were getting ready to leave she said I didn't have to check on her. I actually did about three times.

When traveling you had to stop at the main gate and state your destination. The Military Police on the gate would document name, vehicle, etc. and notify the Base I was going to what time I left. There were times assigned to prevent speeding on the roads so if I got to the destination ahead of the time I would get a ticket and a trip to the Commander's office! One time I was in Taegu when I got a call from the Commander. He notified me that a typhoon was going to hit Kunsan and he wanted me back NOW to lead the shutting down of the Base team. When I mentioned the time/distance problem he said he would take care of it and I was to get back as quick as possible. I blew into the front gate nearly two hours ahead of time and nothing was ever said to me but "thanks" from the Colonel.

While I am on the typhoon, I called ahead and told all my guys to be ready and assigned them shut down tasks. David was always getting in trouble. I was near taking a stripe because of it but he had connections. His father-in-law was a General. I mean he would do stuff he should be busted for. If you wanted to borrow my truck it had to be Air Force business. If taking it out to the flight line or where the aircraft were parked you had to pull to the side and leave the keys in the truck in case of an emergency the truck could be moved.

One day David took my truck and wrote on the sign out board that he was going to the Flight Line. I got a call from my friend at the Motor Pool. He asked if I was using my truck? He asked because it was parked by the massage parlor! I told him David had taken it to the Flight Line. In a couple minutes he called back and said David was in getting a very frisky massage! He picked me up and took me to my truck. I drove it back to my office. When David walked in he said he had my truck parked out on the Flight Line and someone stole it! I filed papers on him, I was documenting everything. I was getting close to taking one of his stripes.

David never reported as instructed for typhoon duty and I didn't have time to find him. I had on my swim trunks and combat boots as the rain was coming down in torrents and wind at sometimes over 100 mph.! I walked into the foyer of the women's dorm and announced I was there. I was making sure the building was secure. One of the ladies spilled the beans on David. He was having a drinking party with some women, all in stages of undress playing strip poker. He refused to leave.

I brought David into my office to discuss disciplinary actions and he laughed at me! He told me he was told he already had an assignment to the base his father-in-law was Commanding! His wife was already there and they had put money down on a house. He was reenlisting and I was nothing too him! He walked out! Problem is, I had already talked to Personnel and one of my friends there helped me with the paperwork. Seems you can only reenlist if there is an available job position! If none existed in his career field, then he could not reenlist! We looked at the documentation I had and Personnel had only job reservations for positions where disciplinary action was not acceptable. David would have to get out of the service at the end of this enlistment!

Within a few days David was in my office begging me to undo the action. He was begging and crying, once down on a knee! He said he had a special job with his father-in-law and it was gone, he was losing money on the house and apparently this was the final straw with his wife! I explained what documentation I had. I asked him if the documentation was correct? He would not answer but made excuses I knew were lies. I finally said I was sorry he messed up his career and I walked out! of my own office!

We worked basically six days a week at Kunsan and I would find myself working a full day Saturday when we were to do only a half day. My very good friend, Willie, worked in Explosive Safety across the hall. He would come by Saturday and basically push me out the door. We would go down to Kunsan City and have a couple drinks.

We were often bothered by girls looking to hook up for the night, for a price of course but Willie and I just had fun. The girls talked about us a lot because Willie is Black and I am white! We guessed they didn't see that often. They didn't know what to do when they started talking about us in Hangul, their Korean language. They would talk in front of us. Since Willie was married to a lady from Portugal and could speak Portuguese and I could speak Castilian Spanish we could basically understand each other. That drove them crazy. Willie and I really had a lot of fun together. One of the girls asked us to teach her how to talk like we did! We could understand what when she said I love you in Hangul was a throaty "Sara Hum Nida"!

One of my trips took me to Jin Ju City where we had a small site and Willie went along. I had explored the city and had been places I doubt any American had ever been. Jin Ju City was where the first man, part Chinese and part Mongolian had discovered the land. He came up the Nam (South) river and settled here, the first settlement in Korea.

Here there was a lot of history. The top of the hill over looking the Nam River was where they built the first Buddhist worship temples. The first were for men only and about 1,000 years ago they built temples for women to worship.

The Japanese invaded and took over Korea for about 40 years. When they did they cut down all the trees so the Koreans could not hide. The Koreans were defeated until one evening a prostitute took the ranking General up on the cliffs by the Women's Temples over looking the rocky cliff down to the Nam River. In an embrace she threw herself and the General over the cliff to the rocks below and their death. The Koreans saw this as a motivation and it ended with the Koreans running the Japanese out of their country. There is a statue of the woman there at the spot.

I took Willie there and we went into the bowels of the City. Here they may never see an American, let alone a black American! It was raining that day so we had on our Air Force blue raincoats. I had learned enough of their language to understand some of what the kids were saying as many ran up behind Willie and lifted up the back of his raincoat. He was getting a little angry and I knew if I told him he would get very angry! He had a temper, and it would not be good. We went back to the hotel and Willie asked the English speaking desk clerk. Willie asked what were the kids doing? I tried to motion for the Clerk not to tell him, but he did. "They were looking for a tail!" Willie was fit to be tied!

One Sunday I had gone down to Kunsan City to do some shopping when I saw an older woman get hit by a truck and thrown to the ground. I rushed to her and immediately saw her leg was broken. I sent people to call an ambulance and I set her leg and made a splint. The people told the ambulance there was an American involved so when the ambulance came there was an American EMT in the ambulance. He immediately saw what I did and told me to get the hell out of there, do not tell anyone! Don't try to find out about the condition of the lady! I had just violated International law by giving aid to a Korean national! I left the scene.

A couple weeks later I was called by the gate guard saying I had a visitor at the front gate. I drove over and met this very attractive young lady. She said the old woman I helped wanted me at her house the next Saturday. She gave me directions, and then she left in the cab.

I took Saturday morning off and when I found the place it looked like an apartment building. I was taken into the bottom floor, which was packed dirt. In a large chair was the older woman, cast on her leg. One of the girls stayed to help interpret. The old woman had many children. When her husband had died she rented the rooms of the apartment building to young ladies of the evening. They knew when her kids grew up to marry and have children the ladies would have to move out of the lower floor rooms. They did but still looked at her as their mother figure and took care of her even if they had moved out! I was the "Special" guest and I had the seat of honor next to her. The room was filled with many attractive women/girls.

We talked for a long time and I remember her saying when the Americans came the jets scared her but she now liked to hear them. She invited me to come there every Korean Holiday and sit next to her. An attractive young lady would come to the main gate a couple days ahead of the holiday with a written invitation from the old lady. I would sit next to her and be treated like a king! The room would be filled with close to 25 or more young ladies. I would laugh because if I went down to Kunsan City with anyone, invariably one of the women would see me and come talk with me! Often there were three or more girls. A lot of rumors went around about that!

When the Korean ruler, Kim Chung He, was assassinated we were kept on the base. When we were allowed to leave again I went down and checked on her. We talked and she told me she had been scared until she got used to the sound but even more scared when the sound of the jets stopped.

One of her girls had gotten out of the bar. Very few did unless they found a steady man. She got out and worked in a tailor shop. I saw her when I went in the shop, we seemed like old friends. Her English was excellent and I learned a lot about culture from her. Something happened and one night I spent the night with her, I had been unfaithful to Peggy. When my tour ended I told Peggy and I agreed to seek help from the church. We agreed not to talk about it again.

We Chiefs; Chief of Safety, Chief of Flight Safety, Chief of Weapons Safety, and me as Chief of Ground Safety were on a C130 Cargo aircraft heading for Clark Air Base in the Philippines for a meeting with all the other Safety people in Pacific Command and were scheduled for a one on one with the General. As we were airborne we felt the aircraft bank and turn in another direction. The Loadmaster came back and said we were being diverted to Kadena Air Base on Okinawa by request of the Base Commander! The Chief of Safety looked over at our Flight Safety Captain and said, "What did you do now Chuck?" The Loadmaster told him it wasn't the Flight guy, pointing a finger at me and saying I was who the Commander wanted to see! I had no idea why.

We landed and immediately a staff car was there for me and the Chief said they would get my bad to the Q (quarters) and to keep him informed if I could.

There had been an aircraft crash and I was wanted for my expertise in setting up Major Aircraft Accident Boards to investigate the aircraft crash. I told the contact who should be on the Board and I briefed the Officers what their roles were and helped them get started and what to look for on the scene. Luckily most were good but they needed an organized, experienced guy like me to bring the pieces together and direct actions. They appointed a Chairman and I briefed him and left feeling we were on the right track.

Since I was still an NCO, not a Commissioned Officer, Bill, the Chief, suggested we go to the NCO Club instead of the Officer's Club as he was not sure he could get me in to the "O" Club. I told him that was not good, the NCO Club was about 7 miles around the runway and the Officer Club was within walking distance. We went to the Officer Club and as Bill was negotiating the Weapons Chief in because he lost his Club Card, I walked in like I owned the place. I flashed my wallet open at the door ID checker and he didn't even bother to look at it, motioning me through into the Club.

When they got in they found me sitting at the corner of this huge table right next to the guy at the head! The table was the longest and biggest table in the area! When Bill came forward sort of hesitant, the Base Commander introduced himself. He also said I was always welcome at his table and since they were my friends, they were welcome. The Colonel and I told Bill about when we first met and why he had diverted the aircraft.

In Vietnam, one of the young pilots had run out of bombs and ammo with a Sampan in the water ahead of him so he lowered his landing gear and crushed and sank the boat! When he climbed out of the dive along side the Mekong Delta, the pylon that held the bomb hit a low tree and limbs/branches were stuck in it where it hung from the wing. Back at the Base he exited the cockpit and knew his career was ended. I told him to go give a clean debrief and not mention the tree he was growing from the pylon. I took off the pylon and replaced it with a new one, you could never tell something had happened!

We were sitting with that F100 pilot, now the Base Commander. He knew what I had done for him. He also knew I was about the best there was setting up Major Accident Boards. And knew we were headed to Clark because his Safety guys were going also. so he'd diverted us to his base. My boss was learning more about me all the time.

Getting near time to return to the States. My Dad had come to the Bases in Florida and North Carolina to visit with us and I was now calling him "Dad" and looking forward to seeing him again. Henrietta had passed a year or so past and as Dad had promised her, her sister Helen lived in his house and was taken care of.

Rich had really screwed up during the year. He told his wife on the phone he was coming home to divorce her, and then he came to me to see if he could get leave to go home? I remembered his wife, she had put on a few pounds after she had been a Bunny Server at the Playboy Club and was still beautiful, but her father was also an Investment Banker so he should expect to be cleaned out when he got home. He was, except for a weapon and a CB Radio, both banned in Korea! He had nothing.

I went home for Christmas and while I was gone he fell in love with a Korean hooker and soon got married. In Korean law, an American can not harm a Korean, but not the other way around. Rich would show up with scratches on his face, etc. Not long after I left they got a divorce.

One trip to Pusan the Chief of Safety went with me. I had arranged some high level meetings for him. The official he met with took him out for dinner. I was with a couple local guys and we went to Texas street! It is known for having the most international prostitutes in the world! It was explained if I wanted to I could have a woman of almost any nationality! I told him I didn't do that but we agreed it was a place to see and have a couple beers.

I was sitting there only sipping my beer and watching all the uniqueness of the area. I overheard a lady from Greece say to her friend that her boyfriend would be there the next night so she was going to tell the old Ahjumma (old lady) she was sick. The next day we finished business early and I had told Bill about where I had gone, including I had just had a few drinks, nothing else.

We went that night and after a suitable time went by, I took the Ahjumma to the side and pointed at Bill, saying he was my boss! I told her I had talked to a Greek woman, I described her, and the woman said we would have a party tonight! Now I am losing face with my boss, what can I do? She asked around and heard the Greek had called in sick. So she grabbed this totally beautiful lady from Brazil and introduced her to Bill and told her she was not to charge him anything! No charge for drinks or your services! The beauty nodded and sat basically on Bill's lap! When the Ahjumma was telling me how sorry she was and hoping her gesture would take care of the problem, I thanked her sincerely in Hangul and started to leave. I heard Bill yelling for me but I left as though I didn't hear him!

The following morning he came in and saw me. He looked tired but refreshed and with a slight smile on his face and in a low voice he said, "You son of a bitch!" We never talked about it again.

One of the guys in the barracks openly stated he has eaten every food there is! He also spoke Spanish he learned during 18 months in Spain. It was more American jargon instead of proper Spanish. I would occasionally politely tell him he spoke junk Spanish, and no, he has not eaten everything! Problem is, he had many friends so if I said anything there was crowd mentality on his side.

One day he said something that pissed me off, so I challenged him! "Denny, you say you have eaten everything and can speak pure Spanish! Neither is true! So I challenge you to come with me Saturday afternoon and I will take you to a place I know. If you don't eat it then you must refrain from speaking crap Spanish or brag about you having eaten everything again!" He hesitated but the same crowd turned on him to show me up!

Saturday afternoon we got off the bus in Kansas City. He had five or six friends with him. I walked through an area he said he had never been before. I walked up a small hill where there was one of those food carts set up. I walked up to the old Ahjumma and spoke to her in Hangul. I looked a Denny and told him the old woman would cut him off a piece. He said "Hell No!" So i calmly said I guess I had won the competition and gave the Ahjumma a little money for her trouble.

Problem is with a crowd it can turn. Now they were saying why should Denny be punished if I would never eat what she was serving? I smiled and told them that I have never declined a food in my life, unless it had milk, I am lactose intolerant. The crowd mentality was still there, so I asked the Ahjumma to cut me off a piece! She did, the crowd seemed to step back a little as I bowed to her and ate the live jellyfish! Dennis never bothered me again.

The third ranked Korean National worked for me so every trip just about he went with me. Because of his high status, everywhere we went I was treated with honor and I learned custom and culture as well as I could.

Mr. Nam had me to his house when I was getting ready to leave Korea and my knowledge was put to the test. Mr. Nam had five daughters before his wife finally had a son. In the room specially made for gatherings, his daughters were not allowed, nor his wife. But his near infant son sat right next to him at the hear of the table. We had close to 20 people there and we all brought presents. Almost all the guys brought alcoholic gifts, normal for these events. I brought a fruit basket! Mr Nam questioned it and I said I knew as guest of honor I could do anything I wanted, and I wanted the gift to include his daughters and wife. He complimented me on my knowledge.

When we sat down, I was at the other end of the table from Mr. Nam. There was another test for me. You start out with small glasses of wine or booze. The guests all around the table drink their drink all the way then shake out the glass into an ashtray like dish. They fill the empty glass and pass the glass to me. Since I had done this before with high ranking Koreans, I was good at it. I had to drink one of the glasses in front of me. Then shake out the glass.

I had to fill the glass and pass it on to the highest ranking in status around the table! I would repeat that until the lowest ranking got the last glass. I did it well. The ovation was loud!

Then I informed Mr. Nam that I wanted to exercise my second and last deviation as the Guest of Honor. He said he was proud I had learned so much but was shocked at my request. I wanted his wife to join us at the table! He told me his wife had never, ever, sat at the table with guests! The wife usually sits in the kitchen. and the men make a lot of noise to indicate the food is good. The noise is usually the men eating with their mouth open! The louder the noise, the better the compliment! She sat with us and I could do nothing wrong.

I sort of stayed in contact with one of the Weapons Safety guys from North Carolina and he contacted me to tell me what happened to the Lieutenant I had told to buy the big black car for his Greece assignment. The Lieutenant, now Captain, had been there for 18 months when he contacted the Agency I spoke of. He went through all the paperwork and a rich Greek businessman met him on the second floor of an old building in the Athens Center Square. He was looking down at the Ford from the table next to the window. He reached into the inner pocket of his suit. He pulled out a gold pen, twisted it, and held the papers for him to sign under his left hand. With the gold pen in his right hand

On

he started to sign the ownership papers.

There was a huge explosion right below the window from the street below! The businessman stepped to the window after he composed himself. He looked down, twisted his pen, put it back in his suit pocket and walked out the door! Apparently there were protestors in the Square and they decided to blow up the big black American car! My friend and I laughed together for a long time, him finally saying, "Must be karma"!

At the barracks I was the top guy, sort of the ranking member. I was often part of fixing problems, referee for disputes, big brother, etc. and friend to most. One guy was so quiet and bullied a little because of it. I sort of became a good friend and people left him alone. He had met his wife when they were in the second grade together. He had never even kissed another woman not a relative and definitely not on the lips! They got married right out of school. He didn't drink, smoke, swear, or even go out with the guys. At home his wife took him to church at least twice a week, often more. He was a squeaky clean all American boy.

I took a couple weeks during Christmas to fly home and spent the holiday with Peggy and the girls. When I came back I was told my very naive friend was downtown! I was told he spent a lot of time downtown! I found out while I was gone some guys took him downtown and he drank alcoholic beverages for the first time! He didn't do well at first, he liked the taste but was drunk immediately. Soon he was doing much better and when I caught up with him he said he had met a woman! He was living with her when he could, and he wanted to introduce me to her! Wow! He was going home in a few weeks to his bible carrying wife and he was now drinking and living in sin!

He talked me into meeting her, so the next Saturday I was standing on a street corner with a friend of mine while waiting for him to show up with his "new love". I looked across the street and ducked down behind my friend saying "I was never here"! I ducked around the corner and headed back to Base. My previously naive friend was walking hand in hand with the fiancé of the guy I replaced! The one I was asked to look out for! The saga goes on.

The day came for my little friend to catch the bus for Seoul and Osan Air Base. He had to catch a flight back to the States. He wasn't there at the barracks and the bus was due to board in about a half hour! He came in slightly staggering! We grabbed him to help him get his stuff in his luggage and catch the bus. He took a quick shower and started throwing his clothes in his bag. A minor problem was he had bought a lot of stuff. He had too much to fit in his one suitcase and was ready to do something crazy! One of the guys stepped up and said he had an old

B4 bag he would donate. We helped him stuff everything in it. The bus had waited as long as possible and had to leave! By now it was already off base without him! So I grabbed my truck and headed for the front gate. The cop told me the bus was a few minutes ahead of me . I sped down the road and we saw the bus. I passed him and we waved him to a stop. My friend took his bags out of the truck and into the bus, and off they went! I could only imagine what his wife would think now. Who was coming home to her was not the timid man she knew a year ago! He now liked to drink and had been with another woman.

Two days later I got a call and had to go to the Headquarters building. I was told my little friend had asked them to contact me when he was thrown in jail at the port of entry airport! Drug dogs had sniffed one of his bags and alerted so they threw him in the brig waiting investigation! I asked and was told to hang on a second as the man I was talking to called the jail he was in on the base. I asked if they had told his wife yet and yes they had. I asked and was told when she heard she got a little hysterical, said they were wrong, and was quoting bible scriptures! As a highly trained investigator I quickly narrowed the information down to maybe one source.

I went to the guy who gave my friend his bag and asked him what he did with the bag before he donated it? He said he had been working as a police recruit with drug dogs! We quickly came to the conclusion he had used that bag to hide drugs to see if the dogs could detect it. Was there a possibility there might have been some residue in the bag? Yes! I got back with the authorities about this and he was released from jail soon after. I thought only that he was stepping out of the frying pan into the fire!

Another time I was meeting with some men on a somewhat official issue. We had a very nice young lady there as an interpreter as a couple of the men did not speak very good English and I did not speak fluent Hangul. Apparently she had some clearance and we also used sealed envelopes. When we were done I bought lunch for everyone, all 14 of us.

We found this corner restaurant that sat down below street level with stairs to get to it. Right after we entered the door and started down the steps an old Ahjumma started saying bad things in Hangul! I caught some of it and one of the men interpreted the rest for me. Apparently the old lady thought the "Ugly American" was buying friends, and the attractive lady with all these men was there to make them pleasure!

A couple of the men said they would talk to her but I asked them not to. This project was a little sensitive and I didn't want to draw attention to our meeting. The old lady continued hissing and talking. We ignored her. When I paid for it she was very ugly with me. I said nothing until we got to the top of the stairs!

At the top of the stairs I looked over my shoulder at her, still keeping my back to her because that was one form of insult in their culture. Then I strained a little, acting like I was having a stomachache and said "Igu, ke Sodi dong y dah"! The place got dead quiet and first the lady interpreter put her hand over her mouth and started giggling! Most of the guys started laughing and when I looked back at the old lady her face was very red and she simply nodded her head and smiled. Outside I was asked I knew what I said and how did I know that? I asked them if it was appropriate to say that after I had eaten her food? They all laughed, I had just insulted about as bad as you could. I had eaten her food and as I left I told her in her language as I rubbed my stomach, "Damn, I feel like dog shit!" By the way, anytime after that if I walked by her restaurant one of her workers would run out and get me so I would come in and eat there, always free to me.

As we left, the interpreter said she would show me an easier route to the bus stop. Along the way I saw a market and asked if we could stop so I could get some stuff to take back to the barracks where I did some cooking. We did and as I was looking at some fresh bean sprouts and picked up a bunch, there was a loud hiss from a small tent where two old ladies sat on either side of two big tubs of Kimchi soup. The young lady told me that men were not supposed to touch food, only women. The old ladies were hissing bad things at me! I went to their tent and apologized, ordering a cup of the Kimchi soup, the hottest food in Korea. The women were sisters and one said she had tried to learn English from her little TV. She then told of the first time she had ever spoken English. She said they had gone to Seoul. She wanted to see the DMZ (Demilitarized Zone) at the border and there was a tower you could ride up an elevator to the top and look over at North Korea. She said she got on the elevator, turned facing the door. When more people came on she stepped back and onto a shoe. She looked around and saw it was a large shoe belonging to a tall black military man. She looked up at him and decided she would excuse herself in English she had learned. So she looked up at him and saiid, "Kiss me, kiss me" instead of "excuse me"! I stopped by to see them when I could and she probably told that story another three times. I knew when to laugh.

I had maybe two weeks until leaving when the Base Commander called me in. He was worried about Rich taking over for me, he didn't trust him. Rich had married the Korean girl and had extended his tour. The Commander asked me to extend for a few weeks. I said I would look into if that was possible since I had a report date to my next assignment. He worked it out for me to extend. Then, just a couple days before I was supposed to go home originally, the Red Cross contacted me to tell me my father had died of a massive coronary!

I told the Commander and he relieved me of duty right then. He told his staff to make my arrangements so I could get home immediately! I called my sister and told her when I would be home. She told me I would miss the Funeral! I would get into Boston about 15 minutes before the burial, and there would be nobody to pick me up! The funeral could not be postponed! I was nearly out of it and maybe the angriest I've ever been! From my working with Red Cross I knew what questions to ask and I found out my sister had not notified the Red Cross for two or three days! Had she contacted them immediately I could have made it. I was upset I didn't get to say goodbye to my father.

I stayed to help the Colonel for an additional 9 days and then went back home to Goldsboro where Peggy and the girls stayed on Base while I was gone. I had been caught in the rain leaving Korea and thought I had a cold. I had a severe headache and then the side of my face started drooping! As an EMT I ruled out a stoke and realized I had Bells Palsy.

26

Final Straw-my Mother

I stayed at the base long enough to get treatment for my Bells' Palsy. I also got some time extension before reporting to Holloman AFB, New Mexico. I wanted to go up to Portland, Maine to see my father's gravesite. I was still very upset with not being able to say good-bye to Dad.

I was notified that I was the only heir to Dad's Estate! Apparently my sister had refused to meet Henrietta and would only meet Dad in a restaurant away from his house. Peggy and I welcomed her and Helen. They were both exceptional people. So when Dad passed I inherited his property. I remembered his promise to take care of Helen so I turned everything over to her. She could stay in Dad's house forever.

I knew I had to take the kids to see their grandmother, so we went. My mother had moved again and was living in a small house that was built on the edge of the entrance to a friend's farm. I believe he built it for an older relative who had passed.

The owner was in High School with me and we worked together on many things. He knew I could easily handle myself on a farm so I could bring the kids throughout the farm.. I took my kids on a tractor ride, we did some light haying, and walked amongst the cattle.

Then it happened. I believe my mother said in front of Peggy and the girls that I had married the wrong girl! The kids were visibly upset and guess I raised my voice to her, I was defending my wife.

Mom came unglued and started to get very nasty with me, out of control nasty. I told Peggy to grab our things, we were going to leave.

I went upstairs to tell her we were going when she lit into me. She started telling me how I had screwed up her life! She went to where having me had caused her hair and teeth to fall out! She berated me for the way I treated her and how much she had done for me but I was too stupid to know, or care. I was selfish, etc. anything and everything wrong in her life, I was the reason.

Mom had not gone to a doctor or dentist in decades, so she had lost all her teeth. The last scene we saw as I got in the car was my mother with her fingers in her mouth spreading her lips out to show she had no teeth and yelling that I was the cause of that!

My kids didn't need to be exposed to that. Peggy and I discussed it and I think we both agreed that was our last trip to Maine.

Later she was put in a home and she refused to use any of the services she paid into. My sister decided we would help pay for the care facility. Her husband was a Vice President of a large company and my sister had a good paying job. I was still in the military and making peanuts compared to them. I still had to give monthly what we referred to as a full car payment without the car!

And I had mentioned my sister taking anything valuable in her "Stack" along the wall, including all my mother's jewelry! There were diamonds and priceless collectables! She had things like antique nightstand bowl and water pitchers that were over 100 years old! I had nothing but the Bible.

I had made everyone promise to never tell my sister that I contributed to her college. I never said a word when she told a stranger that whenever she needed money for college that my mother always came through. My sister would tell perfect strangers some of her life stories. It was quite evident my sister and her husband thought my mother was an angel while I despised her entire being.

Back to my assignment following Korea.

27

White Sands New Mexico

Holloman Air Force Base is in Alamogordo, New Mexico. I was assigned to the Air Wing but basically reported to the Air Division one Star General. The base was on the edge of White Sands National Park.

I also had responsibility for running the Test Group Safety Program when the Safety Manager was on leave or similar. The Test Group had the infamous Rocket Sled, the one John Stapp rode and became the fastest man on Earth. More interesting stuff to follow.

The office was staffed heavy, so when I walked in there were a lot of guys and the secretary. I was introduced to them all. I settled in my assigned desk and almost immediately there were seven guys around my desk, one guy with a notebook. They said something about there were a lot of problems, especially traffic accident because of the flat land and straight roads. Okay, then the one guy opened the notebook and I saw the first gory picture!

Apparently a guy was driving his motorcycle in front of the base and had come up fast behind a truck loaded with steel. He didn't see the steel protruding out the back of the truck. They think he was turning his head to check traffic before passing the truck. Instead he hit the steel and it was a real mess. The guys thought they were cute and I found out they had done this before to new people to see their reaction. Unfortunately for them, I had seen much worse and had medical training. I started describing the injuries in a very graphic manner. "I can see where the steel hit his right orbit (eye socket bone) and pushed it

158

into the frontal lobe"! I went on for a couple minutes. My description of each picture was very graphic. The only guy remaining in the group told me to "Shut the hell up"! He grabbed the notebook and left! I could see I was going to have fun.

I fit right into the Test Group when I filled in for the Manager. There was a lot of very cool experiments and projects going on. Unfortunately, they are all sensitive or classified so I can't talk about them.

I investigated a couple unique accidents. One was on the engine test/run up facility involving an F15 engine run test.. One of the Techs disconnected a fuel line and forgot to reconnect it. So when the test equipment was connected the lead guy got in the cockpit and the engine was started up. They checked performance at idle but when they advanced to full throttle and started into after burner, the entire engine and side of the aircraft burst into flames!

There was a lot of finger pointing and blame going around. After I completed my investigation and briefed it to the General, I got a lot of attention. I have to admit I did it well. And I got to do some really good stuff that advanced my professional standing.

I was asked to write the Specific Safety Plan for the Alternate Landing Site for the Space Shuttle! The Site was on the military section of White Sands. I got intimately involved with the Safety training for crews and support people. I was working with the Fire Services and Crash Recovery people. I met a couple astronauts and NASA people. Of course the Shuttle never landed there while I was assigned.

Alamogordo, literal translation means "fat fort", wasn't a large town. The town was near the mountains to the east and White Sands West and South. We didn't do much in the city but we went down to El Paso quite a bit. The brother of a good friend I was stationed with in Spain lived there. We had met before and became friends. We stayed with them and went across the border into Juarez. We would pay a kid a dollar to watch our car so we didn't worry about that. We partied and ate well, the cost was so much lower than on the US side of the border. Our friend used to go across the border for gas up at half the US price.

I was doing a lot of work at some of the off-site bombing ranges.

At one we came across an Arizona Rattlesnake, similar color to a Diamondback. I went to catch it but one of the guys beat me at it, he wanted the rattle for his son. I still got the snake to take home and skin and eat. I took the skin and rubbed it with salt and stretched it across a piece of plywood at let it sit in the sun a couple days. Then I cut and sewed the skin to make a hatband for my cowboy hat!

You see, I had started wearing harness boots back in Maine and now had transitioned to cowboy Western style boots. Thats all I wore. So another reason for trips to El Paso was the Tony Llama boot factory and stores. I had a couple custom belt buckles so with the hat, boots and buckles, I fit in well.

One town, Cloudcroft, had a ski area and there is where I really started to snow ski. I wasn't very good but I did was persistently poor style at everything but falling! One day I was riding up on the lift with Susan and she started playing around. She ended up falling out of the lift! I jumped down into the deep snow and when I got her out I went back to get one of my skis that had fallen off. I left the other ski with Susan while I did. When I came back to her she was crying! "What's wrong?" and she pointed down at my ski she was supposed to be holding. It was building up speed by itself! Luckily it didn't hit anyone. I didn't get much better time skiing that day..

We ventured south of there and found a mountain town called Timberon. We bought a little plot of land at the Timberon area. We thought with what I was doing we would be there for a while. I wasn't very good at skiing but thought I would get better as time went by. That didn't happen, I had another "By Name" request to go to Japan! I think we had been there only 10 months.

I did get a nice plaque and accompanying letter for my work with NASA for helping write the safety procedures and training for Shuttle Support crews at White Sands.

28

Yokota Air Base, Japan

Yokota was where I had stopped both going over and coming back from Vietnam. I had little time then to see how beautiful it was with Mount Fuji in the background. My job was Chief of Safety for the 1956 Communications Group! I was working directly for the Commander of the Year for the previous year, a "Bird" Colonel. That meant he was one step below General and his rank was designated by an eagle.

We flew in and got transportation to the "Q" (transient Quarters) units for families coming into the Base. I got Peggy and the girls settled and then went straight to my new office. I had heard there were problems, the reason I was requested "By Name" so I could fix it. Yes, it was bad.

I went to the office and the guy I was replacing was there. I kind of caught him at what he did best, sit at his desk reading books. When anyone came down the ramp into the office he would fold over the top corner of the page he was reading and throw the book into a lower open drawer! He would close the drawer with his foot! He had been there three years and still had not been to all 16 sites around Japan! His records were all messed up and he faked mandatory reports. The Safety program was the worst I have ever seen! He was upset that I was there! He expected I would not come there until I was processed in, expected three days. He had scheduled no time to brief me! He and his family were leaving early, about four days later. He had claimed hardship reasons with his son so was allowed to leave close to a month early. He knew he had a problem and wanted to leave and dump it on me.

The third day I had just finished processing in and went to the office. I was told the Colonel wanted to see me immediately in his office! I went up there and after introductions the Colonel stated he knew the Safety Program was a mess! He stated that the coming April we would be having a Command MEI and ORI Inspections. He wanted an "Excellent" in Safety on both those inspections! He added that if I didn't think I could do it I might just as well pack up my bags and leave, he would find someone else who could! He went on to say he thought I would have a rude awakening when I finally got to my office and got into the Program! My turn.

I told the Colonel I knew how bad the program is, I had spent the last three days in the office and saw what problems I had to deal with. I also told him I would guarantee him an Excellent in both inspections and if that didn't happen he could kick my ass off the Island! He looked at me, asked a little about me being in the office as soon as I got off the plane. "So you think you can fix my Program?" "And you think you are really good at Safety?" My response, "Sir, I don't think I am good, I know I am!"

As I was leaving his office I talked with his secretary and his clerk, Mel. We hit it off right away. Mel and I would go eat Unagi (Fresh Eel) for lunch every Wednesday!

As always, the guys had to test the new guy. In a day or two I was told by one of the technicians there was a problem on top one of the towers nearby. Okay, and I went with him to the tower and we started climbing. It was a 300 foot tall communications tower. At about 200 feet up he finally stopped, he had been watching me as we climbed. He turned to me and before he could say anything, I asked if there really was a problem or was he testing the new guy? He confessed. I told him I would not do anything this time but if he ever brought someone up this high without ensuring the person had a High Climb card, I would have his ass! We became easy friends.

I traveled to all the 16 sites, including one way up north at Misawa, a Navy Base. I traveled south to an adjacent island where we had a Comm Site at the top of a mountain called Suburi Yama. It was outside the city of Fukuoka. The city was famous because it is the original place where you could find Hakata Dolls. I went there every three months and the things I did and learned and who I met are unbelievable.

One trip to Fukuoka I flew down on a 747 and had seat 1A, the bulkhead where it was curved because it was the nose of the aircraft. The runway is very short for a 747 and it was raining hard! When we touched down the pilot slammed on the brakes and the rain was coming hard against the nose. It was very loud and I had no flat area to brace myself as the aircraft slowed down fast! I was glad to get off the airplane. One of the military guys picked me up and he asked if I minded if we stopped in a camera shop before heading up the mountain. The owner of the shop loved Americans and you could tell. Seems he was 13 days from graduating from Kamikaze school when the war ended! I bought a half-frame Olympus EES from him and he charged me about half of what it was worth.

Another time I met a guy who was the nephew of a man who lived in Nagasaki when the bomb was dropped. He took me to the hills overlooking the City. We sat on some boulders and he told me about some of the survivors and pointed out areas of the City. It is hard to describe the feelings I had that day. Unbelievable. Sad. Wow!

I went to all our sites within the first two months there. I rewrote the Safety procedures for many. We had a lot of programs going, not all Safety business. I took one of our conference rooms and set up a Santa and his Wife hotline for the Christmas holiday. It was mostly military kids.

I had a seat belt challenge! The average number of military wearing seat belts was less than 15%. I set up a challenge and all the Staff Officers joined the Challenge. I proposed to the Colonel that if anybody caught me without wearing a seat belt where they were available/functional in a vehicle I would pay them $500 on the spot. The boss asked me if I was independently wealthy? No, I didn't plan to be without my seat belt! Not all the Officers bought into it as a commitment. When the program ended one Officer paid $1,000 and another $500, the rest of us paid nothing and seat belt use was over 80%, highest in the Pacific bases!

We had the Base Safety Office and other separate organizations, like the Mobility Squadron had Safety Managers. My position as Chief of Safety was actually a higher position than the base Chief of Safety! I organized the other Safety Managers where we met monthly to help each other. A good example was a project, a new building being constructed near our 300 foot tower. The Base Photo Office lead photographer was sent to my office for permission for them to put a camera on top the tower to shoot the progress of the construction. I asked a lot of questions and found that someone would have to climb up once or twice every week to change the film. Also, there was only one camera. Other cameras were positioned on low buildings and hangars. While he was in my office I called my Safety counterpart in another unit that flew helicopters. I basically set the plan from my desk!

The squadron had to maintain flying hours for certification so we arranged for the photographer to ride in a helicopter a couple times a week on a set pattern and take pictures of the progress! He got an award for that! The Unit Safety Manager got due credit for the support.

Peggy and the girls had a great time. They went skiing and we did a lot of things. Susan stayed with a Japanese family and their daughter stayed with us a couple times. Susan's Girl Scout leader came up with this idea in an effort to support her husband's promotion to Colonel. She wanted to take the girls for an International trip! All girls must have a chaperone with them, in this case each had a parent. We asked if Carrie could go also? That meant both Peggy and I had to go. The destination was Seoul Korea. Four fathers had tours in Korea so they worker with her on the planning. They were going to lead the troop while in Korea.

We flew a C130 Cargo plane from Yokota to Osan Air Base Korea and went to the hotel. In the morning we saw the Troop Leader out front and in tears! Apparently the four fathers were up most of the night playing cards and drinking! They had caused trouble with the hotel staff and not a one of them made it downstairs for our gathering.

Oh well. Then Peggy goes up and volunteers me! She told her I not only lived in Korea for a year but I spoke the language! Me to the rescue.

First I had to win back the hotel staff. I saw one of the Staff getting on an elevator with a Mican, the sweet little tangerine type fruits, so I hopped in the elevator. He and I talked in mixed languages about the Mican coming from Chegg udo Island. He was surprised I knew that and other things about Korea. I came down in a couple minutes. The word had gotten to management and I was warmly greeted by the Staff. I apologized for the behavior of the fathers and was forgiven. I was complimented for my pronunciation of Korean words. I told the Leader and then did something they didn't expect. I asked for four girls to volunteer, I was taking them to breakfast while waiting for the men! My two stepped forward and soon a couple more. I took them to the food market and we ordered foods for breakfast. Much of it was food they had never seen or heard of. They loved it! And the next and each morning after I did the same and nearly all hands were raised. I tried to take a girl each day that had not been yet.

We did the same thing a couple times for dinner. Only there were many more girls and parents. I would teach them the Korean name and what it was. Many of the girls ate stuff their parents wouldn't! More than once they would gang up on me and say they weren't going to eat it unless I did! Unless it has milk, I am lactose intolerant, I have eaten everything ever put before me! I have eaten pig brains, both rattlesnake and python meat, live jellyfish, Rocky Mountain Oysters, fried grasshoppers and scorpions, etc.

Peggy and I took a couple hours to visit the Eastgate Shopping Center, the largest in the world! It may not cover as much space but there are more stores than any other. They sold everything. As we came to a store that sold sneakers, I pointed out a pair my friend Bruce had bought while on vacation back in the US. He paid almost $60 dollars for them. Of course they would be cheaper here because they were made in Korea.

Peggy was back in the price game again. We used to go to Mexico and I taught her how to haggle for a lower price. She started with the lady selling the sneakers and I believe they had agreed on $15. Peggy turned to me and bragged she was better at this than me! So I had to prove her wrong.

I started talking to the woman in Hangul, her Korean language. I said she was ripping us off at that price! She swore at me! I swore back! This went on for a couple minutes. We drew attention from a few people and soon she threw one of the shoes at me! She had a big smile on her face when she did. I asked her about the other shoe to the pair? Smiling, she threw that at me and made a gesture with her hand to swoosh us away! I had both shoes now. I bowed at her and said "Sara hum ne da"! Many other vendors laughed, a few clapped. As we were walking off with a pair of free sneakers I told Peggy the only way she could beat me at haggling would be if the store paid her! She hit me and asked what I said to the woman that caused everybody to laugh? "I love you!"

Then it was time to fly back to Japan. The Leader was trying to find us a ride back. Her husband didn't have the pull he thought he did so we were stranded at the Passenger Terminal at Osan. It was estimated it would be between one and three days before we could all get out as a group. The Leader said some of the fathers said they might be able to get a couple out. So the Leader agreed and basically said if we could, do it. I called Mr Nam, my old friend and coworker when I was at Kunsan. Between 2 and 3 hours Peggy, the kids and I were on a flight back to Japan. The full Troop didn't get back for another four days.

I was at the office area when the Colonel sent a message for me to meet him in our "War Room", a specific small conference room we had a wall of monitors. This is where we handled emergency responses like Typhoons or massive outages, etc. This day we had intercepted emergency messages and also followed reports of the crash of Korean Airlines 007. Reports were coming in about it being shot down and numbers of bodies floating in the sea. I had written the Emergency Response Plan but besides monitoring and coordinating events, we couldn't do much.

I was notified of an urgent call from Dr. Winett Warren! I had heard Winnie from our days in North Carolina was stationed in Japan but hadn't truthfully had the time to contact her. She was at the Base Hospital. So why the urgent call to the War Room?

The base had to get about 1,000 military troops prepared to respond if called upon for this incident. They all had to be current on CPR training and Winnie needed my help. I told her I hadn't trained in a long time and my training certificate was long expired. She said she had talked to the Hospital Commander and told him she wanted to bring me in. When he asked if I was good, she apparently answered the best she had ever seen. He agreed to sign my authorization if I could come in and do CPR on the test dummy and get a perfect strip! Adding, of course, that some of the certified teachers at the hospital would find it hard to punch a perfect strip. She sent an orderly to get me and I went to a classroom. She met me there along with the Hospital Commander and the first thing I did caught everyone off guard. I walked up to Winnie and embraced her! It was not expected because she was a Black officer and me a white enlisted guy! We embraced for maybe half a minute, I didn't realize how nice it was to see her again. In the embrace I whispered to her and asked what would happen if I didn't punch a perfect strip? She laughed, saying she knew I would but would still love me if I didn't.

I punched a perfect strip and the next couple of days the team I was with trained nearly 1,000 military members. That was a proud day.

So my first half year there I was very busy. In the second year, 1982, I had the opportunity to march with five other Air Force men with the Japanese military forces honoring the Shogun and Samurai! It was at the Budokan in downtown Tokyo on January 15th. Paul, a Major I worked with, was married to a Japanese lady and he owned one of the Samurai suits of armor. It was considered a national treasure so he could never take it back to the US. He was friends with some very important people. One of those was to be the Shogun in a couple years and between Paul and him they arranged for some Americans to march and honor the fighting man. The Americans would wear traditional Japanese fighting armor. The Japanese would help us dress correctly. It was quite a spectacle. There were thousands of people there. Demonstrations of fighting techniques and the Shogun broke open the Saki wooden barrel with a huge sword! Ladies were making traditional Mochi on one side in front of the stage. There were thousands of people in the stands!

That second year while I was being dressed in my Japanese armor I was smoking a pipe. One of the Japanese helping dress me hissed and told the other one I was basically bad for smoking a pipe. I spoke Japanese by then so I told him in Japanese that my father had passed and I was the oldest male in the family. Japanese culture only allows the eldest male to smoke a pipe.

Word got around and in 1984 I was asked to train more than 25 Americans on how to properly wear the Samurai outfit. There are many customs to adhere to, such as, you never show the unsheathed blade of the sword or knife because by culture you must draw blood before you can put it back in the sheath. So I taught them tricks like a small piece of a toothpick to make sure the blades don't come out. I taught them the names of the armor pieces and how each part of the armor fit. Paul taught them phrases you yelled when about to charge forward, etc.

Then, by the request of the soon to be Shogun and Paul, I was asked to do the same prior to the marching and festivities, but this time on international news The morning on January 15th I stood on a round pedestal with just my undershorts on. There were about 85 people in the room with both UPI and AP cameras on me. Two Japanese I knew from the previous year were dressing me. I explained in English what the name was for each item they put on and what purpose it served. It was all going great until they went to put on the breastplate. It weighed about 40 pounds! That meant it was a real breastplate! The "Hollywood" ones they made only weighed about 10 pounds. As they were fitting it and tying it on, one of the Japanese whispered in my ear. "Brown san, we found this one special for you, it is the same ranks as you are!" I had trouble talking for a second or two. I got emotional about that moment, there may never have been a moment of greater honor.

As I had said earlier, when my Dad passed away I had honored his promise to take care of Helen, Henrietta's sister. I had started to call him "Dad" after all the trouble he had gone to come see us when we were stationed in the US. I had accepted Henrietta, I knew Dad was happy, however my sister would never do that. If she saw him it would have to be at a restaurant by himself. So when Dad had his massive coronary, everything he had went to me. I honored his commitment and turned everything over to Helen. His house, classic car, everything. It was a good thing I did that, she was able to live a couple years in an assisted living situation before she died. One of the caregivers became the executrix of everything. Both my sister and I got checks for $7,000. Peggy and I paid off a little debt we had, leaving more than $5,000 that we had no idea what to do with to honor Dad.

Then one day it hit me! Dad had always talked about all the traveling we had done and how he wished he had done more, so I suggested we use that money for travel, Dad would have loved the idea.

We left the girls with friends and we took a 16 day organized tour of Bangkok, Hong Kong, Singapore, etc. all over the Orient. We bought jewelry and clothes, had unique experiences like me standing near the Reclining Buddha with a 44 pound python around my neck! We became friends with a Marine and his wife so we took taxi trips to many of the places. We ate food so hot that a waiter was standing by the table with a wet cloth to wipe the sweat! Wonderful trip, thank you Dad, wish I could have said goodbye.

The trip was unique beyond just what we saw. Six of the people with us were Diplomats! I believe they were at the US Embassy in Tokyo. They acted as though we were lesser beings. They had gotten Blue Passports and left their Black "official" passports. The Air Force had issued me a Red Passport. I didn't think about what that meant when crossing borders or getting on a plane. I was stopped at every crossing and asked who I worked for, what job did I do, was I very important, etc. The dignitaries jumped on that. They laughed about the trip being slowed because I didn't get a blue passport. It was like that a lot, especially since they had herd mentality with six of them. I was waiting my time to throw their "stupid" comment back at them. Them calling me stupid nearly spoiled our trip. Then the time came.

I was telling someone about the swashbuckling tales at the Singapore docks about Frank Buck and the Sultan of Johore. One of the dignitaries heard me and now there were all six talking about how gullible I am! Now I believed in Fairy Tales! I was stupid!

We had been to Newton's Circle, an encampment that had dozens of international eateries, most in tents. We met the tour bus. When we were all seated a very tiny lady boarded the bus. She was our guide. As she was telling us the itinerary, one of the dignitaries said something about Frank Buck and they all started laughing. She asked what was so funny? The loud one spoke up and said there was a fool with them that thinks comic books are real stuff. She asked a couple more questions of them and then asked me where I had heard such a story? I told her I read a lot and Frank's story was interesting. That brought another outburst from them, saying the stupid fool reads comic books, etc.

She shook her head and smiled. She said our first stop after we crossed into Malaysia would be at Johore Barru and we would visit the home of the Sultan of Johore! She added the Sultan and his good friend would cross the border to here when they got in trouble! You could hear a pin drop. Then she looked right at me, "Don't worry, you are not the stupid fool here!" The dignitaries didn't say much to me after that!

We had the chance to go to Raffles Hotel. This is where old movies were filmed and where the Singapore Sling was first mixed! I had a couple. Probably more impressive was the area next to the hotel about a block over. Located on Arab Street are the most colorful and beautiful Mosques I have ever seen.

We went to Hong Kong twice, once on the way and again on the way back. We stayed mostly on the Kowloon side. I had looked at some tailor shops, always asking how much and what materials I could get. We were on the Star Ferry landing and I saw another Tailor Shop. We walked in. I asked if they had Worsted Wool? They pulled out many colors. I picked a beautiful blue pattern. They started sizing me and said

I could come in on my way back for a final fitting. I then asked how much it was. We left and the first thing Peggy asked was why I didn't ask them price up front like I did at the other? I told her I had this feeling when I walked in there. On our return I found out they were the oldest Tailor on the Kowloon side of Hong Kong. I knew there was something special about the shop.

On our way from the hotel we passed by the famous Peninsula Hotel. Very impressive, especially with all the green Rolls Royce they had there!

We took the Star Ferry to Macau. It was owned by the Portuguese. It had numerous casinos. It was also the area adjacent to China. Three months before, China had opened her borders to guests.

Through Immigration/Border Control I was detained longer than usual. "Who do you work for? What do you do? Are you a spy?" and many more questions. I left and joined our group walking into the first little town. I noted I was being followed.

Right off there was a man holding a Black Mamba snake with it's mouth wrapped shut with a small rope. I recognized it and knew it was one of the deadliest snakes in the world! He wanted to let people hold it for money. I wanted to but when I approached, one of the guys I had seen at the border stepped in and ushered the snake handler away from me. Yep, I was being followed.

A short distance there was an old church-like building with a lot of kids running around inside the fenced courtyard. It was an orphanage. After what happened in Vietnam, I visited orphanages a lot. I stepped up to the gate to the courtyard and when I started to open the gate I found a hand grab my wrist, stopping me from opening the gate. Another hand appeared and roughly pulled the hand off my wrist! The same follower was chewing out the guy who grabbed my wrist! The grabber stepped back as if at attention. The follower reached over and unlatched the gate.

They tried to control the kids but could not. I was the center of attention for a small group of young kids. I was sitting on the steps and had one child straddling my left leg, two straddling my right. On my right leg the little boy got so excited he peed his pants! The follower came fast to grab him but I put up my hand to stop him. He spoke some English. I told him there was no problem, I had a clean pair of pants in the bus. Then I added, "If you or anyone else harms this boy, I will be back! You know I am important!" He backed off and said weakly "Yes sir, yes sir".

We got on the bus again. We traveled through some open spaces and small towns. We stopped at what appeared to be a school, possibly a college. We were there to see a statue on the campus. All the windows to the school were boarded so we could not see inside. We heard the students talking. We saw the statue and back on the bus.

We stopped at a building with a huge open room that looked like a meeting room with an small elevated stage up front. I was escorted to the stage where a table was set up. Tables were also set up on the floor area. I was told the special table was for me, but Peggy had to sit with the others. No way! I expressed my anger and they soon let me sit on the floor tables with everyone else. We were served lunch.

After lunch we got back on the bus and headed further into China. I fell asleep, as did everyone else! I never doze in the afternoon! We all slept so we realized they had put something in the food so we would sleep as they traveled through an area they did not want us to see!

We stopped at a village and were told we could see how the Chinese lived. We were also told to just walk into the houses! I don't do that. Others did, but I stayed outside the houses. Soon a man came to me from inside the house. He motioned for me to come in. I didn't. When he stepped out he was joined by another man who spoke broken English. I was told the town gets paid from the Chinese Government to show their open houses to visitors. I asked if that was really how they lived? I was told first that it was but then quietly told the Government had directed how the town would look. It was apparently in much better shape than how they normally lived.

Soon we were back at the border with Macau. The exit questioning was more intense! I believe they wanted me to tell them what I was going to report back to my superiors! Back to Kowloon. And on to Bangkok!

When I was in Vietnam and some guys took an R&R (Rest & Relaxation) to Bangkok They talked a lot about wild times. However, they also talked about a great city. Bangkok is a great city.

Gold everywhere, especially near the Presidential Palace. So many beautiful and colorful buildings with gold roofs and trim. And the gold being sold, especially in Chinatown was unreal! The City sanctioned Chinatown to sell only true gold as advertised. That way you could buy a chain that was 23.7 carat gold and be assured it was. The City didn't have to push that law anymore, only an occasional inspection. If you went into a gold store, all you would see was gold! The Baht claims hanging from the walls were so many they covered the entire walls! Baht is their currency and also their weight. And you could trade in your gold for new gold products. I had bought a 2 Baht serpentine neck chain years back and intended to trade it in toward a new chain.

I watched as they went to what looked like spaghetti hanging from the walls and brought the chains to people. There is no haggling, the state-controlled price was set. When they would get a call from a store wanting gold chains they would send a runner. The merchant would take large handfuls of gold chains, weigh them, and wrap them in newspaper. The runner would take the package and leave for the store.

While walking in another store that specialized in precious stones, we looked at blue and black star sapphires. I was looking at all the stones, many of them being "Lindy" stones. A lindy is a man made stone that actually has a more brilliant star in low light. I had researched them and I could tell from the back of the stone and the price which ones were real stones. I looked down at one small group of stones and said to Peggy that they didn't look very good. A woman I didn't see that was standing back from the case stepped forward. "Sir, I don't think you know what you are looking at."

She opened the case and pulled out the tray of stones. I was introduced to the Gold Star Sapphire! They were not a brilliant stone like he blues but when a direct light was applied the most beautiful star appeared! I asked what the difference was? She said the Blues and Blacks sell from $5 to $35 a carat. The Golds are quite rare and sell from $30 to $300 a carat! The one I was looking at was $650! I didn't buy it.

Like Hong Kong, Bangkok has some very special hotels. Here it is the Oriental Hotel. In front of it there is a sweeping curved driveway that looks like a large arch from a distance. When we had taken the three-wheel taxi, the driver told us he was not allowed to take his vehicle up the drive! He would be arrested by the Hotel Security. Later in Chinatown we ran into a young American teenager. She was on her own at that moment. We struck up a conversation. I explained the gold and stuff like that. She said she wanted to visit certain areas she had heard about. One of those areas was the Oriental Hotel.

I explained to her that we could not take one of the three-wheel taxis, they are banned from driving up to the front entrance. Don't remember how we got there, but we said the three of us should get one of the drivers to take us to the hotel entrance! We found a three-wheel taxi driver that would do it, for a price! We paid him extra. When he raced up the driveway with the little engine sounding like it was going to blow up, we jumped out before he came to a full stop. We watched him go at full throttle again with about four Hotel staff in bright white uniforms chase after him! He got away! We were scolded by the Hotel management!

The tour took us through the City and we stopped in the "Red Light" district. Among all the pleasure establishments was the Bat Boat! They had the freshest seafood, lobster, crab, fish, etc. You ordered a meal for two and they brought it to your table in a wooden boat! In the City there was great food everywhere. The Marine's wife was from a Mediterranean City that ate spicy food. When we ate together as a group both she and I would order the food spicy hot. They would serve her but refuse to serve me the really spicy food. She would tell them that I could eat it hotter than she could. They would serve me the hot food but have a waiter or two standing there with a damp rag to wipe my forehead if necessary! It was never necessary.

We were introduced to the Water Taxis. They ran a boat back and forth on the river. You could go to almost any place on the water taxi without getting in a traffic jam. Very few Americans rode it. We got off the boat and visited the presidential palace and government buildings. Police were dressed similar to British "Bobbys". There was a lot to see. All the building had gold on them. Quite spectacular.

Not far from our hotel was the American Embassy. The Marine and his wife spent a lot of time with us. We four entered a jewelry store next to the Embassy. It had a long display area. Directly behind the counter in a chair facing sideways was the owner's wife. She had a cash register. The owner had set up small diagonal stands raised off the counter a foot or so. Each had a small pad of paper. He also had his son and nephew as runners to get gold things as necessary from the big guys in Chinatown.

We asked if he was governed by price like Chinatown? No, but he knew well enough that if a customer from or visiting the Embassy got a piece of jewelry or gold chain that wan't good, he would go broke from a bad reputation. He guaranteed his was the same as Chinatown. His wife spoke to him a lot to make sure he didn't make a mistake. He would take care of all the people in there by writing the cost of the item on the pad, tear off the sheet and place it on the counter with the item. When we first walked in he was very busy and had apparently he made a mistake. His wife was still cussing him.

The Marine's wife picked up a beautiful Cornflower Blue Emerald and the owner put down a price. In his rush he wrote a wrong number and the Marine's wife was going to get a very special price, more than half off! The owner's wife yelled at him and he went to the Marine to say he had made a mistake, but he would honor that price if she wanted the stone! The Marine's wife looked in the counter and told her husband she really liked the other one better! He told her if she put it back he could not offer the same mistake. She put it back and the Marine looked at us with wide eyes, "She just cost me $6,000!" It was the most beautiful stone.

I saw where he had four Gold Star Sapphires and I asked to look at them. He asked which one I wanted and before he rushed to take care of another customer he wrote down a number and went on. I also got another Baht Chain and he put the cost on another slip of paper. The Gold Star was priced at $80. I looked at it and knew something was wrong. The stone was genuine and it was 5.5 Carats! When he came back Peggy asked if he could give us a better price? He didn't look at the stone, only the paper. He said he could not bargain on gold, the price was set. Then he looked at the $80 and changed it to $75. We paid him and immediately his wife went high order! In his rush he had apparently written $80 instead of $800! He gave it to me for the $75! It was supposed to be $145 a carat!

We fell in love with Bangkok, but it was time to head back to Hong Kong.

Not only did I get the final fitting for my suit, I met with a trusted jeweler who took my Gold Star and mounted in a hand made Castle setting. Beautiful ring by itself, but even more so when seen in bright sunlight. A Lindy will display many stars at a lower light. A genuine star will display a single spectacular star in bright light. The jeweler said she had never seen a gold star and she said she made the castle to bring out the beauty of the Star.

We got back to Japan from one of the greatest trips we have ever taken. I spent some time by myself. I may have shed a tear. I asked my father if I did what he wanted. And I apologized for not being there to say Goodbye to him. I get real calm as I feel he would have been happy. See you later Dad.

I drove or had a license for every Air Force vehicle on the base. If there was an accident and the vehicle involved was in the way, I could legally drive it. That included the 28 and 40 passenger busses. I drove one down to an orphanage we supported in Kamakura and other places. So it seemed logical when the Girl Scouts wanted me to drive the Air Force bus to the new Tokyo Disneyland! It had only been open a couple weeks. It was great hearing songs like "It's a Small, Small World" being sung in Japanese! We had a blast! The very next week the Boy Scouts asked if I could take them to the new Tokyo Disneyland? Of course

I could! So Peggy and the girls went to Tokyo Disneyland twice in two weeks!

I had taken two semesters of Japanese in college. Yes, I was still proving to my mother I wasn't stupid, but I don't think she knew or cared. The Air Force had a degree program that when mixed with basic college level classes they would award an Associates Degree! Mine was in Occupational Safety and Health! I was taking Japanese Language classes and spoke quite passable Japanese. We went to a local amusement park, Toshimaen. While walking around some young school kids came up to see the Americans, especially my tall daughters, one a blonde and the other a strawberry blonde. Their designated spokesperson, a little boy in his school outfit, came up to us and asked in this tiny voice,"Do you speaky Japanese?" I answered, "Nijongo Hanashimasen", in Japanese that I didn't speak Japanese! He bowed and turned back toward the other 10 or so little kids. He got maybe four or five steps away, stopped, turned to look at me with big eyes, and then put his hands in front of his face and started giggling! I don't know what it must have looked like, but we stayed for another couple hours and those kids stayed with us the whole time! Must have been like the Pied Piper. We practiced English and Japanese.

The MEI and ORI came as the Colonel had predicted. Overall we did great and the Safety program rated Excellent across the board. And, this was the first year that Clark Air Base in the Philippines did NOT get the best safety program in the Pacific! My program did! When we received the plaque I was awarded it during a Staff Meeting. I told the Colonel I would put it in the trophy case and he did something never done before, he told me I had earned it and I was to take it home! He told the staff the Safety Program was nothing, and seven months later it was the best in the Pacific! I was also put in for Safety Professional of the Year!

I investigated an accident where a young Airman was struck and killed by a large truck as he supposedly was crossing a main street. Luckily I spoke very good Japanese and was able to do a thorough investigation. I asked for a meeting with the Colonel and we talked about it. I told him I could not write an accident report on the young Airman because my investigation indicated the Airman had committed suicide!

The Colonel was livid! He said he was not going to tell the parents their son died in a foreign country by suicide! He demanded I write an investigation that showed it was an accident. When I refused he came unglued! We had some words and finally he said he wanted the report I had submitted on another accident. He took it, used many of my suicide briefing facts and removed the suicide portions, and signed it himself. It took a while for us to get back the outstanding rapport we had.

I was scheduled for some training and it was in Denver. I got to see Peggy's mother after her surgery. Apparently being around all the chemicals she did by being a hairdresser caused throat cancer. She eventually had radical surgery and now was having to use a small megaphone pushed up against the new stoma (hole in the throat) to talk. I was concerned because she complained about pain that lingered on. She was stubborn and said she was okay. We both worried.

The First Sergeant and I were friends and worked a couple projects together. He came up to me one day, leading off with the story of his daughter getting married in Las Vegas and how he had borrowed $10,000 a few months before, went to Las Vegas and said he wanted the casino to put his money in their safe. That action made him an immediate "High Roller" and he was now getting the comps! He was about to fly home, meet his daughter in Las Vegas and the casino was picking him up from the airport in a limo and his daughter in a Corvette, which she could use during her stay. She was getting married at the casino also. He paid something like $40 to borrow the money for a few days but he was now getting the comps of a high roller without spending a dime!

Then he got to the meat of his insanity, he had told the Colonel he did not trust Frank, the chef of Human Resources, his designated backup, and wanted me to fill in for him while he was gone! This was important because he was going back to the states for a few days so I would have to make management decisions for the organization, not just Safety! The Colonel loved it!

I had so much fun bailing drunks out of Japanese jails, one guy resisted arrest and broke the wrist of the Japanese Police! I had to do a lot of stuff not normally on my shoulders. And of course Frank was not happy about it!

I guess it didn't help when one day one of my friend's wife came in and headed right for my office by the HR office, passing Frank. You could detect some odor and by the time she happily walked in and gave me a special gift, many people were aware of the odor! She presented me with what is called a "Century Egg". That is a large egg buried underground for 100 days. When dug up and the shell broken you can see the egg has changed colors and formed into layers. Man does it smell! But my little friend knew I ate stuff like that, and it was a gift to me. I was forced to leave the building! And yes, we sat outside and ate the Century Egg!

We bought a Yamaha 1200cc touring motorcycle, all black. Japan had strict rules about nothing larger than a 250cc motorcycle unless you belonged to a sanctioned Harley Davidson group, or you were American military. Even at that I could not take Peggy with me on the freeway because "two up" was not allowed. We had to take side roads. We had to worry about getting run over because car drivers would pull up next to you and want to look at the big motorcycle and in doing so would drift toward you!

I was still teaching a select few bikers and one guy from the Base Hospital came to me and said he was thinking about a small motorcycle because of the gas and a few more reasons before I told him I could see he just wanted a bike! He agreed and he got something like a 350cc motorcycle. I taught him and he asked what would be his biggest problem? I told him it would be when for one reason he had to roll the throttle a little more than usual and feel how much power he was sitting on.

He saw me a couple weeks later and said that exact thing happened and he was wanting to speed all the time! He had done something that got back to the Doctor he worked for and the doctor said he was not allowed to drive a motorcycle if he worked for him! My friend asked me to talk to his boss.

About the first thing I saw as I walked into the hospital clinic was a sign that read, "Buy your son a motorcycle for his last birthday!" An 8X10 red sign with black letters! Could not miss it. The meeting was somewhat a draw and I told the Doctor to take the sign down and give it to me. He refused. So I talked to the Base Commander and told him I thought the sign was a deterrent to my Safety program and Motorcycle safety program. He agreed. We got in his staff car, and I now own that sign!

One secretary I saw somewhat often when I visited the office area she supported asked me after I had known her for a few months if I wanted to go out with her! I knew she was married, for one, and when I looked in a mirror all I saw was scars. Yeah, thanks Mom for waiving my rights to medical treatment following the car accident. Anyway, I asked a couple friends and they said she was known to have flings with guys other than her husband.

The young lady was attractive with a very nice figure, blonde hair that when pulled back showed her large forehead, but still attractive. Nice voice and she had a lot of charm when she asked if I wanted a date with her. Me and all my friends knew that would never happen but apparently she didn't. Then one day I was really stressed and came by to see if her boss was in, I had to see him.

She said he was in and reached across to touch my hand that was resting on the end of her desk. "When are you going to give me that date?" She had her hair back and I could not resist. Her sort of lazy Susan holder for her ink stamps was sitting on the front of her desk blotter. There was the stamp for classified data, stamps for mail, etc., and a self inking stamp for today's date. Yes, I reached across to her stamps and got the date stamp and pressed it onto her forehead! I did a good job and she never asked me again!

There are a thousand more stories about Japan, too many, so we were getting ready to return to the US. I was preparing for another "By Name" request to go to Ohio to take over a Major Command

Safety Manager position. We started preparing for the move when I got another priority "by name" assignment to the Air Force Weapons Laboratory at Kirkland Air Force Base in Albuquerque New Mexico.

29

Chapter 10

Kirtland Air Force Base, New Mexico

The Weapons Lab had requested me because one of the Lieutenants fried himself to a crispy critter while attempting to align a very high voltage LASER. I was needed to do something to prevent recurrence! I would review the programs and fix them so something like this never happens again. I was also the Safety Consultant to the Space Technology Center.

One of the first things we did was go see Peggy's mother. She was not doing well so I left Peggy with her and I went back to Albuquerque. During that time she was gone I chose to quit smoking, cold turkey.

Peggy came down to Albuquerque very worried about her mother. We made another trip and basically said our goodbyes, Marie was bed-ridden, frail, and dying. She told me to take care of her girls, meaning Peggy and out two girls. She died an few days later at the age of 59.

The problem with Engineers is Safety is usually an add-on, never built into it. So some of these remarkable engineering feats didn't have great Safety programs and procedures. That was now my job, and a lot more. A whole lot more! Often there is only one thing you can tell an Engineer, nothing! Fortunate for me the person who designed and built the LASER is a NCO, not an officer. We could talk and work together.

The killer LASER was called EDCL1 (Electrical Discharge Coaxial Laser). It could maintain a beam hotter than the sun, continuously. As a LASER usually will admit a beam only 1/3 the power input, we had isolated the power from inadvertent contact.

The Laser is what we called EDCL is basically a Carbon Dioxide LASER. All Lasers have to use more power than output. The Laser beam hardly ever gets more than 30% as strong as the power going into it. The reaction between chemicals and in this case, electrical power causes the reaction inside the chamber. When a small portion of the chamber is opened, a laser beam is emitted. The reaction/interaction continues inside the chamber. The opening is small and the beam has to be concentrated. On EDCL the power input, electrical, had to be isolated so we had the power generator in a cage raised up so the base was 8 feet off the floor. The heavily insulated wiring went down to a junction box and then over to the control panel on the other side of the Laser. The Laser puts out a round flat beam. Flat being the end of the beam. If the beam was not flat it had to be realigned. It is aligned by small bolts along each side and ends of the mounting table. The lieutenant was attempting to align the table with the Laser running. He would take a wrench and turn the leveling screws until the beam was adjusted flat. He had the metal wrench in his hand and moved to the side and back to observe the Beam. Either he or someone else had left the door open on the junction box! The J-Box we could use to shut power off to the laser. In operation, the J-Box cover should have been closed tight. On that day it wasn't! We assessed the door was open and the Lieutenant, holding the metal wrench, became the path of least resistance between the Power and the Laser through the Box, He moved too close to the Box and the electricity arced across and through his body, frying everything immediately.

The EDCL will quickly burn through anything solid but a clear object like glass or plexiglas it burns through much slower. Our fix was to make Plexiglas squares we would mount and fire the Laser at. When the Laser beam was off, you would shut down the power. Then get the Plexiglass. If the burn of the beam was not flat, we would adjust the table until you got a flat beam. Nobody had to touch the adjustment table while the Laser was being fired. We engineered away the possibility of a repeat fatality. Now I solved the problem we had a chance to get to know Albuquerque.

Albuquerque was a remarkably versatile and pretty city. In the background were the Sandia Mountains, named Sandia for the reddish color seen at dusk, Sandia meaning "Watermelon" in tribal language. Whereas Homestead Florida was the number one city to get shot in, Albuquerque had the largest number of drunk drivers! Any Friday night it was estimated 40% of the drivers on the road were impaired! Luckily, I was definitely "Key Personnel" and we went directly to Base Housing. The Base was separated in two major areas. Personnel, Base Exchange, Motor Pool, Hospital, etc. was on the east side of the base. Sandia National Labs was also located on that side. On the west side was the Weapons Lab and Space Technology Center. On both sides there was base housing. The small area just across the street from the Weapons Lab was a nice small area. That is where we got a nice house.

There were 16 Indian Pueblos surrounding the City. All were considered Federal Jurisdiction, meaning state or local laws were not enforceable. The highest number of hit and run accidents were where the person went back to the Pueblo. Therefore, unless he/she left the Pueblo they could not be charged. That is also why the insurance rates were very high. I was hit twice and my insurance had to pay.

Another time I was driving up the road toward the Base at exactly 37 mph in a 40 mph zone. I was going through the intersection on a green light when a car from the other side of the dividing island turned left in front of my car! The driver, a 16 year old Hispanic with his mother in the passenger seat ran the red turn arrow and caused the accident. We hit so hard a spare tire flew out of the trunk of his car! I put my flashers on and watched the car he was driving go up onto the center island of the cross street and stop. I watched closely in case one of them was hurt but instead watched the mother and son change places in the car!

Soon a police officer came and I said I was not hurt so he went to the other car. I listened and the woman, speaking in Spanish to the Hispanic Cop, told him she was driving! She said I was speeding and that my car ran the red light! I think one of the witnesses said something because the cop asked again who was driving. I could not hear what she said to him in a very low voice. He walked the boy off to the side and talked with him. Then came and told the mother he was writing the report that the mother said she was driving. And she stated the speeding car in the opposite lane ran a red light and struck her car. I acted like a typical Anglo who spoke only English. Little did they know when I came back from four years in Spain I tested bilingual, and back from three years in Japan I tested trilingual!

Next day I went back to the intersection with my investigation tools.. As I was taught in Police Accident Investigation training I timed the lights. I timed the seconds of transition from green to yellow to red. I did extensive timing so to set a proven sequence. I then measured my skid marks. I measured and recorded the striation marks his car made while turning through the arrow. I thoroughly checked all my findings. I documented what the Hispanic driver's mother and Hispanic Cop said. I wrote my investigation and finished it with my credentials, education and training. Then had it notarized. I took it to my insurance lady. After reading and commenting she didn't know I was all I said I was, she faxed the letter under her letterhead cover to their insurer. After just a few minutes she called the insurance agent.

The conversation started with the other lady telling my lady she was glad she called! From the insured statements and police report, we were going to pay! New Mexico is a Comparative Negligence State. She determined I was 80% negligent and my insurance would have to pay for damage to her insured car, loss of work, bodily injury, etc. The cost was staggering! My Agent lady said that was not acceptable. She asked if the insurance lady had received the Fax? Yes, she said she would look at it later. She didn't know I was sitting in the room listening to her on speaker. She was told to get the Fax and read it now! We heard the papers and soon she came on the line. When she read it she said things like nobody has those qualifications, and since I am a Military guy she was sure I was lying! And besides, how can he say what the Cop was saying if they did indeed speak Spanish. I spoke up and said, "Por que,

Yo Hablo Espanol" She was shocked! Then she proposed we split it 50/50 and each insurance will pay their own damage. My lady laughed and asked again if she had read all of the letter,? She stated a hard copy was on it's way to her and being filed against my citation? We demanded 100% their fault but settled for 80%. That showed them clearly at fault. My citation was dropped! The lady charged with false reporting. Her son could not get his driver license! He was driving under a permit then and "at fault" for an accident. The cop received disciplinary action, they would not say what.

Justice! And it really bothered me that other people may have similar experiences but don't have the knowledge, experience or ability to do what I did, so they get screwed. God I wished I could help some of those people. It depressed me. And the other Insurance lady speaking out loud that she thought military people were stupid and not trustworthy! I felt like I was still fighting my mother even in New Mexico! I only had two college degrees then, I am not stupid. And I married the woman I fell in love with, not the woman my mother said I should have married.

I got heavily involved in the Weapons Lab. I talked to all sections and filling my head with as much as I could. I was at one of our laser sites and the site manager asked me how much I understood? I impressed him with how much I had learned. He walked me through the upcoming shot. We were at one of the test ranges. He then asked how much Nitrogen should we put into the mirrors to cool the mirror when the laser was shot? Without Nitrogen the mirror would shatter from the heat of the LASER. I can't remember but it was only a few seconds of Nitrogen. The operator said it was within range and set the Nitrogen flow. I actually hit the firing button! As the laser fired, the first mirror exploded! $25,000 mirror! We went through all the data and most likely I directed one second too much Nitrogen and the mirror was too cold. I was told that happens, not to worry. We were doing experimental tests and that had happened to about every operator at least once. I didn't like the outcome but I understood the experiments.

I was concentrating on laser since we had to do something about the death by laser of the Lieutenant. After that there was so much going on in the Lab. Our mission was to simulate the effects of a nuclear weapon through conventional means and to ensure if a nuclear weapon was ever released, our airplanes and equipment would still function uninterrupted. All our equipment, especially the lasers, were used for contractor experiments. Most had slowed or postponed due to the accident.

Before speaking to what we did to achieve our mission and scope, here are some basics.

There are four elements of a nuclear blast:

Explosion

Intense light and heat

Electromagnetic Pulse (EMP)

Plasma generation (Altering molecular atoms)

We simulated all this, the explosion done by underground blasts, the light and heat by use of lasers, the EMP by very specific creation of EMP, and the Plasma by specialized equipment. I am being vague because of the sensitivity and classification of some of this. I take my Top Secret clearance seriously. Since we were working with one of the most powerful lasers in the world, the one that killed the operator, I'll explain what I can.

The EDCL Laser maintained a heat hotter than the sun, continuous. To simulate the explosive (Over Pressurizing) effect of an atom bomb we did underground explosions in the dessert. And to simulate the Electromagnetic Pulse (EMP) we had many EMP devices. And Plasma generation is quite an in-depth process.

We actually had the greatest number of Lasers in the free world. Mostly Defense Contractors would set up experiments and tests that used our Laser beams. For example: one contractor was testing the vulnerability of a metal they were developing. It would be a part of a aircraft. So we set up the beam to go through a concave mirror to narrow the circumference of the beam to fit their needs. They placed the metal on a stand and we fired at it with the Laser. It immediately burned a hole through the metal. Then we turned on the wind tunnel to simulate the aircraft going through the air and then we fired it again. With the wind on they could tell if the wind caused the burn to maintain the same hole diameter or would the wind cause the hole to burn outward? We did so many experiments, but again I am not at liberty to speak openly.

We were famous for our Trestle! The Trestle was the largest totally wooden structure in the world! All wood, including the nuts and bolts. The top of the Trestle was approximately 278 feet off the floor of the arroyo it was built on. That was because when we fired the EMP on whatever we had on the top, we would zap the object and take the readings before we got a bounce EMP off the ground below. The test equipment we had in the test object would tell us our vulnerable areas. We would then use means to isolate or protect those areas so our aircraft could still fly even after a nuclear blast. We tested equipment from all branches of service, I was there during testing of the new Black Hawk helicopter and the first B1 Bomber and others. We had a lot of visitors to the Trestle and quite a few times when the PAO (Public Affairs Officer) was unable to take the tour they would ask if I could. I had learned quite a bit about all our equipment.

I worked for a Civilian, a GM13 (General Manager level 13). I was supposed to work for a lady GS12 (General Supervisor level 12) but everybody realized I was so far ahead of her it wasn't feasible to have me report to her! She had her own problems.

The GM13 was not great either but blew his own horn very loud, louder than his knowledge back up. I tried very hard to work with him. Ralph believed anyone in uniform was stupid! Now where have I heard that before? Problem is that now I had two college degrees and was 6 semester hours short of a third degree when I left Japan. I was already enrolled in the two classes and upon completion I would get my third degree.

One day we had the top Colonel in Safety come out from Norton Air Force Base (AFB) in California. He saw the B1 on the Trestle and asked the GM, Ralph, if he could possibly get a tour of the new bomber? It was the first one in production so it was a hot item. Ralph started saying what he was going to do, who he had to get approval through to take the Colonel aboard, etc. and he started making calls. While he was doing that, I simply asked the Colonel if he wanted to see it? Of course he said yes and I pointed my head toward the door as if to say "Let's Go"! I told the secretary we were going to the Trestle and around. We got in the truck and off to the Trestle.

The Colonel asked if I thought we could go aboard the B1? I told him one of my jobs was to give Safety briefings to all crews using our test facilities and I knew the crew chief of the B1. We got there and were not allowed very close. Security with M16s stood all around it and would not let us near it. One of the crew was coming or going so I asked for the Crew Chief by name and soon the Chief came out. We shook hands and I introduced the Colonel. I told him I would love to get the Colonel aboard. He asked the Security Clearance of the Colonel, he already knew mine. He went back in the aircraft. About 3 minutes later he came back out.

He cleared us through the guard, and we went into the B1! Two super secret panels were covered up but all else was left uncovered. He showed us through. The Colonel got to sit in all but one seat and the Chief answered almost every question. He seeming very impressed with questions asked. We exited after about an hour with a truly great tour. We shook hands all around and the Chief joked that now I owed him one and we walked back to the truck. Just then Ralph drove up with the Public Affairs Officer. He was sweating as only an overweight man wearing the same worn brown sports jacket with the patched elbows as he wore every day would sweat. He announced he had gotten a written approval for the Colonel to go aboard the B1. However 7 panels had to be covered for security. He said the Colonel would not be able to sit in the Pilot's or EWO (Electronic Warfare Officer) chair. The Colonel turned slightly away from Ralph and winked at me with the eye Ralph couldn't see. He turned toward Ralph and the PIO. "Ralph, I appreciate all the effort you put in on this, but I have a lunch date with someone, maybe next time"! I looked at the Colonel and suggested since I had the truck I could drop him off at the Club or his car. We laughed a lot of the way back. He asked if Ralph found out I had done that, would I be in trouble? Oh Hell no, I would just say we had to look at a Top Secret item, Ralph only has a Secret clearance!

As far as the "Overpressure" effects of a nuclear bomb, we had tests in the desert that exceeded any tests up to that point. Again, the results verified what actions we would have to do to keep us flying and fighting.

The last effect from a Nuclear Weapon is "Plasma" generation. That is the next level of rearranging molecules. Looking at places like Hiroshima and Nagasaki where shapes were sometimes not recognizable, our experiments showed the shapes and forms being altered. A metal object would be transformed into a totally different shape from the rearrangement of atoms. Sandia National Labs across the base and us were amongst five laboratories trying to split the atom peaceably. This was an important step.

We used a "Shiva Star". It was a six legged star made up of capacitors the size of baseball bats. They were imbedded in water beds and stacked quite high. All connected together and attached to the center ring. In the center we would put handmade foil around the inside the ring. We used sold metal and placed it in the very center. We charged up the capacitors to full power. Then we left the room. The walls were thick with iron built in them so the pulse could not penetrate. We viewed through cameras, all remote viewing. The electrical surge would go down through the arms to the center. The building would shake and the Star would rise up a couple inches off the floor! We had to wait until the electricity was dissipated before we could enter the room. The solid metal in the center was now a totally different shape. It might look like modern art. It was unrecognized from it's original shape. We had rearranged the atoms!

I got invited to a meeting of the American Society of Safety Engineers (ASSE). The president of the New Mexico Chapter was Margaret Carroll. We talked and she found that with my experience I should be a member of ASSE. I soon was and Margaret soon became my Mentor. I guess I can say between her and two other Mentors, I owe them my professional career. She was also the one to get me to attend remote classes taught by Central Missouri State University (CMSU). The other university classes taught on Base didn't have a Safety or Environmental degree program.

Carla, the GS12, worked with me somewhat well. I was invited to a gathering where I said I would be a little late and not stay long. As I went to the venue, grabbed a beer and soon saw Carla. Mind you, Carla is Hispanic, a little short, very pretty, and very large breasts. I could see this guy was trying to touch places he shouldn't. I didn't think he spoke any Spanish so I asked her in Spanish if he was bothering her. She said yes but asked me not to make a scene. Okay. I walked up to her and said to the guy "excuse me" in Spanish. I got between him and Carla, leaned over and kissed Carla on the forehead. I turned to the guy, "I'm sorry, I promised our mother that I would take care of my little sister" Carla called me a fond name in Spanish and kissed me on the cheek. She said she may have had a little too much to drink and this nice man had been kind enough to offer a ride home. I said you know what happened the last time you did that! Then she laughed, gave me a big kiss on the lips! The guy walked away from us. Carla gave me another kiss and a thanks, "keep it between us".

We had that little secret between us that didn't affect our work, Pat Watkins did! Pat came in from Germany. She was black and made that clear. After she challenged Carla on everything they resorted to passing written notes. I was doing some special projects and basically reporting to Ralph. He asked me a couple time what I would do about it, and if I could help Carla? My response, Carla is a GS12, makes considerably more money than I do! If she claims to have earned the promotion and not because she has huge boobs, then she has had management training and should be able to handle the Air Force female! He didn't ask me again. They were like oil and water! They weren't together on anything and Pat argued Carla didn't know how to do anything! They literally passed note so they didn't have to talk to each other!

Then Pat came up to me and asked why Carla treated me so much better than her? I simply stated "It probably has to do with professionalism." I got a call the very next day from my black friend in the Equal Opportunity Office. "Bruce, a Pat Watkins has filed a discrimination complaint against you!" He asked if I knew her? Then he added that she has a record of destroying white men, and this complaint would destroy me! He asked if I had indeed told her she was unprofessional? I said I did not. I repeated what I had said. He said it must have been important for me to remember exactly what I said! I told him that I had a near photographic memory. I then told him what I said was correct, I was recognized as a professional, she wasn't!

He told me I was on thin ice! He didn't know if whatever I could do to prove it would help me. Adding she hadn't lost a complaint case yet and I was number 7. I pulled out my Professional Certification cards. I showed him my signature with the letters behind my name. I added that if I signed an official document it was against the law for anyone to change it. My certifications were the equivalent of a lawyer or engineer's official document. He made copies and notes, conversing with me on the notes. He shook my hand and wished me luck. From there I went down to see another good friend and we talked. From that conversation I contacted Air Force Personnel Center in Texas and asked for another good friend of mine. We talked and by talking with my friend here in Personnel I knew what to say to him. He said he would get back to me.

I had unofficially found out I had won the case against Pat! She didn't know yet that her case against me had been dropped. However, when she got off the phone and started yelling something about, "They can't do that to me, it is against the law!" I figured she had just found out. I was wrong! She had just been given orders to report for Duty in Korea on October 1st! She had been back from Germany only five months and said it was illegal for them to send her overseas without a full year Stateside! She was yelling, blaming everybody! She was headed to Personnel to set their asses straight! We talked when she drove off, and laughed a lot in the office. Nobody liked her, glad to see her go.

The call came from Texas a little while later and my friend asked if she had been notified yet? Laughing, I told him what happened and then asked what and how in the hell he had done it? Yes, the Air Force member has the right to be stateside for what is thought to be a year but actually it is not a calendar year but a Fiscal Year. That runs from October 1 to September 30! So it was legal to reassign her at the next Fiscal Year! He said the hard thing to do was have her report to Korea on October 1st!

When Pat got back to the office she was still ranting and raving. Now she was blaming me because of the complaint, blaming Carla because of their situation, and when she was about to blow a gasket, I talked to her. I told her, if she didn't know, her complaint against me was dropped. She started on that and got even madder and blamed me again! Then I assured her that none of us in the office had enough power to get her reassigned to Korea, it must be her outstanding service record that got her the assignment. I added that my trip to Korea was a "by name" assignment, maybe hers was too. Carla was with us in the big office area so Pat's angry fit carried on as she went into the office she shared with Carla, slammed the door shut and told us loudly not to come in! We could hear her on the phone talking loudly, sometimes in anger. Carla looked at me and asked if I had anything to do with that? "Who, me?" I went into my office listening to them laughing and saying they knew I did it.

I was getting very good at knowing and understanding the research. I had created a Laser Safety course for all Support people who might be exposed to a laser beam unintentional. They were required to often be in the same room with the laser in operation but didn't have the same physical protection the operator or engineer had on. I got that policy changed also.

I also attended a Laser Safety Course taught by Dave Sliney and Myron Walbarsh, the undisputed experts in the Laser Safety field. Their book on Safety with Lasers and other Optical Devices were a must read for Laser Safety. I was the only military attendee. One day I was approached by Jim. He was the first person to open a commercial Laser Company. Their claim to fame was cutting transmission mounting holes in Oldsmobile transmissions. He said he knew us guys in the military did some really big, special stuff, could I tell him any. I asked how far was he propagating a beam? 27 feet, he said. Then I told him we had just declassified our Airborne Laser Lab. We were firing at a 14 foot by 14 foot target. He said that was a big target! I responded it did not look that big from 330 nautical miles away and in atmosphere! I told him some more unclassified stuff and his mouth remained open with awe the whole time.

I was knowledgeable of all the stuff we had or did. I was sometimes asked if I had the time to take over one of the tours when the Public Affairs Officer couldn't. I was doing minimal stuff for the Space Technology Center, so I had a little time to work on projects. One project that came through was a surprise.

I guess my motorcycle expertise was noted at a high level. I was asked to set up an experiment using three and four wheel ATVs (All Terrain Vehicles) to determine stability and safety concerns. I took four different levels of riders from novice to expert, excluding me as the most qualified. Each rotated diving both the three-wheel and the four-wheel ATVs. I took them through sand and dirt areas, roads, etc. and through simple to difficult scenarios. I wrote my report and turned it in. It was one of three reports that helped ban the use of three wheelers. The reports causing companies like Honda to discontinue manufacturing the three wheeler. It also helped to improve safety and training

One of the American Society of Safety Engineers (ASSE) meeting I was talking to the Chapter President, Margaret Carroll. She worked as a Engineer and Safety for Sandia National Labs. She was also very active with the Tribal Women and with ASSE National. We talked and she said with my experience and college degrees I should have joined long ago. She wrote an editorial about me and it was printed in Professional Safety magazine and she truly became my first great mentor.

She introduced me to Dr. Semonisc from Central Missouri State University (CMSU) and soon he became another great mentor. Together they had pulled the right strings and were setting up a satellite program with CMSU for Occupational Safety and Health (OS&H) and I was soon enrolled.

I was working on my third college degree, taught by Central Missouri State University. I was told there was a 16 semester hour requirement to be on campus to graduate. I went through Personnel and applied for Operation Bootstrap. This is a program where I could go to school on a college campus if I could graduate within one year. It was for Enlisted members to come back and apply for Commission to become an officer. I declined the Officer stuff, I wanted to continue with what I was doing.

I drove to Warrensburg Missouri and stayed at Whiteman Air Force Base. I had 37 semester hours to complete and it was questioned if I could do that in a year. Bootstrap was not without a commitment of three time the school time and was considered "terminal" as you had to get the degree in one year. A one year school time meant I would have to serve an additional three years! I graduated with a 3.85 gpa in 8 months! It was unheard of to do 37 semester hours in 8 months! I did it and I owed the Air Force only two more years instead of three.

I now had three College Degrees! My sister who bragged about her going back and getting her four year degree called me up and said I was the first one ever in our family to have three degrees! I thanked her and mentioned maybe Mother wouldn't think I was stupid anymore. She didn't understand and was appalled I said that, "Mom has never said that"! So much for keeping your head in the sand, sister of mine.

I was still trying to take Peggy somewhere every year for our anniversary. I was now a Professional Member of ASSE and I was elected a Delegate for the Annual Professional Development Conference (PDC) so I took Peggy with me when she could go. I took her to Seattle, Las Vegas, New Orleans and Washington DC. Otherwise we would plan a trip to Hawaii or overseas.

The secretary came into my office and told me a directive came that said all military members of the Lab were to participate in a special ceremony and would wear their Dress Uniform, etc. It was from the Public Affairs office, so I called up the office and told the person I was assigned to Safety and regulations state clearly that Safety Personnel were exempt from all additional duties. The person responded that the

Lieutenant organizing the "Review" stated that all military members would be in attendance, no exceptions. I simply stated that Lab protocol does not rise above United States Air Force regulations, so please tell the Lieutenant to count me out!

Within minutes the Lieutenant called me and informed me, by orders of the Commander, I would stand in uniform for the Review. I told the Lieutenant the same thing, I am exempt from any additional duties and even the Commander can't overrule USAF policy. He ranted and raved and soon came to my office. I wasn't there but heard he was livid and told Ralph to order me to be there! Finally I got a call from the Commander and he asked if I would as a favor to him? He said this simple thing has gotten way out of hand and is embarrassing the Lab. He asked if I would please stand for the Review? I said I would for him, not the pain in the ass Lieutenant.

We met on a parade field and were put in formations. The Lieutenant walked the formation as if he was General Patton reviewing his troops. He told a couple people things that were wrong with their uniform. When he got to me he stopped with daggers in his eyes. He looked at my five rows of ribbons and Missileman badge! He instructed me to take them off! "What?" He said that I was just wearing them to cause him more trouble! I looked at his two ribbons and told him that I didn't wear the Organizational Ribbons, even though I was authorized. I only wear the ones I earned. However, if it bothered him, he could wear the Organization ribbons and maybe it would make him look like he had a full row! There were snickers all around! The Lieutenant yelled "Attention" so everybody had to stand and be quiet. He ordered me to remove my ribbons from my uniform! I said, "Sir, with all due respect. I cannot do that. I would be considered out of uniform! Sir!" He dismissed me from the formation! Later, with a slight laugh, the Commander contacted me and asked me to go a little easy on the young man! Only one person in the Lab had more ribbons/awards than I did.

I had been diagnosed with my fourth case of Bells' Palsy. No doctor knew of anybody having it more than twice. And no doctor knew exactly what caused it! It could not be officially stated that it most likely came from my exposure to Agent Orange. I got a call from the Army and I was given orders to go to Fort Bliss near El Paso Texas. I was to meet one of the top doctors in the Army, he was a General. He was dabbling into research on Bells' Palsy due to the negative affect on the readiness if a member caught the disease. The eye drooping, inability to protect the eye, and exposure to environmental problems. I waited in an examination room in the hospital. I waited for quite a while before the Doctor came in. He verified that I had it multiple times. He said he was a working on the theory it was stress related. I believed that was a contributing factor since the first episode was when my Dad died while I was in Korea. He talked a little bit longer, mostly to himself Then he left the exam room. Someone tried to put another patient in the room I was in, thinking it was empty. The doctor had left the building about a half hour ago, so what was i still doing there? Love the professionalism.

I will say one good thing about him, he didn't trash other doctors by stating he thought I was misdiagnosed. I got that from most doctors. The third time I had it I went to the doctor, a Major, and said the first episode was a disaster, the doctor had screwed up on administering Prednisone and had to up the dose and not correctly stepping down the dosage. The second was better but I still had the nasty side effects from the Prednisone. I had major problems with depression, sleep, etc. I told this doctor I didn't want to take Prednisone again!

He talked intelligently about a study from Great Britain that basically explained the use of Prednisone by itself broke up the virus but in doing so allowed the virus to travel and avoid a concentrated defense. By using an antibiotic with the Prednisone it tends to drop the virus from a four month battle to a few days! It worked but did serious damage to your LDL, HDL, Triglycerides, Lipids, and more. Less than a week later you would look normal but have months trying to get your system back where it should be.

I had talked with doctors about following the drug regime but all still said previous doctors must have misdiagnosed because nobody has ever had so many episodes. I have! Oh, and I would gain weight when I had an episode and took the drugs. Substantial weight. And I found when I was able to lose weight again I would have another episode. This did not happen with the cocktail. I just planned on having an episode every 18 to 24 months! I still believe it was a result from exposure to Agent Orange.

Ralph was supposed to be the "expert" in Systems Safety but he had a couple problems. I believe he was handicapped by trying to follow the writings of an out of date author. My training was more complete and up to date. He only had a Secret security clearance where I had a Top Secret. Meaning, there were a lot of things he didn't have the security clearance to do the job. He was sly at it but I often caught him trying to do stuff that would make me look bad and therefore make him look good. I told him we had to have a talk about it. We took a day off together to have lunch in Santa Fe. It didn't solve anything, maybe made it worse.

I had this very special project that fit right in with my experience with Ordinance. I was probably the best guy to do this project. It involved one major section that was Top Secret so I had to have a small safe for it. The classified secret stuff and the project was in a locked desk drawer special for it. Ralph had access to that but not the Top Secret materials. Ralph was apparently still doing his tricks, worse than before we had the talk. I believe and think I could confirm that he thought anybody in military uniform was inferior to him, and stupid. So one day he asked how I was doing on the project? I told him it would be hard to tell him because I was using calculations and processes that didn't fit the standard norm. I said I could not do the job in the traditional way.

I locked everything up and left for lunch. When I came back I found my entire project was missing! Except the Top Secret stuff. I asked him what happened? He was the only other person with access to the project? He told me since I had told him I could not do the project, he had sent it to Brookhaven Labs for them to look at. I was so pissed!!!

A couple months later I got a call from the past, Gene Farrington! We talked like old times. He casually said he would see me at the meeting that afternoon. What meeting? It was to brief the project I was working on! I can't tell you what the project involved, but that Ralph was briefing it today! No, the project was sent to Brookhaven to review and supposedly complete it. Gene said Brookhaven had reviewed it and remarked at the manner I had gone about doing it and thought it ingenious! They had sent it back! Ralph was briefing it today to the three star General I had known when he was a two star. I laughed. I wasn't invited, for which Gene said the General expected to see me there. I laughed again and said I didn't know how Ralph could brief it since I still had the key section of the project, the Top Secret stuff. We both laughed as we both know the General has a photographic memory so when Ralph tries to cover what he doesn't know he will be caught. Yes, I will be there.

As you walk into the conference room it is a long room with the long wood table. There is a podium by the door at the near end of the table. The General will preside at the head of the table on the far end. Behind that is an obviously secured room where we could go if discussion involved Top Secret materials. I took a seat against the wall adjacent to the podium. Ralph was there with the same brown tweed sport coat with the leather elbow patches. I could see a faint line of sweat when he saw me! He made a gesture that I was to leave. He even bent over the elevated podium to order me to leave! He made all these gestures and now everyone could see the larger ring of sweat from his underarms! I am surprised he could even talk he was so bothered I was there.

The General entered the room. Everyone came to attention! The General told them to sit so we could get on with this briefing. He checked with the Master at Arms if the back room was secure? He asked if he had names and security clearances of all attendees. Gene must have taken care of me.

The General said to begin. Ralph stumbled through the introduction and purpose of the project. I shook my head more to myself as Ralph said things that were wrong! He kept going and in his fourth paragraph he said something many of the attendees kind of shook their heads. The General spoke up somewhat loudly, "In your opening you said this". He repeated almost verbatim what Ralph said., "and now you are saying something different! Which is it?" Ralph stumbled some more. The General yelled, "Is there someone here who can answer my question, or am I wasting my time here with idiots?"

I stood and raised my hand. "Sergeant, who are you and do you know the answer?" I answered his question. Then he asked why I wasn't on the podium instead of that fool? I told him it was my boss on the podium and he was capable. Then the General did it! He asked me another question for which I said I could not answer. He went high order again and asked why! "Simply Sir, the answer would be discussing Top Secret Materials and I know not everyone here has a Top Secret clearance". He and Gene got up, I was motioned to join them and the Master of Arms was to validate anyone coming into the secure room. Inside the room everything was smiles, handshakes, and catching up on a few years. We got down to business when people came in and I briefed the program and answered questions, big success. Ralph was not in the room.

Ralph was behind his desk and already yelling at me to come in his office! I was met by yelling and how I embarrassed him! Sounds like my childhood! So I turned around and walked out of his office to him yelling for me to come back, NOW! I drove over to the other side of the Base to the Personnel Office. I went in and told the assignment guy that I was declining my assignment to the Philippines! He told me that it was a Special assignment, for which I said I already knew. He told me there was no way I knew the real purpose of the assignment. I was about to tear his head off, "Of course I know the assignment, me and two other guys, John and Larry, developed that assignment for the PACAF (Pacific Air Force) General! I am not going!"

He followed it up with telling me I had a line number for promotion, to E8. I would lose if I declined the assignment. I would have to get out of the USAF at the end of this enlistment! I looked at him and said, "If Personnel and a certain First Sergeant hadn't screwed with my award of the Purple Heart I would have already been an E9!" I referred to the fact the Purple Heart carried 25 points toward promotion and at last count I had missed upward promotions 7 times by less than 25 points! He finally gave me the paperwork and I signed away a promotion, assignment, and the right to stay in the military longer than this term. I believe I did it out of anger, having to work for an idiot! I also know Peggy had already refused to go to the Philippines. She had heard all the stories about that place. And knowing I would be constantly traveling around the Pacific. I thought I really should have talked to her before I made my decision.

When I got back to the office I headed straight for Ralph's office! His already elevated voice was telling me I was in trouble for what I did! I ignored him and walked up to his desk and dropped a copy of the declination statement on his desk and spoke, "Fuck You" and walked back to my office. I sat for a minute and then called Peggy. I told her what I had done. I was waiting for a delayed response from her but her response was immediate, "It's about time".

Peggy and I never lived beyond our means. We had good cars, food on the table, clothes for the girls, etc. So when I told some of the guys in the housing area that I was retiring I was surprised that most said they wished they could afford to. One pointed toward his house and the new truck and boat in the driveway. He said he would have to have a great paying job waiting for him to get out, he couldn't do it otherwise. He, like many, accrued a lot of debt.

Ralph was distant and understood he had basically lost control over me. I had sailed past him professionally. So one day he came into my office and handed me a job posting. He said he called around to his friends and one said he had an open position I could possibly fill. Ralph added he was trying to do me a favor. I looked at the posting, it was for a GS7 Safety Technician somewhere in the Midwest. I looked at him, "You don't get it, do you?" Did he realize with my service time, rank and qualifications I would never be offered a job lower than a GS9! I already had an offer for a GS11 position, promotable within six months to a GS12/14 position. I asked him if he truly thought those of us in uniform were stupid?

I still had a couple years before I could retire. I still owed two more years because of Operation Bootstrap so we enjoyed our time. As I said, Ralph had lost control and I did work as hard as before but looked at it differently, I didn't have all the BS from Ralph and it seemed things came easier.

I spent a fair amount of time on the Golf Course. I worked down the hall from a friend of Lee Trevino. He was also a great golfer and I learned a lot, and played a lot.

One day I was across Base getting my hair cut. My barber had become a friend and while he was cutting my hair he asked if I could get the next day off? Sure! So we talked about going snow skiing in Santa Fe! I told him I skied about four times a year and was probably advanced beginner by now. He had started skiing at age six and was an expert skier.

We had a couple bottles of Peppermint Schnapps in our parkas when we hit the ski lift. At the top he told me to start down. It was icy and I looked amateurish! He stopped me, explained about edges and soon he led with me copying and following him. All other times I had made maybe four or five runs on the mountain, today was different.

We would ski down and right onto the lift to go back up. We sipped the Schnapps on the lift and talked about what I had to do better. By the end of the day we had not stopped for lunch, we drank two bottles of schnapps each, made 21 runs on the mountain, some were advanced slopes, and I was now a strong intermediate skier!

Sandia mountain had a good slope, smaller than Santa Fe but when the snow was good it was a great place to ski. A couple times I would drive Peggy and the girls up to the ski area, drive back down and play a round of golf and then go back up and pick them up.

We enjoyed Albuquerque because of the food and culture. But I would guess we really enjoyed it during ski season. We could go to Sandia, Santa Fe, and north to Colorado. We went with a group from the Base, about 16 of us, to Durango and Purgatory ski slopes. There were three 20 something ladies who had bad experience with past boyfriends who might have taken them on slopes too difficult. They wanted to ski but had to do it at their pace.

Of course, Peggy volunteered me! She said I usually did a couple easy runs to get my knees loosened, both had been operated on, and then I hit the tougher slopes. She was sure I could help them. I did. We took it slow with me showing them some basic control steps using edges, like my barber had taught me. We did three simple runs and then went to an Intermediate. After one run I left them and aggressively attacked the mountain. I was skiing the Advanced slopes all afternoon.

In the end, all three young ladies did me proud. They moved to Intermediate slopes and one took on an Advanced slope. They thanked us a lot, they got past their bad experiences and were loving what they were doing now!

Another trip to Durango and we met an older couple originally from Germany. They had been skiing all their lives but due to age problems, the husband had to slow down a little, just about the right speed for Peggy. However, his wife, maybe five feet tall and beefy was hell on skis! She and I took on the Black Diamond (Expert) slopes and had a blast! One time we had gone down and back up while Peggy and her husband were coming down. We started at the top and she split to the left track, me to the right. When we joined up near the bottom, Peggy and her husband stopped to wait for us. I had just gone through some fresh powder and was covered with snow! Peggy thought I had crashed but the woman said I didn't.

When we got home we called Susan and I told her I hadn't fallen once all day! She kindly ignored that I said I was on Black Diamonds all day and responded, "But Dad, you don't push yourself!" Love that girl!

I was heavily involved in the American Society of Safety Engineers (ASSE) and when a call came from one of the ASSE members in San Diego Chapter asking if anybody was driving out to the National Conference in Las Vegas? I said I was. He asked if I could bring out a big chest his father left him in Albuquerque? His father just recently passed. I told him I was driving out and had a van, so it would be no problem. I even refused payment.

So sort of as payment, he talked to the Safety Manager for another Division of General Dynamics. He worked in the Electronics Division and his friend was in the Convair Division. He was hiring. I was set up for an interview during the Conference in Las Vegas.

I interviewed with Randy. He was trying to fill a Senior Safety Engineer position. He was not sure if he was going to hire from outside the company or from within. If from within he would still have to fill the vacant Safety Engineer slot.

It wasn't long before I was sent a package which indicated I was being offered the Senior position. It included a lot of information, including salary. I was ready to turn down the job because the pay was $2,000 below my expected entry salary.

I had just been to Cape Canaveral and turned down an offered job as the Head of Safety at the Space Shuttle Vertical Assembly Building (VAB). There was just something with one of the answers that bothered me. I turned down the job and told the hiring manager to look up my friend Larry as I believed he was the right man for the job. After he told me nobody in his entire long career had turned down an offer and recommended someone else! He contacted Larry and after interviewing him he gave the job to Larry!

For the General Dynamics position I was hesitating because of the $2,000. Peggy's boss knew me well and sat me down. We talked about that little amount of money was nothing compared to me getting my foot in the door of General Dynamics, one of the top Defense Contractors. I took the job when they agreed to delay it a couple months until October when I retired from the USAF.

Since we were a unique organization on the base, and we had five people retiring the same day, Personnel came to us with all our paperwork. While all five were waiting, the four of them, three Commissioned Officers, one Chief Master Sergeant (E9) were talking about what they were going to do once they retired. I listened to them all. There was nothing exciting. The Chief asked me what I was going to do? I told them I was going to San Diego. The Chief asked if I was going to kick around some sand until I found a job? "No, two days after I leave here I will be the Senior Safety Engineer for General Dynamics Convair Division!" The others started talking all at once, "How in the hell did you get that job with GD?" Seems all had put in resumes to GD and all were rejected!

As I was actually standing in that room, I reflected on what could have been. First of all, had my Purple Heart not have been wrongfully taken from me. I tested many times, even getting E5 the second fastest in the Air Force. Every rank after that I would have achieved first time testing if I had the 25 points from receiving the Purple Heart. If I stayed Enlisted I would be the same rank as the Chief sitting in the same room.

If I had accepted the free ride to becoming a Doctor, I know I would have outranked the Officers in the room. Twice more I was offered a Commission, once to be a Munitions Officer and the next to be a Maintenance Officer, I would still probably outrank the officers in the room. The irony of this is I didn't outrank any of them, but I got a job they couldn't get! Most of them had one college degree. I had one in Safety Engineering, one in Occupational Safety and Health Engineering, and had satisfied the requirements for a degree in Psychology. I guess I made the right decision.

I was also offered a job with a company on Kirkland doing Defense work. They wanted to hire me as a Systems Safety expert! It payed an awful lot of salary, but when Peggy found I would spend six months on travel and six months in Albuquerque, she didn't want me to do it. I turned down the job offer.

Susan was going to college in Albuquerque and she was able to stay with a close friend of hers who graduated High School with her. The girl we knew quite well and agreed to that, so we left Susan and took Carrie with us.

30

Chapter 11

San Diego California

General Dynamics put us up in a nice Condo until we could find a place to live. Which we did, moving into a small house in a small community in Escondido, in the North County about 35 miles from downtown.

I felt the hostility immediately. I soon found out that three of the current Safety Engineers had been contenders for the Senior Safety Engineer position. We also had an old former Army woman with a very sharp mouth and talked very rough as our secretary. We had a guy running our Workers' Compensation section. He knew everything, just ask him! And we had a PhD Industrial Hygienist in our office.

Our office suite was separated from Human Resources by a coffee machine and a Conference Room. Our building was located just inside one of the gates and the entire compound was fenced in and guarded. There was a long, narrow hallway opening up to the center with a hangar to the right and on the left was a building that housed Firefighters and the Medical offices where our Company Doctor and nurses were. The entire complex was huge and sat slightly north of Lindberg Field Airport along Pacific Drive. You could easily see downtown San Diego from where we were.

Here we also built the McDonnell Douglas MD-11 and in another facility the Tomahawk Cruise Missile. We also had the longest continuous Machine Shop west of the Mississippi. The Convair Headquarters was there and the Senior Vice President had his office there. I actually came to know him quite well as we were together on an intramural golf team but never knew what he did until I got my first ass chewing in his office!

Further north in Kearney Mesa we had a second complex where the Electronics Division had it's headquarters and facilities. Convair had a building there . Our design and Engineering sections were in the major buildings. My second office was a shared trailer with the Locksmith. Further north a few miles we had an area where we stored explosives and some components for our Cruise Missiles! We helped comply with the Russian and US INF Treaty that reduced the numbers of nuclear weapons.

Scattered around we had facilities where we performed special and often very classified research and development. I was heavily involved with the R&D because of my work history with the Weapons Lab.

On top of all that I was heavily involved with the American Society of Safety Engineers and worked often on projects with people from CALOSHA (California Occupational Safety and Health Administration), a State program under Federal OSHA. I met infrequently with Dr. John Howard, head of CALOSHA. He was appointed to manage NIOSH (National Institute of Occupational Safety and Health) under CDC *Center for Disease Control and Prevention) in Washington DC.

Yes, I was extremely busy and I made a name for myself because of my knowledge and experience. One Safety Engineer from a large company was working with me on a project for ASSE. He asked how I knew all this stuff? He was a trained Boiler Inspector, so he knew boilers, and thats about it. I had to tell him that in the military where you run Safety for the entire Base you have to know a lot because each Base would have all of the facilities of a small city. I had to know all that.

When the Russians came to inspect the INF Treaty I ended up taking over the job of giving them the mandatory safety briefing which I did through an interpreter.

My boss was a very good friend with one of the Safety Engineers and it was something that got in the way. There was definite preferential treatment and I wondered why he wasn't selected for the Senior job? It soon became evident in many ways, mostly because one of the Engineers was very experienced and what I brought to the table was over the top. I had retired from the military as the second most qualified Safety Professional in the Air Force. I had also done something that made me a very valuable resource.

I remember one day the Safety Engineer came in swearing, "That Oriental is frigging stupid!" He went on that he had found the Oriental worker not using a rivet tool correctly so he taught him how. He said the Oriental kept nodding his head so he knew the guy understood, and then he went right back to the way he was doing it before! I asked him if the man was Vietnamese? He said he didn't know anything but the guy had funny eyes and was stupid! I informed him that many cultures will nod their head in recognition you are talking, not that they are understanding. He muttered something like we were both stupid. I told him what was needed on his part was to test the person along the way to determine if he/she understands, or get a bilingual to help you. He said something like I had a problem and I had just tried to make a fool out of him!

While at the Weapons Lab I tried to learn all I could and soon ran into a roadblock called the Bio-environmental Engineers. They were an elite group, mostly degreed engineers, who had a strangle hold on en-vironmental issues. If I detected an atmosphere that was affecting the workplace by either a reduction of oxygen or infusion of chemicals, I had to turn it over to them. That was when I tested and achieved Profes-sional Certification as an Occupational Health and Safety Technician. Meaning, I had the qualifications to go into their world, which I did.

Now at GD we had an Industrial Hygienist (IH). I would go to a certain point and then turn it over to our IH but still help him with the problem. I had my Merck Manual and my Book on Hazardous Chemicals, and the experience working with exotic chemicals while at the Weapons Lab.

If ever in my career I wish I hadn't done something it was when one of the ladies told me her sister was terminal with a disease caused by her exposure to missile fuels. She talked openly and I listened. She told me General Dynamics had already paid close to a Million Dollars for her treatment and would pick up all funeral expenses! As I said, she talked, I listened and I believe I only asked a couple questions.

I stored the information she had told me in my head, as it didn't sound right. I talked to our PhD Industrial Hygienist and researched my Merck Manual. He said it was possible. I did a lot of research and confirmed it with my reference materials. I had the chance to talk to her again and from that put the pieces together. I presented my case to our Industrial Hygienist and he confirmed my theory. I presented it to management. Another investigation I performed further proved my theory.

The sister was not dying from exposure to missile fuels, she was dying from exposure to lead! Her husband made jewelry and used lead and lead solder. She helped him often by holding some of the pieces as he soldered them and therefore was directly exposed to lead! GD turned her care over to her insurance and discontinued taking care of her. They didn't ask her to pay back, they just didn't pay any more. When her sister found out what I did, a group of people had to pull her off me! She was screaming at me and hitting my arms as I was blocking her blows! She was moved to one of the other facilities in lieu of firing her for her actions. Like the first guy I killed visits my head every day, she does so a couple times a month. I still question why I did it, knowing I'm an excellent investigator. Guess I can't lessen my ethics.

The incident that got me to the VP's desk happened at our weapons storage site. We had one of the Company Policemen driving a truck on the facility with a passenger. The truck veered off the small access road and down an embankment. Both were injured, I can't remember which one was hurt the worst but he was hospitalized for quite a while. The driver said he was doing under the posted 15 mph speed and something like a coyote came across the road and when he swerved to avoid it, the tire caught the side of the road and pulled him off the side over the embankment. His boss signed off on it saying it was just an accident.

Of course I could not accept that theory that it was "Just an accident" so I investigated it. Amongst the bushes and snakes I looked at skid marks and angle of descent, length of travel, whether braking as the vehicle left the road, etc. I proved he was traveling at 27 mph, speeding, and the curve he went around was not made for 27 mph. He saw he was not going to make it so he overcompensated and lost control of the vehicle. The most injured was not wearing his seat belt, as is mandatory. So the driver was speeding, which resulted in the crash that resulted in major injury and property damage, and he lied about the accident

My boss was not happy, he didn't want the conflict it was causing so instead of supporting me, he threw me under the bus! I was called to the VP's office, along with my boss for the meeting that included the Chief of Police!

We were brought into the office and I saw for the first time where my golfing partner worked! He was the Senior Vice President. My boss deferred to me, basically saying he did not instruct me to investigate the accident. I presented a folder. We were made to stand while the Chief and VP sat there at the conference table as though I was reporting to the guillotine! I started to lay down the folder to pass it along but was told the two of them had read it. They were in general disagreed with my report. The Chief saying he trusted his officers much more than a "stupid" safety person, the report was flawed.

I basically went over my investigation and my qualifications. I included I was trained by Police and worked with Police on major incidents, including drownings and fatalities. I said I doubted if anybody in his Force, including him, had anywhere near my qualifications. Him insinuating I am stupid boiled my blood, I may have been a little harsh. The police chief was livid! He rose from his seated position, leaned across toward me while swearing and threatening me! The VP had to tell him to basically sit down and shut up. The Chief had words for that also and said if I was so damned smart, what would I do about disciplining the Police Officer? "Not my job" telling the Chief that I was not the man's supervisor, he didn't work for me, so it is not my job, it is his!

The swearing and yelling got worse and the VP got control back with the meeting. My boss had backed up a ways, not supporting me at all. The VP finally asked me what I would recommend for disciplinary action against the cop? I repeated that I was not in a position to, I was not his supervisor nor in his chain of command I am an educator and I presented the evidence for the Chief to do his job! The Chief was still saying stuff, just not yelling it, and it included a few more Stupids aimed at me. So when the VP asked again if I would recommend disciplinary action and I said I would not, he responded "What if I told you to?" I looked at him and reached down to my security badge, unclipped it and threw it down on the table! I added something else like, "If you pick it up you are no better than a two-bit whore!"

The room went quiet. I could hear Randy behind me telling me to pick up my badge. I ignored the spineless bastard. The VP spoke up in a calm voice, "I don't think your choice of words are very conducive to you working here. Bruce, pick up your badge, I'll take it from here."

Nothing ever came out of it but Randy chewing my ass. I never told anyone I would be seeing the VP on the golf course that weekend. On the Golf Course we talked about not talking about it again. He seemed like he had more respect for me.

A few months earlier, before we left Albuquerque, Susan had a discussion with me after her Counselor told her she was pretty, tall, and would make a nice Stewardess! Susan was crying. We talked for a couple hours. She wanted to be an Engineer! We discussed what we thought would be the best for her. She wanted to be a Chemical Engineer at first but after we talked she said she wanted to pursue becoming a Mechanical Engineer. When we left Albuquerque she was in the Engineering School at the University. I liked working with Engineers and I had one level of Engineering myself. That helped me with Susan and was now helping me with our Engineers at Kearny Mesa.

I would tour facilities and review Engineering plans before I signed off on the Plans. I was the only one in the Safety Office that was able to sign off drawings because of my Professional Certifications. Seven letters behind my official signature. At the Engineering Office I had two main Engineers I worked with the most. When their secretary contacted me to sign off on drawings she would always ask me how much time I needed at their office? I would ask who did the drawings and if she said George I would say 15 minutes. If she said Rebecca I would say to plan on more than an hour! George always had it right or very close, Rebecca was the prime example of an Engineer who designs something and then takes it to Safety to add to it, not building it into the Plans. Her reviews sometimes changed major sections of the project. George just had "it" and once I asked him how/why he was a so good to me? His response was that he saw me at work on these drawings and projects so he understood what I was a looking for. So before it was ready for my signature he said he would look at it and ask, "What would Bruce do?" I occasionally miss him, he was so good.

I was involved with ASSE and maybe it was Dr. John Howard, then with CALOsha, that said something about I should do more with my speaking. He said I was very good. He had read many of my published works. I respected him greatly. He was a medical Doctor, a PhD, and he had a photographic memory. I started looking into getting my Masters Degree. My sites were set on USC.

Randy told me to talk to our resident PhD Industrial Hygienist as he taught for National University. Terry, the PhD, told me only practicing scholars taught at NU. The students got real life education and NU was set up to complete a 3 semester hour class every month. This allowed students to get the classes with the flexibility necessary with their working schedule. Besides, there was a Campus in San Diego instead of me driving to Los Angeles for USC.

I talked with NU and started setting up classes. The schedule fit perfect so there was no break in classes that covered my degree program for EH&S Management. The counselor warned me that my schedule was extremely aggressive! Maybe I should take a break or two between classes. I told her when I went to CMSU that I completed 37 Semester hours in 8 months! She signed me up for the class schedule.

Classes seemed easy and I had a 4.0 GPA and found myself going for my Dissertation worth 6 Semester hours. I chose to do a Research Project that I was already doing for work. It was titled, "Foreign Body

Eye Injuries on the MD-11 Aircraft Assembly Line". I found that my teacher to be very unprofessional. I felt he was only doing it for the extra cash. Then when I had to do a review on my Research paper he said he didn't want to see a Hypotheses with my research. All R&D I had ever done had a Hypothesis and this project had a tri-hypothesis! A hypothesis is a scientific process that basically states that if you do an action it should result in a planned response. If I do this then that should happen. If it doesn't it is then a null hypothesis and still an important part of your research. I told him I had been doing research for years and every one of the projects had at least one hypothesis! He said I could do it, but it would reflect on my grade.

Three things happened when I completed his class; I graduated after 10 months! It was the fastest recorded time with NU for a Masters Degree, I received a grade from the research, dropping me down to a 3.85 GPA! And I submitted my Research paper to ASSE. I submitted it to see if I could get to present it at the annual Professional Development Conference (PDC). A few weeks later I was told my paper was one of four selected worldwide to be presented in Washington DC at the PDC!

GD was very pleased at my success. Unbeknownst to each other, the Human Relations department funded my trip to DC and so did the Engineering Department because my research was incorporated in the operations. My research showed more than an 80% reduction in Foreign Body eye injuries! The dilemma was easily fixed, they funded for Peggy to join me on the trip! I also got a call from my sister telling me I was the first person ever in our family to get a Masters Degree! She finally realized I was not her stupid little brother. I wondered what she told my mother and my mother's reaction? It still didn't stop my sister from using the word "stupid" and even worse was her husband calling me that!

Peggy and I went to DC. My classmate was selected also. Her project was on International Traffic Signs. I was surprised because I had never heard her presentation. We all did a presentation in class. We asked her if she had ever been to DC? She hadn't so we invited her to join us. She said she had to stay in the hotel and practice her speech. I asked her how many times she had presented it at class? She hadn't! How? She said she made excuses every time so she never had to present. She said a couple times she told the teacher it was her "time of the month"! The worthless professor let her slide.

The presentations were in front of 600 people! The audience could direct three questions to each speaker. When my classmate presented, they were not kind to her. Her project was for people whose English was either not spoken or a second language. But she did all her surveys/questionnaires with students at NU! The questions caused her to leave the stage crying. Questions to the other two were mostly clarification questions to fully understand what was presented. I was questioned last. The first question was why I had developed the research matrix as I did? The person said he thought what I did was brilliant! The next two questions came off as positive comments. There was no doubt that I took the honor. I received a Jefferson Cup for my efforts. Then Peggy and I flew to Boston, got a rental, and drove up to Maine and on to Canada for a week.

When I got back I was contacted by NU Dean and asked to meet with him, and bring the cup so he could see it. We met and soon he proposed I submit a complaint about the teacher. He said just about all the students protested their final grade. He adjusted their grades. It was the last straw and the professor was let go! I told him that I would not protest. The teacher had warned me about the hypothesis and I had not developed another means of research assessment. I got what I earned! Then he blew my mind! Apparently my answer was all he needed. I was asked if I would teach classes at NU? The two classes he suggested I teach were two classes the teacher that gave me the "B" had taught. I started developing lesson plans and was soon teaching.

I have so many wonderful stories about teaching at NU and others but a couple with NU stand out. I was coming in from a facility we had in Imperial Valley. I picked up mail and headed to teach an evening class. So tired when I got home I almost threw away some mail but didn't. The class got me a little rejuvenated. I opened up the thick letter I expected from the Board of Certified Safety Professionals. It was thick, I had received one before. I thought it contained a rejection letter and information on study materials. I was shocked in a couple ways. I had taken it before and missed by one question, This time I was too busy to study, so I took the test unprepared. Instead the letter told me to add another three letters to my signature! CSP (Certified Safety Professional) is the highest peer reviewed Professional Certification in the Safety world.

I was teaching a class and right at the start of it I announced, as always, each student would have to present a five minute speech before they passed my class. I believe all your knowledge is for nothing if you can't communicate it. I asked them to think and give me a short synopsis on the topic each was presenting and I gave them the criteria for the speech. Just about everyone in the class started laughing, pointing to one student and telling me what he would speak on. Seems he has a specialized job he was always bragging about. Whenever he was to chose a topic it involved this special process. When I talked to him he quickly stated he had a 4.0 GPA and in his mind, the smartest person anywhere. I also told the class the criteria included only two excused absences from class and some other stuff. Everything reflected on their grade for the class.

He missed the first class because of a headache. He missed the second class because his house had been broken into! And the third missed class was because his wife was afraid to be alone after the break in. I heard rumblings he did stuff like that often. Apparently he was so smart that rules didn't apply to him. There were some other things I documented. In the end I looked at my very complete notes and gave him a grade in the "B+" range!

He called me at my home, at work, whenever he was mad enough! Then filed a formal complaint against me! I had to take all the papers, schedules, attendance, etc. to a meeting with the Dean. We sat down with it and he commented he had never seen anything as complete and comprehensive as what I had. When finished reviewing it he said to me, "You were very tolerable with him. Looking at these records I would had graded him even lower!" Case dismissed but I got more disturbing calls for weeks, I was the villain who took down the 4.0 Man!

Now I will admit I sort of cheated with my classes. The first night I would pass out index cards and ask the students to write their name, desired degree, and what they expected from the class. I asked what was important in the class and the profession? I would then slide the cards under a clear plastic sheet so the students really thought I was good at remembering their names. I got the one card from Linda and it read in bold letters, "I JUST WANT THAT DAMNED PIECE OF PAPER!"

When I asked her what she meant she said she knew more than any safety person there, me included! She had worked for a company as Safety for 14 years and the only reason I was up on the podium and her down there was because I had that damned piece of paper!

I told Linda I was glad she was there because when I get in a bind I can use her help! I transitioned into the fact I wanted to build a matrix so we can prioritize our learning elements! I saw what the students wanted. I would try to get the best out of this class for their needs. I asked how many had used a Probability and Severity Matrix before? A few hands. So I drew five horizontal lines spread out about three inches apart and then five vertical lines at same distance but crossing the horizontal lines to make boxes. I wrote "Probability" across the top and numbered the top horizontal line with 1 through 5 lined up over the columns. The I wrote "Severity" down the left side and wrote "A" through "E" so each box had a number and letter corresponding. So the highest block on the left was "1A" and the lowest on the lowest right corner was "5E'.

If the Probability was "1" it was going to happen NOW and the severity of injury or property damage was catastrophic it could be rated 1A. A lesser severity possibly 1C, etc. same for Probability reduction. When everybody understood I looked at Linda. "Linda, help me on this". The owner of the company built the company around one large piece of equipment. The equipment is old, parts have to be made specifically custom for the unit and they were expensive, So to increase the safety they built a wall around the equipment/machine. They gave extra pay for those working there. They all knew it was going to blow soon, and when it did, someone might die! "Linda, what would you rate it in the Probability/Severity matrix?" She rated it a 1A immediately! I told her we can never rate a 1A because if we do we must close down the operation, too much Risk.

We rated the severity down one to a 1B and I asked Linda what she would do? She laid out a plan to go to the CEO with a proposal based on ROI (Return On Investment) to move toward replacing the machine. "Nice job!"

Next scenario for Risk Assessment. Same factory. There are seven supervisors who have glass offices and their secretaries work in a small clutter of desks in the Secretarial Pool. This one manager uses real #2 pencils and he has an electric sharpener. He has set it behind the books in his bookcase. He puts it there because every time he puts a pencil in the sharpener the point is broken off and flies off! By placing it behind the books the lead is only allowed to sail against the wall and drop! The floor behind the bookshelf is thick with pencil lead. "Linda, whats the Risk Matrix on this one?" She rated it a 4D, not very severe.

Change of environment! The boss is gone on vacation and his secretary has been using an old hand crank sharpener. The boss wants her to use pencils also. So while he is gone she takes the electric sharpener from behind the bookshelf and sets it on her filing cabinet. It is now in the middle of the seven secretaries. "Linda what would you do about it now?" She said her priority was still the 1B! And her project to the CEO. I asked if the sharpener had become more of a possibly eye injury? She agreed but was working on the CEO problem.

"Linda, the pencil sharpener is what we call "low hanging fruit", It is still a hazard. While you are passing by the office area on the way to the CEO, stop and confiscate the sharpener and dispose of it. You have just eliminated a risk/hazard before it got bigger!

We had a great class. After it was over I got another call from the Dean and another meeting. He said he had reviewed all the critiques. All were outstanding but there was one he wanted to watch me when I looked at it, "Must have come from Linda" I said. He smiled and handed me the one from Linda. The front was all rated at the top! But her's had an arrow pointing toward the back side of the paper. I turned it over and in big letters she wrote, "When I grow up I want to be just like BRUCE!"

I was working in almost all of our facilities. My security clearance got me into some unique research and development areas. I can't talk about much since much is still classified. I was given oversight on the Tomahawk Cruise Missile group. They were still involved in the INF Treaty. When the Russians came to town I gave them a translated safety briefing.

Randy supported my Safety activities so I went to a few Professional Development Conferences, I was teaching at National University, I was Co-Chair of the Southwest Safety Conference, and I was Guest speaker at conferences and universities. I worked with Dr. John Howard of CalOSHA and was one of seven people signing the bill to get 6 semester hours of safety training into every state university Engineering class!

The HR group had a fun golf tournament and I was put in different teams. Then I was put with Michael who loved and hated the game at the same time! That was because he could not hit a ball off the fairway, I took the time and worked with him and soon he was starting to hit better. We ended up being partners and good friends for all HR golf outings. Michael was working on his Jurist Doctorate, very intelligent and about 6'4". We became good friends, possibly even better when while we were golf partners. I basically would hit my ball and help him with his club selection and ball striking. He became pretty good at it.

I don't think about it often, all the lives I have saved. I was known to be the guy you didn't want to be around. You might need your life saved being around me. On the other hand, if something happened I was the best to have around. To list a few:

Pushed Harolds head back in our September 23 near fatal accident

Car accident in Colorado. I stopped and assisted until ambulance arrived, my efforts were said to probably save the driver's life.

Drowning teenager in Athens Greece, took off my boots and swam to get her.

Girl fell off a sea wall in Massachusetts, I did triage until ambulance arrived

Aircraft Mechanic sucked into the intake of a fighter jet, I pulled him out and did CPR until he was breathing.

Pulled a 305 pound document safe off a man that was being crushed

Now with a total of six saves, not including what was done in the ER. However, nothing would top January 1992 at General Dynamics.

I came out of my office to go to the coffee machine. Michael was heading to the Conference Room, followed by a shorter black man. He was dressed in all blue. Blue jeans and a loose fitting blue jacket zipped up to his neck. He had a yellow Visitor's Badge attached to his left collar. He was followed by a thin and tall older man. They were followed by more HR people. Micheal and I exchanged a couple words. He asking if we were both signed up for the HR Golf Tournament and were we playing together, as usual? I could tell he was upset or troubled about something but didn't know what. Our conversation was a short few words in passing before he entered the conference room ahead of the gang.

A few minutes later I heard loud voices from the hallway and saw Michael and the taller man coming out, followed by the man dressed in blue! They were loud and appeared upset! A few seconds after Michael turned left into HR, The taller man followed by the black man in blue went straight down the narrow hallway toward the exit into the fenced compound.

The sound was loud and I recognized it immediately. Everybody was standing there or sitting at their desks wondering what it was. I automatically responded. I told each office I entered to hide! Get behind the filing cabinets! Get under their desks, etc. I did all that in maybe 20 seconds. Then I headed for the hallway. At the end of the hallway lay a body partly in the building and partly in the compound! It was the tall older man. He was flat on his back. The upper half of his body on the pavement with his right arm out from his side. The arm was hooked around the end of the partially open door! It was such I knew immediately I could not pull him inside the building. I would have to raise his right arm before he could be brought inside.

I turned back inside to assess the situation. As i did, the shooter, the black man with the blue clothes and the yellow Visitor's Badge was coming toward the exit! There was little room in the narrow exit aisle. He was coming through the narrow hall with a long barrel .38 pistol in his hand! He was pointing the gun at me, I was looking straight at the barrel! I dove to the floor and covered my head. I heard a gunshot just as I pulled my head down and my neck gave a popping sound like a chiropractor was adjusting it. Only thought was I had been shot!

I reacted and found I could move so I sprinted to my office and locked the door. Some lady was pounding lightly on my door, "Let me in, please let me in"! I opened the door. My psychiatrist later said I probably reacted because of my wife and daughters made me more reactive to a woman's voice. I took a couple seconds to compose myself.

The first thing I did was alert everybody. I went to each office telling people again to find a hiding place! I ran to the hallway and to the open door. I was about ready to go out and get the guy's arm free of the door! One of the Company Police shouted for me not to! We could hear another lady yell "He's got a gun and shooting people!" One of the nurses from our medical department had come in the other door and was yelling that we had to get him in to save his life! Behind me were a lot of people, including my coworker. He had on his Navy Reserve uniform! He had been to his one weekend a month Reserve Duty. He just happened to be there before reporting for duty.

I told somebody to hold the door for me. One of the Police stopped me and said the shooter was in the office about 30 feet away and he could shoot if anyone came out! The nurse was still screaming someone had to get him in to save his life! I started to step out into the compound, knowing fully well I might get shot at! Across the pavement about 20 feet I could see the top of a man's head! Looking at the color of his scalp I knew immediately the person was dead. I didn't know who it was. I ignored the police telling me not to and I stepped out, pulled the man's right arm up and clear of the door. I grabbed one of his legs. I lifted his leg and pulled him into the door. Someone reached for his leg and pulled. I grabbed the other leg and we dragged him into the building. I helped get him into an open area and started checking for pulse, etc. A couple Paramedics surrounded me and said they had it. I said I was a former State Certified EMT and they didn't push me away. One handed me the bag of normal saline drip as they started fluids and working on him. One of our nurses assisted and I held the bag the whole time. I was unaware the bag was leaking a little and I was getting wet down my front as I held the bag up to assist the flow. I don't know how long it was but they finally stabilized him and took him out on a gurney.

The police were there now and one of the HR people said the guy in blue must be Robert Mack. The police started calling him by name. He had taken two hostages into a small office right outside the hangar. Later one of the hostages stated when he heard his name being called he visibly relaxed. A short time later he surrendered.

I found out the guy I helped save his life was Jim English. He was Robert's boss. They were in a meeting to discuss Robert's claim of Wrongful Termination. Robert was 45 minutes late for the meeting. He was loud and argumentative enough the meeting was postponed. As they were leaving, Robert pulled out the gun and shot Jim in the back of his head! And when I met Robert in the hallway he had jumped over me and ran into Michael who was trying to calm him down! Robert shot Michael in his left eye and killed him immediately.

I worked with the lead Homicide Detective and finally convinced him I knew what I was doing. I talked him into letting Jane, our former Army secretary, back into the office to get her cigarettes. Under control of the cops, she got her cigarettes and handbag. She would not stop talking and was disrupting the investigation. They let her go. That left 23 of us sequestered, including a very pregnant HR person which they soon let go. We were now 22.

Helicopters overhead and news crews just meters away outside the fence, it was now news. I talked the Detective into letting me write a statement, which he could approve, and I would take the 21 people into the doctor's office next door. They could call their wives/husbands and read off the script to tell their loved ones they were okay. They could not talk about the shooting over the phone. If they swayed from the script I was going to hang up the phone and cut them off. The Detective agreed and I checked off all 21 of them. Then I called Peggy.

Monday morning we came in to EAP (Employee Assistance Program) psychiatrists! One of my degrees being in psychology I ignored most. However when I went to the pregnant HR lady and touched her arm to ask how she was doing, her husband in Navy uniform started yelling at me! He said to not touch her and wanted to fight. He was getting right in my personal space! A gentle grip on my elbow and a very quiet female voice spoke into my ear. As she was gently pulling me back, "Just step back, just walk away from it". That person ended up being maybe a life saver, Gina. She was great and helped me for weeks to come. My PTSD came back full bore! Had she not been there I have no idea how sane or insane I would be now. I was in such a terrible place now knowing that was Michael on the pavement and I didn't try to save him. I now have another vision besides the face of the Vietnamese I killed to visit me at night.

The company organized a trip to Phoenix for those of us involved to go to Michael's funeral. I signed up for it and Randy, who was not even on site when the shooting happened, said I could not go! He said I was not even involved in it so he said if I went he would have to fire me! I told him not to worry, if he did that shit I would quit and sue his ass! The HR Director, George, knew what I did and told Randy to back off, I was going! I was wondering why he would say I didn't do anything? Then I heard my coworker in his Weekend Warrior Uniform told Randy that I wasn't there! He claimed he did what I did! He claimed he dragged Jim in and helped save his life! He even got a special Award from the Navy when he claimed he did it all! Later Randy wrote an article in one of the Safety Periodicals about how he managed the scene. He went on about how he did it and lessons learned from his handling the shooting! He was not even there! So I wrote an editorial that basically told the truth. Since I had been published in the Periodical a few times, I got the Editorial on the back of the front page!

Phoenix, the funeral, emotional. I met his family. I had pictures that had been taken of Michael and me during one of the HR Tournaments. I started crying and could not stop. His brother was a Russian Orthodox Priest. He remained so calm when we talked. I was so mad at him for taking this calmly and me crying my soul out! Then he spoke firmly but so sincere. He said the family knew how good friends we were. They knew if I could have I would have saved his life. Then he said if I had done so, Michael would have been forever in a vegetated state. The family is very glad I did not save him, they want to remember Michael as he was in life. I could not stop crying.

I went out to the bus we had brought from the airport so I could think. I found one of the young ladies who worked right inside the hangar next to our office. I also knew she lived in the same apartment building as Michael and was a single mother. I asked her how long she and Michael had been seeing each other? She became upset and wanted to know if Michael had told me? No, he didn't. She said since she barely had a High School diploma and Michael going for his Jurist Doctorate, they wanted to keep their "affair" quiet. I told her I knew Michael very well and could tell by the way he looked at her when she came by, I knew they were together. Then she asked me a question, "If you had a gun when you met Robert in the hallway, would you have killed him?" And, "If you believe in Capital punishment, would you like to watch him die?"

I later told Gina what I had answered and that as a Safety guy protecting people and already 7 lives I saved, why would I have answered as I did? Her answer was right. "That's your dark side, live with it!"

I couldn't testify at the hearing, I had said there were three shots, everybody else said two. I believe people talked and if anyone had heard three but everyone else said two, they folded with the majority and said only two. When I was told that by the lawyer, I didn't say anything until I showed him the one shot nobody talked about. There was the first shot to the back of Jim's head. The second shot went over my head when I dove for the floor. I showed him where the bullet went through the awning over the door. The third shot was in Michael's left eye.

There were 11 of us intimately involved with the shooting. We all got under the table free trips to Hawaii. We could not talk about it since Robert was Black and the Black community circled the wagons and stated if anyone was awarded or rewarded for the incident that put Robert in prison, they would be targeted. Peggy and I went to Maui for a week, all expenses paid.

Peggy had said when I asked her to meet me in Hawaii that she thought it was overrated. Actually she said that because we didn't have the money! When we got to Maui and to our rented Condo on the beach, Peggy threw herself into my arms! "When are we coming back?" We were just west of Kaanapali. We drove around the Island. Most everyone was restricted from the road past Hana because it really wasn't much of a road. When we got our rental car we were given a soft top Jeep. Problem was it had no place to secure valuables. I had an expensive camera and different lenses. They gave us a Ford Explorer that we could drive on the road around the island.

I talked to some locals and we were told about a perfect place to Snorkel. We had been to Hanauma Bay and snorkeled through the reefs, but we were told this was a special private beach. It was! We had to walk in past small picnic areas to a little cove. We immediately saw what was so special. It was the fish, turtles, eels, etc. Everywhere there were beautiful sea dwellers! I was following a Moray Eel and stuck my head up to call Peggy. She was off swimming behind a sea turtle!

There were a few locals there, not many. I went back to shore and grabbed a little styrofoam boogey board. I took it out and tied it to my wrist. I opened a small bag of fish food and placed it on top the board. My plan was to take a few pieces at a time and lure the fish it for a picture. I had an underwater camera. So many good pictures, until! One of the kids swam by and kicked my board with his flipper. I believe it was unintentional, but the board flipped over and the entire bag of fish food slowly drifted across my face! Thousands of fish attacked the food. They nibbled at my fingers. There must have been some bigger fish because one actually bit my finger!

We went next door to the Kaanapali Hilton Hawaiian Village one night when Charo was performing. We only knew her for her "Koochy Koochy" humor, so we didn't know what to expect. She joked around, did some singing. Then she turned very serious. She had her guitar on her lap. Her smile disappeared. She was a different person. Then she started playing the guitar! Until then we did not know she was rated the second best Flamenco guitarist in the world! My God, she was phenomenal! Such beauty. We had heard many Flamenco guitars when we lived in Spain. None was ever as good as she was then!

When I got back to the office the pressure around us was so high. I was involved in writing an Emergency Response Plan. I helping with ideas on how to better get someone out the door when being terminated. But worst of all was Jim going on national TV stating he wished whoever had dragged him in hadn't! His short term memory and his depth perception were very poor. He said he did not want to live that way, why didn't I let him die? I was devastated! Gina told me, "He had only one option until you gave him a second one".

I think of Michael often and many of my nightmares I see a bright yellow badge on a blue background. Add that to the guy I killed in Vietnam, the drowning victim, the electrocution from a high power line, the numerous accidents with some severe bodily injury, the attempted suicides, the Vietnamese orphan, and the few times I visited Dr Fernandez at the City Morgue! I don't sleep well. Right before I left the military I taught a class to other Safety Professionals. It was Accident Investigation. I was discussing the process when I saw blank looks on a lot of faces. It was a sequence you deviated from normal if the accident involved a fatality. I evaluated what I saw and asked who had investigated a fatality before? One person had assisted in one. A person in the class asked how many I had investigated? I clarified I was considered an expert at motorcycle fatalities. I answered, "more than

40". And I was called in to consult on at least that many more. Is there any wonder I have nightmares? But still all that did not take away from the worst nightmares I have from Vietnam.

With all this going on and bullseyes being painted on the ground where Michael was shot, and looking at my boss and coworker and their lies,I knew I had to leave. Besides we were closing down Convair. I was four months before being Vested. I could not wait. I found another job. I had finished my section of a book on Workplace Violence one of the psychiatrists was getting published. I had a couple choices. I could stick around and get Vested. I was offered the job with Hughes in Tucson where I would run the Tomahawk Cruise Missile Safety Program. Or? Peggy and I left San Diego for the San Francisco Bay Area. My mental health was the issue.

3 1

San Leandro, California

Airco Gases, headquartered in Murray Hill, New Jersey, owned by BOC (British Oxygen Company), the West Coast Regional Office was here in the San Francisco Bay Area. I was the Regional Safety Manager. I had responsibility for the Western third of the US, to include part of Canada, and the Hawaiian Islands. They put me up at a hotel where I could see San Fransisco across the Bay. There was a golf course a few yards away, and one of the best Mexican restaurants between me and the golf course. After Peggy sold our house in Escondido she joined me and we lived in a condo at the golf course!

I replaced the Regional Safety Manager because of California Law. Legislature passed a law fondly referred to as "Become A Manager, Go To Jail"! I believe he either didn't understand the law or was unsure of his future under the law. Either way, I got away from the remlrants of the shooting.

Our California revenue/sales was higher than any of the entire countries where we were in! We supplied industrial gases and oxygen to hospitals, factories, fire services, any where there was a need. We had several air separation facilities where we took nitrogen, hydrogen, helium, etc. out of the air and purified oxygen for hospital use. We supplied gases for barbecue, welding, canning, etc. operations and in stores.

There was a lot of travel, not only between sites but for meetings with the other Regional Managers. Peggy and I also visited a lot of places, Napa and Sonoma Wine Country was a big high point. And when I was passing through Fairfield from our Sacramento sites I could be found stopping by the Jelly Belly plant and main store for a bag of the imperfect jelly beans, Tastes just as good but didn't look as nice as the ones in the stores! They were a lot cheaper!

When at the office I tried to work in a couple days on the golf course. One day after a long trip I took the morning to play golf. Two big black guys from SF were there and we played a round. We hit it off and just about every week we tried to get together for a round. All three of us were long ball hitters and we challenged each other. One day one of the course marshals knew we had a competition between us to hit every Par 5 green in two shots! We basically did that and the word got around, so the three of us were minor celebrities.

I had been directed to use Veteran's Administration (VA) medical facilities but instead used medical provided by my company. However, at GD I had gone to our company doctor and another couple doctors about a spot next to my right eye between the eye and nose that was not healing. I knew I had the skin for Basal Cell Cancers because of my dad being Scottish, but all the three doctors I saw said they thought it was nothing and that it would just heal.

I had a meeting very close to the VA in Oakland so I stopped in and had them look at the sore by my eye, I had also just had another episode of Bells' Palsy. They sent me up to a specialist. As I was looking for the clinic, a man in a hospital white coat was coming down the hall talking with a Med Tech. He was twirling a golf club and using the grip on the floor like a cane he obviously did not need. Without breaking stride he pointed the grip end of the club at me, "You are about to be my youngest cancer patient!"

He confirmed it without a biopsy. He knew what it was and gave me two options. One was he could take care of it with a "triple burn" that would leave a small, flat scar. Or he could send me upstairs to another doctor who could cut it out and after the stitches were removed I would have a small, thin, straight scar. He immediately did a triple burn with nitrogen and I have a small flat scar. He did it all in less than 20 minutes! He was good.

We had the 16th largest motor fleet in the US! Besides traveling to sites, I was always asked to attend celebrations such as awards for million accident free miles, and general celebrations. I helped dedicate a Totem Pole as our facility in Seattle, stuff like that. I also challenged one of the citations a County was trying to fine us a considerable amount of money! They interpreting our slight oxygen escaping due to temperature changes with our tanker trucks was release of a hazardous material. I mean, the cost was staggering and if they won, we knew other counties would follow suit! They didn't win, and I was the main person in the middle of the action.

A manufacturing facility in Hayward had a chemical leak that was contained on the property. However, they didn't have an Emergency Response Plan (ERP). On TV you could see things like a man standing beside his old sports car that paint was obviously bad due to age. There was a young teen using a sander on the paint. He said the chemical did that to his car! Since there was no Plan, the company had to pay for such damage. It cost them dearly. The surrounding community was low income. The company paid doctors bills, house repairs, a lot of auto paint damage, etc.

Because of that I got involved in the local Community Action group and I wrote a standard ERP so they could write one for their companies. I had written the Emergency Response Plan for Los Alamos National Labs when in New Mexico so I didn't take much time for me to help the community companies.

In the City of Industry, a suburb of Los Angeles, we worked a deal with a local school. If there was an earthquake or other disaster we could use one of their buildings for our guys who had to stay at the Air Separation Plant. We did that to ensure we could get oxygen to the hospitals. I can't remember what we were giving in return, but twice while I was there we used to facility and we were able to support the hospitals.

A horrible accident happened in Hawaii. We operated stores there under the name Gaspro. We sold things like coolers and barbecues. We filled the bottles for personal barbecues. A local small business, not ours, had one person filling the bottles. He was well trained. One day when there was a waiting line for him, the owner of the store said he would help and took the next person, a woman, and went to the fill lines. He did not inspect the bottle, it was too rusted and should not have been filled. He connected the fill line and turned the gas to the full open position. He still had the wrench in his hand. He had not connected the hose correctly. When he read the gauge he thought the needle was not reading the flow, when in reality the needle was pegged open beyond safe levels. He hit the gauge with the wrench and the bottom of the rusted bottle exploded! The bottle went up like a rocket through the air for over 300 feet! The owners decapitated head still on top of it.

Even though there was a full and complete investigation, our Gaspro guys refused to fill any more bottles. We had stores on just about every Island, even those where only Hawaiians were allowed on. No person with less than 75% Hawaiian blood was allowed on. We hurriedly got a waiver from the Governor of Hawaii and the trip was set for me to go. Stephen, having more than 75% Hawaiian blood, his wife was a 100%, was my escort. We traveled to all Hawaiian Islands where I did special training on proper safety procedures to all our guys. There was no-one in the company or that I have ever heard of who traveled to all the islands and not full or near full Hawaiian. It was a Wow trip! I visited almost every Island! And many of the people I met gave me gifts, usually Macadamia nuts!

Peggy had gone over with me but stayed on Oahu. Stephen's wife took her to places we hadn't been. On the day she was to fly back to the Mainland, they had a liquid lunch. I got off the small inter-island flight and went over to see her off. I was carrying a couple large boxes of Macadamia nuts. I was going to get her to take one back with her. She wasn't at the Departure Gate! I started calling just as I saw her come down the walkway. She was not walking straight! You could tell she had a little too much to drink! I met her, gave her a kiss, and handed her one of the boxes. She didn't take it. She asked me what it was and I told her. She smiled, said "Thats nice" and left me standing there with the boxes. She boarded the flight. When I talked to her next she asked if she was supposed to take one of the boxes?

I used to tell friends that it was just terrible I had to visit Hawaii at least once every three months. During one visit my boss from New Jersey and his wife and our Industrial Hygienist, also from New Jersey, joined Peggy and me. My boss had made a special deal with the Prince Hotel, a fully Japanese owned high end hotel. We had a Lincoln Town Car rental and when we pulled up at the Prince we all got out and started in. Japanese women opened the hotel front door for us and I thanked them in Japanese! The front desk had heard that and one lady said something to me in Japanese! I answered and we did small talk for a couple minutes while we were being checked in. Somehow I got the biggest room with a wonderful view!

While there we stopped by the Wyland Galleries and I noticed a beautiful painting by Tabora. As an artist he was considered a reincarnation of the great artists even at the young age of 26. We looked at his painting, "Tempest" and I remarked he painted the water too green, water is blue. That night Peggy and I sat on the patio of Michael's in front of the rock formation called the "Crouching lion". While sipping drinks we were watching the waves crash over the rocks along the shoreline. I'll be damned! The water breaking was the exact shade of green we saw in the painting! I went back and found I did not make enough money to buy the painting! However, the lady I talked with contacted me a couple months later and said Tabora was leaving to open his own galleries. She said she could make a deal on the painting she had in their gallery. I still could not afford it, but I did and for Christmas I gave the painting to Peggy for a present!

Another trip over to Hawaii I went into Tabora's gallery. Roy Tabora was there! We hit it off and have become friends ever since! I have another few of his less expensive paintings, one titled "Moon Over Diamond Head" that is mounted in Kona wood from Hawaii. For Peggy's birthday he gave her a small painting he signed for her. I am one of the only people, and he told me that, from the Mainland who has met his wife and two daughters. I actually was able to paint a couple strokes under his guidance on one of his paintings.

I traveled a lot between sites and across the US for Safety meetings with the other Safety Managers. Between the traveling with Peggy and the girls and this traveling I achieved 50! I have been in all 50 United States! And that is not just passing through on an airplane. Feet down in 50 States!

We spent a lot of money at most of these meetings. Bob, my boss, would hand me the wine list and tell me to pick out at least one red wine and one white wine. Cost was not an object. I could not believe how much we spent on food at very well known restaurants. We picked the best wine.

Why did Bob ask me to pick the wine? Easy, I had learned from one of the best palettes in Wine Country. Darrell worked for Peter, the owner, and each said the other had the better palette! I learned from them and as I was told previously, I had a natural talent for taste. I soon was teaching friends of mine how to use their senses to know what to expect from the wine before they actually tasted it. Many of my friends went from "It's just alcohol" to appreciating the grape.

On one trip to Houston, Bob was acting a little funny. As we were checking in to the hotel he commented if I wanted to work at Corporate I would have to get rid of my boots and buckles! All the years in the Midwest I only wore Cowboy boots. Not cheap ones either. That night I believe I had on my Luchese boots and one of my western belt buckles. I asked him if he though I should wear Wing Tips? He thought that would be nice. When we met again for dinner I had on a pair of Tony Llama that was smooth Ostrich with a wing tip of bumpy rough Lizard, just like a wing tip shoe! He was upset. I believe he was going to offer me a position at the Corporate offices.

We met with one of his friends, now a Vice President. Bob used to make fun of me. He told his friend that I was a mess. He said I wore Cowboy Boots, flashy belt buckles, was from Maine but lived in

California. And I carried a purse! It is actually a Man Purse that I carry ever since I severely hurt my back. Carrying a wallet in my back pocket threw my hips off and my back would hurt. So I carried the purse. We were sitting at the bar in a Cajun restaurant. The VP looked at me and asked if I was screwed up? I answered,"Not yet". He then said he would teach me another talent and reached for the crawfish from the tray just delivered. He said he would show me how to eat a "Crawdad". As he said that I grabbed one, split the head from the body, put the head to my lips, and sucked the juice from the head! He shook his head, looked at Bob and said "You didn't tell me he was Cajun also!"

When I had been with the company for about a year, Bob showed up and informed me BOC had taken over the company and enacted a reduction in force. I was the last one in so the first one out. The other guy hired a few months before me had been let go also. I thanked Bob for a good year with them and went job hunting again. I played a lot of golf and then one day I interviewed with a guy from Dallas Texas. He hired me as his Account Manager, meaning I ran all the Safety and Health Consulting for his company.

32

Dallas, Texas

Consulting was something I did a lot in my jobs, but usually in-house, this was now nationwide. One of the guys reporting to me did all the cold calling and set up my clients. I wrote programs, taught programs, public speaking, etc. all the stuff he found that I could handle.

I went to VA on Lancaster Street. I had applied for VA Disability previously and it was a nightmare. I was sent down to Waco at the Regional VA Office. I was evaluated for my injuries. The female doctor was rude and acted quite superior to me! A couple times she called me "Sergeant" in a demeaning way. The items we talked about was my continuing problem with my back. She said she did not have continuous doctor reports on my back so it couldn't be as bad as I say it is! When I told her my last doctors had said they could do nothing more for me, they would not recommend surgery, so I was seeing a Chiropractor. She said she didn't have records so I would only get 10% disability. Next was the scar on my head that should have given me the Purple Heart, but she said it was too short to be used as disability. And the big thing was my PTSD, for which she candidly said, "You were in the Air Force! The Air Force saw no action." That was denied. I took all my Chiropractor reports back down to Waco VA and the receptionist signed for them. When I checked back, VA said they didn't get the records and there was no record of me delivering them!

I raised a lot of hell at the Lancaster Avenue VA. They were just as caring as Waco. I stopped using VA.

I was asked often to do investigations that would be entered into law suits. Most often my deposition was adequate, most lawyers remarked how comprehensive and logical my reports appeared in court. Then I was called in on a $3.5 Million case! I did the investigation and they would not accept it because in the report I called one of the lawyers by his first name! I rewrote the report and was told I missed the time to get it in, so I would have to appear in court. I was tying my necktie before heading to court when the lawyer who hired me told me I didn't have to come in, the opposition had seen my report and decided to settle! They could not tell me how much but a slip of the tongue put it at over $1 Million. Of course the company I worked for got their piece, I questioned why I didn't get anything? Screwed again.

The company was using Harvard Graphics, an out of date graphics program but one I had played with when I was a Programmer. We had a booth at one of the major conferences and he wanted to show some film he had someone produce for him. I said it didn't have an opening that would catch anyones eye, so I was going to try something.

I was told by many Programmers that using Harvard Graphics was so limited they didn't like it. My boss had refused to update to a new system so I played around with the program. At the Conference it was the attraction! I had programmed semi dark background to look like a wall. Then a little guy walks from right to left and stops at a string and loop and pulls down a movie screen. When down, he just continues walking and as he walks off the screen, the presentation comes on! His narcissistic son claimed he had done that, so I got no credit or bonus.

Soon I heard about and found out more of the things the owner of the company did were unethical. I planned to correct what I could and if I could not I would start looking again for another job. However, I got a big job for a Federal entity and spent nearly a month traveling to their sites and doing training.

One of the things in my contract was if I brought in work I would get a Finder's Fee and a portion of the profit. While on this month long trip I was confronted by one of the guys in the class. He owned his own business. We talked and I contacted my assistant and we signed a contract. Basic calculations was my Fee amounted to $153,000! My boss refused to pay me and said he didn't have to because he had sent me to do the consulting work so therefore if he hadn't sent me I would not have got the follow on contract! Royally screwed again!

I got a lawyer and was going to sue him but after my lawyer researched he talked to me and asked if I had $100,000 in my back pocket? No, of course not! He said my boss presently had seven law suits against him! With his liquid wealth in the millions, it would cost me that to even get in the door! He told me one of the ladies I knew, but I never knew she worked for him, had filed a sexual harassment case against him and had won $100,000! But she and her husband spent an estimated $113,000 on the suit!

One evening my assistant had to run back to the office. He went to his desk and heard noises coming from the big office. He looked and saw the boss screwing the secretary! We now understood why he gave her a Company Car, a Mercedes, and why he was paying for her son to go to a private school!

My boss found out I was asking a lawyer and immediately started harassing me. His son, a crook also, publicly claimed I stole something from him! They were going to smear me. My assistant left, don't know if he was fired, he refused to talk to me again.

I left the company. He was a preferred vendor with ASSE, but not after I was finished. I was a Professional Member with ASSE and was writing questions for the Board of Certified Safety Professionals, so my word was solid. He tried to blemish my record with them but never succeeded.

I left the company, and was glad I did.

33

Fort Worth, Texas

We had bought a house in Plano, north of Dallas. Every morning I would leave North Dallas and drive to north Fort Worth where I belonged to a fitness club. I worked out every morning, showered, and dressed for work at a Computer manufacturing company in north Fort Worth. The headquarters were based out of Irvine, California. I was the Safety Director.

The first thing I ran into was my new Assistant who handled Workers' Compensation. She had an attitude and the first thing out of her mouth was that she was leaving, she would never work for someone like me! I found out she had been good friends with the Safety Manager I replaced. The company wanted to take the program to the next level, so I was hired. He lost his job because of me! Apparently, his limited knowledge and education was evident and management didn't think he could move forward with the Company. I also found out my assistant was not getting paid for what she was doing. She was actually recommending people for Administrative jobs and they were getting more pay than her from the start!

I asked her to give me some time, a couple weeks until I got into the job and tapped her extensive company knowledge. She agreed and one of the first things I did was get her a pay raise. We found we actually worked quite well together and she stayed. We became friends. Peggy was very cautious of her, saying she didn't like her. She was very pretty and Peggy thought our working so close and the time I was at the site was too much. We weren't moving to Fort Worth and my working situation was driving a wedge between us.

I also helped her with her education. She wanted to get a degree but didn't have time with her two girls, so I did some research and talked to about 4 on-line colleges and determined which was Certified and Accredited. One stood out and I contacted them. While I was trying to work something she could work into her schedule, the representative asked me about my educational needs. I told her I had four Degrees, one Associates, two Bachelors, and a Masters, and what they were all in. She proposed I look into their Doctorate program! I did, the company supported it, it would be the first where I didn't use the GI Bill.

As usual, I burned through it and in a relative few months. When I got to my Dissertation on "Safety Within a Multicultural/Bilingual Workplace" I had a problem. I didn't want to finish the PhD program because I knew if my mother ever called me "Doctor" it would be with malice. I also thought my sister would make comments since I had blown past her one degree. Quite the opposite. Both her and Susan urged me to finish. I told Susan why but didn't dare tell my sister, it would have been another useless fight. So I settled in and finished my Dissertation. It was actually very easy. With learning the language of many of the countries we lived in it always involved learning the culture. By that time I spoke fluent Spanish and Japanese, and could get by with somewhat limited Hangul (South Korean), Italian and some Turkish. Since there was no other documented writings on the topic, I did not have to defend it! I did get some comments about my writing style, but not about content.

I had earned my PhD, Doctor of Philosophy majoring in EH&S (Environmental Health and Safety) Management! Things just don't change immediately. The degree really didn't mean anything to me, nothing shot off any fireworks. Nothing in my office changed, I did the same things I was already doing. A week or two after I got it and updated everything, I went to our bank satellite counter in the local grocery store. When the line was dwindling down, the head teller walked from the back office to a vacant counter and announced she would take the next person. When I had finished the deposit I was making, the teller said, "Will there be anything else we can do for you, Doctor Brown?" I truly thought she was talking to someone behind me! I recovered pretty good and thanked her, I didn't need anything more, I smiled, thanked her again and then sat in my car for a few, just absorbing Doctor Brown!

One day one of the guys at the facility told me about this red pickup that the driver had taken out a gun when my friend honked his horn at the pickup! The pickup merged across lanes into his lane almost hitting him. I knew quite a bit about guns in Texas. I had met the senator who authored the Texas Concealed Carry Law and actually helped in the final product Legislature Bill. I put out a message to everyone to be extra careful and added the specifics on the new Law. About two months later I was driving the quick trip from our manufacturing plant to my office and as I merged into the main road I was almost hit by a red pickup that moved over into the free lane I was entering, almost hitting me! I was driving a yellow sports car, so I know he saw me and there was no right turn there so his moving into my lane was on purpose. I instinctually blew my horn and sure enough, he pulled a gun!

I slammed on the brakes and swerved way to the left and stepped on the gas! He swerved to follow me. He could not hear it but I saw the flash and where the bullet hit the roadway! I stepped on it more and called my assistant. I told her to call the cops, mentioning one of the officers I knew well and hatched the plan. I was on a loop road and he was still following me and trying to catch up to me in traffic. I took the loop and a major highway and back on the loop again. My assistant called me and said the police had done what I suggested and were ready. I made a turn, him still following a distance back! I entered the parking lot to my company. As he followed me into the lot, a police vehicle pulled in behind him and turned on his lights. As I passed an opening in the lot another police vehicle pulled out and turned on his lights! They had boxed him in and soon had him in custody. My assistant went crazy, telling me I was crazy and something she said triggered my PTSD.

I didn't have Gina around any more and thought I could handle it.

My head was getting cloudy and I was having trouble trying to get coherent thoughts out. I was really having trouble and a heavy feeling of depression. I hid it from some but I believe Peggy read it as me doing something. She thought I was having an affair with my assistant when I was really distant from everyone. I was in deep depression again.

About that time there were about six of us in the office and we talked about getting my assistant a nice birthday gift, I believe one of the girls knew she was having problems with her husband. So they came to me and asked if I wanted to contribute to a joint, nice gift for her. Then one that knew I lived in the Dallas area suggested a gift card from Nordstrom! We all thought it a great idea and they gave me the money they had. I added to it, and bought her a $100 gift card for Nordstrom! Peggy thought it was from me and fueled her idea of an affair even more. Then when my assistant used it to buy clothes for her girls, I called her up! I was doing something and she was in the office. Jokingly I said, "I had a dream last night I bought your daughter a dress" referring to her buying the girls clothes instead of something for her. I didn't know Peggy had put a recorder near the phone and as far as she was concerned, that message validated my affair. The next day when I was walking to my car at the gym, Peggy pulled up on the side of the road next to the parking lot, rolled down the passenger window, and through tears told me she was leaving me and she drove off!

She went to Colorado and stayed with her brother. That sent my depression and PTSD into a deeper hole, I was truly ready to kill myself. Between me losing any professional edge I had, maybe a little of the drinking I was doing, and the fact the company had sold out to a noted bad player in business! Soon my whole section and the company was folding. Add to all this again, I was now one of the unemployed and maybe on the brink of divorce.

I had always had problems, or thought I did with having a clear mind. Someone might ask me a question and maybe my answer was not that clear. It was worse now and everything was a fog. I realized I had not been nice to Peggy. The PTSD had put me out of touch. I was very depressed. I was not a nice guy. I drove the woman I love away from me. It was a good thing someone had stolen my two guns during a household goods shipment. I was ready.

34

Gⵣ⊘

Dallas, Texas

Windows and doors was what we manufactured at numerous sites in North Texas.

I was the Safety Director and had an office, glass enclosed, right across a narrow hallway from the female Vice President. I was harassed from the beginning because a Hispanic Manager had been promoted and unofficially was told he could have the office next to the VP. He got the glass office at the end, as far away from her as possible. He was always trying to get me kicked out of that office. I think he thought he would have a relationship with her. I had the office so I was the barrier and the problem.

He wasn't my only problem, I had die hard supervisors that liked the way my predecessor had done Safety, by not doing it! I cracked down on supervisors pretty hard. They had basically done what they wanted in a very unsafe manner. I started doing things like telling them away from their workers that their unsafe practices were making my job harder. Most ignored me. So I turned on my mean side! That appeared to be getting more results. Then we had one of the top Union guys come into one of our factories and caused some problems. When I kicked him out, the problems got worse.

Add to that, someone found out I was separated from Peggy and the women came out of the woodwork! I drove a yellow Nissan 300ZX Twin Turbo and I believe at least three times a week one of the women would ask for a ride. We got a new supervisor in and he loved himself, bragging about everything he had. One day I was standing by the window talking with another Director when this guy comes up and interrupts. He pointed at a very nice looking BMW M3 and proclaiming he probably had the fastest car in the company. The other Director looked at me and kind of laughed, so did I. He tried to push his point and said there maybe one car out there that might be faster. The Director asked him if he was talking about the yellow car? He said if he was, he should talk to me! "Is that your car?" he asked me and I smiled, simply saying it was faster than his, and walked away.

I walked into the big warehouse and factory we had and probably the supervisor I had the most problem with was standing there smoking with another worker. I heard him say that he had really screwed the Safety guy, see what is going to happen! When I confronted him he just roared laughing and walked away while giving me the "finger".

I found out within days that someone had contacted OSHA with a false report about something I allegedly did. Although it was deemed a false report that sometimes happens when someone wants to get back at someone like me, it did prompt an OSHA inspection/audit! Since it involved me, I could not participate. The VP brought in supposedly a consultant she knew. The guy was not current on standards or procedures/processes. He was a dinosaur well past being an effective safety person. He made suggestions that were in conflict of current directives and standards. When I pointed them out he told the VP that I was hampering his consulting. I knew this would probably be the end, but it wasn't. Something totally innocent and in violation of Human Resources guidelines was my downfall.

I had the four bedroom house to myself and a fellow Director asked if I could do something for one of his workers in the office, a single mother of two. She lived in an apartment that had been badly infected with, I believe, rats. She and all the other residents were being forced out for about a week and his lady didn't have the money for a hotel, etc. He asked if I would agree to them living in my spare bedroom for a week? I met her, very nice, about 18 years my junior, and I could see she needed help. Mostly for the two kids, I agreed.

Her daughter was the sweetest little girl, maybe 11 or 12, and her son had a real problem since his parents divorce. The first thing he said to me was that I hated him! He was screaming that no matter what his mother tried to do to stop him! So the first hour I sat down in front of this 8 year old and asked him why he thought I hated him? After about 40 minutes we were talking and even laughing. I stood up and he grabbed my hand and followed me around the house. I found out he loved trains and I brought a picture book of trains back to the house for him. As they were about to go back to their apartment I took them out to Joe's Crab shack. He came up to me, leaning against my leg and asked, "Would you be my daddy?". I did everything I could do to keep from crying, all the while explaining I was not married to his mother, I thought she was a very nice lady, but we were not married. I had to promise him I would come see him,. I think I loved that little guy. I remembered the boy in Vietnam that was killed and wondered if this little boy was his replacement.

I had to wipe any thought of that from my mind if I was going to win Peggy back. Getting involved with the boy beyond being a new friend would undermine any purpose. I could not get my head on straight.

While I was having all the problems at work, a truck had rear ended my car! While in the shop I got a rental car. I was driving a convertible! I heard about a small fair nearby that had a miniature train ride. I contacted his mother and asked if I could take them to the fair, mainly as a promise to her son. She agreed and that weekend her kids had a blast with the top down on the car and going to the Fair. It was also a good break for her and while the kids were riding a ride, the mother was thanking me. She hadn't seen her son so happy in a long time! She gave me a little hug, nothing else. We were just standing there waiting for the kids on the ride, Apparently one of the Managers saw us and reported to Human Resources that we were apparently having an affair! I was brought in to see the VP! I was read the riot act about me representing the company as a Corporate Dircector and was apparently having a fling with a common worker many years younger! The lady was brought in and she told them the same thing as I did that it was a surprise for her son! She was counseled and I was set on the path to being let go. I think I was glad, because my PTSD was even worse.

I heard noise about a new Safety Manager. I was told I was being moved to an office in one of our smaller companies. A couple days later I was told I was being fired, apparently because of the OSHA complaint but I believe it was the Fair incident, the Manager, and the other Director who wanted my office. One of the good guys told me the Manager was bragging how he had really screwed the Safety Guy! He also told me who the new Safety Director was and he was getting a new office at our largest company. To me, the office away from Headquarters was another sign of manipulation by the other Director. I laughed! The guy who came to replace me had been fired from his last job! Oh well, I just got fired from this one.

35

❦

High School and Sports Center

Rowlett, a suburb of Dallas, was building a new High School and Sports Center. The builder was looking to replace their Safety Manager. They saw no reduction in accidents or rates it was causing a rise in their insurance and delays. This included delays by OSHA visits. They brought me on and I had a few days overlap with the current safety person before he left and I took over.

Standing on the second floor looking over the temporary wood railing at the edge, the Foreman had introduced me to everyone but Rickie. Looking down to the floor below. He pointed out Rickie and his "raising gang" the group that raises the steel on cranes to higher levels and "walk the steel" to attach it all together. "Are you going to introduce me to Rickie?" "Nope" I was on my own.

When I approached Rickie I first noticed he had on a complete one piece coverall that when you unsnapped the legs it hung down like the old fashioned gun slinger "dusters". I walked up to stand alongside Rickie and introduced myself. His only comment was, "Safety people get hurt around me!" I said okay, let me try this again. I stepped back, then forward to again stand next to him and introduced myself again. "You aren't going away, are you?" "Nope".

The first thing I noticed was all the unsafe practices. I went to where the soon to be replaced safety guy was. I wanted to hear his reason for the unsafe conditions. I was expecting him to blame management or Unions. Instead, I walked up on him showing a worker how to cut a hose off and replace a connector to the hose. It was a high pressure hose. He was resting it on his leg and cutting down so if the knife slipped it would get his leg! I stopped him and asked what he was doing? He told me and I told him to meet me at the Forman's trailer. He argued and I strongly told him to get out! Then I showed the young worker the table vice. I had his supervisor show him the correct tool and procedure for replacing the connector. The safety guy did not go to the Foreman's trailer so the foreman and I went to find him. When we did he was bad mouthing me! When I said he was showing the kid an unsafe practice, his only response was that I didn't know construction! I asked him if he had a Certified Safety Professional (CSP) certification, I saw the letters behind his name? Yes, and I responded not for long. I did a thorough report and recommendation and sent it to BCSP (Board of Certified Safety Professionals). They investigated and about three months later I was told they had removed his Professional Certification.

I got along with all the people. I gave impromptu briefings, walked the site and found out what everybody was doing. We talked about fall protection and instead of telling them what was right, I explained why. For instance the new rule that came out about people wearing a safety harness on a scissor lift. I took the time to explain why it was imposed. When the guys understood it was for their safety, I was for their safety, compliance came easy. One time they were laying tin on the roof and instead of walking the steel and starting on the far side and working back, they laid panels without welding from the ladder to the other side and started back from there. A new guy saw this and asked the lead roofer why he was doing that? He simply said, "So my safety man can get up here!"

The raising gang was tough but I was making roads. One evening they had a truckload of steel come in. It was raining hard and I was standing there watching them unload. The next day Rickie came up to me and said I was different, and maybe a little crazy. Okay. He then told me when they had night delivery and it was raining, the past safety guy would sit in his car, staying dry. Any complaints about safety was not revealed until the next day! "You stood out in the rain with my guys last night!" Okay. He said from that action I probably earned more respect from his guys than anybody on site! It was a different ball game after that.

There were some wild people there! Constructors sometimes get a bad rap, and some live up to it! Again on the second open floor. We were preparing to put the steeple over the entrance. We heard loud steps. someone running! I was alerted, thinking there had been an accident. No, it was a tall guy with blond hair flowing under his hard hat. With all the noise it was hard to tell what the banging noise was until he came running by us. It was gunshots! Out on the road close to the building was a red Camaro diving slowly by. The female driver was firing a hand gun at the guy running by! We ducked. We could hear the guy say as he ran by, "I didn't know the bitch knew where I worked!" No one was hurt but the blond guy was escorted from the site.

When my contract was up we were near finished and I had found another job, Rickie's crew asked me to go to a local Cajun restaurant and join them to eat a bunch of crawfish and drink some beer! I asked Rickie if he thought it was a good thing, I was sometimes hard on his guys? He told me I was either going to have a wild night with those guys, or get my ass kicked as a going away present!

Wow, that was one of the best nights I have ever had! All but one of the Crew came and we ate God knows how many platters of Crawfish and so many beers! I didn't drink and out of respect, the crew had designated drivers who didn't drink. I still smile thinking about it.

36

Chapter 12

Coming Home

Fog was all around me when I woke up! I sat up in bed alone and knew immediately it wasn't a fire! The mist like fog around me scared me! As I was sitting on the bed the fog lifted. For the first time maybe ever, I could think one thought! Usually any input, written or spoken was caught in this tangle of thoughts I had to rumble through. But now I had only one clear thought in my head!

I had been diagnosed as Clinically Depressed. Whether it was growing up being called stupid or killing a person, I had problems. My visit with medical professionals basically determined my young verbal abuse started my depression early. I didn't know any better. I was skeptical because most psychologists/psychiatrists will blame a family dominate figure. Why would this be anything different? Looking at my degree I didn't want to self diagnose. I was able to follow reason and understand my growing up was faulty. I didn't know better.

The second thing I thought of was how much better I could have been if I could have had the clear mind I had at that moment. I said second, because the first thing I thought of was what have I done to Peggy? She had been such a saint to stick with me when I was mentally low and I know I was not always nice to her. I had to blame someone and she was always there. I was between jobs. The construction job was finished and I was getting things ready for my new job. I had nowhere I had to be. I went downstairs to where I had set up my computer and I sent an email to Peggy. tI told her I was so sorry, please forgive me. She later told me when she received my message she muttered that she could not go through this again and almost did not respond. But she did.

I've always had a motorcycle and now had a big Harley Davidson. A couple weeks after I sent the email I hopped on the Harley and drove straight through to Denver. It was almost like a first date as we were very cautious. A couple more trips and my courting her again got us back together and she returned to Texas with me after another couple months.

We talked and I admitted that I was the problem all along. My depression had come from Vietnam and doctors thought most likely from my mother and such things as her calling me "Stupid The more we thought about it, the more sense it made. I told her I could do nothing about my PTSD. I never got a warning when it was going to kick my ass. By using the Transcendental Meditation I was still practicing I thought I had a little control over it. As far as my depression, I didn't know since I had come out of it without medication. I could still feel it always there and ready to pull me back to the "dark side". I found if my brain was singing a song, no particular song, I was okay. If my brain was not playing me a song, I wasn't. Often I could use my TM to help my brain out and get back to the bright side again.

We agreed to be tolerant, to help each other. And I was back with the Love of my Life! I am so sorry for the way I treated her. We had traveled a lot. Recently to Hawaii and the East Coast. We agreed we needed to get away more, I was always working. The last time we went out of country she had booked us a week in Cozumel Mexico. We agreed to do more together and travel more.

I love you Peggy.

37

Chapter 13

Austin, Texas

Broadwing Communications had posted for a Safety Specialist, but the job description was definitely for a Safety Manager. I applied for it and went down to Austin for an interview, and what an interview!

I stopped for lunch and the young waitress started talking to me. I had been through Austin many times but was mostly passing through, I told her that and that I was interviewing for a job here. She basically told me that Austin was a young college town. I asked if she was saying I was maybe a little to old to fit in? Before she could answer I asked "does it make a difference that I have a PhD and drive a Harley?" She smiled a huge smile, turned to walk away but turned back, "You will love it here!"

I met the HR Manager at the Broadwing Headquarters on Capital of Texas Highway. She was very cold to me, not friendly at all and she tried to rush me through and out the door! She was even telling me I probably would not fit in or enjoy it there! I found out while waiting for the Vice President that there were internal applicants and she wanted one in specific to get the job. I also found out Broadwing was owned by Cincinnati Bell. Now I understood why a VP was running the site, he reported to Cincinnati Bell.

We met with the VP in his office and every time I started to say something, the HR manager would interrupt. She would add or detract from what the VP was saying, even telling him that both she and I had things to do! The VP was looking at my resume and asking questions, often before I had a chance to answer the HR lady was doing it for me. I was getting frustrated, along with the VP but we didn't show it. When our eyes connected we could both tell the HR lady was disrupting the process. Finally I came out and asked the VP a question. The HR lady raised her voice and said I was not allowed to ask him questions. I said I thought I was there on an interview!

I was looking at the VP and he kind of had a smile and a slight nod toward me. I caught the gesture and addressed the HR lady by her first name, "I am sure you are well versed with personnel interviews and must realize it is not a one way conversation. An applicant who does not have at least a few questions during the interview is one really not looking for a job." The VP almost laughed and told her he welcomed my questions When I delivered my first question, she actually sat forward in her chair, "You can't ask him that!" The VP leaned over and said it was one of the best questions he had heard in a very long time and gestured me to continue. She was physically upset so the VP and I talked and she soon left the office! He laughed a little, kind of letting me know he would not say or do anything to upset her. He was very candid and when it was over his handshake was firm and positive. I still had no idea what the outcome would be and checked out and back on the road toward home.

A few days later I got the offer for the job and it was for a Safety Manager and a salary significantly higher than posted, plus a moving expense! I accepted the offer and I/we got ready to move to Austin, Texas! Peggy had moved back to Texas.

The first thing that happened was I was now reporting to another VP, the one I interviewed with went back to Cincinnati. I was now reporting to another VP who nobody in the building knew yet. Roger and I got along very well, he said he had reviewed the other VP's notes and agreed I was the top candidate. He warned me without saying why, that I may find some resistance to my hiring. I thought he was talking about the internal candidates. Later I quickly found out he was not!

I met the internal candidate the HR lady was trying to get promoted into the position. I actually felt it went beyond just friends. She was better with me but still not very civil. The internal candidate was a large man and he apparently though his size, ignoring his large belly, would intimidate me. He said he should have got the job and may still prove he is better, after all he has more experience in Safety than I do. I kind of laughed and asked what experience he had? He had been in the military and served as a unit safety office, no formal training. He had worked in another company as a Collateral Duty Safety Officer He counted his nearly 10 years in a safety position as a certification, again with no formal training. I kind of said, "So, you have a lot of experience!" He said he undoubtedly had more than me. I just said okay and started to walk off.

One of the people in the little group around us spoke up and asked what kind of experience I had. I simple said that I didn't want him (the internal candidate) to feel bad, I'll just say I have a little more than he does. I was asked again so I told them I had over 25 years as a full time Safety Professional, had five college degrees, including the PhD, and four of them were Environmental Health and Safety degrees. I added that I had 10 letters behind my signature, including the CSP and OHST, both professional certifications. The big guy just kind of huffed and stated they didn't have the right to bring someone in, I had screwed him out of a promotion.

Then I found out what Roger was talking about when I took my first trip to Cincinnati for Orientation. I met all the Safety Staff. There were four Safety Specialists, the Chief of Safety and other staff members. I was treated kind of cold and soon found out why. One of the safety guys was given the opportunity to go to Austin for the Safety Specialist position. He had turned it down, as did another Specialist. I got the reason very abruptly and very much in my face! They had turned it down because it was a lateral position, not a promotion, the pay the same and no relocation bonus! Then I come along, got the Manager position, a significant pay raise over them and relocation expenses! He was getting nasty and one of the other guys called to him telling him he had better be careful, I technically was his boss! We got along but I don't believe ever mended fences.

Roger and I got along quite well. He was an action person and soon found out a lot about me. He respected my education, knowledge and ethics One time he was supposed to discipline me for something I did, instead he told me face to face he wished he had thought of doing what I did! We laughed about it.

I was inspecting one of our sites at 60 Hudson, New York City. We had two communication sites in the building and there was work being done on one of the sites, but the work had come to a standstill. I went to where the electrical panels were along the wall in the underground parking lot and asked the workers what the hold up was? There was a switch, an industrial strength toggle switch that had to be closed to connect power to the finished work. The crew said that was all there was left but they had to wait on a Union Electrician to flip the switch! I asked how long and one of our contractors said he was told probably another hour or two! I told them I was a little upset, their inability to flip a switch was causing us unnecessary down time and higher cost for our backup system. They reiterated they could not touch it because of the Union. So, I asked him if he knew how to flip the switch? His response was he was not an electrician! I said that I was a Safety Manager and one of the things the Union could not file a grievance on me was if I did something once for training. I then said to the guy that I interpreted his answer to be that he did not know how to flip the switch or didn't have enough training. I would safely train him in the operation! "Watch how I do this, I can only train you once" and I flipped the switch!

The Union was all over me, big guys too! I calmly said I was doing some training and the Union Charter says a Safety Professional can demonstrate, once, how to safely perform a task, which I did. They countered I didn't have training and I countered I have been training on electrical safety for a long time! Not only did I teach Electrical Safety, I was an Electronics Technician in the Navy! They continued to complain and I walked away unscathed, except the report to my supervisor. And Roger told me approximately how much money I saved the company, "but don't do it again" with a laugh.

A lot of things happened at Broadwing. We were the first fully fiber optics communication company in the US. We were the ones large companies would use to connect coast to coast meetings where we provided ultra clean images. Most used a standard provider for daily use. A nationwide company wanted to have a teleconference with all sites, we could do that over the much clearer and more reliable fiber optics. Recently the company was concentrating on the big companies, not the smaller ones. Our Tech Services said it was because big companies normally had their own IT office and smaller companies didn't. The smaller ones used our services as their troubleshooter and repair. We could concentrate on more business and profits if we didn't take on so many small companies and their problems. So our culture was changing.

In the middle of all this was our NOC (Network Operations Center) where we tracked everything. On the wall was a screen that was covering most of the wall and showed the status of everything. Seated were probably 40 operators updating status, discussing problems with customers, orienting new customers, etc.

I was talking with one operator and looked to his left. The female operator had one of the best customer voices I had ever heard! Friendly, accurate, easy to listen and talk to, all really great customer service. She also had a chart up on her computer I had never seen before, it was a simple customer log but done so much better than anything I had ever seen. She told me she had developed it. I was impressed and sat next to her.

A few minutes later the VP walked into the NOC and the Lead who was standing and watching over everything, announced him by Sir and his last name. Everybody stood or sat rigid because he was the new boss and most had not ever talked with him, he was to them, untouchable. I looked up when everybody went quiet and saw my boss walking toward the front. He was close enough I could say without yelling, but still loud in the NOC, "Roger, you need to see this!" There were gasps and even more silence because he was Mr. to them and I had just called him by his first name! He walked over to me still sitting in a chair next to the young lady, and I repeated that he should see this. His response, "I would love to, if you would just get the hell out of my seat!" The place was quiet! I got up and Roger sat down, smiling at me, and I walked out with all eyes on me! We laughed about it later.

I was at my desk later in the day and this same young woman came up to me, I told her to sit down. When she was at her computer I saw a confident young lady, the person who walked into my office was anything but. I could not tell her height because her shoulders closed in front of her chest, making her look feeble and flat chested. She could not look me in the eyes when she talked. She had problems speaking as if I really intimidated her. I waited for her to say something and was surprised when she said in this weak, unassured voice, "How did you do that?"

We talked and I soon found out she was talking about how I had talked to the VP as I did, very self assured, and she knew there was not a single person in the NOC, even the Director, that dared call the VP by his first name! We finally got to what she wanted, it was for me to help her be like me! I had mentored many a Safety Person and had done inspirational speaking, but still I don't know why I agreed to mentor her. Yes I do, I felt pity for this frail girl with the wonderful voice she used over the telephone that could not even look you in the eye if she was face to face. I remember my problems with stuttering and looking in a mirror. I had to help her.

I worked with her for weeks and saw a lot of improvement, it was simply building confidence in herself. I then contacted a friend I knew in the local Toastmasters Group and he agreed to help. She soon was involved in the Group and I basically stepped back. Probably nearly six months later I got a call from her and she asked if I could come to a gathering where she was getting a speaking award! I said yes, but I could not get there until about the time her gathering was finishing and I would meet her in the lobby of the hotel the ceremony was being held. I hadn't seen her for a few months. I had talked to her but could not tell if there was any improvement because she still had the great telephone voice. I was not prepared for this slightly taller than average woman walk out the door with something in her hand. She stood tall, a great smile, definitely not flat chested, and headed straight toward me! She started to slouch a little, probably not sure I would approve. I told her to stand tall, put those shoulders back, and let me see that smile! She hugged me and showed me her Toastmasters award. I kept helping her when she asked, but she was getting to be confident. Toastmasters really helped her bring out herself. She left the company but called me and emailed me for a while. She had met this lucky young man and last I heard he had proposed to her. Maybe my greatest mentor success.

I had another run in with the HR lady. There was a complaint about the lack of adequate lighting in the parking garage across our driveway. She said it was too costly for the additional lighting and she wanted to know who complained! Of course I didn't tell her but she continued to bug me and said she wasn't going to submit a useless safety work order, the lighting was adequate. I looked at her and told her we had a responsibility to employees and guests. Then I said I had seen her daughter come in often late afternoons as it was getting darker. I could tell she was about to blow, so I continued without giving her a chance. I told her I was concerned the way her daughter dressed, she often wore the coveralls, as many teens do, and she wears her hair in a long pony-tail! I said I have spent time talking to criminals and one guy, a rapist, used to tell me and others that he loved seeing girls in coveralls with the straps crossing in back, and especially if they had long hair. He said they made it so easy, he would come up behind them, grab both hair and straps where they crossed, pull out his box cutter, slice the straps and the girl was helpless to fight him. The HR lady was crying then, called me a son of a bitch, and signed the Safety work order!

Then came 9/11! From the sixth floor of 60 Hudson we could look straight down the street to the Twin Towers. Roger had me join him in the War Room where we had the feed on the wall sized screen. We had the site managers on the speaker system. I guess the little thing I did with the switch rubbed him the wrong way because one of the managers was always argumentative to me after that. So when we had him on speaker I told him there were N95 masks in the emergency locker and he should make sure all windows were shut and if anybody left the building they should have a mask on. He argued with me, even though he knew Roger was sitting next to me.

He went on about me not knowing what their situation was there so I should just keep my stupid masks where the sun don't shine, he was not going to issue masks! Roger said for him to hang on and asked me why I wanted them to wear masks? The manager interrupted and said wearing masks was stupid, the dust was too far away and there was nothing in the dust. I asked him how he was so sure and he said he had talked to one of the engineers who worked on the Trade Centers and there was no problem. I said I didn't think he had talked to an experienced engineer because if he had he would have been told during the 1993 bombing in the parking garage under the towers the air was sampled and at least three percent Asbestos! And above ground the first 64 floors were done in asbestos until it was banned! The higher floors had another fire protectorate other than asbestos. I added that asbestos was a natural carcinogenic fiber that the N95 can stop. He didn't respond, but Roger did. "Get out those masks, apparently Bruce knows a lot more than you do about the hazards!" He then added that anything I told him to do because of Safety or Environmental concerns, he was to follow to the letter. If he didn't there was going to be problems. Roger and I watched and coordinated all the actions we were to take. I still have bad dreams about what we saw and was angry when one of the professional organizations I belonged to donated 10,000 N95 and set up a training and fit test table at ground zero. Cops, firemen, etc. said they didn't need them, didn't we understand that was their brothers in there! They kicked us off the site and went in with no masks. 40% of those people that refused our masks could never go back to full duty, some not even to work, because of the stuff in their lungs! They developed what we call pneumoconiosis. I understand, but don't understand. When tremendous tragedies like this happen, safety and environmental health go out the door. I saw that in Vietnam and at Ground Zero. Amen.

Our policy of taking the big companies backfired on us. The big boys had no idea what was going on with the economy so they cut things like our services because the Ma Bell slow system they had to have, our system they didn't. Customers were dropping like flies, we lost 91% of our business and one of the companies we had bought, bought us out! I was one of the last ones to go.

I checked around and there were more safety people laid off than jobs available! However an audit of the City of Austin had caused the Human Resources people the need to hire an additional Safety Specialist. I threw my name in the hat the day before the position was closed to any more applicants. Because if my PhD and Certifications I rose to the top and interviewed. I got the job with the City of Austin, Texas!

<h1 style="text-align:center">38</h1>

City of Austin, Texas

Capital building within site, I was the new Safety Specialist. Problem was the politics! You got many jobs because of who you knew and once you got in the job, no matter how bad you were, it took basically your death to get you out of the job! Nepotism ran rampart.

Start with my new boss. He got into the Safety Officer position through a friend high up and he didn't have the qualifications nor ability, nor knowledge, but he was my boss. Our HR Manager was called "Trailer Trash" behind her back and her voice was gruff and she was nasty. She didn't know what she was doing either and her mouth got her in trouble, plus she was sneaky and vindictive. Many years earlier I inadvertently got an unknown chemical in my lungs and along with exposure to Agent Orange it resulted in nonallergic rhinitis. Basically, I get around chemicals and I get an instant headache. The worst one is cheap perfume. I had complained about one of the large Hispanic ladies who used perfume in lieu of personal hygiene! I told Trailer Trash I was having a problem with it and her response was that it didn't bother her so she as not going to do anything! The only thing she did do was when we moved to another building, she set up the seating, putting me right next to the perfume source. I told her boss, I took days off and finally moved my desk to an area that wasn't ours but they let me use it.

I visited every office and in most cases got along with most people. I did some special projects and was recognized as a team member when those projects worked out well, many getting awards. The Safety people in the separate departments were mostly collateral duty, only two departments had actual trained Safety people. There were a few departments that safety was not welcome in, mostly because of poor previous management. I started teaching an Ergonomics class, I was formerly trained at the Joyce Institute and had written many articles in safety periodicals. I would teach the class while sitting on an exercise ball and soon every class I had was full.

I followed up on a complaint from our 911 Call Center and had to meet the lady who was complaining in the lobby. They didn't let safety people into the Center! She had complained she needed a new chair and Procurement told her supervisor that if the new Safety guy did an assessment and recommended a new one, they would get her one of the new Ergonomic chairs. So talking with her and her supervisor I basically said I could not approve a new chair unless I could see how she was sitting in it, her posture and uses, etc. so I was allowed in just to see her work station. I did an assessment and told her how to properly sit, location of keyboard and screens, all that. She wasn't happy I wasn't going to authorize her a new chair and I could see the supervisor seeing the value of my assessment. I took advantage of that and pointed to another lady and asked the supervisor if that lady had complained about her shoulder? She had and the supervisor took me to her and I was able to adjust her work station so she was not putting strain on her shoulder. I pointed out another woman that I guessed had back problems, and was right again!

The supervisor had to lead me out because she knew management would not be happy I was there, but to my surprise upper management contacted me and asked if I would come back to the 911 Center! I ended up going to all the Police facilities and did more than just Ergonomics! I was told by my management, Police management and the City Manager that Safety had never been in a Police facility, I was the very first one! My boss tried to take credit for it in his weak little way.

Ah yes, my boss. He had worked his way through positions in Corpus Christy and was promoted to Chief of Safety with no formal training at all. It was a small department and the program basically was lucky he only had a few major problems. When his City Manager moved up to Austin and took over the prestigious Austin Energy, the most powerful City Department, he talked HR into bringing my boss, his friend up to run the Safety Department! I got hired in and made him look good, mainly because I was telling or helping him do his job. Very political.

I was asked to be on a project and a group of us met in a large theater style conference room at the City Headquarters. As I walked in I moved aside for a couple ladies coming in and one had a wrist support on. I asked what had happened? She asked if I was a doctor and I replied yes, although I have had extensive medical training, I was a PhD doctor. She laughed and I asked again and she described what we call repetitive Motion Syndrome. I asked if her doctor had said to wear the brace? She said no, but the pain in her wrist was so bad she had trouble even driving and someone had recommended she get a brace. He doctor basically told her if it worked, it was good.

I spent only a couple minutes with her but recommended she not wear the brace during the day but at night when she went to bed, then explained why. That was Thursday and she tried it that night. I got a call from her Monday and it started out with, "I love you!" She said she tried what I suggested and by Sunday night her wrist had stopped hurting as much and she could drive her car in without the terrible pain!

Those are the things that make me love what I do.

The city had food contests all the time, and I loved to cook. So when they had a Salsa contest I had an entry! I made a Salsa Fresca and as soon as I turned it in one of the ladies commented it wasn't like the salsa people made! She said she was not even sure it was real salsa. Then another lady said it really didn't make any difference, she said this one woman always won! We were not supposed to know who submitted what but I overheard one of the women ask which one was the lady they say always wins. She did, I placed third but got the most requests for my recipe! The girl who placed second talked with me and verified the lady always won, no matter how good it was. She added it was not right to have a "Gringo" cooking Mexican food! I smiled and told her I could cook most as well as anyone. She challenged me to make Tamales!

The following Monday I brought her in the number of tamales she had requested and then she told me her mother was considered one of the best making Tamales and her aunt sold them for a living! She was going to take mine to them to see what they thought of them The next day she said her mother said they were great, asking which Mexican made them? She would not accept they were made by a Gringo, let alone a man! Her aunt asked if whoever made them was selling them also, admitting they were as good as hers!

Later the City created a cookbook and it was open for City employees to submit recipes. The book was going to be sold with profits going to one of the charities. I wrote the Spice Section again along with two recipes. They used both my recipes and made my long Spice Section where I talked about all the spices, their common use, what they enhanced, etc. as the Forward behind the dedication page! In all, this was the third published cookbook with my Spice Section!

In honor of the publishing and sales of the cookbook, the head chef for Whole Foods, Chef Doug came to do a display of cooking. It was to be televised. We had the cooking tables in a large "U" shape and we had set up cooking stations, two at the head of the U and three on each side. Chef Doug chose the person he wanted to cook with at the station next to him. I was chosen to cook along side of him and I cooked one of the recipes I had submitted. We got along well and I think we actually learned from each other. He asked how I knew so much about international foods and all I had to tell him was where I had been stationed while in the Air Force.

When we moved offices it was just a half block from the Capital Building. I used to take a walk during lunch and sometimes went into the Capital Rotunda to see the six flags displayed in a circle on the floor around the center. We had our granddaughter out from California just about every year. One year we took her with us to Massachusetts for my nephew's wedding This time I told her I would take her to see the six flags. Like when we took her to Massachusetts she had said before we got there that the trees in California were bigger and greener. That was until she saw the trees in the Northeast. Now she told me that Six Flags was an Amusement Park in California, not Texas. When I showed her the six flags of the countries that had owned Texas at one time, and was actually a country itself, she was impressed. Even more so when I told her when the United States flag was flown, all state flags had to be lowered, except Texas because it was once a country, she was really impressed!

Whenever my granddaughters came to visit I would buy them a pair of Cowboy Boots. That was all I wore. My California granddaughter got boots because I was buying them. My Boston granddaughter really wanted them. I got the best picture of her as a young girl standing with her hands on her hips in front of the mirror where you can see your boots. I had bought her a pink pair and the look on her face was precious!

One day I decided to talk to the Veterans who sat on the curb not far from the Capital. I spoke to them and I got punched, basically because I dressed nice and was clean shaven! They said I was not a Vietnam Veteran as they were! A few more attempts, meaning being hit by a newspaper, a fist again, a tennis ball thrown in my face, etc. until finally they let me convince them I was a Veteran. We talked and I was accepted.

The unofficial leader of the near dozen Veterans was a large guy with an unkept beard called "Big John". He was scary but often quite nice. I would sit next to him often. We enjoyed each other's company. I never took them anything about my education or job position, it would not be accepted by them and would make them think I thought I was better than them. We just talked

One day another 'so called' Veteran came into our group. I walked in while he was chatting away about what he had done in Vietnam. I thought, and John spoke what I was thinking so that only I could hear, "I think he is a poser". I agreed. A "poser" is someone, in this case, that thought being a Vietnam Veteran was a badge of honor. But he was lying about his experiences there because he had never served there. It was all bullshit he was repeating from what he had heard from others.

I told John that I might be able to flush him out. John told me to go for it. I spoke up, "Remember that smell?" All the guys there, except the Poser, looked at me with daggers! The "poser" kept talking and started talking about some smell! John nearly yelled at him, "You fucking poser! You got to the count of five to get the fuck out of here or I am going to kill you!" At about the three count the guy left. John and a couple others basically said the same thing, if I ever mentioned that again, I was dead! I had mentioned something we never talk about but all of us who had been in Vietnam knew well, the smell of death.

I started teaching Safety for Texas A&M as an Adjunct Professor or Associate Visiting Scholar, depending on the venue. They had just got a contract from the Army to teach at the Safety Center at Fort Rucker, Alabama. We were teaching safety and engineering classes for those Soldiers wanting to get their Masters Degree. I took vacation and drove to Enterprise, Alabama, the city nearest Fort Rucker. There I met a Medal of Honor recipient! He was a helicopter pilot in Vietnam and risked his life rescuing downed fighter pilots. We spoke briefly about Vietnam. He looked at me and said I needed to go back as a returning Veteran. We thought that might help get rid of some of my demons and skeletons.

Later I told the guys on the sidewalk I was going back to Vietnam. I told them I had met a Medal of Honor recipient and during our discussion he said he could tell I was carrying many Vietnam skeletons that probably would destroy me if I didn't go back. So I was planning on going back to Vietnam. It was met by a lot of "Hell No!" "I will never go back!" "You are crazy Man!" etc. Then it turned to they wished they had the money I would be spending, but still not to go back. They again said I was not like them, and the good clothes and good job came up again as to why we weren't the same. The one said another divider was whenever they tried to do anything, society put up barriers, roadblocks that maybe I had never experienced!

The irony was when I tried to plan for the trip I ran into those barriers. I was apparently classified because they could not see me and apparently thought I might be one of those guys. It took me 8 months to find an agent or company that would take me back and to where I was stationed, Phu Cat. Many travel companies were quick to tell me where they went but got interruptive when I told them where I wanted to go. Basically it seemed as though they used the barriers for Vietnam Veterans, one even asking if I could afford the trip.

During that planning time there was a parade downtown for Memorial Day. For the first time they recognizing the Vietnam Veterans! Peggy and I went to the parade on my Harley and met some other Harley riders and other bikers. We had met a couple guys who had come up from South Texas on BMW motorcycles. Unlike most Harley drivers, we talked to them. We were standing there talking with them as the parade turned the corner in front of where we were standing. There were some soldiers on a military vehicle in the group. It was warm that day so I had left my motorcycle jacket in my bike so there were no patches or the like to identify myself as a Veteran. But that didn't stop one guy from saying something to the guy next to him on the truck and then point at me and both gave a hand salute to me and finished with a nod. The guy with us leaned over and said to me, "They know, don't they?". I was so emotional I was about ready to cry, but didn't, I just said a sharp "Yes". Peggy moved up a little, we were probably in the second row but a clear view of the parade. She kept looking at the truck for as far as she could see and they apparently didn't do it again while she was watching. She turned back to me, "They do know don't they?" and we said maybe it was in my eyes, whatever. It was eery and scary as hell! Was the guy in Enterprise right that he could see the pain?

By the way, Enterprise, Alabama has a unique statue in the center of town. It is a woman in flowing dress holding up a very large Locust! Enterprise was a cotton growing town and one year the Locust came through and destroyed the cotton! Some out of towner told them they had perfect soil to grow peanuts! That area around Enterprise is now the largest peanut producer in the world!

The Austin City Manager had a lot of help getting to where she was and she owed a bundle of favors. She promised one person that she would hire his son about to graduate from Florida State. She just had to post a job, it was with Austin Energy, and the job description would be something nobody in the City was a qualified for. And about the time his son graduated she would offer him the high paying job! That went to hell when they posted the job and I submitted my resume! They had to interview me as I was the only person with those qualifications to submit a resume. My boss' friend, the head of Austin Energy, interviewed me and remarked he had no idea someone like me worked for the City!

I didn't get the job, the son got it and they left Florida for Texas. A couple months when the family took a vacation to go back to see her family in Florida. Then he called the Head of Austin Energy and said his wife hated Texas! If he went back, she was leaving him, she would not go! The job was posted again, I submitted my resume again, and I was not even considered for the job! It was given to my boss! Who, by the way, was not even remotely qualified for the job! Politics and the "Good Old Boy" again.

Meanwhile I was doing some special projects. One was I volunteered to assist the Church run schools who could not afford to hire a safety person, so I did it for free. I was contacted by the HUD (Housing and Urban Development) group needing help with AAV (Air Accumulation Valves) with the houses they were renovating for low income people. I had seen the plans and would not approve them The AAV was located in the cabinet next to the toilet in the bathroom. The AAV allows air to come in and void the vacuum caused by flushing the toilet. If it malfunctioned it would or could cause a buildup of methane gas. And methane gas at first exposure causes the olfactory nerves in your nose to not work. Shortly you can not smell the gas. Due to the location it was a possible for a person to be asphyxiated from the methane gas displacing oxygen. If they could no longer smell it, by the time they would notice the effects it was probably too late. And don't even think about someone smoking in the bathroom with the methane fumes. The AAV needs to be located above the room so the vapors can escape versus kill.

The HUD Engineers were argumentative as that put a big design fix that wasted time and money! Besides, what the hell does a simple safety guy working for the City know about AAVs? They called a formal open meeting/debate. I was the target.

It was run like a judicial inquisition with about six highly respected Engineers behind a long table and me in a single seat and small, very small table in front of me. I brought the folder for reference, but never used it. I spoke without notes. Whereas, they had quite a few folders and papers to apparently intimidate me with their expertise and knowledge, they were, after all, Engineers and I wasn't. I never told them I went one deep on Engineering, had a near photographic mind, and had done extensive research. No, it became quite obvious that I was either a fool or I was the intimidator.

Everything they brought up I countered with facts and science and Environmental concerns, never reading a single note! They had a camera or two there to apparently show someone how good they are and maybe to boost their own ego, it didn't work. They agreed to re-engineer the plans and project to my recommended specifications! The lead engineer in the center of the panel leaned over and stared at me, "Who in the hell are you? The City doesn't have people like you!" He didn't believe me when I said I worked for the City.

The tape of the meeting was seen by thousands who watched the local news. I soon had a request by both the Governor to have lunch with him, and later the Mayor wanted to talk about a project for him. I ended up writing the City Smoking Policy for Austin, Texas!

Returning to Vietnam was in some sense just another trip. Peggy and I had lived in Spain four years and Japan three years. I had spent a year without her in Vietnam and another year in South Korea. We both had traveled throughout Europe and the Orient. I had traveled to Turkey, Greece, Philippines, and other countries without Peggy. I traveled a lot for work. I had visited all 50 states, Peggy had more than 45. This could be just another trip but I spent 8 months trying to find this company where we could travel to Vietnam, Cambodia, and Thailand on a private tour and where I had a say in some variance with the itinerary. It was basically a private tour where we would have a driver and guide or a single person doing both tasks at the places we wanted to go. I would get to see where I was stationed. In case I was bothered by sights or memories, we scheduled to go to Hon Tre Island, a resort, so I could decompress if necessary. Otherwise we would start in the North and fly/drive to the south, then fly to Cambodia. After a couple days there we would fly to Bangkok and go north to Chiang Mi. We had always gone south when we visited Bangkok so this time we wanted to go north.

Peggy and I left Austin with a couple stops before landing in Hanoi, Vietnam. During our hour or more layover in Seoul Korea, Peggy and I got to eat some local food we loved! This was a great way to look forward at the trip and not back toward work.

In Hanoi we stayed at the Hanoi Opera House Hilton. Our Guide and driver took us there and we planned a night itinerary that included the water puppet show. We were also taught how to walk across a Vietnamese street. You don't see any crosswalks or traffic lights to help you cross the street. So you slowly step out into traffic and take short, smooth steps across the road! The cars and motorcycles either slowed or went around you. Have to admit the first crossing I was still shaking a little.

At the hotel we went down for breakfast. We could see the river and countryside in the light of day. It was beautiful. Even more so because when I fought there I said Hanoi was North Vietnam and I would never see it.

There were a lot of German and Russian visitors for breakfast The waitresses mirrored the stoic attitude of the guests. So when we talked to a couple we became surrounded by smiling waitresses! They insisted we try this food and that. The Dragon Fruit was the best I have ever had.

We toured and saw a lot of military museums and where some bombing had taken place. We saw where John McCain landed in the lake after being shot down. We toured and saw Ho Chi Minh laying in state.

Then we went to the Hoa Lo prison, as we called it, "The Hanoi

Hilton". One of my friends was a 6 1/2 year POW. He talked freely about his experience in the prison. Most of us did not talk about our time in Vietnam during the war. My friend did so, saying that if he could tell one person who had the power to never let something like that happen again, he would talk. We had talked so much that I had a graphic picture of how it was there. Our guide had a Masters Degree in teaching but found being a guide paid a lot more. He knew I had a PhD so he allowed me to dispute him.

When we walked in I saw some very disturbing things. I saw the "typical" cell. I told the guide that was not correct. He started to argue and said something about the history books. I interrupted him and said, "The french were in Vietnam for 77 years. Your history book has a chapter dedicated to the French War! The "American War" has only three long paragraphs! This is how the cell was set up for Jane Fonda's visit!" Our discussion moved to a learning moment. We both learned something. The most disturbing thing was not the photographs, it was the French Guillotine! After the French left, the Vietnamese understood the fear and power of the Guillotine so for years they used it to maintain fear.

There is not much left of what was a sprawling prison. Most of the prison beyond the front has been torn down to make way for apartments.

We flew down over what was the DMZ (Demilitarized Zone) that marked the area between North and South Vietnam. We landed in Hue (pronounced 'way'). It was considered the Provincial Capital of South Vietnam. It is where the Nguyen (pronounced 'wen') dynasty ruled. The walled compound was where the Nguyen dynasty were buried. There was a lake and beautiful burial sites and impressive headstone. It was a true history lessen.

I still have problems from my exposure to Agent Orange. While we were walking through the compound I got some severe stomach cramps. There was a guide at a large counter at one of the open overhangs. We asked him where the nearest bathroom was? He said the bathrooms were closed, I would have to go back outside the compound! That was near a mile away! I would have big problems if I had to go that far! We tried but he held true. So I told my guide that the guy must have a facility nearby, he is not going all the way out as he said we have to. We finally won the argument and was pointed to a very old and small outhouse behind the building.

I barely made it! The little one-seater had a lot of stuff stored in it. As soon as I sat down there was a thumping against my leg! I had no idea what it was so I grabbed a wood board they stored in there and used it to block the animal, snake, whatever, and herded him into a corner. When I was finished I opened the door so enough light to see what it was. It was a poisonous dart frog! He had made contact with my skin but I was apparently lucky, it would have been a bad thing if his poison got to me.

From our hotel we could look down at the "Perfume River". It is actually the Hue River but one time there was a typhoon that uprighted many trees upstream. They floated down and many piled up at a sharp turn in the river. The trees had a sweet smell to them. Before they were able to break up the trees the river was fondly named the Perfume River and that name stuck.

We saw a lot, visited shops, etc. But the Nguyen Dynasty compound made everything else kind of ho hum. It was there that I learned I was wrong in many ways with the Vietnamese language I learned many years prior while eating fish heads and rice with the housemaids. I thought I was saying "hello" to the women but now found out the Vietnamese will use a term like "great uncle" to a man. My "hello" was actually "Great aunt"! That was an eye opener of how many mistakes I made, but also what I did remember was well pronounced!

Hue was so beautiful and when we left we drove down through China Beach and Da Nang. We stopped for lunch at this little restaurant near where across the street they were making lawn figurines and larger statues, very beautiful. When we went to eat we were taken to a small room with a table and chairs while our driver and guide ate with the locals. I would have loved to eat with them but we were told special people got served privately. A young possibly brother and sister were our servers, he spoke some broken English but apparently she was either too shy to talk or didn't. We ordered mostly by pointing at the menu, even though I think that made no difference, we were going to get what they wanted us to eat. Again, we have been to a lot of places and liked the foods, and this was good also.

The young teenage girl had her phone out and we found out from her brother that they had never seen an American couple up close, only at a distance! I believe the girl snuck our picture and I know she called her friends because just about the time our food had been served and we were starting to eat a group of about 7 young teenage girls were staring at us through the big window-like opening out onto the second floor balcony and walkway! We tried to talk to them but it was mostly big eyes, cute little giggles covered up by hands, and a lot of head nodding when we talked. The Vietnamese culture is when the person is talking, head nodding is not necessarily understanding or saying you understand, it merely acknowledges that you are speaking. Quite an experience and cute to see that like kids all over the world, the phone is an important object!

We drove on down through to Qui Nhon. We stayed in a beautiful hotel right on the South China Sea. Very tranquil. I needed that because the next day we were going to Phu Cat where I was stationed for a year.

This happened to be the only sour note of the trip. Don't know if they misunderstood, or what. We were greeted at the regional airport and the airfield manager was under the impression Peggy and I were there to see if the airport was good enough to fly in and out of! When I started toward where I used to work, they stopped me. I probably could not have seem much anyway because all the buildings had mostly been abandoned years before. I still wanted to see it, but we were escorted off the airport. I did look to the south and there was the same prayer tower I saw for a year.

I didn't have any tragic emotion as we thought might happen. We had booked a night following on Han Tre Island, a resort. We believed it would give me a chance to relax if I had problems. I didn't, but it was a nice day of relaxation. While there we saw the restaurant had American hamburgers! Peggy got hers and asked for mayonnaise. They brought some on a piece of foil. I warned her not to eat warm mayo, she ignored me and the next day she was sick with a mild case of food poisoning!

She was able to travel to Cam Rahn Bay where we caught a flight to Saigon (Ho Che Minh City). We stayed in the hotel that night and the next day she was doing much better but not good enough for the Cu Che tunnels! She stayed in the hotel and I went with the guide to the tunnels.

So much propaganda! There was a picture of Troops running through a stream. The caption read that the Vietnamese were such a feared force the American ran from the Vietnamese! Their movie presentation and more pictures all heavily put down the American. I walked out. We went to the tunnels and saw all the traps along the way. There were false ground areas that if you stepped on it you would impale yourself on sharp wooden stakes! They had traps that sprung up with panels having long spikes protruding! And more.

When we got to the tunnels I saw the diagrams of the areas within that were expanded to form space for tables, etc. You still had to crawl through the tunnel to get to the habituated areas. They said they widened the tunnels for us Americans, but I didn't believe it. Between the stories from the "Tunnel Rats", the Americans who volunteered to go in the tunnels after the enemy, and my cautious claustrophobia, I started in one tunnel and then backed out after maybe 10-20 feet! I could not handle it.

The next day we made it to the Mekong Delta. We went upriver and saw things like the shrimp harvesting, the majority of farm raised shrimp in the world comes from Vietnam. We went ashore and met vendors holding snakes, monkeys, etc. for the guests to get their pictures taken with, for a price. We rode a small sampan down this very narrow river cut out of the jungle. We had lunch at the end. Very interesting. I did not think the Dragon Fruit was as good as in Hanoi, it wasn't as sweet and was quite a bit less juicy. Then back to the hotel.

We walked out of the hotel and went to cross the street. There was a British couple there on this side. He was tall and she much shorter and was hugging his arm, visibly shaking! They said they didn't know how to get across the street. No problem, we will show them how. It looked difficult, more so than usual as this was the Universal Day of the Woman! Everybody was out on the road. Motorcycles had as many as five people on one bike! This is going to be testy.

With the couple behind us, we stepped slowly into the traffic lane! We didn't get hit! Very slowly we took baby steps across the three lanes of traffic. At the other side the woman was crying, she was still shaking and scared. No matter how much you helped her realized we had just crossed one of the busiest streets in one of the biggest holidays, without any problem, it still didn't calm her.

Peggy and I crossed a few more streets so we could go shopping and made it back unscathed. We saw the British couple in the hotel and asked how they did? Not so well. They made it to the next block with us but then were still too scared to do it again. They visited a couple shops on the block and to get across the street to the hotel, they hired a taxi to take them around the block to get back across the street!

We flew over to Cambodia and stayed in a hotel very near the Angkor Watt. At the hotel we ate on a patio looking down at the street. It was very busy and I remarked to Peggy that it looked like a lot of Americans in the crowds. We also had fun looking at all the Geckos all over the wall behind us! We slept under the nets that night. I had a chance to do some shopping there and I walked in on a former American Soldiers sitting in the store with a Cambodian woman. Appears many that got out of the Service found both the cost of living inexpensive and the women very friendly.

At the Angkor Watt you could not help being impressed! In the Buddhist practice everything is an odd number, i.e. 1-3-5-7 etc. In front of the Angkor Watt you could see the 5 spires atop the compound. We had to dodge through and around many large black elephants before we started down the large path to the temple. Our guide knew I had a PhD and that I was versed in Buddhism. When we started down the path he stopped and pointed a at a small but impressive building to the right. "Doctor Brown, If you were here during the time it was in use, you would be in that building. It is the library!" You had to understand Buddha was not a god, he was an educator.

The compound was huge. The guide told us the three doors entering the compound were for Educators and important people through one. Workers and common people through another. And the last was for elephants, livestock, etc. Inside the buildings were taken over by time and large rubber trees growing over and through the walls. Carvings in the stone were everywhere. He showed us the only woman's face on a wall that showed teeth! The small engraving in the thousands all had mouths shut, except that one. You could see the history and read stories made by etching in the rock walls, The stairs up to higher floors all showed massive wear and tear. The large corridors through the buildings showed wear on the support columns and walls.

The guide knew I was very learned in Buddhism. As we walked down a large hall and back into an open area, he looked around a corner and turned back to stop me. "Doctor Brown, I hope you are prepared for this". We rounded the corner and across an open area there was the steps leading up to another building. On the area above the stairs were two Monks and the "Wheel of Nirvana"! I could not believe my eyes.

In Buddhism it is believed to be seven personal attributes that if achieved would bring lasting self peace, Nirvana. Those seven attributes are represented in a wheel with seven spokes. I was looking at a Wheel of Nirvana! I talked with the Monks, mostly through our guide. They understood my knowledge and spoke softly to me. They led me to it so I could touch it. I was holding it with both hands. The monks stepped a little closer and put their hands on my shoulders. The said something that resembled a mantra. Something came over me and I felt a peace I have never felt before. I get heavily involved in my TM, but this was a different peace. I will never forget it.

We finished in the buildings and left the Compound. We went to some outlying buildings. Impressive in a much smaller way. We learned a lot. And our guide was so great. He saw that Peggy did not have the understanding I have. I think when I was talking to the monks our guide could see Peggy was basically left out. All the years I have learned could not be explained in a couple sentences so Peggy could understand, and appreciate. So the guide talked to her and showed her some other stuff. He was very respectful to her.

We flew to Bangkok and flew up to Chiang Mi on the Burma (Myanmar) border. All Other times in Bangkok, except when we spent dad's money, we usually traveled south toward Phuket. This time we went north, All the buildings were similar to Bangkok with all the gold. We saw so much stuff. We were leaving one palace and we saw the "Diamond Factory" across the way from us. Our guide took us there and we didn't want to leave! We asked about some particular stones and jewels, we were told the Factory in Bangkok had a lot more selection.

The next day we went to see an Elephant Training Center and watched the elephants perform. The Mahout stays with the elephant for life. If the elephant has a calf the Mahout's son will grow us with the new one, for life. We got on one and rode through the jungle for a long time. We emerged out of the jungle and into the river. We rode the elephant up to a restaurant where we parted ways. We ate at the restaurant and we questioned by the servers about our use of chop sticks! Where they use them mostly to push food into their mouth from the dish, we learned while in Japan to pick up food. We had a good time with them.

Now we were going to take a raft down the river we had recently come up on an elephant. The two pole pushers guided us down the river, We encountered young people wading out to the raft with floating displays of food and trinkets to sell. At one point we came up on some grazing elephants and one black one started aggressively toward us in the water! He was huge! The pushers were able to slap the water and yell enough for him to back away and we went down to our waiting guide.

He said he had two things all the older guest wanted, cold bottles of water and a ride back to the hotel. We said we were not ready to go to the hotel yet, but his plan was to drop us off and do something else. Okay! But could we stop at the Diamond Factory first? We were there for a while and bought some pieces. So when he dropped us off we went to the desk and got one of their tours, we weren't ready to act like old people!

The next day we decided to go over to the Palace and some of the museums. When we got downstairs there was a crowd waiting in line for the concierge. We didn't want to wait so I walked up to the side of the desk and simply asked if someone could tell us where the nearest Water Taxi station was? The man stopped what he was doing, smiled widely, and yelled at one of the staff. They were so excited an American was taking the Water Taxi they provided us free transport to the station!

We boarded the Water Taxi and headed down the river. Peggy was playing with two young boys. They had looked at us like we were aliens, but when Peggy started playing some silly game with them and they acted like kids around the world. One of the boys hugged her as we were getting off. The Palace station was like most with two distinct paths to take. At the top of the ramp you could go left into the souvenir shops or right where locals passed freely. We went right and saw a restaurant sitting on the pier. Everything was open, you could see the open kitchen. It smelled great. We got maybe the best Pad Thai and Coconut shrimp ever! A Canadian couple walked by and stopped to question why we would eat at such an unhealthy place? We laughed and pointed toward the locals eating there. "They are not dead, so the food is edible. And it is great!"

This trip was therapeutic and did clear some of the skeletons from my soul because of what happened in 1967/68 in Vietnam. Peggy with me as she should be. She could not imagine someone fighting a war in the conditions she saw, but on the other hand she understood better what was taking this extreme mental toll on me. Was I better for doing it? Hell yes, many times over. Vietnam was and still is to me one of the most beautiful places in the world. The people are friendly and helpful, the sights spectacular. But most of all I got to share it with the woman who married me less than two months before I was there fighting. The woman who stuck with me through all the mental problems I had, and some I still do. Simply speaking, I would be dead now if I didn't have that commitment to her in the late '60s. I believe that loving support was a medicine that helped me through Agent Orange problems and my severe depression. I love you Peggy!

We flew back to Texas the next day.

I was having major problems with"trailer trash" and her boss. She put everybody down with her raspy voice and I had asked her to please have some respect for my qualifications and education. She just thought she was cute and could get away with it, until she said in Staff Meeting that we had a survey to complete and that she knew it was a stupid report because a stupid PhD wrote it! I asked in a slightly raised voice that I have a PhD and believe her comments were abusive and please keep such comments to herself. Her response was, 'Who gives a fuck about a stupid PhD, all PhDs are stupid!" At least when my mother called me stupid it was not nearly as nasty like the chain smoker sounding raspy voice of "trailer trash"! I filed a formal complaint on her and we went before an Arbitrator. We both had seconds, mine a close friend, her's one of her minions.

I presented my case and when she was to answer to it she said she could not be touched! When I asked her if she did or did not call me a "Fucking stupid PhD?" she refused to answer. The Arbitrator said she was required to answer! She repeated she could not be touched! Finally the question of why, and she answers that she had already been disciplined for her language so that was not admissible! In the end, she won, and my life was just starting to get worse.

I was already doing my old boss' work while he was there and still after he left. His job was posted and my resume was submitted. So were others like the guy at Austin Energy that I know they wanted to get rid of at AE. His claim to fame was a related degree that was fluff, especially to my four degrees in EH&S. He was not a good speaker, had minimal experience in planning, but was good at making PowerPoint Presentations! So was I but I didn't see a need for them at my interview.

He got the job! I protested but was told he got it because of his

PowerPoint presentation! I asked where in the job description does it say he has to have good PowerPoint skills? The response was to ask me why I hadn't brought my PowerPoint presentation?

After a couple weeks he was driving me crazy! He was on a ego trip and trying to undermine what I was doing. One of my longtime friends, a safety guy at one of the departments, told me my new boss had come down and said he was new manager! My friend was supposed to tell him everything I did when I came there, and not to listen to my direction now, he was my boss!

I went looking for work and answered a job posting for Lawrence Berkeley National Labs! I took vacation and did two serious interviews for the position as Director of Safety for the Labs. I was a grilled and knew I did well. When I came back again for what I thought was another finalist interview, I was met with sturdy handshakes and slaps on the back! I realized I was the candidate of choice! The top lady came out and we went to a quiet place. She said she knew the interviewers from all departments wanted to hire me, as she did, but not for this position. What bothered her was this position had about 30 people reporting to the position. I had never had that many direct reports! #2 and #3 candidates had managed that number so she was going to pick one of them. However, she was creating a position for the new Nanotechnology Lab that she wanted me to run it! It should take not more than four months and I would take over the Safety for the Nano-technology Lab at the same salary of the big position! Good, that was enough time to put my plan in place.

I contacted Procurement and stated that I was already doing a lot of the training they were contracting for. We talked bout Ergonomics, Accident investigation, and a couple more that I could, and in some cases did teach. It ended up we could cancel near a half million dollars in contracts! I was assured, they were long term contracts that now would cost a lot more to renegotiate! I said I could do the work and the contracts were cancelled.

I put on my teaching brain and wrote scripts and program elements such that a simple person, safety or not, would not have trouble with understanding and executing. I started teaching the classes and was told I had saved the City a lot of money! Then I told boss "dipshit" that he might want to sit in on my training in case I could not be available, we had the responsibility now. He first sat in on the Ergonomic class, the one I taught while sitting on an exercise ball. I just happen to know he could not balance on the ball, nor did he understand the science behind what I was doing. In other words, he could not teach the class!

A couple days later I brought in my own computer and ran the Accident Investigation class. He was not in the entire class, he had areas he didn't understand so we would talk later. Since I had been teaching as an Adjunct Professor and Associate Visiting Scholar for a couple Universities, I understood the different between using my computer versus plugging a drive into their computer. Plugging into theirs allowed them to have all your presentation and notes whereas by using my equipment I still owned it! Later when I asked him if he wanted to sit in on the class again he claimed he had work to get done and patronizingly that he was not needed, I was doing a great job. I actually started laughing when he left the area. God, I felt devious!

Since the shooting in San Diego I had been writing and teaching about Workplace Violence. My part in the book one of the psychiatrists had authored was okay, but I felt a need for more. When I spoke to groups I talked about the entire spectrum to include Diffusion Techniques but I could feel the knowledge was there but it lacked a verification that would happen from possibly a Police Officer. So I went to see my new police friends and one name popped up just about every time, Scott Stephens, a cop. I talked to Scott and found he was already doing Evacuation and Threat Assessment of City facilities. For example; he worked with a City group that filled four floors of a building. The people worked closely with the public and apparently there had been a situation where an employee was threatened by the visitor! It showed how ill prepared the department was. After training, the people had a signal code they could use so others in the building could react, and they were able to evacuate the entire building in less than 3 minutes!

Very impressive! The building became the Poster Child of what an evacuation program was. I believe they even got an award for that.

We started working together, me assisting him on some risk assessment audits and him taking a progressive role in Workplace Violence training. Soon I got us a gig and we ended up teaching all over the US, often for International Conferences. He added credibility to the defusing scenario and also the different threats and what actions people could expect from Police with each scenario. We spoke for a few City Management Teams and for the American Society of Safety Engineers (ASSE) and the National Safety Council (NSC) across the States. He could not join me in Alaska where I presented and taught a couple topics as an Adjunct for the University of Alaska, Anchorage.

When the ignorant one took over I found it funny that since he was so great and did so much, it was harder for me to take a day or two off to teach! Speaking of the sorry soul, I was getting ready for the word from Lawrence Berkeley. I was getting updates from the secretary at the Labs. It was a slow but certain process. There was no doubt I had the job but waiting for the new Lab was tricky. I didn't want to spring it on too soon or say anything that might get back to the HR Department, so I told nobody, just bidding my time. I grew increasingly angry every day at the stupidity, ignorance, and incompetence. I wanted out. Problem was that Peggy didn't really want to go back to the Bay Area but I convinced her I would make enough money to live in a very nice area in Berkeley.

I had kept in touch with some of the EH&S Recruiters and I was home at our place in Cedar Park. One of the recruiters contacted me and said there was a company interested in me and wanted to talk to me. I explained to her that I already had a job on the horizon and was not interested. She told me that was a very bad attitude, you never turn down an interview, if for nothing else it was good experience and maybe would be something. She said the President wanted to talk to me! President of the Company? No, President of Construction within the Company. I said, "Shit, I don't want to go back into construction!"

Her response was, "Bad word, you owe me for that, I'm going to schedule the interview!" I agreed but planned on basically blowing off the interview.

I was in the kitchen with Peggy when the phone rang. We had a phone on the kitchen wall so I picked it up, it was a going to be a short call. Far from it, I was on the phone for one hour and ten minutes! When finished, I hung up the phone and Peggy was saying something to me when I shook my head and said, "I want to work for that man!" Peggy stated that I had never said that before and I responded that I have never talked to a man that really understood as he did! I've never worked for anyone like that.

He sent me tickets and I met with him. He was as great in person as on the phone! I wanted to work for him and soon after I got home I received the offer! Without hesitation I signed it and sent it back, notifying the hiring people I had to give a two week notice to my employer, the City. We set a date about three weeks from then to get my things picked up and start work. Now was the time for my plan to come to volition!

I had successfully cancelled four contracts where the City had contracts for safety and health services because I was there and could do the work. I also had a couple high level audits planned, plus a project for the Mayor and the City Manager. Oops, I was leaving! I put in my notice and then told the incompetent that he should have listened better in my classes, he hadn't been told yet that I was leaving. He asked why and I simply responded that it was his training now, I was leaving!

I have to hand it to him on one point, he actually admitted he could not do the training I was doing. He had never done it before and he just wasn't able to do the training. He was stunned and soon anger came out and he told me I couldn't go! Then he said I would have to find someone to do the training! I told him that he would have plenty of time to find someone to replace me after I was gone. If he could get approval for someone to replace me now I would have a few days to train them. He said that I would have to find a contractor to do the training! I told him it was a long approval process and Procurement had already told me to reinstate the contracts they would have to go out for bid and most likely would cost considerably more than original. The proposals would have to go to the City Manager for approval, adding it would probably take at least four months for that process.

I then said I would print out my commitment schedule. I suggested that one of the department safety reps was probably a lot smarter than he was at a couple things and maybe he can get help from him. He was getting pissed and said he would do something to make me stay to do my job! I told him that Texas was an "At-Will" employment state, meaning an employer could fire an employee at any time for almost any reason. The City made that a hard thing to do. It worked both ways and I was abiding by state law and was willingly terminating my employment with the City! Then "Trailer Trash" and her boss got very angry! She used very bad language! She actually threatened me, saying I did this on purpose! "what me, a stupid PhD?"

I left them, and even though I got respect from the Mayor, City Manager and all the department safety people I worked with, the send off from my department was nasty. The HR Manager tried to be social and courteous but ended up apologizing for the treatment I got from everybody else. He was acting sort of like he could offer me more money to stay. That was until he realized he was doing that and nastily walked away. I stopped by to see my Vietnam Veterans friends and bid ado. I was glad to leave.

39

Chapter 14

Los Angeles, California

Leaving Texas and finding myself in a place we had said we never wanted to go, Los Angeles, we found a rental on Venice Beach until we found a house to rent in Manhattan Beach, six blocks off the ocean and a really neat place. It was an old house, close to falling apart. The landlady kept half the detached garage for her storage. The garage was so small and old a car could not fit in it. Peggy kept her car in the driveway, mine on the street. The area was called the "Tree Area" and the road by our place went down, across, and back up in the alley behind the house. So it was like a dead end street with little traffic. However, the Doctor across the street was a terrible driver and didn't care about anything. I would find a dent in my car and nobody would say anything! My car, a 1992 Nissan 300ZX Twin Turbo, bright yellow, was struck so hard the last time I ended up selling it cheap. I was always in the air flying to one of our sites, so a $20 taxi ride to LAX alleviated my need to have a car, and I could fit my motorcycle in the garage. I had the biggest Harley Davidson Anniversary Edition but when it had major problems I traded it in for a new BMW like the ones we saw at the parade in Austin.

My office was in a building in West Hollywood and the Company had contracts all across the US, including Hawaii. I worked exceptionally well with my boss. the man I wanted to work for. We established mutual respect for each other as I did so much more and much better than my predecessor. I went to all our sites, 64 around the US. We had government contracts that required specific Site Safety and Health Plans, and some specific Site Accident Prevention Plans, and more. I created baseline reports for both Government and Commercial projects where I researched all the information, talked with Project Managers and Site Superintendents. I reviewed construction plans, blueprints, state and local laws and directives. I had the entire EM385 (Corps of Engineers Safety Directive) on my I-Pad! I was prepared for all of the creation of Plans. I was even instrumental in getting the word "Accident" removed from use because of its effectiveness!

To explain; we were finding in Safety that new people were not taking accidents as something that could harm or hurt you! For instance; a kid is running through his house and he knocks over a vase and it crashes in pieces to the floor! He is upset, maybe even crying, but everything is almost magically good again because his mother is there, holding him and saying, "Its okay, it was just an accident!" So now an accident means nothing to worry about. So I proposed a solution to some fellow PhDs and others, coming up with the use of the words "Incident" and/or "Mishap". Slow but sure we changed the wording and we could do Incident Investigations and Mishap Prevention Plans, etc. and be talking serious prevention.

I will add at this moment that I grew up with a mother calling me "Stupid" and well after she passed I have my sister and her husband carrying that banner. I was explaining to them once about the name change when we were visiting their house. The response was her husband looking up from his computer "That's stupid, it means the same thing" and my sister laughing along with him and saying,"That is really stupid"! Guess the rotten apple doesn't fall far from the tree.

I met with all the managers at all levels, including the big President. I was at a site when he showed up. John was a soft spoken man but could show you he meant business and also show his savvy intelligence. We were getting ready to walk into an area where hard hat and safety glasses were required. Just as we started to walk in I handed the Site Superintendent a couple pairs of Safety Glasses to put in his jacket pocket. We were maybe 100 feet into the building as a group when John pulled off his Safety glasses to look at something and then continued to walk on without his glasses on. I quietly said so everyone that could hear would say I was being polite. I said to the Site Super "Do you still have a pair of Safety glasses John can have?" The Site Super pulled out a nice pair and handed them to John! He put them on and looked at me, nodding his head. At the end of the tour he handed the glasses to me and asked, "Are you always so nice about compliance, or was it just me?" We laughed and he said he could see why Bill hired me. I told him the glasses he got were special glasses, not the cheap ones we get for normal visitors! So if he wanted to keep them, he could. He smiled and said he would pay for them. I told him not to worry, he already did pay for them!

Supervisors and I got along well because I supported them. I was there when they needed me. I remember one of the projects we were doing I got a call from the Regional Manager who was on site telling me that OSHA was at the door! One of the subcontractors that we had to let go decided he was going to call OSHA with a complaint about Safety! So the OSHA inspector was there! I told the manager to ensure nothing was said, the site super was famous for bragging about what he had done on the site. The inspector was to tell them what the complaint was and if he would not wait until I got there, I was in California and this was Colorado, the Site Super was to ensure the inspector was to be taken outside the building and then to where the hazard was, no where else. Then immediately back out. No way was he to be allowed to walk through the facility!

I got there the next morning and found the inspector in the middle of our facility writing stuff in his notes! What the hell happened, I asked the Regional Manager? He said he told the Site Super and the Super laughed at him and said something like this was his site! When the OSHA Inspector started taking about the complaint the Super starting telling him about this multi-million dollar project and what he was responsible for. Then he took the Inspector for a tour of the site!

I went into the site and walked up to the group. One of the guys said that the Company Safety Manager was here. The Inspector turned, stared at me for a bit, "Dr Brown, I didn't know this was yours!" We started talking and it was quite evident he was star struck by my presence. I looked at the list he had. I told him I had identified all the problems he had seen. I had all the site reports and corrective actions identified. I would show him when we got back to the trailer. He said it was good if I could just send him the response to the complaint showing it was taken care of. I told him the complaint came from a disgruntled contract employee we had dismissed. We talked for a bit, he shook my hand and said it was an honor to meet and work with me. Then he left. The Regional Manager and I ascended on the site super and chewed his ass for disobeying my orders and that of the Manager, He wised off and told me I had no right to talk to him on his site. I told him when OSHA comes I am his boss! The Manager suspended him for what was a few days. Then the Manager looked at me and asked what the hell had just happened? I told him I was the second person in the world to be awarded the Award of Excellence by the Board of Certified Safety Professionals and the OSHA guy knew it. He "respected" me for the achievement, that was what we were talking about in our little conference. He asked if OSHA did that often? I said I was somewhat used to it, many of the OSHA Inspectors I personally trained. I had quite a reputation. I was known as one who did it right. I sent the response to the inspector and never heard another word from him.

One of the big managers was in a meeting with my boss. The discussion was about a project we were doing and they worried if the team they set up would do it right? The guy said my boss spoke up and asked if my name was on the team? He was told yes. He responded that if I was on the team he knew it would be done right.

I did a lot of construction safety before but you always have some guys who have been constructors for years that don't respect anyone. One of those was a Regional Manager who I thought didn't want me around. I was at a site on the East Coast and one of our subcontractors was setting up scaffolding while I was there. I saw it and asked him who was the "Competent Person" on his crew? He responded that he was the boss and he was competent, adding he knew a lot more about scaffolding than I did! I told him I doubted that, especially since a Competent Person was a person designated by the company to have experience, training and the authority to shut down the erection if something was wrong. If he didn't know that I could only guess I knew more than he did about scaffolding. When he shouted back at me I just simply called the Site Superintendent over and told him to take the individual off the site! He was fired and the owner of the company would have to send a Competent Person to replace him, or the contract was void.

He started yelling and threatening me. I hadn't noticed the Regional Manager was there. The guy told him he wanted me out! He told the Manager that he knew the Manager was in charge and only he could kick me off the site! The Manager looked at him and said he was sorry. Correct, he was the big person in charge, however when I was on site I was the most powerful man with the company on site and that he answered to me and not me to him! He nodded to the Site Super and said to do what I had said and to walk the man off the site. If he chose to come back for any reason, call the police! I guess I had the manager all wrong, we worked together well after that.

So many things happened with the company, so I'l highlight a couple. One day I was at the office, a rare thing because I was flying more than 150,000 "Domestic" air miles a year! My boss stuck his head in and asked if I was here for the day? Yes. Then he said "Let's go" and we headed for the garage and his SUV. Where are we going? San Diego. What are we doing there? Wanted to see the projects and talk to some of the people. I laughed, "You just wanted a carpool dummy!" adding he could have called one of the project managers there. We had five or six projects going on. So on the way we talked and he asked me if I had any airline frequent flyer points? Yes, and named specifically three airlines I had more tan 300,000 air miles with. He suggested I pick one as my favorite and accumulate all the miles with them and get better Status. I did and chose Delta as my airline of choice.

Soon Delta took notice and when they started Frequent Flyer Forums in many of their main hubs, I was asked to join the LAX Flyers

Forum. We met every month and at first it was to tap our minds at what other airlines did that made them special. Then Delta started changing for the good. The leader of our Forum was the Senior Vice President for Marketing and he encouraged us to talk. We had a very lively group and I remember one heavy traveler said she heard me suggest something and saw what I was getting at and she would join in and elevate it into very viable options. I fed off her also as did many of the members jump in and we were very productive.

Delta showed their appreciation with many of us on the Forum being invited to special events Delta was sponsoring. One time we went to an Emmy party in which the singer "Lorde" performed. Peggy was close enough to touch her and once when she flipped her hair around she struck Peggy and a couple others with her hair!

At the same Hollywood party. I was standing there talking with a senior pilot friend of mine when three of the Flight Attendants I knew walked up and waited to interrupt. I asked which one of us they wanted to talk to and it was me! They said they knew of nobody as calm and able to do things nobody else could do. I stopped them and said that was enough foreplay, what did they need? They motioned over toward a bar that was not in use and the two women standing there leaning on it talking. The girl on the left was Julianne Hough! They said she blew them off when they asked for a picture. Okay, okay. I walked over to Julianne and stood in front of her. She looked briefly at me, I nodded but said nothing. She then said she was not signing autographs. Told her I didn't want an autograph. When I didn't move she asked what I wanted and I moved closer to her, slightly turned and pointed toward the three Flight Attendants. I told her that first, these were some of the greatest people I know, and if I didn't get a picture of them with her, I might get my butt kicked! All they wanted was a picture with her. She immediately said no pictures, but I didn't move. Finally she said okay and turned, put her arm around me and posed. I stopped her, "No, No, No, this is for the ladies, not me, I am just the negotiator!" The three had their picture taken with her.

These weren't the only perks. Soon I had enough status that 97% of the time I was upgraded to First Class on the flights. I forgot to mention that I have never been star struck so it has never been a problem with me. Peggy said one of the doctors on TV said that people like me who grew up like I did were always trying to prove themselves better. We were borderline or actual Narcissist! Yes, I am borderline but never mistreated anybody nor put them down to raise me up.

When Delta merged with Northwest the transition was not always the smoothest. I was standing in front of the overhead board in front of the departure gate when a woman came up to me and asked how come the flight was delayed? I glanced at her and told her the pilots were taken for an old Northwest flight. The backup crew was called in, should be here in about 20 minutes. She asked if I was a pilot? No, just a very frequent flyer. She said okay and that she was going to go get a newspaper and was sure they wold call her when the flight was ready. I simply asked if she thought calling her name might be a problem? She said, "Hell, I have been famous for a long time!" and added it didn't bother her. As she stepped away, four guys jumped up and offered her their newspapers.

When she returned I was standing at the head of the Priority boarding lane by myself. I was talking to Peggy using my wireless ear piece. Cybill Shepherd walked up to stand beside me and started talking about I must really know this flying business. I raised my hand and pointed to the ear piece and kept talking to Peggy, I didn't tell her I was standing with Cybill. When I finished with my call I apologized and told her I was talking to my boss, my wife. I don't know if this is her standard practice but immediately within the first minute she was talking about her two German Sheppards that the "Dog Whisperer" Cesar, had trained. I really didn't care to hear that so I said, "He wouldn't touch my pet". She asked what I had? So I opened up my I-Pad or laptop to my pictures. I showed her a picture with Peggy, me, and a giraffe! The giraffe had her head between us and resting against my shoulder and head! It happened at the San Diego Wild Animal Park. It was verified this was the first time the giraffe did that to anyone! Cybill didn't believe me! I told her the picture was real, not photoshopped. It broke the ice. We talked like normal people and talked a little on the plane. You could see it in everyone's eyes wondering who that talking like a friend with Cybill Shepherd?

I sat next to Allison Stoner for about five hours. I told my daughters and granddaughters when I got home and I was chewed out by the girls for not getting an autograph! I sat next to ODB, the world champion female wrestler. She was okay. I sat next to this very nice guy with a beard, AJ from the Back Street Boys.

I talked with many stars. Again, not being starstruck I had no problem just talking with them. Possibly the one I will never forget was a party sponsored by Porsche and Delta at a Hollywood mansion in the hills. Peggy and I were up on the top level where the pool was and a half floor to the side rose a barbecue area on the top level. It was a small area. I was talking with one lady from the Forum and her sister, both past beauty queens. John Stamos stepped up and while the ladies started giggling and watching, I shook John's hand and, calling him John, i started talking with him. We talked a few minutes as John and Bruce, him finally saying the young ladies seemed to be having a good time. I agreed and told him they were really great ladies. He asked if I lived with them? Oh no, my wife is down by the pool, just a few feet away. He responded that I hadn't introduced her to him and I motioned for him to follow. I introduced him to Peggy, "John, my wife Peggy. Peggy this is John" and they talked a couple minutes before starting to go back down. A firm handshake and partial man-hug, a hug for Peggy and we followed him and his entourage down the stairs. He went right, we went straight and after a few steps I said to Peggy, "Now you can tell the girls you met John Stamos!" I did?! And I was chewed out for not calling him John Stamos, just John! She didn't recognize him and I am a very bad person for saying only "John"!

I met a lot more celebrities, talked to most of them. Back to the job. My boss kept me posted on everything. With the bonuses and pay increases I was making a lot of money! At the Porsche and Delta gathering I drove there in my new Racing Yellow 981! My boss had me doing a lot of management stuff. He would ask me to step up above my Safety position and take care of management problems since I was traveling there. Then came a real big ask.

He called me up on a Friday night and asked how soon I could be in Hawaii? Who am I supposed to meet? I knew the Army Corps of Engineers (COE) top dog on site so I knew I had to fly over Sunday too catch Walt coming in early. If later, he would be busy and ignore me the rest of the day! I heard something but still asked what happened. Simply, one of our subcontractors was using a building ventilation system to exhaust fumes. It could be done if the pressure was set on low and did not exceed the capacity of the piped or exhaust system. Something happened and there were complaints of toxic smelling gas in the working area! The Site Super and the Regional Manager were there but said they had corrected the problem. They were not going to test the system. The COE guy wrote a "Cure" Letter, which meant we had a date to fix or "Cure" the problem or the contract would be null and void! We would be kicked off the site!

I asked my boos what he wanted me to do? His response, "Fix It!"

I flew over on Sunday with a scheduled return flight on Wednesday evening. I met Walt at 7:30 in the morning and we talked. He went through the problem and said both the Regional Manager and Site Manager had said they fixed the problem but would not check the exhaust system. Walt stated there was a toxic odor in the building the next day after my guys said they had fixed it. I told him I would report my findings and then I left for our trailer.

Both Managers were there and started asking what I planned to do? I said I was told to "Fix It" and I would. It told the Regional Manager to move his operation into another area, told the Site Manager to send out a request for a teleconference with all the Subcontractors, I would be leading the meeting. We had the meeting a short time later and I explained I was now in charge and I was halting all work for a day in the area of concern. One Sub protested and said she would have to have that in writing from the Regional Manager, then hung up! I told the manager to fax a message to her and he started saying I was not to tell him what to do, he was in charge! I challenged him to take it up with my boss, which was his boss also. He realized he would lose that battle, so under protest he sent the fax to the sub.

I took the Site Manager with me to the facility and he took notes. I interviewed the sub who had over pressurized the system. We discussed why and who was responsible for lasting corrective actions. I interviewed all the people in the section and others in the adjoining work spaces. Our Site Manager was flabbergasted! He said he had no idea the extent of the failure and asked how I had gotten so good at investigations? I spent the rest of the day and Tuesday doing physical inspections and double checking my hypothesis. I felt my investigation was as complete as possible. Then I tried to set up a meeting with Walt for early Wednesday to make sure I had time to catch my flight back to California. That night I visited with some of my good Hawaiian friends and packed my bag, planning to check out in the morning.

Walt asked me to meet him at one of the nice trailers on site so I could discuss our actions with some key people running the site. The first thing I told him was we were not going to do a complete systems check, even though I knew he had insisted we do it. I explained that through my investigation, handing out copies, that I believed there was no loss of any integrity. A functional check verified my findings. I went through all the elements of the problem, and what I had instituted as corrective actions, lasting corrective actions, along with my summary of the investigation.

I then addressed his assumption of a second malfunction, assuring him it had nothing to do with our operation. He protested! I told him what my investigation reveled. He told me to continue. I told him that two of his maintenance people had opened a door onto a lower roof, placed some metal panels out there and spray painted them there instead of taking them to their maintenance facility. They had propped them up on the air conditioning unit and spray painted them there! This action allowed fumes to be sucked into the ventilation system and through the open access door. He asked me if I could variety that? I showed him my notes, only to him, of the identified maintenance work-ers and the names and location of the witnesses! He was part upset, angry, and somewhat blown away because some of those same people had blamed my company for the fumes released into the work area.

He dismissed the meeting and told the others he had to discuss some stuff with me. We talked but he did not reveal any action he was going to take for or against us. He did offer some problems he had with both the Regional and Site Managers! He told me what he had and that he would show me the next day. He also asked if it was possible to discuss some other stuff with me the next day. I told him I would have to change my return to Thursday evening if he wished me to stay another day. He asked if I could do that. I contacted Delta and was able to change flights. I went back to the Hilton and got the same room I had for another day. I changed and went downstairs to go next door for the best Mai Tai on the island! As I was walking I was talking to my boss on my cell phone.

I told him some of the stuff Walt spoke of that both our mangers were doing or had done. It wasn't pretty nor professional. My boss wanted to argue with me, mainly because the Regional Manager had been with them for years and my boss didn't believe he would do that! He didn't defend our Site guy nearly as much. I raised my voice at him! That was something everybody knew not to do to my boss! It caught his attention and he said he would listen to me. I could tell that when I finished telling him he was not that pleased with me. He asked what I suggested he do and when I told him we were back to raised voices! I finally swore at him, nearly yelling it but not too loud to draw attention, and he listened. He asked if I could verify what I was saying? I told him Walt had promised me the records, he would give me copies the next day. We ended the call.

The next day when I got the copies, Walt and I stepped out on the patio and leaned on the wood railing, both of us looking across the parking lot toward the trees. It was as though we were two friends that maybe had just come back from trout fishing in the local stream, that comfortable. Neither looking at each other just discussing the things we wanted to discuss, both talking in a low, friend like voice. I went to the airport, turned in my rental and waited for my ride home across the Pacific.

I got home late and had a site meeting the following morning so I never made it into the office. I hadn't had time to discuss the trip with my boss yet but had sent him my report. I truly did not know what to expect when we did talk or meet as I had broken that unwritten rule and raised my voice at him. Two things with my boss, besides him being a really great guy and tremendous manger, he was not quick too stay "thank you"! He believed in why get thanked for doing the job you are being paid well for,? And secondly, you do not raise your voice at him. So I was shocked when he called me at home that Friday night and started it off with "Thank you, thank you so much"! When I asked, he told me that because of my taking over the site and fixing it, the Cure Letter was torn up! We were going to finish the contract! He said Walt was extremely impressed with what I did and that I had saved the company an $8 Million contract!

If you are wondering the outcome of my suggested actions against the Region and Site Managers, One was demoted and transferred, the other was relocated and told not to consider Hawaii as his territory! The subcontractor that demanded the letter from the Manager had been the wife of a close friend and I knew her well. Since then, she has not talked to me and my friendship deteriorated. I guess she thought I was not honoring our friendship, but I was doing my job and I treated her as the CEO of a company, not a friend.

We were an Engineering Company that decided to do some construction work. However Construction was becoming much bigger and me being the only Safety Professional in the Company I was infrequently asked to assist the Engineering side.

My boss called me in and I was asked if I could go to Egypt with a Senior VP from the Engineering side? They had designed a Water/ Wastewater plant on an Egyptian Air Base. They had finished the training of the operators and wanted me to train the Safety representative and do an audit of the facility. I teleconferenced with the Senior VP. I honestly did not like him, he had this "I'm greater than you are, and you are in Construction" attitude. I almost said no but knew I had to.

I flew from California to the East Coast and then on to Switzerland where we would meet and go together into Cairo. He was still a little aloof but we talked about the site while walking through the terminal. Of all places, I heard my name being called and there was a guy I hadn't seen in years, a friend when we were in the military! I remembered his name, we did a man hug. When I introduced the VP I was with, I introduced him as a Vice President with the Company. Before even shaking my friends hand, he announced rather obnoxiously, "I am a Senior Vice President" emphasis on SENIOR! My friend slowed a little, thought about it, then told me it was good seeing me again as he sort of rolled his eyes toward the VP. He said Good Luck, and maybe we will run into each other again one of these years! I think the action and his statement made it as though my friend was below his intellect. He never said a word nor even commented about me meeting an old friend in Switzerland. But that was only the start of his reign and my problems with him. It was going to be a very very long trip and I needed to make sure I didn't turn my back to him.

It started at the Cairo Sheraton when we checked in. The American representative of the project and his wife picked us up at the airport and we went straight to the hotel. I started walking to the check-in huge curved desk while I was talking to the wife and in doing so, the VP stepped in front of me and started to check in. He was telling the clerk that the US Sheraton hotels did not issue loyalty cards and that he was a loyalty member and wanted the perks. I stepped up when another clerk came to the computer next to him and asked if he could help me. I travel so much I have all the Airlines, Rental Cars and Hotel loyalty cards. I pulled out my Sheraton card and loudly stated here was my card! The look I got from the VP and the smirk across the face of his clerk was something to remember! I was definitely on the VP's shit list! The wife caught that and I could see I had a new friend. I also had a better room than the VP, which added additional venom.

With people like him I don't get bothered. I don't let them know the person they are treating as stupid has five college degrees. Not stupid. He either did not hear the desk clerk call me "Doctor Brown" or he was going to make a bigger point of his position. Having a PhD under his control was probably an ego thing for him, not a respect for the PhD.

So the first chance he got he started telling me that since he was a Senior VP and I wasn't, that over there he was my boss and he started to tell me what I was supposed to do! I mean starting right now! I looked at him and asked him how many layers of management does he have to go through to get to John? Never mind, I already know it is four layers for him. Whereas, my boss works directly for John and I work directly for my boss, so I have two layers, maybe one in many cases because I am a separate entity as Safety! I asked him if he reported to John as a direct report at all? End of conversation. I walked away and he stated loudly that if he wanted me to do something, I would do it! He nearly yelled that he was my boss over here. I continued walking.

At the site I talked with the Egyptian Site Manager and the safety rep who had minimal safety training not much more than basic. I was going to tour the facility with the Safety Rep and one of the supervisors. The VP said he thought that was not a good idea, he had stuff he wanted me to do. I told him I needed to see the facility and was going to do some training while at it. The VP said that was not possible, the Base Commander had just told him he didn't want any visitors in the Plant! The Rep and another worker laughed a little and motioned for me to come with them. As we walked outside the worker said the man with the bald head (the VP) was lying, the Base Commander was not on station today! He also questioned why the Commander would have said that? I hopped into one of the cars and four carloads of Egyptian workers, with me went to the site. I did an audit and training, then back to the assigned room in the on-base quarters. The wife cooked for us and we talked a little, I could relate as I had taken Peggy to many overseas locations.

The next day I had my overheads for the training for safety that all workers were to attend. I gave some training but turned most of it over to the Safety Rep and he trained as we had planned. The Manager was extremely mad at me and the VP jumped in on the ass chewing! He said I was supposed to do all the training and I was supposed to give them a test! I simply told them that was not going to happen! If I trained them and I represented Safety to the workers, then when I left so would the Safety Program. The Rep there had to be the face of safety or he would be ineffective with ensuring compliance or program management. I in turn, turned the program over to the person who owns it and has to foster it! The Manager did a slow burn but finally said he saw I was right, especially the fact if I was Safety to them and I left, his job and that of the Rep would be much more difficult. The VP still chewed on me, saying he should have had final approval on my overheads and he would have changed them dramatically! I just asked him how many degrees does he have in Safety, and answered before he could say anything, "I only have five degrees, four of them including the PhD are in Occupational Safety and Health Management and Engineering or Environmental Health and Safety Management! Plus I have about 45 years as a Safety Professional! He still said he was my boss and he would have had me do the training differently.

Then I asked what time the next day we were going back to Cairo and he said it would be late, not enough time for me to do anything. When we met a short time later with the American Manager and Site Manager, and VP for a tour of the area I mentioned something to the wife before we left. She smiled and said she would take care of that. A while later we had driven off the Base and soon were standing there watching the ships queuing up for the Suez Canal.

Back at the quarters after dinner, the wife came up to the VP and asked what time he wanted to go to Cairo, she hoped it was early because she had to pick up a prescription. She talked him into leaving early, and then snuck a wink at me when she walked by.

We left in the morning and I got some shopping done and we checked into the hotel again. The VP was still being an ass and I believe he was upset about me getting my way by coming back to Cairo early. So he throws another one at me. I already know he was not planning to get there until later, but he tells me he wants me to come with him, he is interviewing somebody. He was still thinking/acting like he was in control of me! That didn't work because I asked him if the person was going to be involved with Safety? He said no, so I responded loudly, "Well then you don't need me and I am going to pay too much for a taxi and too much for a camel to take me to the Pyramids of Giza!" As expected, a person was right there with his taxi outside, a nice Mercedes, and we went out to his taxi as I waved ado. The wife was nearby and actually laughing a little as she gave a little wave at me.

There is a meaning to my madness. If I took a regular taxi it would pick up fares along the route. A private, more expensive taxi would not pick up fares and would wait for me while I was on a camel. For the taxi and camel were both the equivalent of $60 each. I have been told most people were taken just to the pyramids and back. I never talked to anyone who walked onto the stones and very few said they went into the pyramid. I did both. And on the camel we went over and looked down on the Sphinx from the sand hills. Also by design, and why only $60 for the taxi, we stopped at a tea shop and gift shop as we went through the city back to the hotel. To go there and to do what I did was so very special. The Pyramids of Giza are one of the Seven Wonders of the world and no matter how I try to explain, there is this thing about seeing and touching, even riding a camel there that sparks your soul. The Sphinx is breathtaking.

There was still no respect between us and I know my boss would hear his side of the story, but I trusted my boss would understand. But for the time being, we flew to London Heathrow Airport and the VP, excuse me, the Senior VP, started telling me where I had to go! When we got on the train between terminals I immediately knew he was trying to get some vengeance back. I had been to Heathrow before and knew it was a mess, but also knew where I was supposed to go! When we got off at the terminal, I did a quick check and caught the train back to where we started. Don't know if he knew I had done that. I imagine he turned around to make sure I was following and I wasn't there! When

I saw my boss, he wasn't in the least bit surprised! We sort of laughed at how it came out between us, again not surprised. We both knew his brother was a commentator on TV and that pushed him poorly.

The Delta Flyers Forum from LAX was apparently one of only a couple remaining and we were told about 80% of the positive changes that took Delta to the top came from us! I went to a lot of events with Delta, almost all with Peggy by my side, except for the Forum meetings. At one gathering we were talking to Jaime and we told him this Anniversary trip. I take Peggy somewhere every year, usually overseas, for our Anniversary. This year we were flying to Australia for a day, then Aukland and catch a cruise around New Zealand and ending back in Sydney. We talked about other stuff. I saw the Senior VP for Marketing, now a good friend, was busy with other people. Peggy and I headed out to get our car from the Valet and just before we were to leave the room, our VP friend stepped in front of us and started talking.

"I heard you two are taking one of my 777 airplanes to Australia?" He then asked what my itinerary was? As I was telling him, Peggy speaks up and asks "Why? Are you doing something special for us?" "Maybe" and then we talked about my itinerary more when Peggy again interjected, "does that mean an upgrade?" He responded that was a possibility, and soon we finished talking, handshakes and hug and on our way to the Valet. While we were waiting for the Valet to bring the car around I told Peggy that we should not expect an upgrade. I explained I was using my miles, I paid $168 in taxes for Economy. I had checked fares and Business Class was about $4,000 a seat and First Class up to $7,000! He was probably not going to upgrade us.

A few days later I got a call and answered "Hello". "Is this Dr. Brown?" Yes I answered and the woman identified herself. "Ester, how are you?" She is a wonderful lady I knew well from the LAX Crown Club! I was very surprised and when I asked her how she was doing, she said she had just got off the phone with the VP friend of ours at the Delta Headquarters in Atlanta! I asked how he as doing and her response was, "Good, but I am doing better than him, because he just authorized me to reserve seats 4B and 4C for you and your lovely bride on the 777 to Sydney!" That was side by side seats four rows back in First Class!

Peggy had never flown in a 777 let alone First Class! I had quite a few times because of my upgrades. So the things she noted like the huge screen, lay down bed seats, etc. I just answered like "oh yeah". Sort of 'ho hum' and she got a little pissed at me until I said I truly was glad we got the upgrades and Happy Anniversary!

The trip was phenomenal! We flew to Auckland and boarded the ship. We saw so much, sailed through the Fjords and did about as much as you can imagine. We did have more ship time than we usually like to do but there was such beauty around us and the trek across from south New Zealand to Australia was really the only sea time we didn't see the beautiful landscape. When we pulled into Sydney Harbor and disembarked from the ship I started looking for a taxi to the hotel. Good thing I am not afraid to ask directions and one of the locals pointed down the main road and a very short block and across the street was our hotel! We went to the Sydney Zoo, the Opera House, the Aquarium, and did a lot of walking. Sydney is a great city, we really enjoyed ourselves.

On the flight back, all First and Business Class was full so they put us in extended Business Class/Economy Plus where we didn't have the bed seats but these were bigger than Economy, and we got all the better food and free drinks. Not bad travel for $168! For later trips we said the better seats and better cruise staterooms were worth the money.

I have to say that New Years every year I don't make a Resolution. I am always on top of news and I pick a person that if I had one hour left in this world, this would be the person I wanted to talk to. Many of my fellow "Road Warriors" I would see at airports and talk with when we did, knew that fact about me and a few would ask "Who is it this year?" I would tell them and some of my travel friends may have flown with this person, etc. Well, one year and probably the next I had picked a very high prior military figure. One day passing through an airport and sitting at my next departure gate, one of my travel friends saw me and came over. One of the first things he said was for me to pick another

"Idol" I wanted to talk to. Why? He explained he had been upgraded to First Class and was sitting aisle seat in a two seat side on row 1 bulkhead. A large man was boarding the aircraft and had the seat against the window next to him. The guy didn't say a word, just made his way into the seat. My friend saw who it was and asked, "Are you who I think you are?" The man said "probably" and never said another word! My friend said by his "holier than thou" attitude and actions that he was not the man I wanted as my idol!

On one flight I was at the departure gate and the lead Flight Attendant came out to the gate desk. I could tell she was upset, even though she tried to cover it. I knew because we had become very good friends through my flying so much. I met her first on one of my long trips to Hawaii and this was another long flight across to Hawaii. She happened to look up over the counter and saw me standing there! She left her papers and crossed around the rope, came up to me and gave me a big hug! When we finished boarding she stopped by my seat and noticed the person next to me had requested an open bulkhead seat because of his long legs, so there was an empty seat next to me.

A while after we were in the air, had been fed, etc. I was laying back about half asleep when she plopped down in the seat next to me saying, "Right now I need a friend! A good friend!" She had a very bad flight before this and she was near tears. We talked for quite a while and some Flight Attendants stopped by to see how she was doing and from there I was better known, enough so I probably saw a Flight Attendant I knew on every third flight.

Then word got around about what I did at LAX. I was at my boarding gate well ahead of time so when I saw a short man with a New York accent and his maybe an inch taller and louder wife berating a young Desk Attendant at the next gate. I could see she was near the crying state. I walked over to the gate and it was so bad with their complaining about the flight delays that people in line were standing well back from them and onlookers increased. He was yelling at her and when he took time to take a breath his wife jumped in and was worse than he was! I remembered my first flight after getting married and smiled. I stepped up to the desk and leaned across somewhat blocking the man and said to the Attendant, "Miss". The man yelled at me to wait my turn and get out of his way! I calmly said, "You two must be new to flying" and he turned on me and she followed with what business was it of mine, I obviously was not wearing a Delta uniform so I was just bothering them, etc. I smiled, shook my head and said, "I assumed you were new flyers because anyone who has flown as much as you two say you have would know that any yelling at this young lady will do you no good. There are two pieces of this gate, the land side and the air side". I explained to them that any delay, malfunction, etc. on the air side affected the scheduling on the land side. This young lady can only get you as far as the door right over there. She cannot tell anybody or help anybody on the air side to get the airplane in the air. "And besides, if your yelling pisses her off and I am next in line she may not be nice to me!"

The man was now full on toward me and the two of them unloaded on me! I was just smiling at them. Then he turned to his wife and said he would take it up later with their travel agent! They walked over and sat across in the seats, still loudly talking about me. The Attendant, a tear showing in the corner of her eye smiled and thanked me. Ignoring the people in line she moved to the monitor in front of me. As she did, much of the crowd now had Delta employees and one stepped up to take care of the passengers in line. She asked me what seat I was in? She stated that she would see about an upgrade for me, the least she could do. I smiled, "That's okay, I am already upgraded on the flight at the next gate, thank you anyway." Her mouth was still open when I smiled, bowed a little and walk to my gate. On my flight, just as we reached altitude I was handed a nice glass of Champagne with the comment, "We all heard what you did! Thank you." That got around fast.

Then when I made my Million Miles my seat was decorated with balloons and streamers and a big card signed by a whole lot of people! The guy sitting next to me simply said that I must be special, he didn't get anything but a card when he reached either the first or second million miles!

We took a short trip up to see Susan and family in Boston. It was late Fall and Susan had some time off, so we went to New Hampshire to do some Christmas shopping. And, of course, get a lobster roll! I can't remember what started the conversation, but we ended up going up to Maine. Susan had not seen her Grandmother since we had that nasty encounter and I took the kids and left. We went to the assisted living place and saw my mother. She was unable to see anymore so we talked. Susan sat by her and held her hand. I did not. I did talk to her a little and I sensed the end was near. I had investigated so many accidents that I could sense things. When we left I told Susan I was glad she saw Mom. I continued that would most likely be the last time you see her. Susan asked why? I told her I could feel my mother had talked to me and now was going to die. Susan was upset. Mom passed three months later.

She was cremated and we had to wait until the ground thawed before we could bury her ashes.

The following Memorial Day, Peggy and I flew up to Maine. My sister, her husband, the caretaker, Peggy and I went to the cemetery. It was on my grandfather's land but donated to the City centuries ago. We knew how Mom had said I was supposed to marry Glenda, and always sort of nasty to Peggy, we joked that probably would not happen now. What did happen was a swarm of Black Flies bothered nobody but Peggy! It was like an omen! Peggy got many bites and not a single other person was bitten! Guess dirt and ashes didn't get in Mom's way of bothering Peggy!

I was at a site with one of our top Project Managers and we discussed Safety Theories. I have proclaimed for years I was an Educator and not an Enforcer. For example; I would go on worksites and see workers standing on the top step of a step ladder and see them scurry down two steps when they saw me or one of the bosses coming. The reason was quite simple, the boss would see someone standing on the top and tell them to step down to the second step from the top! They would comply, until the boss left and then would climb back up to the top step. When I saw it I stopped and explained when climbing a ladder you should have three point contact; one hand and two feet or two hands and one foot, otherwise it is easy to fall. Now they understood why climbing where they could not retain three point contact was very unsafe.

In our discussion he mentioned he had worked with many Safety people but I was different. I did indeed educate and I was researched and prepared for meeting with owners and representatives. Most Safety people he knew did not research and were only weakly prepared. I took that with great pride, it is what I believe in and was glad another person saw that. Then he really humbled me. He said of all the people in the company he only trusted two people, me and another Manager! That said a lot!

I was sitting in an outdoor patio of a new restaurant across from Walter Reid Military hospital in Silver Spring Maryland when something very hard hit me on the left side of my head! It continued forward into my jaw and almost took off the bottom of my left ear! The shaft went forward over my shoulder and one of my guys across the table caught the end. It was a table umbrella that was not secured and the wind blew it out of the center of the table! The shaft was like a javelin thrown into the back of my head! I have very strong upper body from my years of recovery and weight training so it didn't knock me off the chair and I didn't hit my head on the table, I just took the blow like a professional. The guy sitting next to me on my left side was looking close because I was asking if he could see any blood, I could feel it flowing behind my ear! He could see none and asked how in the hell I wasn't knocked out or over? He added that if something hit him that hard, he would probably be dead! The sound of the impact caused people at the tables on the outside look at what caused the sound, We finished eating, I got all the information of the restaurant and noted only one server asked me if I was alright! Management did not respond nor were any medical services contacted! Management did not care!

I went across to Walter Reid and went to the ER. A Med Tech spoke to me and said if I needed to see a doctor it would be a very long time since I had no visible injuries. He did check my eyes and gave me a layman's diagnosis that it appeared I may have a minor concussion. He said a doctor would have to confirms that. If I didn't feel any problems it would be best to see my doctor or make an appointment. I hurt but felt okay and continued my visit to a couple other sites in the area. On the way south, looking at another 60 miles to my destination, I started to lose focus with my left eye! Since I wore mono ocular contact lenses and my left eye was for distance, I knew I should get to my doctor. I took the next flight home and had an appointment soon after I landed.

My doctor was not the best I've ever had but when I had my last episode of Bells' Palsy he had agreed to the mix of meds I needed. With my second or third case while overseas, the military doctor listened while I told him I didn't want to take Prednisone again. The side effects, especially the depression, was not good for me. He talked about a study out of Great Britain where a mixture doses of Prednisone and another antibiotic had amazing results! The effect was almost immediate cure from the affects and return to normal in days, not months! But it did mess up a lot of your bodily things like cholesterol, lipid count, triglycerides, etc. I took the chance and although inward my system was messed up, outwardly in a week you could not tell I had Bells' Palsy. This doctor had let me do the mix or else I would have found another. Now I was seeing him for my head injury. He noted the damage to the left side of the back of my skull. He said he saw some swelling by my left ear and jaw, saying it must have been from me hitting my head on the table when I was knocked from the chair. Even though I told him many times I was not knocked from the chair and did not strike my head on the table! He did not believe me!

I saw a neurologist and my eye doctor, both saying they could see the damage to my head and side of my face. My eye doctor said it could possibly have been the impact that actually popped out my left eye! The muscles pulled it back before it went out of the socket and possibly the smooth muscles were stretched. That was not good news because fibrous muscles tend to go back to original shape, smooth muscles do not. A few months later I was sitting in First Class next to a gentleman. When I talked to him he looked at my left eye and asked if I had been in an accident or in a fight? I asked why he said that and I found

I was sitting next the a world renowned eye surgeon who was rated if not number one in the states he was number two! He said my left eye was not aligned and he suggested what could have caused it and he was right on! He gave me exercises to do, saying my eyes would adapt but it would take time. Since I had mono-ocular lenses I started reading again where I could read with my right eye and let my left eye relax and hope it would adjust. It never did fully adjust, I adjusted to it. Now I found I was now on pace to read over 125 books a year! I love reading.

The lawsuit was long, difficult, and nasty. I had to find a lawyer in Maryland and although I thought he was okay I found out too late he was one of those that settled, not winning a trial! They presented an Expert Witness that never examined me, only told them what he would recommend for Physical Therapy for my injury yet didn't truly find out what my injury was! He also said I should not be called a doctor since I was not a Medical Doctor! I told my lawyer for him to tell the ignorant medical doctor he should look up the definition of Doctor!

The title Doctor came from Latin, referring to an academic achievement. The first time "Doctor"was used was more than 2000 years ago, about the time the word "University" evolved and a Doctor was one possessing a higher degree of education, i.e, a Doctorate Degree. About 200 years ago medical practitioners from Tonsorial Parlors and Dentist units were given the opportunity to get their Doctorate in Medicine and therefore instead of a PhD for a Doctorate in Philosophy, they could have an MD, Doctorate in Medicine. However, in 1956 one of the Dear Abby types answered a question. Her "opinion" being that a Doctor should only refer to a medical doctor in social circles. The United States is the only country in the world that has adopted that theory, most PhDs are more revered throughout the world than medical doctors.

When I asked my lawyer how we were coming on the whiplash part of the trial he told me weren't going for whiplash! It was then that I found out my doctor had put his thoughts instead of the truth into my records and I was now fighting that! And since he had said it a doctor who examined me in Maryland agreed with him even though he initially told me his theory, which didn't include banging my head on the table!

Then the judge was told they had pictures of me working on my car! The girl who thought she was being cute was not, I even spoke to her as she was a sneaking around taking a video of me washing my car. The lawyer for the restaurant told him I had been seen with the hood up on my car and working on the engine! Kind of impossible, I was drying the water from my front trunk! If anyone had checked the video, which apparently my lawyer never did, anyone who knows what a Porsche Boxster is would know it is a mid engine car that both front and rear compartments are storage, the engine is not accessible. Maintenance has to be done by dropping the engine.

And just about then Peggy was diagnosed with breast cancer so I decided I could not be running off to Maryland for an extended trial, I needed to be there for her. I took the meager settlement, much less than what my salary was for a year, but I was around for Peggy. I still traveled but not for more than a day or two at a time where before I would be gone all week to multiple sites. She came through it well.

So I was able to travel again but I still kept it less than I did. That was until I got an invitation to be the Keynote Speaker at a Safety and Security Conference in Goa, India! Besides speaking Internationally on Workplace Violence, I had created and published an article about how companies should look at their Visions and Strategic Goals for the company and the position. Then they could hire to those strategies and expectations for the position in relation to existing and future goals. This was based on the number of people who look at personal wants and objectives and not the hiring or placement to match the company goals and strategies. For example; if I applied for a job and the hiring person looked at the 10 letters I have behind my name and hired me for that, then it might be a very poor decision. Let's say the job was Safety for a Pharmaceutical Company and I didn't have laboratory experience but was hired because my 10 letters were impressive, I most likely would fail. The hiring manager should find someone with Lab and safety experience that could understand and help move the company forward.

I had published that theory and had presented it at a lot of venues, even the University of Alaska. I was asked to present the lecture in an international forum attending the conference in Goa. My boss talked a lot about it as far as cost and time away from work. I explained that he now had site superintendents that understood what was needed, I had trained them and was very proud of their Safety knowledge and application. He said he would think about it and only a few hours later he asked me if I really wanted to go? Yes! So he had arranged it so the company miles accumulated from travelers using company credit cards and company arranged flight could be used for my First Class ticket to India. And I was supposed to see one of our US Ambassadors in Bangalore to discuss more opportunities for our company to work in India. That made it more of a business trip than a lecture trip. Many people asked if I could speak Farsi or Hindi because that was their language. I can't remember the number of times I told people Indian was a British Colony until 1956, so most speak English.

First Class to Mumbai, a long layover, then flight to Goa. Goa, the Cashew Capital of the World, was first settled by Portuguese so the buildings are white and resemble what you would see in Portugal. We landed at the airport and were told our hotel was only a short distance across the bridge. In the van was another PhD from a foreign Polytechnic University, just the two of us and the driver in a medium sized van. The bridge was closed for repairs so we had to travel down and cross over the river, adding 60 miles to our trip to the hotel! We got to see the land and I didn't know if I could accept the dirt! We saw workers digging a large trench alongside the road. It was obvious they were digging with shovels and they had a blue tarp they were using for a tent. They would dig all day in sweat and dirt and set up the tarp tent while still wearing the same clothes 24/7! They were and looked extremely dirty.

I checked into the hotel and into my room, a small room where the water didn't quite work the best, etc. I wasn't sure if that was with all the rooms and I was tired so I took a power nap. That afternoon I enjoyed the Indian festivities. I was told by the organizer the event was in my honor, I was the only American attending the Conference! The following day we started the Conference and were told how the presentations were going to go. Following each speech we sat as a panel and talked about the points of interest in the speech followed by the organizer, a CEO of his company and organizer of the Conference, presented individual awards to the speakers. I met Safety Professionals from around the world. It was noticed by all that when the host had something that took him away from the Conference, he had personally asked me to present the awards in his absence. Apparently this was a much bigger honor than I realized. Many more people wanted to be my friend.

That included the Safety Manager who oversaw the construction of the then tallest buildings in the world in Indonesia, and his wife. They both wore bright clothes and because of what he had done he was given a medal and he wore it on his suit and native dress, making it look like he was in uniform. His wife was large but her way of dress and her dignity made her look great. I enjoyed their company and the wife really helped me throughout my stay, keeping me from buying or doing something I shouldn't because of my lack of cultural understanding. For example; the van we were in touring temples outside Goa when we stopped even at stop signs all the kids were crowding around begging for a handout or selling stuff. My friend in Chicago who took Archeology students into Northern India had told me that if I gave a penny to every kid who was begging, two things would happen. I would go broke and I would not make a difference! The wife agreed with that so she was there to help me. At one stop where we got out of the van, the kids crowded around the van. One was selling very nice earrings initially for $20 a piece. She told me not yet. She haggled. He had 16 pair of earrings, all different colors and shapes in a flat box with dividers, $20 a piece. After nearly 15 minutes of her speaking Farsi, I believe, she asked me if I had $10? Sure, it was apparent she had haggled him down from $20 to $10 a pair. I passed the money to her, she to him, and he gave her the entire box! At least now I had gifts for all the ladies in the office and more! I bought silk for my bosses wife and similar for Peggy and others.

I spoke to this obnoxious guy from Great Britain and his overweight wife with a big mouth, he told me there may have been a mistake. He said he got this huge room and had flowers and sweets and fruits delivered to the room! One of the waiters addressed him as Dr. Brown! He said something and discovered he was given the room I was supposed to have! His wife spoke up and said she thought it wasn't a mistake because her husband was the most educated and experienced person at the conference and he deserved to be treated like that! I never said anything to either them or the host, I didn't want to put up with that.

I did get back at the Brit. When he talked he put up slides and on the cover slide it showed he had 23 sets of letters behind his name! I looked at them and knew at least what half of them were. I knew most were those that didn't require peer review or testing, you just had to fill out a form and pay money! Then it was my turn to speak. I got to where I talked about the right fit to the Mission, Vision and Goals of the Company, I said I would rather hire someone that does not have a degree but good experience. I would not hire someone with so many letters behind their name as it tends to be self promotion and not an advancement of the profession! Plus, their letters may be irrelevant again to the Mission, Vision and Goals. Just about then, the Brit was sitting about in the middle of the room with his wife at the table. She gasped, then she spoke in her loud and screechy voice, "He's taking about you!" to her husband! About half the people in the conference either laughed or put there head down smiling. I got the highest review from the panel and after we finished for the day I was interviewed by one of the Indian Broadcasters.

I am Lactose Intolerant and many of the snacks had Yogurt. I thought I could handle it but the last night I was supposed to receive an honor and attend the banquet, but I could not. I was tied to my room and the toilet. When I went to check out I was asked at the front desk how was my stay? I said it really wasn't that well, the room was small and the water didn't flow that well. It was then they discovered they had given me the Brit's room and them mine! Management was all over the front desk! I just left, glad that I didn't have to hear all that, and it was too late to make amends.

I flew to Bangalore. When I had made my travel plans I had found the nearest reputable hotel near the Ambassador's building. I was blown away when I entered the compound! I hadn't realized that for $160 a night I was staying at the Taj West, the number one hotel in all India! The guard at the front gate was dressed like a British guard at England's Queen's palace! The vehicle was searched. At the front entrance to the hotel built inside this huge and beautiful compound I was greeted, a dot placed on my forehead, and a small ceremony! I was escorted to an individual reception desk and all was done perfectly in order! I was taken to my room and found a had 24 hour butler service that was right next door to mine so they could respond immediately to any request I had. The fruits, flowers, etc. were exceptional and the people even more so. I think the second day I stepped out of my room and started down the hall when someone asked if they could help. I said I was heading down to the lobby to check what time my taxi was coming. The person addressed me with "Dr. Brown" and told me exactly when the taxi would be there and where it would take me! All staff was briefed on anything you might ask.

My room had a balcony overlooking the compound. The smell was enchanted, the fruit trees and flowers just smelled so beautiful and my room was nearly as big as one of the houses we lived in! I didn't know what to expect in the dining room. I was greeted by a chef! He told me what they had and asked what I wanted! I don't remember looking at the menu at all! I told him I had problems in Goa from the yogurt and he told me why the Indians use yogurt. Indians use many spices and to prevent the spices from flavoring the food unevenly, they use yogurt to spread the spices evenly! He then said he could cook a meal using Olive Oil instead. We had talked and he knew I cooked a lot, so he invited me to a special set where he could cook and we could talk. It was fantastic! I did ask why there were no Indians at the hotel as guests and he said that was because they could not afford to stay there. If we sent a computer engineer to Bangalore and paid him $100,000 a year, his Indian counterpart, doing the same job, would make $16,000 a year! They could not afford to stay in this hotel.

I met with the Ambassador and even though were talked freely and comfortably you could tell he went through many similar exercises. Our meeting was short and he gave me the same promises he probably gives many times a week, nothing we could bet or plan on. I left his office and grabbed a three-wheel open taxi to go downtown to the shopping areas. The taxis all do what they can to save gas. Their little three wheel small two stroke engine vehicles were zipping around in no sane manner. Every time they stopped, even for a few seconds, they would shut off the engine. Starting it was done by a long handle on the left of their seat. It usually took at least two swift pulls up on the handle before the engine would come to life, it looked like everyone was pumping up the vehicle. You could look around and see it with the hundreds of these everywhere. Stop for a few seconds then wildly pump this handle and jump ahead into the bumper car game. Mixing all the cars with these three-wheelers was also a mess! This was mostly because of the three-wheeler cutting in front of the car and stopping immediately! Twice we were hit by cars unable to stop, once very hard and my driver cussed at the car driver but not once did he turn to see if I was okay!

I shopped and walked. I am always aware of my surrounding, especially having been in two workplace violence episodes. So when I caught this guy saying something to another guy in a cloth store, then dropping what he was doing and jumped out behind me, I knew I was a target. I thought probably to pickpocket or worse. I altered my direction many times, he followed. I stopped and looked in open doors and glass window fronts and he managed to try to look innocent. He stayed behind me. I came to an intersection and he sped up a little in case I crossed the street. I caught him off guard! I spun around and stepped forward right up almost against him! We were face to face about 18 inches apart. I asked, "What do you plan on doing to me?" He was stunned and actually stammered a little as he said he didn't know what I was talking about, he was just walking! I asked him if he saw where we were and before he could answer he then saw I had stopped less than ten feet from a Cop. I then told him if he chose to walk off and then tried to follow me again, I would explain to the officer why he was laying in a heap on the sidewalk. He walked away.

Another great evening at the hotel and I ate in one of there great restaurants inside the compound. The walls were high and thick enough and trees inside enough you could barely hear the traffic and chaos outside. Very nice. The next morning another flight to Mumbai and we landed at the Domestic Terminal. I ended up walking to the International Terminal because traffic between the two was at a standstill. A few steps into my walk two men/boys tried to grab my bag and said they would show me the way. I told them to leave me alone, I had my bag and knew where I was going. They ran alongside me and when I got to the terminal they stepped in front of me and demanded money for showing me the way to the terminal! I pushed through and my bag wheels ran over one of their feet! He was of course in sandals, so he was yelling at me demanding I pay for his injuries! I got inside and checked in my bag The guy checking in my bag said I had to stand in line on the other side of a long wall. I was required to identify my own bag to the guard so it could pass along to load on the aircraft. I told the guy my flight was leaving in a little over an hour and he said I probably would not make the flight! I waited on the other side for a few minutes, identified my bag and was directed to Customs and Immigration to show my passport. There was over 300 people crammed in there and the line was not moving at all! It moved ahead only slightly. I knew I was a going to miss my flight! I heard a woman yell for anyone going to some destination to come forward on the left. A few minutes later the same woman called for anyone going to Amsterdam and I quickly moved to the left. She stopped the few of us and saw I was not going to Amsterdam and I told her which flight I was on. She told me to stand with two other guys to the side. The line through Passport check was basically stopped.

A few minutes later the same woman came back and told the three of us to follow her. Seems they segregate the women from the men and women have a single line! They are much fewer in numbers, so she had us hug the wall beside the women in line. At the end we were put in front. She talked to one of the people checking passports. He tuned around and in really quick time processed us through! I rushed to my gate and there was a Flight Attendant at the door to the ramp to get on. She held the door open, addressed me, "Dr Brown?" and glanced at my ticket and opened the door to the ramp, "They are waiting for you!" A man was coming back up the ramp and I immediately recognized him as the man who checked my bag in! " I took care of you" and smiled as he walked by. I rounded the last turn of the boarding ramp as the Flight Attendant was putting another tag on my bag, "didn't think you would make it" And she passed my bag to a guy waiting at the outside stair landing and he took it down to the handlers below. They threw it in the baggage hold of the aircraft and when I was seated I heard the door closing under me. I made the flight and when the Flight Attendant came back to make sure I was settled and bucked in, I asked her if I had missed the flight, when would the next one leave? She told me they had only one flight a day, so I would have had to stay in the airport or a hotel for 24 hours! Later I kind of wished I had missed the flight because that would have given me time to go down to Agra and see the Taj Mahal. Maybe next time. Really I wanted Peggy with me to see it together.

Plenty of time to digest my trip and despite the dirt, the beggars, the chaos having to put toilet paper in a can next to the toilet instead of flushing it, lack of clean water, way too much perfume, crazy traffic, etc., if you can accept that you will find India is truly a beautiful place. With all my travels to third class countries I was able to look past a lot and see the beauty. I don't know how many Westerners could?

I try to take Peggy somewhere every year for our Anniversary. This year after my trip to India was no different and I believe we want to Costa Rica that year. Totally opposite from India, Costa Rica is one of the cleanest countries I have ever seen. It is also considered the most Environmentally Friendly country in the world. We landed in San Jose and after a night in the hotel where we met others in our group, we set off in the morning toward the east through jungles toward Tortuguero, famous for the turtles laying eggs, all the wildlife, etc. The paved road stopped abruptly and it was all dirt from there! Why? because they didn't want to infuse the air with the chemicals necessary to pave the road, and the unpaved road discouraged a lot of travel, again reducing the pollution. We soon got on a boat into the jungle and our first stop!

We stayed on the east coast for a couple days. We saw every kind of bird you could imagine, snakes, leopards, alligators, huge spiders, types of monkeys, just about everything. We walked in the jungle, took swinging bridges, rode lifts up into the jungle tops, we saw leaves the size of cars! The jungle is so thick and the soil so rich the trees grow huge leaves to catch sunlight trough the dense jungle. In the US normally the rich growing soil is down 12 to 18 inches below the surface. Here the rich soil is on top so you have growth, bugs, and other creepy crawlies on the surface. I hear all the time about people coming back with foot infections because they walked barefoot or in sandals.

We moved west to see the dormant volcano and the hot springs. Walks in the jungle and at one place we had a choice of water rafting, zip lining or horseback riding. Peggy and I chose the horses, we both love riding. We were told all events had guides who either spoke English or there was an interpreter. Wrong! The ranch we went to was beautiful and as usual they ask who has the most experience. It is usually me, so I get a spirited horse! The owner/guide spoke little or any English so I got to ride ahead with him and interpret for him. I believe that totally enhanced my experience! He showed me stuff and I would interpret for him. I would tell the others to follow a trail while he and I checked out to see if something was passable or open. We would go off the path with him showing me the wonders of the land. Peggy said she loved the ride and joked with me that I had way too much fun! The horse I had was very spirited and with the owner and his horse we crossed rivers and went up steep terrain! I think my smile lasted for days!

When we got to the west coast past Liberia we did a lot on our own and saw a river filled with crocodiles from the bridge above. We walked in a very different jungle and saw a very different side of Costa Rica. We talked to students who went there for work on their degrees and we saw some of the stuff they did. We went to an arachnid center where they studied spiders and similar large insects. The guy brought out a tarantula spider and we talked about them. He said their main defense was to rub their legs together and produce barb-like hairs that would stick in your skin and really aggravate the skin. He said the spider could detect things like fear or danger and spread the barbs. He asked if anybody wanted to hold the spider. When I asked what if the spider took a bite he asked if I was allergic to bee stings? No, so their venom is similar to bee stings and although their mandibles will hurt, they seldom bite. I said okay and he put the tarantula on my hand! The spider up close is really beautiful and I was busy looking at it and not at all afraid of it! One of the other guys, Stephen, was the only other one who even dared to try. He stood there, I guess anticipating, nervous from what I could see, but he wanted to step up to the plate and try. "Let me try it" he said and the guy took the spider off me and put it on Stephens outstretched hand. It was as though Stephen had just climbed a mountain or something like that as he held his hand away from his body as to say look at me, I did it! Whereas I had my face within inches of the spider and was talking to it. The guy sort of quickly took the tarantula off Stephen's hand and nobody else volunteered. Still, at least three hours after the encounter, Stephen was still rubbing his hand vigorously on his shorts, "Doesn't your hand itch at all?" Mine never did. With all my encounters with animals, snakes, horses, etc. I truly believe they know when someone will not harm them.

We saw banana picking all done by hand using strung cables to push the large stalks to the processing area. We saw many three toed sloths, we saw so many poisonous snakes and other creatures. Right by the door to our room at one place we woke to find a viper snake curled on top a large leaf! We had to walk under it and make sure we didn't wake it! The leaf was no more than ten inches above our heads and we could see him very well as the sun shone through the leaf. Someone said to me that it isn't like a tarantula, don't try to hold this one!

When we went to leave, our aircraft was large and we were told the runway was very short and the winds were not favorable. We had to take off with tanks too low to make it back to the States so we would take off light, fly to Panama, land and refuel with enough fuel to get back home.

I remember telling our guide that I wanted to come back and be her assistant! I loved the country and the Environmental attitude. I could live there forever.

Back at the office I found out a lady in a different department had gone to the West Coast of Costa Rica while I was there. I talked with her and she wanted to compare/share photos. I told her I would like that after I get mine sorted. She asked why I would have to? She took 64 pictures, I took over 1,400!

My boss took his family somewhere in the world every year. We compared notes. We did a lot of overseas visits but also within the US. That year we went to Maine. We went back to Maine for a late Anniversary trip so I could attend my High School Reunion. We did that every few years and each time we traveled somewhere else in the North East. It was always enjoyable in a sadistic way for me to attend the Class Reunion. My graduating class was only 24 people and because I didn't stay back a year when I had that terrible car accident, I graduated at the very bottom of the class. I was voted least likely to succeed and nobody expected me to go on to college, etc. However, because I had to prove something to my mother, I would go to the Reunion as the Most Educated person to ever graduate from the High School! I spent as little time as possible with my mother. When we did she was still telling me in front of Peggy that I should have married Glenda! So we traveled in Maine, New Hampshire, Massachusetts, Rhode Island, etc.

I grew up 11 miles from the Lobster Capital of the US, Rockland Maine, and 11 miles from the most photographed inland waterway in the US, Camden Maine. Camden is famous for the first filming of Peyton Place! But usually we traveled north of Camden up to Lincolnville where we got fresh lobster at the Lobster House. Probably our best Anniversary Trip to Maine was when we drove up to Bar Harbor and stayed there for a few days. We relaxed, went to Acadia National Park. We ate some of the best lobster, clams and mussels we have ever had! One place where we had superb lobster their claim to fame was their blueberry pie! I think I can still taste it while I am writing about it. My cousin lives in New Hampshire and my sister used to live in Rhode Island but now lives in Maine again. So we left Bar Harbor and went down the coast to a resort a little south of Wiscasset and my sister and her husband come over to see us at the resort. My sister used that word again and said I was stupid for paying for a hotel instead of staying at their place. Then we went south to see my cousin and our oldest daughter and her family in Brant Rock, Massachusetts. Speaking of movies, the second Equalizer with Denzel Washington was shot partially in Brant Rock, mostly the storm scene ending.

We drove up along the coast and when we got to Waldoboro, one of us said "Wonder if Glenda still lives here?" I can't leave out the time early in our marriage when Peggy got to meet Glenda! I am talking about this because we looked at what Mom always said about how I should have married Glenda without even knowing Peggy and Glenda had met, and liked each other.

I had been showing Peggy around the local communities when we drove through Waldoboro. I looked up this sloping green lawn and said I thought that was Glenda! Peggy said for me to go closer and if it was Glenda she wanted to meet her! It was and Peggy did, and it went very well. Glenda, not being able to have children, now had married a man whose wife died on the German Autobahn and left two beautiful girls now calling Glenda their mother. We visited and when her husband came home I don't believe he was too happy. Apparently Glenda must have talked about me and he was a little cautious or standoffish.

We agreed to go out that night as two couples for food and then to the Blue Goose! It is one of those places I used to frequent and learn how to dance from older women. The band would play a series of three instrumentals in a sequence of one fast, one slow, and the third fast. The next set was three but slow, fast, slow. I had won some dancing awards before my knees went, I was very good. Glenda and I danced often and we were very good together. Her husband drove and we sat in a side booth. Her husband didn't participate much in conversation nor dancing. Peggy and I danced a lot and all at once while sitting there between sets, Peggy commented that she had heard a lot about Glenda and I dancing and would love to see it! Glenda and I both protested a little and then she asked her husband if it was okay. Whatever, he unenthusiastically agreed and I took Glenda's hand onto the floor for the next set; slow, fast, slow. The first slow dance we kind of shook off the cobwebs and soon we were in rhythm and were dancing a little like we used to. The fast dance was us talking a lot and basically relaxing with each other. Then came the third song in the set and as if old times, we meshed close. We chose to do our favorite dance, one we won an award with, the Old Fashioned Waltz! We slid, stepped, dipped, and spun as one! We didn't notice but the people on the floor around were stepping back to watch us! We were "clearing the floor"! We finished it with a twirl, dip and applause from all around us! Still in the dip, Glenda gave me a quick kiss on the lips as she said she missed that. We stood to see he husband had left the table. Peggy said he didn't say anything. She said it was quite obvious we were dancing very close to each other, Peggy said it truly was beautiful. Glenda's husband apparently was not happy watching us. We waited, thinking he had gone to the bathroom, and then we went outside to see he had taken the car and left! A lot of people either Glenda or I knew stopped by to tell us how beautiful our dance was. One couple said they would drive us back down to Waldoboro. At her house she asked us not to come in, she would take care of it, and no, he does not hit her, etc. So we left and have not seen nor contacted her since. I also didn't want to rub it in, Peggy and I danced a lot but never as good as Glenda and I.

During one Class Reunion, Peggy and I spent a couple days in Maine seeing some of my old classmates and friends. Gary, the driver of the car we were in when we plowed into the truck, did not come to the Reunion. I understood he was not doing well, the steering wheel to his abdomen did lifelong damage. The guy on my right in the car, Harold, showed up at one. Apparently his facial scars didn't heal as well as mine, he kept his hair long and covered most of his face.

His comment, "Last time I saw you, you were hanging upside down in a car!" left me wondering. I thought I pictured much in my head what happened, but that was not it. As a highly trained and experienced accident investigator, something was wrong. The car was totaled, I saw it a month or so after the crash. It was crumpled and flattened some. I don't believe it flipped over. I don't know how I could be hanging upside down because the car had no seat belts!

I probably should have talked to him more but it was hard. He had been medically treated for many years. His settlement lasted years and was enough for him to build a huge house! My mother settled almost before I was out of the hospital for $1,000! There was no medical treatment for my teeth, my scars, my elbow, etc. because she wanted the $1,000. Meeting Harold brought up some deep scars and renewed anger. We left shortly after the encounter, I needed to find a better place in my mind. I guess I still wasn't totally passed the pain.

We agreed to stay at my sister's house before moving on. When we arrived at her house we soon walked out behind their property to see the land, trees, etc. and one of the first things my sister said to me was how hard it was for her and Mom to sell my car! I was blamed for just leaving it there for Mom to sell! My God, that was over 50 years ago and my sister was still blaming me for that without knowing her mother had refused to give the car to the guy who was selling it for me! I didn't say anything. How can you fight ancient history that is based on such a devious lie? I had asked my sister what Mom did with the money she got from selling my car? Then I asked about the money from selling our grandfather's farm? She could not answer, only speculate it was spend for hospital bills! I didn't tell her I was waiting for my friend who owned the gas station to sell my car so I could have some spending money, but my mother didn't turn it over to him. I again asked who took the money from the sale of my car? I didn't get any money and it was my car I paid for with my money!

And I still was upset that my sister didn't contact the Red Cross for a few days to get word to me my father had passed. I was in Korea and the Base Commander could have got me back immediately! However, I was told they could not delay the funeral and there was no-one to pick me up at the airport. I never got to say "Goodbye" to my father. When I brought it up it was always someone else's fault. For God's sake, I worked with the Red Cross and death notification is priority! If they had been notified when Dad died, I would have been home. It seemed to me that I was again the stupid little kid that was easy to forget.

We had taken a short trip to Rhode Island with them years earlier. We went out to see lighthouses and huge mansions. At one of the lighthouses my sister started talking to a perfect stranger about her life story! She did that often. In this case she talked about that she had student loans but if she needed something, he mother always came up with money for her, she always found some money. I kept quiet but thought, "Hell yes she had money for you, I was giving her 50% of my paycheck for her college and Mom never told her that"!

Peggy and I talked about never coming back. I want to point out, we make the decisions together and we experience the pain together. Both my mother and sister have bad things to say about both of us. And what affects one of us affects both of us. We spent seven years living overseas where we had to support each other. We survived by our love for each other, and the kids!

I also think that was the trip my sister and her husband told me that I had told someone that I really did not have a PhD! I stated I have a PhD from a duel Accredited University! She said some gibberish about someone saying I said It wasn't real! Then the truth came out! She said and was echoed by her husband, "Well, don't ever expect me to call you Doctor!"

We left!

Back home it was still a lot of travel and some disturbing news. Our company was an Engineering company that did construction. The construction became about three times the revenue of the engineering side so the company was trying to solve that problem. The construction side was being sold if they could find a buyer. Unfortunately, they did.

40

Irvine, California

Local wanting to get into global was what this company wanted to do, so the local talent bought the global construction company. Since there was no need for my level of Safety with an Engineering company, I went with my boss to the new company.

There were assurances, promises, and big problems. We eventually relocated from West Hollywood to El Segundo, right next to LAX on one side and Manhattan Beach on the other. We lived in Manhattan Beach. Peggy worked for a Defense Contractor in El Segundo, so it was perfect for us. I was still traveled a lot and had to be at the new headquarters in Irvine a couple days a week. On those days it was a sizable drive. I usually took my BMW K1600GTL, BMW's six cylinder, #1 touring motorcycle in the world! It was so smooth and in California I could ride in the HOV lanes. If traffic was stopped or near that I could legally split lanes. Let me make it clear, I did that legally. According to California law, a motorcycle can "share" lanes if he can do so not exceeding 40mph or 15mph faster than traffic. This was started in the 1980s when we had gas prices rise tremendously. This forced many to revert to driving high gas mileage motorcycles versus gas guzzling cars. Problem was that most motorcycles then were air cooled. When traffic stops on California freeways it stops completely. With no air flowing on the engine it caused bikes to overheat and stop! It was making the traffic jams much worse. That is when California started allowing motorcycles to share lanes. Unfortunately, many bikers didn't know the law and were splitting lanes at high speeds, causing many incidents and often deaths. I followed the law. Don't ask me about speeding, I kept up with the California traffic, making sure to flow safely, at any speed.

Peggy was getting very tired of the work she was doing and she wanted to retire. I told her I could live anywhere if it was close to an airport, so find us a house in San Diego and then retire! I was thinking close to the same thing because of this new company.

The first mistake they tried to do was put their supervisors in charge of our projects! Not only was it against our agreement, it wouldn't work! My boss and a VP told them that was impossible because we were working with people like the Army Corps of Engineers that knew and worked well with our management. We knew if new supervisors come in we would lose the integrity and trust, therefor the contracts. They agreed to that and then they said they had a VP there that assessed all contract risk. The VP was very narcissistic and would not work with us. And he did the unthinkable! Again, global projects looked at by local mentality. He told management there was too much risk in most of the projects and we would not be pursuing the contracts! On one contract we had been designing for over a year and a half was worth more than $100 million! The dumb ass said it was too risky and we lost the contract!

I tried working with their local geniuses and got aggressive resistance! They didn't understand what professional safety was about. For instance, we had a project at a hospital where they were going to put up traffic cones where construction literally met pedestrians coming from the parking lots. When I said we have a responsibility to protect the public from our operations, the site super first said anything above what he had budgeted for would have to come out of my Safety budget! Of course it can't, I don't have a budget and federal and state laws say it is our responsibility! So our next step was to put up a fence and I argued that would put people in the flow of traffic. Many of the patients are temporarily or permanently handicapped. The law also says we have to protect them from traffic. We were putting them in a hazardous situation. I talked to one of the Foremen and suggested we put up a double fence with openings every so many feet so pedestrians can slip into the safe corridor between fences. By the time the Site Super told the VP, I allegedly was not welcome on the site! That is against the law, but the new management told me not to go there any more. Later there was an accident on the site and I had to investigate it. The first thing I saw was the double fence system I basically designed! I mentioned it to the Site Super and he got very upset!

The company violated their promises to my boss and our VP which ended up forcing my boss to resign and join another global company and the VP to take his right hand guy and start a business of their own. Neither could take me with them, although the VP had a job in Florida he wanted to hire me to go there and be the onsite Safety person. I told him I would give him a month and would train someone for the job. He never called back. His assistant called me a couple times, we had been friends but these were not friend calls. The guy they got for Safety was totally lost on many issues so I was asked to tell them how to do it right.

The company had never had a Professional Safety person but now they had bragging rights. Soon they had me as part of the staff for business purposes, bragging about my PhD, my Adjunct Professor qualifications, my BCSP Award of Excellence, etc. I was getting jobs for them but I was not allowed on the job sites! It was back to the engineers designing a project and then asking safety to make it safe after it was built! They decided to offer me a consulting position at a much lower salary. The intent was to keep me with the company and get a consulting fee. Problem is, they asked for a lot but had an excuse every time why I was not getting paid! Finally, I told the VP to send by the dumbass that lost the contracts for us, I knew he lived near by, and he could take your computer back and put it anywhere you felt like, I quit!

41

New Job, but first!

Unemployed again! I started looking for a job around San Diego, but we had already paid for one of the trips from my Bucket List, we were going to go on a Safari!

Every year I would take Peggy for a trip for our Anniversary. My old boss, the president of Construction, was also a world traveler and we compared notes, often as if it were somewhat a competition. Of course he made a lot more money so his trips were spectacular and we, I believe, did more earthy things. He went to spectacle and we went to seeing people and cultures, etc. We rarely went to the same place twice unless it just fit. For example, we have been to Bangkok many times and usually it was a short stay as we ventured to other places. The first two times we went south to places like Phuket and last time after Vietnam and Cambodia we went north to Chiang Mai.

All the times we have been to Italy we never made it to Rome so we planned a trip to start in Rome and travel by bus up through Italy, stopping in Lucerne, and finishing in England. Our granddaughter is married to an Air Force guy and they were stationed in Japan. She flew over from Japan and joined us on the trip. It was a great trip and it was Peggy's idea and planning. As we finished up in London, Peggy looked at me and said it was my turn to plan the next trip, but she would not go to Kathmandu or Tibet, only a little sure she would agree to a Safari. She knew those were my top three desires. One may ask why, and to put it simple, I was on an airplane sitting next to a man who had returned recently from Tibet. His son's best friend had gone to tibet and did a photo journal and National Geographic had contracted him to go back and do a movie that would edit and show on their TV channel. He was told he could take a friend and he asked his best friend but he could't go but his friend's father, the man next to me, asked if he could go? So he went and when they returned National Geographic used his, not his son's best friend's journal! He tried to show me but the format they made his copy on would not load on his computer. I took out my computer and it worked! Beside the narrative on the CD I got a first hand narrative! It was now on top of my Bucket List! But Peggy would only agree on the Safari. I don't think we will ever make it to Tibet or Kathmandu.

So we contacted a friend who was a travel agent and she said she had the perfect Safari for us! It was with one of the more expensive tour groups but also one of the most reputable. She had us starting in Kenya or Botswana, traveling through Tanzania, down through Victoria Falls and down to Cape Town, etc.! I could have bought a new Porsche for what that costs! Through a lot of hype about how we had to do it right, never will have such an experience, etc., I had to threaten to go to another Agent! Told her I have always dreamed of a simple Safari with the animals and not touring a damned city! Still expensive but not outrageous, we were going to Kenya and Tanzania.

42

Kenya and Tanzania

Our travel agent arranged most of the basics, very few changes made, and that was our land trip, we would take care of the air travel to and back. I was still faithful to Delta and had enough points, but Delta said we could not use points because they would fly us to Amsterdam where we would have to fly KLM to Nairobi. KLM didn't take Delta miles and we could not split it up by using miles to Amsterdam and then paying for KLM. We could buy a trip to Amsterdam and a trip to Nairobi. So I asked how much for Coach and Business Class for the trip? I got quoted fares for each. Peggy did her great research of other airline fares and she came up with Etihad Air where it would cost us less than $200 more to fly Business Class than Delta's Coach Class to Amsterdam! And since our layover was more than 8 hours in Abu Dhabi, the airline would put us up for the night and feed us! Abu Dhabi is a beautiful city, especially at night, but the hotel we didn't think was very good. We told them that and on the return trip we had a 5-Star hotel

I had bought Peggy a new mirrorless digital Sony camera so she could take pictures. I had my Canon and a couple telephoto lenses and I took most of our pictures. She wanted to have her own camera, hence the new Sony. She hated the camera and it didn't do what is said it should! The night before we left she told me she truly hated the camera so I told her to leave it! I tried in San Diego Airport and LAX and could not find what I wanted. But in Abu Dhabi the Duty Free Shop had a beautiful deal on a new Nikon and she loves it. The Nikon I believe has better color quality than my Canon.

Nairobi was a unique city. Our contact with the Safari Company left us a couple warnings, so we were cautious and had no problems. When we stopped along the way I would talk to the natives and I learned a little Swahili! I practiced a little with our guide. He was going to be with us through Kenya. At the border going into Tanzania we would change Land Rovers and drivers. The first day leaving Nairobi we went through the city and then out onto the plains for a long drive to our first camping area. We saw some animals, not a lot, but started noticing more as we climbed up to a land mass that looked over the Masai Mara. Masai means plains and is the name of the indigenous people and Mara means "dotted" representing the trees dotted along the plains we could see very well from up high.

The camp was very nice and we had a great cabin slightly down and on the edge so we could look out at the Masai. If we had to venture between the cabin and clubhouse we might have a Masai Warrior go with us. The first day after breakfast we went out on the Plaines and our guide would point out some animals and we would try to get closer to see them. I wondered how he saw them but on the third day I saw a few before he did! But that first day after the morning safari we had lunch and we were asked if we would like a Walking Safari? Oh YES! We met John, not his Swahili name but the Christian name he was given when he started in the schools. He was dressed in the bright red clothes of the Masai Warrior and traditional shaved head. He had a walking stick and a second stick about 30 inches long, all wood, one end a large ball shape and then the shaft was tapered down to a point on the other end. When I asked him if while we are walking, what will we do if we meet an animal that sees us as lunch? With a still serious smile he said, holding up this pointed stick, "Then I will just kill it."

My research again, why John was so sure was because the ritual all boys did to become a man, they had to kill a lion! They would be sent off with a full head of hair, kill a lion with only the pointed stick, and when finished they would meet with the elders and be designated a man and his head was shaved bald. They don't do that anymore. Both the Masai nation and the state made killing a lion a thing of the past. The new ceremony into manhood is now quite different and painful. Now they have to meet with the village council and be circumcised in front of all the people. If he can take it without showing pain, when he comes back from healing he will be determined to be a man and have his head shaved. Often during the recovery the soon to be man will leave the village with other new candidates. They will often paint different black art on their faces. When I asked what happens when they show pain I was told they were sent from the village like a young lion leaves the pride until strong enough to fight for control over a pride.

Again, more research. The young male lions are pushed from the Pride when they start reaching maturity. The young lions will gather with other young lions and run together until they feel like they are strong enough to challenge the older male lion leading the Pride. If successful, the young lion will kill all the new cubs in the Pride so the mother Lioness will go into heat and the young leader will impregnate the lionesses and it will be his bloodline as the Pride increases by new birth. While we were there word was sent to all the drivers to be on the lookout because five young lions were coming up from Tanzania to Kenya and we should be concerned and keep away if we saw any challenges.

Back to our walking Safari. John took us out on the plains away from the campgrounds, still up on the plateau, not down into the Mara. We saw Wilder-beast, Zebra, and my favorite, Giraffe. I have always had a love for animals and I believe they know it. I mean, how else was I as a kid been able to pet a skunk and not get sprayed? I have actually pet three skunks. And during one of our Anniversary celebrations we stayed overnight at the San Diego Zoo Safari Park, called "Roar and Snore". I paid extra for us to climb aboard a truck and drive out amongst the animals. During a feeding for the giraffes, our guide was taking pictures of us with a giraffe taking acacia leaves from our hands. We were facing the guide and as he was taking pictures he said "something is happening!". He said it a couple more times but assured us he didn't think it was anything to worry about. Peggy thought different when the giraffe leaned in with her head and put it on my shoulder and pressed her head against the side of my head! She held her head there for maybe 40 seconds and our guide was just shaking his head. It was the first time any giraffe had done more than licked a finger with the long tongue, none had ever touched a guest like that!

So with John, we were out in the open with all the animals and from the trees to our left came three giraffe, beautiful and one was very tall. As they emerged from the trees I went slowly toward them. When I was within 50 feet of the tallest, I put down my camera so not to frighten this beautiful animal, and I slowly walked toward him. When he stopped, Peggy said to John that she was concerned. John said, "I feel his soul and I think the giraffe does too. I think if Bruce gets too close the giraffe will just turn his head and walk away". That exact thing happened at about 25 feet from the giraffe, he just turned his head and walked away. I didn't get a close picture of him, I was in the moment and it just didn't seem right.

Then we did something nobody had done before. Peggy had her camera and was also using her I-Phone. John said something like would the pictures be good from the phone? Peggy held it up and gave it to John and showed him how to zoom, etc. He was doing that and Peggy reached over and hit the button to switch the camera so it was now a Selfie! John took a double take and in a high voice, "That's me!" His voice even higher repeated again "That's me!" and Peggy pushed the button as he was holding it and it took the picture of John! He said he had never seen a picture of himself! After we finished the Walking Safari we said goodbye to John and we went to the clubhouse and talked with two of the ladies in the office. We found a piece of photo paper and Peggy was allowed to connect to the printer and soon we printed the picture of John on an 8 X 10 photo sheet. The next day while we were out on a safari in the Mara, they gave John the picture of himself. They said he was due to travel to his village that afternoon and back in a day or two. We were gone when he came back but one of the ladies emailed Peggy to say John showed the picture to the head of the Masai camp. The photo was posted in the center of the camp and John was treated like royalty! It was the first time he ever had a picture of himself!

We continued through Kenya and saw so much, I could write a entire book about our Safari. Then we went into Tanzania and did the same. Here we were in the Serengeti looking at the beautiful Mount Kilimanjaro! The guide and I went out very late to catch some sites and pictures, Peggy stayed at the campsite. Rules say there will be no vehicles there after 6:30 pm and it was after 6 as we were heading back. A unique thing is all the animals, the elephant, hippo, wilder-beast, zebra, etc. all head across the Serengeti to the thick trees every night for protection from lions, etc. I got some beautiful pictures as we got basically in the way of their nightly retreat. I got pictures and a movie of two springbok locking their long horns in a fight, elephants wading through marsh waters, etc.

A quick explanation about marsh waters in the Serengeti. Kilimanjaro still seeps volcanic waters heavy with acid. As the water goes through the heavy grasses it is literally filtered so the retaining waters that create the marsh are safe for the animals to drink and walk through.

Whenever I could I would interact with some locals. At one stop we made I saw some kids that looked like they didn't have much so I took the apples from our boxed lunches and walked to them. We talked a little and when I gave them the apples it was such a look on their faces, they were so happy. I not only learned much from the people I also learned enough that I respected them. That was said when one of the ladies at a stop where we bought a couple things made the comment that I was not like so many visitors, I paid attention to especially the kids and the woman said they don't usually smile at visitors like they did with me. I like being me.

On one of our daily safari we saw a cheetah going through the tall savannah grasses. Our guide said he thought he could guess where he was headed so we did a wide circle and came up very near an ant hill. Sure enough, the Cheetah went to the ant hill and on top of it looked like he was looking over his kingdom. Such a beautiful cat. We waited for a Rhino to come out of a wet ravine, we saw lions everywhere, saw a river full of alligators, huge alligators, and a mud hole where over 85 hippos were laying in the mud. We missed the Great Migration by two days but still saw thousands of animals in numbers that made the scenery look like a moving black carpet! We had lions within easily 10 feet from us, once one rubbed right next to the Rover less than three inches from me! We saw kills and the birds and Hyenas scavenging the left overs. I was seeing the animals as fast as the guide and even saw some before he did.

I bought a painting for Peggy and she bought me a silly one of a giraffe and a vase with an etched giraffe. I bought her some Tanzanite. We went back up to Kenya and back to Nairobi, back through Abu Dhabi and back home. My dream of a Safari was realized and despite having traveled around the world twice, my heart is with the animals we saw and in the beautiful places we went in Africa. Possibly the best trip ever.

We saw animals in their environment and I often looked at the beauty, even in the hierarchy of death and survival It was as though I understood some of it knowing that if I had given to the verbal and physical abuse as a child, I would be like one of the weaker animals waiting to feed up the line.

I have killed animals for food and people in self defense, or war. You get the understanding and when you get past it you can see such great beauty in the animals. Of course I now shoot them with my camera.

Would I go back on a Safari again? In a heart beat! I put that right up there with flying in a jet fighter! Don't stand in my way if the chance comes along again!

43

Looking again

Unemployment sucks. I interviewed for the top Safety and Health person at a University, for the first time not teaching but trying to be staff. I was the chosen one and then they dropped the pay bomb on me! They offered a salary about $50,000 below what I was making! I told them I would not take the job for less than what was about $20,000 less than what I was making and she hung up on me.

Another really interested me and I decided to take it, wish I hadn't. It was a company that handled all the Human Resources, Payroll, Workers' Compensation, Hiring, and Safety for companies. We had maybe 60 companies in each section. We had four sections and a safety person in each. Right after I signed and just before I started working, they were still reviewing the necessary documentation, the lady I was going to be working for met me for coffee so she could "get to know me". I drove up on my BMW K1600GTL motorcycle, number one touring motorcycle in the world, and basically said this is what I do, I'm a biker at heart. She never said anything about it, but just before I reported for work she told me the company did not allow anyone to drive a motorcycle for work, we had to drive to customers, and if I showed up on a motorcycle to the office I would be immediately fired! If I knew that before I signed then I probably would have looked somewhere else. But, this was after signing all my papers! I wanted to walk away, but didn't and instead drove my Porsche to work.

Next, I found out the company only paid reimbursement for using your car at $0.40 a mile, government standard was $0.55, and I had to drive a lot! Her Human Resources guy was super friendly with her and it left some questions in my mind, and some others in the office voiced they thought so also. He was going for his Masters Degree and everyone reveled at his accomplishments, that is, until I showed up with my PhD. It was so evident there were people there out for themselves and nasty too others. One lady asked me about what my PhD was in and another lady complained I was over in their section bothering people by talking about myself! And the big boss at our location was the most narcissistic asshole I have ever met in my life! He drove a new Tesla and used to let the ladies drive his car. He said a lot of sexually inappropriate things to ladies and blew it off!

I was chastised because I talked too much with new customers, even though many of the new and existing customers talked readily that it was good to have a professional Safety guy, finally. On the hard new customers, the marketing person had me go to the first meeting with them because I could relate to them and as far as Safety, I knew so much more than the other Safety guys. So I would talk them into joining with our company but their rep was another guy and another team. The lady running our team was promoted to the asshole's assistant and she put the HR guy in charge of the team. He didn't like me, and things just happened all the time he didn't like. Even simple things like when he got his Masters he had a party at a bar along Pacific Coast Highway. The nearest parking was a small dirt lot across from the bar and a couple slots in front along the curb. When I got there he was talking to the people there and standing on the sidewalk. Just as I drove up the spot right in front of the bar opened up and I pulled in. His friends took their attention away from him to look at my Racing Yellow Porsche Convertible and you could see he was pissed. His actions later were so blatant that Peggy and I left. And also asshole showed up.

We were encouraged to have an off-site social within each team where we could talk freely. We had drinks and the conversation got around to one of the ladies saying she felt really weak on one of her duties and was seeking help from another team. I thought to myself, another thing, the lady had already made so many mistakes but they were all forgiven, I would have fired her a long time ago. So that became a question that was asked of all, "What do you feel is a weakness with you?" Everyone added their weaknesses, I didn't say anything. Our Masters Degree leader even leaned over toward me and in a raised voice asked me what my weakness was! I kind of shrugged my shoulders and said if I see a weakness I correct it and learn from it so it now is probably a strength. He almost lunged at me berating me for saying I didn't have any weaknesses, he knew I had a lot and I wasn't man enough to admit I did! He challenged my manhood three times and the other team members seemed to jump on the wagon when in hindsight I think they wanted me just to say something so the shouting and berating me would stop. I ignored him and kept my cool but soon left.

This is where I stepped on the sharp rock and bruised my foot. I told him as I should that I hurt my foot and had to go to the doctor. It was on-the-job and by law he was supposed to report it to Workers' Compensation. He never did, didn't even take any information down. When I saw my doctor he told me to stay off it for a week. I went to him and told him I was directed by a doctor to take a week off, he said I didn't have enough vacation! I had to walk around with an Orthopedic boot on my foot! It was a short time later I told the other three Safety guys that the lady, now working for asshole, was trying to set me up to fire me, she was saying I was talking too much! The guys were very surprised and said that would never happen, I was the most qualified in the office, and they didn't think I talked too much. We talked and I told them I was not going to speak at all during our weekly all-hands meeting she said I was interrupting others. I never interrupted and now I didn't talk. This went on for five weeks and I was brought in to be counseled on that four of my customers had said I talked too much about myself, which only two I had seen during the previous month, and by chance they each said exactly, verbatim, of what our boss lady was saying about me. Hmm. Then she claimed I had interrupted someone else during the weekly meeting and we knew I had said nothing!

One of our clients had a very bad accident and I was asked to help with the investigation, which help meant I did the investigation. I came back and was talking to our receptionist when asshole came in. I said I had just got the retro license plate, black with yellow letters and personalized. I told him I saw one of the retro plates on a new Tesla and it looked good! He turned to me with rage, "What the fuck are you saying? That's so fucking stupid, no, you are so fucking stupid!" There were visitors in the lobby and they were shocked as he said that and went into the conference room. Everybody got very silent and nobody would look at me. And that wasn't the end of it!

I got to my desk and was buzzed on the intercom to report to the boss lady in her office. I walked in expecting to be briefing the accident but instead the dynamic duo started telling me they had to take away my customers because of what I was saying and that my employment was terminated! I hobbled out to my desk and Masters Degree followed me as I cleaned out my desk. Did I say he was very short, had a weasel like face and black rimmed glasses. Him following and watching everything was just disturbing. I walked out through the receptionist, said "bye" as I did, walked to my car and drove home! With a smile on my face.

I basically said this was bullshit but still had my foot to worry about. As I sat there I did more research and decided to write an email to the CEO of the company. A couple weeks later I got a call from one of the top ladies in the company at headquarters to tell me they had conducted a thorough investigation of my incident and one of the managers from their Denver office had reported she found nothing illegal in what happened to me! I told her that I was going to accept her findings because I wanted nothing more to do with them, and by the way, my boss, Michael, had broken California law by not submitting Workers' Comp on my foot injury, and secondly had broken the law by refusing a competent medical authority when he denied me time off for an injury that occurred while on the job! He should see heavy fines and possibly jail time! She scrambled and said she would put me in for Workers' Comp, for which I laughed because if she did that long after the injury it would be denied and probably investigated. The Company was sitting on a lot of legal issues and lot of liability, but I was not going to push it, I didn't want this resolved that I would get my job back. It was then she said I would not have to worry about the two anymore, they resigned! Then I asked if the big guy, the butthead was gone? She said he was chastised for his language and sexual innuendoes, but he was still a Senior Vice President with the company and was actually, I think she said, an investor. So he will slug on with his nasty and illegal ways that others would be fired for as much.

44

Cuba!

We had another cruise already paid for so we flew to Miami and boarded a ship bound for Mexico, Belize, Honduras, Cuba and The Bahamas. We had been to Cozumel before so now we stopped in Cancun. We did the tourist thing and realized it was not that much difference between the two except the population.

Our next stop was Belize. I had worked with a wonderful lady from Belize when I was doing construction and I promised her I would see her country one day. Now I have and it is beautiful! The most beautiful beaches I have ever seen, and with my foot problem I could only sit in a lounge chair on the sand while Peggy and a new friend went out into the water. The friend's husband was doing something else and we met up with them that night. He owned his own business and when he cruised he did it in style. He smoked cigars and he said he came along for the ride so we could go to Cuba and he could get some Cohibas!

He also had the largest cabin on the ship! All the amenities were included, stocked bar and all the specialty restaurants were just a couple benefits besides the room and view. Peggy and I talked and said a cabin upgrade might be a thing to think of, but not to that extreme.

Next was Honduras and we took a taxi tour to an animal sanctuary that rescued birds and monkeys. As usual, when we walked into the monkey cages the monkeys all jumped on me! After some nudging from one of the caretakers, a few lit on Peggy and the other couple in the cages with us. The lady asked if I was wearing something that attracted the monkeys? Peggy just said no, all animals do that to him!

Almost the same thing happened when we went into the bird cages. I had one Macaw on each shoulder, one on an arm, and one on my head! Finally one of the Macaws flew and landed on Peggy's head. She said the talons hurt. I didn't think about it because I get very attached to animals and don't think about such things.

There it was, the island of Cuba! Another place I thought I would never see. We had to register ahead of time with one of the organizations Cuba was letting in so we could visit. Stepping off the ship into the main seaside area of Havana and seeing the 1950-60 American cars and the old buildings was like a time warp. I again researched and found the American car makers, mostly General Motors, sent their new production models to Cuba for pre-sales testing and operation. Therefore, it was common to see a 1957 Chevy driving around. They used them for taxis and charged a lot. Our new friend said he rented a 57 Chevy to take him out to the tobacco farms. He said he got to drive it a little and he said something about the cost to hire the taxi in the hundreds of dollars!

Another bit of research proved most of their profits went to the government. That was good and bad. First bad because it was feeding a Communist government, but good because you could haggle the price down. For example; I smoke about one cigar a year but had many requests for me to bring back some. So I went into a market and talked the cigar dealer down on price about 50%. I could only get one box per customs and the vendor did not take credit cards, so I went back to the ship and got cash. On the way back I found another vendor selling a nicer Cohiba and talked him down even further! The guy with the huge Suite bought about six boxes and was able to get them in through Customs!

We went to what was described as a Rum and Cigar tour but the Rum plant was closed for operations, looked like it had been for quite a while. We saw a model of the factory and explained how they distilled rum. We then went upstairs and tasted rum and each of us given a cigar. They had a small singing group there as we sat in front of the stage at tables drinking rum and smoking cigars!

We then went to the alleged Cigar Manufacturer and found similarly it was not operating. More cigars and we could buy rum and other liquors at a good price.. Again, Customs said only one bottle per person so Peggy and I picked a really nice Rum and a bottle of Anise. We finished that tour at a school and it was so apparent the school was Communist! The pictures and displays left nothing to question.

More touring the city. We might see a glamorous hotel on one side of the street and what looked like a bombed out old building on the other side. We walked past what appeared to be a rolled up garage door and a room about the size of a two car garage where there was a barber chair and a young child getting a haircut. Peggy said I needed a haircut, so when the kid was done the barber cut my hair quite well for the exorbitant cost of $5!

Then on to the Bahamas. We docked and went shopping at the nearby stores. I asked and was told which bus to take and which stop to get off on to cross over to see the Atlantis Hotel. We had been told taking a cab and crossing the bridge to get to the hotel was very expensive, the bus much easier and cheaper. We got off the bus, walked the long bridge and wound through the streets to the harbor and the Atlantis Hotel. We passed by the docks and the Yachts were huge and ostentatious! We tried to guess how many millions of dollars were floating at the different docks we passed!

We could walk around a portion of the Hotel and even into the entrance foyer, but not a step further! Guards were there looking at wrist bands and if you didn't have one you could not even step inside enough to get a good picture! Another couple we met on the ship were getting into a taxi at the circular drive. They were heading back to the docks and told us to come along. We got in and a few minutes were back shopping just off from where the Ship was docked.

A good trip. We saw a lot, especially Cuba. I never expected to see Cuba so it was special.

45

Medical Incompetence!

When I had the blister on the pad/ball of my foot I went to the Veterans Administration (VA) hospital in La Jolla. My incompetent general practitioner said it was just some kind of a bruise. However, his assistant talked to me after the doctor went back into his office and suggested I go to the Emergency Room, it looked bad.

I did, waiting over 3 hours to be seen by a doctor. He agreed it was bad and the next day, thanks to him putting some urgency to it, I had an appointment with the Podiatrist. Nice, fairly young guy who seemed to know what he was doing. He started by lancing the raised bruise and then scraping away dead skin around it. I questioned if it was getting infected but he assured me he was taking care of it. My history with being an EMT and working in an ER made me question his competence.

When we took our Safari, the skin was still not closed so I treated and covered it daily. It didn't get worse nor better, so when we came back it was as though we hadn't left, pretty much the same condition. I kept with him and a few months later we took the cruise to Cuba and returned again to no change, my foot was not healing and my doctor still saying he was taking care of it.

I got to a point I believed he didn't know what he was doing, I suspected the wound was getting infected and in near a year it did not improve. I said I wanted to go to a Hyperbaric Chamber to help with the healing. He said I could not do that, no local hospital had one the

VA could use! I kindly, well sort of kindly, told him I didn't need him, I knew the doctor who ran the department at a local hospital that had a Chamber. I saw him once more to tell him I was not seeing him again.

The Chamber was in the specialized Wound Care Center and when I was examined it took less than 15 minutes to set up an appointment for me to get an MRI on my foot. That was followed within a couple days be nerve testing and a Nuclear Dye injected and X-rays taken. So a week after I met with them I was scheduled, through them, to meet with a surgeon, one of the best in California. A few minutes with him and a review of all my tests, and I was scheduled for surgery to remove my left Great toe! It was clearly explained that if I had waited another few months under the care of the VA Podiatrist I would have lost most of my foot due to the increasing infection! The big toe and the ball of my foot was amputated and the surgeon moved muscle and bone to reconstruct the ball.

I did research on support shoes, specifically those that offload pressure on the toes. I visited the store having the highest rating, but was not sure they would be right for me. The salesman could not answer my specific questions and called over another salesman that was much more knowledgeable. In the end, he agreed with me their shoe was not what I needed and recommended a pair of Hoka shoes. Never heard of them but did find a store and bought a pair. When I met my new Podiatrist at the Wound Care Center, he recommended I get a pair of Hoka shoes! If it were not for Hoka shoes and custom Orthodics, I don't believe I would have the mobility.

My civilian Podiatrist worked well with me and the second toe, right next to the one amputated soon became disjointed and a classic "Hammer Toe" so it was also removed. Ironically, I got another bruise on my right foot very similar to the one that I initially had on my left foot. My Podiatrist cleared it up in three weeks! Why couldn't the VA do that?

Since diagnosis for many of my problems could be related to Agent Orange I went to VA and attempted to get some disability for it. First of all, when I retired from the military I was told I had to use VA, which I tried to but was totally turned off by what I thought to be shear incompetence. And I guess VA thought the same thing because all I would hear in their newsletters and general propaganda that they were going the extra mile, making their services and staff better! I didn't hear any of the medical services we got through work putting themselves down by saying they were doing everything to make themselves better! Then I needed to use VA for Disability. I found another racket and roadblock to disability called AMVETS, short for American Veterans. They hired people to help in the process of getting disability. I started applying in 1991 because of illnesses and diseases related back to my exposure to Agent Orange. It wasn't until much later when I was fighting for earned disability that I used AMVETS and found all I got was headaches from someone telling me how great they were, giving up fighting for me, and sending a letter to me agreeing with the decision of VA when the decision was so wrong!

A good example was when I applied for disability for PTSD and the answer I got back in person from the VA Center, "You were in the Air Force and we all know the Air Force didn't see any action"! True quote, VA denies it was ever said. I went to the VA hospital on Lancaster Road in Dallas and sought treatment, if I can remember, for my Bells' Palsy and my Ulcerative Colitis. It took a long time and the doctor had his theory of Bells' Palsy that was recognized as a valid theory. Remember, I have had multiple episodes and each doctor I see says I am lying, he/she has never seen anybody with more than one or two, and each one would slam the past doctors treating me as incompetent and they misdiagnosed my condition. When I worked in a hospital Emergency Room, one of the first briefings I got by the Hospital Commander was the "Them vs Us" talk about what we do in the hospital, bad or good, stays in the hospital and we never share any problems about other doctors nor do we put them down in public! The VA doctors apparently never got such a briefing. One doctor told me he knew what caused Bells' Palsy and I asked what and was it printed and peer reviewed in the American Medical Journal? He didn't answer that but told me it was caused by canker sores in the mouth! I never saw him again. We also had moved from Dallas.

Ironically, with Bells' Palsy I have been called in by doctors to talk about the disease. For example; one Doctor called me and I was available. At his office shortly thereafter he wanted me to talk to a wife whose husband contracted Bells' Palsy. One of the reasons she was attracted to him was because of his outgoing "life of the party" being, and now she was not sure the marriage was going to work because all he did now was sit on the couch and watch TV. He didn't want to go out with his face drooping! I explained the disease, how it affected a person and also asked if he was on Prednisone because that also had terrible side effects, including depression. She listened to me since I appeared normal after multiple episodes, I didn't tell her that one episode crossed over under my lower lip and resulted in paralysis of my lower lip and I had to learn how to properly speak again. No, I didn't tell her that, I told her to support him and soon he would be back and she would have to encourage him too move forward, I gave her some suggestions. She was pleased, hugged me and a small kiss on the cheek. I even gave her my number if her husband wanted to talk with me.

For years I traveled as part of my job, more than 150,000 Domestic Air Miles a year! I thought I was functioning well with stress, but I was wrong. And then this screwed up company caused me to have to get out of the workplace because of a workplace injury! I did continue lecturing and traveled for speaking engagements but something was going on with my voice and I had to stop that. Nine months of complaining to my San Diego VA doctor before I took the issue in hand and went to the Emergency Room. Another 3 1/2 hours waiting, they took 3 minutes to scope my throat and tell me I had polyps on my vocal chords! VA operated and OOPS, they didn't get them all and I had a second operation. This time they said the polyps must have grown back! No, they screwed up again and I ended up at University of California San Diego (UCSD) Medical Center. The UCSD doctor did a great job where VA could not. My speaking had taken a back seat and when I was finally fixed I didn't have the connections, I had been out of the profession a little too long.

Another thing I loved and had been doing nearly all my life was being a motorcycle enthusiast and driver. My daughter questioned when I would get off the bikes and Peggy said I would probably never, adding I would probably be buried with one! The last company said I would be fired if I drove one even to work and thinking I was going to be with them for a while, I sold the motorcycle and wished I hadn't.

Then I was still seeing a Chiropractor for my back, which VA still did not compensate. I complained about my sciatica and X-Rays showed what he thought to be a misaligned hip. By then I had another motorcycle and was having a few problems because when I rode I wore boots and because of my two toes I needed special sneakers, so when I drove I didn't walk far in the boots. Now with my sciatica it was getting harder to mount and ride my BMW 6-Cylinder Touring motorcycle, the number one Touring bike in the world! Hip adjustments didn't work as well as my Chiropractor wanted and because I had such a high tolerance for pain, he pushed harder! And the pain was through the roof! I was now diagnosed with needing a hip replacement and it came as COVID-19 hit! My scheduled surgery was cancelled/postponed for more than ten months! I could not drive the motorcycle and justified I had my convertible Porsche and sold that motorcycle also. My back which I had controlled and endured since 1976 was now getting the worst of my hip problems and my back was constantly in pain to match my hip. No way could I go back to work.

Numerous VA visits, compensation disputes, a personal letter to the Secretary of Veterans' Affairs, and in what became a 28 year battle with VA, I was still fighting the system. If you added up all the 10% here, 20% on others it totaled more than 80% but the VA math is not standard, so I had 50% disability. Until I met an even more incompetent doctor that really crossed that line and I was there fully loaded.

I was protesting my disability rating, each time bringing out their incompetence! One protest was send concerning my latest rating and I submitted it within the 30 days I had to protest. This was 2019. I got the letter back that denied my claim based on my response not submitted in time! They quoted the rating I was challenging was from 1991! My response was brutal. Shortly thereafter they said they were using a new program between VA and contracted services to review each of my physical complaints. This where I met the truly incompetent!

I went to a clinic near downtown San Diego, about 40 miles of packed freeways from my house. When I was directed into her clinic it was obvious she didn't want to be there and between her mouth and attitude it was obvious I was a much lesser being. By the way, many Veterans I have talked with, especially many Veterans with problems, many said they were treated similar. Anyway, she talked down to me and was reluctant to touch me for validation. Then we got to the scar over my right eye, you know the Vietnam injury I didn't get the Purple Heart for, she said it didn't look bad. I spoke up and quoted their VA regulations they had used to say the scar was too short but they failed to recognize the raised skin of the scar did meet the criteria! You could tell she was pissed at me challenging VA! I continued by asking her not to put any pressure on the scar as even the pressure of a hat on the scar caused a mild migraine headache, greater pressure caused a disabling headache!

Her reaction/response to my comment was to aggressively rub her thumb back and forth across the scar pressing very hard! I saw flashes of bright light coming out of my eyes and the headache was like an explosion in my head! "Why in the hell did you do that?" She answered by grabbing my right shoulder and walking me toward the door! She told me to go to the VA Hospital across the freeway to take a urine test! My head hanging and in obvious severe pain, "I can't drive." Her response as she pushed me into the lobby, "Use your GPS!", and shut the door behind me.

I staggered out to my car, mostly staggering because I could only barely see the steps or any other obstacle. Realizing how wrong it was for a doctor to tell someone obviously incapacitated to drive across an extremely busy California freeway! I made it to my car, put on my sunglasses and pulled down the windshield visor and slowly moved my car to a spot under a large tree. Seat pulled back, eyes closed, and transcendental meditation in full force, it took over 40 minutes to get to where I could even focus. Another half hour I thought I could go over to the hospital. It took me much longer than it should, so I sat under another tree at the hospital, went in and did the urine test, back to my car and near another 90 minutes before I felt I could drive home!

I raised so much hell over that and was contacted by the top administrator who the doctor reported to. I believe the doctor was disciplined and either let go or put somewhere away from patients. The boss inadvertently admitted to it while trying to say they were taking actions from my complaint. He explained the doctor's report was reviewed and they would do a competent evaluation of each problem I had identified.

Also I had complained about the AMVETS actions and a phone call I made to VA. VA had sent me a nice pamphlet about my VA benefits and had identified my primary VA hospital was on Lancaster Street in Dallas and the VA regional office was in Waco, Texas! Only problem was that I lived for over 10 years in California. I was getting all my correspondence at my house so I knew they had kept up with my address changes. I called the number on the pamphlet and was connected to the VA headquarters.

I told the person who answered what was wrong. I didn't expect the response I got. He went into a tirade about being sick and tired of us stupid GIs not smart enough to complete a change of address form and expected him to do their job for them! That complaint added to the mix and I got a thick letter about my disability rating, followed by a personal call from VA. The person did not apologize, he said he did not believe anyone at VA would ever talk to a patient/Veteran like I said he did. He also said VA does keep up with change of address and does not make logistical mistakes like telling me my VA hospital was in Texas!

I basically told him he must think similar to the others, does he really think us Veterans are stupid? He did raise his voice and said if there had been a problem it would have been corrected. I asked him to please tell me his name again. I validated with him it was his name on the letter back to me. And he said all problems were reviewed and corrected? He was getting upset and was interrupting me. I raised my voice and told him he was as bad as the man who cussed me out! He basically started more aggression, which I spoke loudly, "Did you review the letter you sent me?" He responded that he did. "Them why on the second from last page in YOUR letter does it say my nearest VA hospital is on Lancaster Street in Dallas, Texas and the Regional Center is in Waco, Texas?" And you are thinking I am the Idiot? I asked if he treated all Veterans like he just did to me? I went on to tell him I knew many Veterans who have little or nothing that tell me they are treated poorly. I feel that I have the advantage because of my education, experience, knowledge, access to resources, and have experience with dealing with assholes! I am very upset many of the Veterans living on the streets or in need of resources and help are truthful when they say there are so many barriers they face daily, VA being mentioned often. The phone call ended

After independent medical evaluations, including admitting Agent Orange exposure, I was rated at 100% Disabled! However, when we were in the middle of the Pandemic I got a recorded phone call from a VA hospital Administrator telling me how important the Veterans are and he wants to make sure I get my Covid-19 shots without delay. All I had to do is come down to the hospital! Then the message repeated the address of the VA hospital on Lancaster Street in Dallas, Texas!

Why was it so important for me to get 100% Disability? Not only do I get a Disability Handicap hand tag, I get all of my numerous medical problems documented and addressed. Also, if something should happen to me, Peggy will have a great portion of the Disability payment. Now I can get medications for all my problems, even my diabetes I didn't know I had until I went it for surgery.

My General Practitioner was another incompetent but he did one thing, he told me about the GRADE (Glucose Reduction Approaches in Diabetes), a National Institute of Health (NIH) program that helped determine the best medications and treatments to help Type 2 diabetes. When I first attempted to enroll they would not take me as my A1C was well over 8.5. It was well into the 9s. They recommended some practices I could do to lower it to the 8.5 A1C that would get me into the program. They said one year to do that was very aggressive and they would test me in six months to help me with my progress.

I didn't know I had diabetes and now it was bad! So I took it on with an aggressive diet mixed with more TM. Six months later I tested and the Study people were blown away! My A1C was now down in the 7s! Nobody in the Study had done that! At the end of the 5 year study I had my ups and downs. After meds taken for one of my surgeries my Glucose level rose dramatically enough I started taking Insulin. At the end of the Study I was called a star pupil, with only 20 units of Insulin daily I had an A1C of 5.6! Anything under 7.0 is considered good.

When the program ended, the results and recommendations were transferred to my new doctor at VA. The Study was in a building on the VA Campus so they knew my doctor and she assured me that she would not change the treatment protocol. Yeah, like I should trust VA to be competent. As soon as my doctor had control she had a very high value of herself, very narcissistic, Laboratory "Professional" take over reviewing my meds. The promise they would keep the medication protocol lasted for only seconds. She changed everything because she knew better! Soon I had another blood test and my doctor's assistant sent me a congratulatory message that my A1C was below 7.0, it was 6.8! My return message was not kind, you are congratulating me for 6.8 A1C when before you took over my treatment it was 5.7! I burned a couple bridges. And to get my Glucose to an acceptable level I had to increase the insulin more than 3 times the level! When the Laboratory phenomenon heard me tell her I was dropping the new medicine she prescribed because of the interaction with one of my other meds, she argued. I had two doctors I was friends with and my nurse sister-in-law say giving me the meds was stupid and an amateurish move. The Pharmacist then told me my expectations for my daily Glucose level was much lower than her standard! I told her to please stay out of my life and got a really narcissistic reply from her, I hung up and texted my doctor, telling her to stop and go back to our initial promise to leave the meds alone! The next response from her was that although she was working on my case, she was taking a vacation!

I still go to VA for prescriptions but very little treatment, I use my Medicare and other insurance to see other non VA doctors. I still get very upset knowing there are Veterans and other people without resources that have to tolerate this literal injustice and abuse. I have lost many friends from exposure to Agent Orange and the effects like Cancer from the exposure. And many friend who have run into these barriers and solved the pressure by taking their lives. I am having an anxiety attack just writing and thinking about this.

46

Life beyond work

I bought another BMW six cylinder motorcycle, even bigger than what I had but soon my foot and the amputations made it too hard to ride. I also was feeling pain in my right leg, which I thought to be my sciatica but was probably the start of my need for a hip replacement. I ended up selling it and put some of the profits to good use.

Peggy's sister, Kathy, had never been outside the US except one trip to Hawaii. So Peggy planned a girls trip that started with a night in Paris, followed by a cruise around the British Isles and another last night in Paris. I was fine with the trip, encouraged it, and even gave Kathy the new Sony Camera. I took some of the cash from sale of my BMW and upgraded their hotel room for both nights in Paris and helped with upgrades on the cruise. I figured Peggy had put up with me traveling all the time in the military to places all over the world without her and now with me traveling in the US for more than 150,000 air miles a year, then she and her sister should go and have fun. They did and even so much that Kathy got out of the Uber from their last night at the Eiffel Tower and left the camera in the car! She started to tell me she was sorry but I stopped her and said the camera was a gift to her and it was hers, not mine. Peggy brought back some literature on the Clan I belong to through my heritage and a great Guinness shirt from} their Irish Brewery. A lot of pictures, not nearly as many as I take, but all good. They had fun.

Not to say I take a lot of pictures but when we went to Costa Rica it was the same time a lady I worked with went. Mind you, we started going to the East Coast and across all the way to the Pacific where my friend stayed on the west, Pacific side. She asked about my pictures and I told her it would be a couple days, I was still editing them. She asked how many I took and it was about 1,400 pictures, they took 64! The Safari I took nearly 1,900, Peggy about 100. But with the new digital media, I take a lot, many duplicates, and then edit them down.

Every year I try to take Peggy on a trip in celebration of our Anniversary. We travel a lot in celebration to overseas locations and some within the United States. We own both our cars, have little monthly expenses except mortgage, so we save and plan for our travels. Not to say we travel a lot, but one of the guys I volunteer with bragged to another that he probably has traveled more than any of the Volunteers, I'll talk about the USS Midway Museum where I volunteer later. So when he says he has traveled more I sort of laughed. "What are you laughing about?" I just said, "You haven't traveled until you have done fifty fifty!" He asked what that was and I asked him if he has done all fifty states and visited, not just the airport, at least fifty countries? His response was he didn't know anybody who has done that! I just responded, "Guess you don't know me."

47

Anniversary Trips and Travels:

I believe Peggy and I survived all that we had suffered growing up in the same way in a different setting. Her mother died from Cancer at age 59 and my mother hung on until one month before 93, the last 14 years in Assisted Living we helped pay for. And still to the end she would tell me in front of Peggy that I should have married Glenda! My sister and her husband, who only spoke to criticize or belittle me, brought up old things that I had done and how hard I had been on my dear sweet mother! The military took us away and we depended on each other as a nuclear family. We distanced ourselves from criticism and arguments that way. When I first met Peggy I told her how my sister would argue and if she didn't have a winning hand she would tell me she was older, and therefore right! The first argument my sister started after I was married to Peggy didn't end as she expected. When she started to use the "age" thing I interrupted and said if age was a factor, Peggy won! My sister has since dropped that defense as Peggy is two months and two days older than my sister! We have thought about moving back to Maine, Peggy never wants to go back to Colorado, but we love living in California.

Growing up I don't think I ever used the word "love" very much, I didn't believe in it and although I tell my sister I love her, I could never say that to my mother. My sister tells complete strangers about how great her mother was and how whenever she needed money for college, my mother always had some for her. Yeah, yet she denies it when I finally told her I gave my mother half my pay because she said I needed to help my sister through college. Yet, my sister quit college to get married, finally getting her single degree while on my own I accumulated five degrees, including the PhD.

Anyway, after I left the military I still dragged Peggy all over the US. I was using the "love" word better and was showing Peggy how much I loved her by the thoughtful and often expensive gifts I gave her and trying to get her flowers on a regular basis. Others got their wives flowers for special occasions but for me it was special when I felt like it, I didn't wait for a reason, I just did it.

And, the one thing we are good at and think it is something special is taking a trip to celebrate our Anniversary. And we travel well together. I had to get over my PTSD restrictions when we travel, but still won't sit with my back to the door, always against a wall. Although Peggy often comes up with the destination, she does most of the travel arrangements, using my miles a lot, even tapping into them for other reasons! I don't mind.

So, our Anniversary trips are special to us and I have tried to take Peggy places where I have been and she hasn't, Alaska and Vietnam are two good examples. So, our Anniversary trips became a reminder of life and love, and I was sharing with the person I loved, even though my mother said I married the wrong woman!

Anniversary for us was May 20 so just about everywhere was fairly good weather at that time, we did adjust a couple trips, like the Safari to try to be there for the Great Migration. Travel is a priority for us, plus I have this thing for years, I won't buy anything that would cause me to have to put one of our vehicles out of the garage. Of course, things like a rental in Manhattan Beach didn't have a useable garage. So when we moved to San Diego I said I needed to buy a car, and a small one, possibly a Roadster! I had my motorcycle that I parked along the front wall of the garage with enough room to drive my car in where there was probably a couple feet between the front of my car and the left side of my motorcycle. I always left the other side fully open for Peggy's car. We owned all our vehicles, even my Racing Yellow Porsche

981 (Boxster S) roadster! It was short enough that I could park both it and the motorcycle in the same bay. Don't get me wrong, affording a Porsche involved some money and time management. I put down a substantial amount to lease my Porsche and then when the lease was up I bought it as I would a new car. So beside the Mortgage and utilities, we could budget for our trips.

Alaska

I wanted to talk a little about our Anniversary trip to Alaska. I had been to Alaska a few times and guest lectured at the University of Alaska Anchorage but Peggy had been at the airport a couple times, so we really planned on having a great Anniversary in Alaska. We flew to Vancouver and caught our cruise ship and started north to Alaska. We made some friends on the cruise and were wondering why we were not running into them in Anchorage? I also wondered why we had such a crappy hotel in Anchorage? I had stayed right across the intersection a couple times I was there and this hotel was embarrassingly bad in comparison. Come to find out the hotel chain is owned by the cruise line and at that moment I was thinking we made a mistake! We did! A few events on the cruise line didn't set well with us. For example, we made reservations at one of the specialty restaurants and we got there a little early, actually a few minutes before it opened. We were standing to the side of the door talking with another couple and when the doors opened the four of us started to enter the restaurant when we heard this stern comment from a woman at the top of the short stairs, "The line forms here, you are cutting the line!" She said it in a superior tone and acted like she was way more a person than us! I was going to say something directly at her but instead said loud enough for her to hear, "You got to be shitting me!" The four of us just laughed at her and when we did get into the restaurant the maitre de asked what was wrong. I said nothing really, we just met some people that we hope stay away from us! He asked what they did and loud enough for many people to hear I said again, nothing, they are a joke, nothing that I want to spoil my trip with. There just seemed to be a lot of people who thought they were important and I found out innocently that a lot of people travel a lot with this cruise line and develop that "at home" attitude where we just don't belong. Another time we were sitting in the top lounge area and were asked in a similar manner to move so the lady would have room for her friends! We didn't.

From Vancouver we sailed up to Ketchikan, a small town that looked like the old west. It is a native peoples diverse area and has the largest number of totem poles in the world! It had unique shops and we walked through most of what seemed to be the town. One day there and up past Sitka, which I wished we had stopped, but didn't. Then we sailed into Juneau where we visited the Rainforest and I boldly licked a Banana Slug! Very beautiful area. I should explain the Banana Slug thing. As we went through the rain forest we were introduced to all the inhabitants by our guide. When we got to some green moss all across the area, he picked up this rather large Banana Slug and asked what were we supposed to do with it? One of the girls on the tour said she heard you were supposed to kiss the slug! She was close. Researchers are looking into the numbing oil on the slug as a possible anesthesia! You are supposed to lick it! Of course nobody stepped up to do it, except me. I licked my first Banana Slug!

We stayed at a great wilderness place where we hiked, saw glaciers, even hiked on a trail where we saw a female moose and two youngsters up ahead. When they crested the rise I walked fast to get up there and get a closer picture, however, as I got near the crest I was confronted with the moose coming straight at me! I said something like "oh crap" and ran down the hill to where Peggy was walking rapidly away from the rise! I grew up in Maine and knew the right thing to do when confronting a moose, and we did run! We sailed in the glacier waters and saw the beauty of it. Up to Skagway and then across to Anchorage. Anchorage has some very beautiful areas and it also seems a little like the old west with some rustic buildings. I think the past earthquakes prevented building taller buildings, so it is a modern city without the tall buildings. Of course we had some very good Reindeer (elk) and many of the eating places looked a lot like bars. We enjoyed ourselves and there we got the idea of flying up to the Arctic Circle.

From there we took train and bus up to Denali (formerly Mount McKinley) National Park. The hotel we stayed in was owned by the Cruise Line and again was a problem for us. It seems that most of the people on the ship and who ran the shops at the town and the hotel were from Belarus. Nice people but American standards did not apply. For example: we took the bus into the National Park and we did see a lot of wildlife. Bear, Moose, Mountain Goat, etc. and they had a zoom camera to spot some at a distance and show them on TV screens, and some, like a pair of Black Bear were almost within reach of us on the bus. Unfortunately, the entire time on the bus we had to have some windows down because of the exhaust fumes seeping through the floor.

At the hotel I turned out of the bathroom through the narrow hall toward the bedroom as Peggy was heading in the opposite direction. I moved slightly right to let her pass and was immediately struck hard on my forehead! They had placed a sharp cornered rectangular light on the side of the hallway wall that projected at least six inches into the walkway! It almost rung my bell, and me being a Safety Professional I realized immediately it was installed not in compliance with federal or state safety laws! That caused me to look more and there were safety violations everywhere, but at the moment I wanted to report the light fixture to their Safety Officer. Good luck there, none of the people knew what safety was, no training, and none knew who or if there was a safety person in the company! I asked to talk to the Manager and he said he would check into it and later contacted me that he had asked their Corporate Office and they didn't know if they even had a Safety Officer!

We never saw Denali from the National Forest because it was never clear enough. We didn't see the friends we met on the cruise, we guessed they had a separate itinerary. We met up with them again after our train and short bus ride to Fairbanks. They had reservation with another Cruise Line and stayed in their hotels. They saw Denali and from what they told us, their tours were superior to ours! We saw a lot in Fairbanks and decided to take our own side tour and booked a small airplane to fly north of the Arctic Circle! We flew up to Wiseman, 63 miles north of the Arctic Circle. As many have said that nothing grows north of the Arctic Circle, I beg to differ. In the background of the picture I took of the City sign is rich green trees and snow crested hills. Back to Fairbanks and the flight home. The trip well worth it, a must see.

Baltics

Another great trip we took for our anniversary was a Baltic's Cruise. The closest Peggy and I had been to the Baltic's was probably going through Belgium. So we decided to see the Baltic countries and Russia on one of our last Anniversary trips before COVID-19 stopped all travel. There were a few places I never expected to ever go; North Vietnam, Communist China, Cuba, and Russia, mostly because of the world we grew up in. Now I can say that with my lovely bride, we have visited all these places. If COVID-19 doesn't mess with travel like it did, I rescheduled a trip we had to cancel, I'll cover that later. Now we were going to visit France, England, Bruges, Copenhagen, Stockholm, Tallinn Estonia, St. Petersburg, Helsinki, and Gdansk Poland! We save about everything, sometimes getting what we want and maybe not need, for our travel and celebration of us. So we usually plan on up-grading air travel when going overseas, but Peggy informed me we ere flying Coach Comfort and upgrading the Suite on the ship! We got a large Suite at the back of the ship and had all the upgrades with it. It was going to be a great trip.

Into France and then through the Tunnel into England and the next day boarded the Cruise Ship in Southhampton. I had tried again to contact Michael but we both knew he had some major medical problems and the Social Medicine system in England, we are sure, delayed his needed surgery until it was too late. I believe I read between the lines the last time we talked that he was in dire straits and expected to lose the battle. His wife did not like us because she could not smoke in our house and we kidded her about her cheap wine she got to get drunk and not enjoy the "grape"! So she never told us of his fate.

Our first stop was Bruges, Belgium. A lot of people take pictures of a body part in front of a sign marking where they were, even though I don't drink that much, I chose to have a local beer at each place and take a picture of that! In Bruges I had a dark Leffe beer. We walked and ate at this very nice little street cafe and asked about the Belgium chocolates! We were pointed to the proclaimed best chocolate shop!

We watched them make all the chocolate products in all imaginable shapes and flavors! It was hard to pick some we wanted to take back to the ship, when in reality I don't remember any getting on board, they were so good we ate them while still in the city. We were basically on our own whereas in most of the cities visited we bought tours from the ship. Bruges is a very quaint town and as we remembered our time briefly in Brussels years past, we remarked the town maintained as it was back then, full of history, waterways, and chocolate! We got on one of the "jump on, jump off" busses and saw most of the city.

Next we cruised through the inland straits and over to Copenhagen. We went to a large food building that was crammed with little stores and restaurants. A nice lunch and walk along the seaside. Visited a beautiful old church and we stopped at all these little stands set up to sell trinkets to the wealthy tourists. We laughed as we stepped under the over hang of this one shop because it looked like many of the Mexican shops in Southern California. We looked at some jewelry and asked where he got this jewelry? Finally he said he got it from Mexico and that is where he was from! During the long tourist season he comes over from Mexico and sells the jewelry. We didn't buy any, why go to Copenhagen to buy what we could get a couple miles from home! Here I had a Herslev Bryghus dark Porter beer.

Stockholm is a very modern city and we found ourselves downtown with except the water, could have been a metropolitan city in the US. As I said, we often took tours and many stopped for some free time, but here we got off the bus and went through the City pretty much on our own, and lucky we didn't have a schedule to meet because we basically got lost! We bought some stuff Peggy saw in a department store and the prices were not that bad, especially since Stockholm is a very expensive place to live. How we got lost was we keyed in on a large building with a name on the side in huge lettering. When we saw it again we knew we had to turn right! NOT! The building, we found, had the same name on three sides and the building looked the same on all three! We found our way back to where we picked up the bus back to the Cruise Ship. There I had an Eriksberg on tap in a restaurant on our small tour.

We did not know what to expect in Tallinn, Estonia. We had a tour that took us through the city and the canals. We stopped in a square and had free time, so to speak. The tour guide told us it was free time so when Peggy and I started to go back to see something we saw along the way, the Guide called to us and told us not to run off, he had something to show us! After seeing the historic clock and tunnel we slipped away and walked in the unique town. We marveled at how the building looked uniform but had enough small differences they made it unique. We got back to the square and we went inside the restaurant to use the bathroom and when we came out the guide told us they had been waiting for us and said how long. We laughed, as did a couple we had been talking to as we were there well before the time he said we weren't! Here I had a Meabear light beer.

Then we arrived in St.Petersburg, Russia. We definitely took the tours there so we could visit the Hermitage and some palaces. Just unbelievable, both the places and the city where we toured. We had a couple days there and we went on tours because there was too much to see and miss on our own. We were told the city is not like Moscow, and I guess it so because we didn't see the large ornate buildings like in Moscow, but such a famous place as the Hermitage we probably would have walked right past it as it was in a fairly plain looking building. We watch a performance and song/dance at one art museum and saw huge gardens and water displays. We spent time in a huge church and saw so many beautiful things and portraits, and displays. And so many people! We could have stayed another couple days and still not seen everything. We were in Russia! I had a Wunyau beer.

We then went to Helsinki, Finland, another place for some reason I never expected to visit. Again, modern and cold. I had in my mind, I don't know why, that it would be like Amsterdam. It wasn't but still had the water nearby but not the canals. We took a tour and saw some museums and northern beauty. It was a beautiful city that I didn't expect. The food was great, and still expensive. I have to admit that seeing seven big cities in two weeks, especially like St Petersburg. we saw so much it was hard to remember where we were when we saw things. I had a local beer that I could not find the name but all symbols, including the glass showed an apparent bear with sharp and long teeth!

Next to Gdansk, Poland and here we booked a tour and the company running the tour busses had a couple stops and after the morning tour we went to the meeting place and were supposed to take the bus for the afternoon tour but we were told to board one of the busses and it returned to the ship! We complained a little but I think we were kind of glad to relax some. What we did see of Gdansk was again unique to a large city where you could tell it got cold because things were protected from the elements. We could go between many buildings with minimum exposure and after visiting more museums we realized the countries all honored their past and displayed it. There were some religious displays but not as much as many of the other cities and you could see what appeared to be a past telling of military force. Very unique and interesting, something I again didn't know what to expect. This tour included a restaurant and it seemed the food was similar to German food. I had a Zywiec beer with the meal.

As we left and took more than a day at sea to get back to Southhampton I can say Peggy booking the upgraded suite was maybe one of the highlights of the cruise. We could eat at any restaurant we wanted, and we went to the Italian restaurant for breakfast just about every morning. We enjoyed the wait staff and they enjoyed us, which made it nice. Because of the upgrade we had access to the upper deck elite lounge and often ate some of the finger food before we went to dinner and returned after a show or such to get another drink and talk to friends. Peggy met one of the performers in the elevator and we went to her show and bought one of her CDs. Our "butler" always greeted us, always calling me Doctor Brown, and making sure we had fresh fruit and chocolate, etc. We were supposed to be gratuity free but I gave him a good tip. The suite was worth it! I had Guinness and Heineken on board. Back to the US.

48

Life After Work:

First of all, I didn't want to stop working but the foot injury I had while at BBSI was a game changer. For my supervisor to fail to report my injury to Workers' Compensation and refuse to honor a medical authority were and are both legal issues. Both he and his supervisor, as illegal as he was, resigned from the company. They knew it was illegal. Maybe I should have sued for both this action and Wrongful Termination, but I chose not to. A special investigation was done to make it look legal but it was internal and the results were said what they did was legal. The investigator was a manger from Colorado and probably didn't know California law or just didn't care. The alternative was my job reinstated but by then I was getting treated by VA and did not want to work with any of them again. I know I am a professional but seeing how so many people made critical mistakes yet they kept on while one very competent person made a comment to the top lady at the San Diego Office I worked in and she was unceremoniously fired!

What does retirement mean to me? I work so well under stress, but now it is much less stress in my life. With my hip replacement surgery coming up and my lack of mobility, it was determined our beautiful Cockatoo was way too much for me to handle. He had imprinted on me and was demanding, so much so we had him "re-homed" to hopefully a good family that will love him. We kept our little Cinnamon Turquoise Conure and she has been so much more a great pet since the Cockatoo left, guess he was stressing us all out. Then we went to a place recommended by our daughter to get a rescue dog. We wanted a Corgi and looked at one but totally fell in love with a brown and white (Blenheim) Cavalier King Charles Spaniel. We named him Charley and on the way home we heard him cough! Soon we had him at Urgent Care and he was diagnosed with Kennel Cough and Pneumonia! We tried so hard, but Charley's heart gave out on him 28 days after we got him. Whatever great things dogs do for someone like me with PTSD, the loss about killed me.

Peggy knew that and the day he passed she contacted a breeder in Los Angeles and we paid for "Pick of the Litter" male. Her dog had a small litter with only one boy. We went up to see him before he was weaned. Susan was out from Boston and we went then. He was so tiny with the most beautiful face, a Tri-Color Cavalier King Charles. On the way home the two ladies came up with the name Stanley! It fits him and his color and markings are beyond belief, but what still stands out is his beautiful face and the most beautiful eyes! When he sits on my lap I can feel the stress and PTSD drain from me, our Veterinarian said it would happen, and added he knows of nobody with just one Cavalier, so a year later we got Albert, a Blenheim, from the same breeder. Not only do the dogs love each other, Albert even relaxes me more when he sits on my lap than Stanley. He is beautiful also, everyone says we have the two cutest dogs! Albert is also so sensitive! Peggy hurt her back and sometimes if she moves or sits wrong the pain will make her yell. Albert will get next to her, look around, back and forth, and whine as if to say "how can I help?" Both watch TV when sitting on the couch with us and if a dog or other animal like a horse appears, they will growl and sometimes go to the TV and bark ferociously.

I still have nightmares and usually come to bed later than Peggy so when I come to bed I am tired and can sleep. If not tired, I will not sleep and end up getting up until I am tired. Stanley more than often sleeps up against my legs. Albert will dive into my neck and often sleep under the covers with me with just his head out and usually resting on my arm. He may get up to turn around so he is facing me and lay his head on mine. Often Peggy has him wrapped in an embrace, but usually within a short period of time he comes over to me and cuddles. Stanley seems a little jealous and will lie above the covers much closer to my head so Albert has more trouble getting to my neck, his favorite cuddling place. I have fewer nightmares with them around. Pets are God's gift to us who suffer.

After being struck by the Restaurant umbrella and my left eye damaged, my left eye is for distance, the right is for near, as was set during my Lasik surgery. I found reading allowed me to rest my left eye and help it improve. So I read over 150 books a year! I love reading and love doing so using my I-Pad. I often think "does a stupid man read all that many books, and retains most of what he reads?"

49

Volunteering:

Can't work, how about Volunteering? I remember volunteering for the American Red Cross, American Heart Association, Seymour Johnson Emergency Room, all the church and school safety work, developing Capital City ordinances, orphanages overseas, school groups, and helping place 14 Amerasian children in loving adoptive arms.

I applied to both the San Diego Zoo/Safari Park and the USS Midway Museum. At the Zoo I would be just one of the volunteers and if I wanted to work with the animals, even at the displays where nobody gets past the barrier or enclosures they have to get specialized training. I didn't find this out for months because they took months to respond to me. When I contacted the Midway Museum I said I was a Safety professional and almost immediately I was brought in for orientation and an interview with the Safety Department. They did not need someone like me. Their mission and goals are laced with security so I was very overqualified. That same day I was asked if I wanted to be a Docent? So I was back for orientation and an interview for a Docent position. Basically accepted on the spot and was enrolled in the next Docent Training Class. I did get accepted by the San Diego Zoo and attended their orientation, but the Midway was operated like a successful corporation that let everyone, volunteers included, the Vision and Goal of the museum. What they really excelled in was allowing Volunteers to be a principle part of the success. The volunteers had something major companies often miss, they have Responsibility, Authority, and Accountability!

I don't believe there is another place like the USS Midway Museum. When the Midway was decommissioned in 1992 at North Island Navy Pier it was sent to Bremerton, Washington, the ship graveyard. Here ships are cannibalized for useable equipment and parts. Then it is a matter of time before destiny shows her ugly head and it is jokingly said the ships end up as razor blades. Actually some are used as targets or are sunk for artificial reefs, and some do end up as razor blades. There are many Naval Museums, old ships docked and converted to museums. There are about 106 ships used as museums in about 30 different states and about 9 countries. There are some we visit to pay homage like the USS Arizona Memorial in Pearl Harbor, Hawaii, and some like the Nazi German Submarine docked in Chicago after it was captured in 1941. So it was not unusual for a Team of former Navy and other concerned people requested the USS Midway to be docked in San Diego Bay and made into a Maritime Museum. The problem was the agencies the team had to go through to get approval These agencies included the City of San Diego that could not see a huge Aircraft Carrier parked in the Bay, they saw it as an eyesore and blocking the sights of the Bay. The Coastal Commission had plans for the area that was proposed and all they could see is problems. The Navy Department did not want to release a ship without guarantees for such things as not having to support maintaining the condition of an old ship, amongst other worries. 12 years of undying determination and heavy costs often borne of the Team members, and the Midway made her way down from Washington state and docked at the Navy Pier. The Team was told there was a chance it would not be received well by the town and there would be unsurmountable problems. Fortunately, on opening to the public in 2004 there was overwhelming acceptance. Not to say there were no problems, but the management that was part of the Team and now the CEO worked it until the Midway now is the #1 Maritime Museum in the World! And almost every step, besides maintenance, safety, staff, etc. is manned by volunteer Docents! And I was asked to join the Docent force.

There were around 20 of us in the Docent Training Class. Most were former Navy, three were women with knowledge but not service in the military, and one although former short time Navy and 22 years Air Force, me. Our training was on the ship and lasted 7 weeks. Our training manual was at least six inches thick, and we were tested and toured every week and then 20 hours of on-the-job training where we worked in areas of the ship under supervision. Finally ending with one of the Evaluation Team doing a thorough testing of our knowledge and skills before we could achieve the status of wearing the Docent Yellow Cap. It may sound easy, however, my final exam took 4 1/2 hours! The evaluator was constantly asking me questions about everything as we visited everywhere on the ship. If a guest asked a question my Evaluator would step back and I would answer the question. Possibly the hardest test was when we went up on the "Island", the superstructure rising above the Flight Deck where we had Primary Flight, Chart Room and the Bridge. Primary Flight is where the Air Boss controlled the aircraft like a Control Tower at an Airport. Then down and forward one level to the "Chart Room" where the Navigator and the Quartermasters plotted maps for navigation. And lastly the Bridge where the ships direction and control was and where the Commander sat during sail. Why it was so hard was that Docents took 20 guests at a time through all three areas and had to give a 4 minute presentation in each area! Not 3 minute or 5 minute, 4 minute talk and then to the next area for another 4 minute talk and then finishing at the Bridge for the last of three 4 minute talks.

When we got to the Primary Flight my Evaluator told me when to start as he hit his stop watch. When I finished he seemed a little different. He corrected a couple small things I said, we didn't have scrips, it was us talking about what we thought was pertinent in 4 minutes. Same in the Chart room and this time when I finished he was kind of shaking his head and then we went forward to the Bridge. This time he did not start the stop watch. I thought I had blown it but later found out I had broken the existing record and had done both the Primary Flight and Chart Room talks at exactly 4 minutes on the dot!

In the training I was often the person to be picked on since I was Air Force. The head instructor might be covering a topic and tell the class, "We had better speak slowly through this, we have an Air Force guy here", and stuff like that. The guy sitting next to me was an Engineer aboard an Aircraft Carrier and had his PhD, he said this was all new to him because all he saw basically was what he was working on and knew not much else! My short time as an Electronics Technician on a Destroyer Escort did little to give me any knowledge, so I studied very hard. I was about the only one in the class that used an I-Pad for training. I downloaded the entire manual to my I-Pad and my search was much easier than those using a PC. If they searched for a keyword their computer would show the first time that word appeared and they would have to "skip" until the word showed up in the context of their search. On my I-Pad it showed all areas the keyword was so I just scrolled down to what I wanted. To put it in perspective, my search for a word usually lasted 15 to 20 seconds while those using their PC some-times complained about 10 or more minutes of searching one word! All this must have helped as I was the first one in my class to get the Yellow Hat! When I got home I threw down my hat next to Peggy and told her I was First! Her response, "you always have to be first and best, always"!

In most Museums there is paid staff and volunteers do sometimes menial tasks. At the Midway, Docents, all volunteers, did most of the work and are supported by Staff. I started volunteering two mornings a week. Reason for mornings is the traffic. The Midway is 40 miles from my house and coming home after an afternoon Watch put me in the worst traffic jam you could imagine! Many on the second Watch would gather at a restaurant to eat and have a couple drinks so they could miss the heavy traffic. I had Watch at many different stations, a few times in Engine Room 3, and in the Combat Information Center, and the Tactical Command Center, but most of all I did the "Island" tours. As a professional speaker I was very good there and my timing was still right on.

During this time I got the invitation to Orientation for the San Diego Zoo and Safari Park. I was elated! I love animals dearly and most appreciated me, most likely because they knew I would never hurt them, as was testimony with the Tarantula in Costa Rica, the skunk I pet in Maine, the giraffe that pressed against me at the Safari Park and the number of times we have met someone with a dog who says the dog doesn't like men and then shocked the dog comes to me. One day at the Midway a lady and her daughter came on with a small dog, we don't see many on the ship. The dog was very quiet and stayed next to the lady, acting as if bored. I was talking to a couple guests and next I felt the dog jumping onto the side of my leg and I put my hand down as I was talking. The dog licked my hand, but I wasn't looking since I was still talking to the guests. The woman loudly said "No" and I turned to her. She started pulling the dog's leash and again said "No" so I looked down at the dog and pet his head, "That's okay, I like dogs" I said and then she asked what I had in my hand? I turned my hand palm up and said I had nothing and asked why? She told me that her dog had never done that before! He had never jumped up and wanted a person to pet him, especially didn't like men! I squat down, rubbed the little guy behind his ear and the lady and her daughter had a nice talk with me.

So, I was enthusiastic about working as a Volunteer with the Zoo and I got the chance to talk to volunteers and some staff, soon realizing just how special the Docents and Staff at the Midway are, and how I can do so much there with people of similar backgrounds and like passion for volunteering at the Midway.

On the ship we have done things especially for the guests. For example; many of the "ladders" were removed and replaced by stairs so guests can see the entire ship. We have listening devices in six different languages for guests to touch on a specific panel in front of most displays and hear, often by people who flew that aircraft or did that job, explain the display. Most of us Docents can tell the guests about each and every display. We also took out a large steam boiler and some structure ahead of Elevator #1 and built a small theater where we show a 14 minute movie with holograms of the Battle of Midway, called "Voices of Midway" and depicts the actual battle where the Navy turned World War II around. The Battle is proclaimed the greatest Naval Victory in US

History. An old guy ran it and when the Pandemic caused shutdowns and they reduced staff members, the theater was closed due to inability to social distance and the old guy was laid off. That was also the time I was scheduled for a hip replacement so I stopped going there.

When we finally opened more of the ship we were told the old guy at the theater had passed away during the Pandemic and the Docents would now have to run it. I was the only one to volunteer to do it Saturday mornings. When I came back I was not fully recovered from my hip replacement so I decided to go only once a week and Peggy asked that I keep it to only once. So again, there was a suggested briefing, but we were allowed to say what we wanted. I immediately said the 14 minute movie was the story so I was just going to have a short introduction and then turn on the movie. Many of the other Watches have two or more people assigned to it, and often one will stand at the base of the seats and tell stories, etc. I don't, mainly because I won't take away from the movie. My presentation is enthusiastic! I tell the guests what the Japanese Empire was doing, how the Task Force was taking islands as they came down through the Marshall Islands, hit Midway, then down the South Pacific to the Coral Sea and the Great Barrier Reef and now was heading back to finish Midway Island, finish Hawaii, and look toward the West Coast of the United States! Then I say the Battle of Midway turned the War around. I speak a little Japanese and tell them if we hadn't won at Midway Island we might all be speaking Japanese! I tell them the Japanese word for the Task Force, "Kido Butai". Then I tell them the size of the Force and how many and description of the ships forming the Force. I turn on the movie and come back in as it is just finishing and I remind the guests that in our bookstore we have some great books about the Battle. At my opening I sometimes get an applause because I make it exciting and I build up to a crescendo and back down so they are enthused to see the movie and the rest of the ship.

I have some people each day tell me how much they like my opening. The head of Customer Service has said how many reports they get on how good I am doing. People come back by and tell me how much they liked the movie and especially how I set it up. I will sometimes have help but usually I do the whole Watch solo. A fellow Docent has worked with me a couple times and I always tell him he can do the intro if he wants to! Last time he said, "Yeah, maybe next year!" and went on to say there is nobody he has seen do it as good as I do, nobody better! And to add to that, since I mention the Bookstore, George is the guy running it and whereas the Bookstore just about breaks even, he is reporting as much as $800 in book sales Saturday morning when I am running the theater! I don't have to ask where I will stand Watch Saturday mornings, I just go in early, warm up the projector and preview the movie to make sure it is running well. Disney helped build the theater and with all the holograms and such, I make sure all is well. Then I go to the Watch briefing and when the head DOW (Docent On Watch) announces the stations, it is always me at the theater and they have no intention of replacing me.

I had another cancer removed from my face and when I told the DOW I could not make it, he simply said he needed to get someone to fill in for me when I could not be there, basically saying the theater was mine. One week, the administrative roster for volunteers signed up for the Saturday morning Watch messed up. My name and others were dropped from the roster. The DOW called me Friday afternoon and asked if I could please come it for Saturday Watch? I said I was signed up and would be there. He said that was great, he had nobody who could run the Battle of Midway Theater, he needed me.

I had to prepare them for me missing one Saturday because my sister-in-law and her husband are coming with us to Boston for a week so we can see Susan, her husband and our grandkids, now young adults. Now, after we have canceled our Mediterranean cruise twice due to the Pandemic, we are doing a land trip to Istanbul, Cairo, and Tel Aviv and I will miss two weekends. So the DOW and others are trying to get some people interested that I can train.

50

Education

Recently there has been a real push for Tuition Forgiveness. Some of the Representatives have talked about how much debt they have on their student loans. One makes $174,000 a year and is complaining her student debt is $17,000 and wants us, the taxpayers, to pay off her loan. Here are some of my thoughts, seeing that I have five degrees.

I will admit that going in the military helped a lot with the GI Bill, however, two of my degrees were not covered by the GI Bill and they were my last two, my Masters and PhD, the most expensive of the five.

I believe schools should be like businesses, their Vision and Goal should be what your Vision and Goal is. When I applied for "Operation Bootstrap" to get a year paid for by the military, I looked at the best schools in the profession I wanted. I was an Environmental Health and Safety Professional and the ranking in schools at that time for that degree were at #1: University of Southern California; #2: Central Missouri State University; and #3: Arizona State University. Bootstrap is a "Terminal" program that means in one year you have to earn the degree, you had only one year. When I applied to USC, and I knew it was expensive, they refused my entrance, stating "People do not become Trojans in less than 18 months", Trojans being their nickname.

CMSU was not as expensive or snooty! I graduated in 8 months with a degree. Why couldn't USC do the same? My belief is many people go to high priced schools for the name, often paying outlandish tuition so people can brag about the pedigree of the school they attended. I have friends and relatives who have asked for Grants and Scholarships. It is a lot of work to get these but in two cases I know the Grants and Scholarships paid for most of their tuition. Again, it takes a lot of work to apply and in most cases your academic history is very important.

Also, I believe our society is now "I want it now" and people attend a university to get a degree as fast as they can. I started going to college in 1969 when I was first assigned to a unit in Spain. I completed my five degrees in 1997. I paid some and the GI Bill paid some. As a Sergeant I did not make a lot of money. The pay scale has improved tremendously since then but I retired from the Air Force in 1988 and still didn't make much. I'll just say there is the Base Pay and then you get money for things like Housing and Cost of Living. My Base Pay as a Senior Non Commissioned Officer was $22,000 a year.

I never complained, I used resources and got my Bachelors Degree through the University Of Maryland while I was overseas. I never took out a loan. My Associates was awarded later through College of the Air Force for performance in my field and a few classes. I didn't take out a loan for that.

Back stateside I attended classes where I could at local colleges. I attended Wayne State, had some classes at Miami University, some at USC, etc. All this while going to work and taking night and weekend classes. While in Japan I basically got my second Bachelors Degree, this one in Psychology. However, I was shy 6 semester hours when I was assigned back in the US. The University of Maryland on Yokota Air Base, Japan agreed to give me my degree if I took two classes when I returned to the US and send them the grades, etc. I did that and was told I had satisfied the degree requirements. The University in the US said I did not satisfy the requirements because now I was on US soil I had to do an additional 16 semester hours on their Campus. It was a game I didn't have time to play and I had my degree completion paperwork from U of M in Japan.

The bad thing about taking courses at accredited colleges where I was stationed is not all those classes transfer to the next school. When I got my Bachelors Degree in Environmental Health and Safety

Engineering I had accumulated over 200 Semester hours for a 124 Semester hour degree!

So now I had an Associates Degree and two Batchelor Degrees. The one I received from Central Missouri State University, I did have to go on Campus. So I used another military program, "Operation Bootstrap" that was intended for Enlisted people to attend college and then graduate within one year and become a Commissioned Officer. I went on Campus, which was a few miles from Whitman Air Force Base and worked a deal to stay on the Base for a much reduced price. I still did not take out a loan. The way the program works is you go to college for one year, you must get a degree during that year and then pay back 3 to 1. For one year on campus you had to extend your service commitment for three years.

When I got there it was questionable if I could carry the 37 semester hours in one year! Since I was not working all day and school at night I completed the 37 hours in 8 months! Was told it was a new record. So my commitment to the Air Force was only another two years. That was a bit expensive because of the books and housing., but again, no student loan.

As I was getting ready to retire from the Air Force there were people who asked two big questions. How could I afford to get three degrees, and how could I afford to retire? I was asked to talk to a group and I basically told them there are resources like "Operation Bootstrap" that you can use to get a degree. It doesn't take much to find programs, just go to an Education Counselor on the Base.

Second question, just about everyone I talked to had a new car, new truck, maybe a boat, etc. that had long loans and often high interest rates. I couple I talked with said when they got an offer for a new credit card that offered great deals, you could transfer other credit to this and save. Many jumped on that feet first. So I asked if they had canceled the old one and I got responses from they occasionally used it or they threw it away! When I told them their credit took the full value of the card so if they had two max $15,000 cards that meant they basically had

$30,000 in debt! Even if they threw the card away and not talked to the bank about cancelling the card.

I brought this up to show there are ways to work within the system and not hold your breath for the taxpayers to bail you out.

Now to the Masters Degree, I was working for General Dynamics and I wanted to further prove I am not Stupid. So I checked out UCLA and USC but the PhD Industrial Hygienist in the office talked about National University, It is one taught by working professionals and I immediately did a curriculum comparison and I could get my Masters from professionals in the field instead of from a book. They were much cheaper also. I did pay a lot there but nothing like the cost of a university like USC!

I sat down with the scheduler and all the classes I wanted just fit in. I was told most people took a break between every class because they were that intensive on top of you working all day! I set my schedule and locked in the classes. My Counsellor wasn't very happy, she believed I was pushing too hard!

Ten months later I graduated with a Masters Degree in Environmental Health and Safety Management. I had just broken the record! And although my final teacher was for thesis or Research, I chose to do Research, something I had done for years. The teacher accepted my topic but said he did not want to see a Hypothesis in the paper! Research always has a hypothesis that states if you do this the specific result would happen.. If it didn't we could still learn from the Null Hypothesis, He said my grades would reflect if I used a Hypothesis, and I had three Hypothesis in my paper. My 4.0 GPA was shattered, his grade brought me down to a 3.85

The Dean was somewhat shocked when I took this "Less than perfect" research project and submitted it to the American Society of Safety Engineers (ASSE) and my paper was one of four papers Worldwide to be presented on Washington DC!

I still never had a Student Loan.

And my PhD was a fluke. I was happy having four degrees, the most ever in our family and the bragging rights of "Am I stupid Now". I was helping the lady who worked for me to find an Accredited Distance Learning curriculum so she could get a degree. She was saddled with two kids and it was hard. I found one and while talking to them they said they had a Doctorate Degree in Environmental Health and Safety Management! I got the information and went to the company management, proved it would greatly enhance out status with a PhD running the program, so they paid the lion's share. No student loans.

Five degrees, no student loans, there are so many colleges, universities, grant programs and even companies that will supplement with grants, etc. to help you get your education.

A recent study approached the topic of "Tuition Forgiveness" and the majority of college students interviewed thought that was great! However, most had no idea how it was going to be paid for. Responses ranged from more money being printed by the President, mothers in the area of the University would pay for it, and the University was just going to forgive! When asked if those who worked to pay off their student loans should get compensated, most responded that it wasn't fair if they didn't and a lot hadn't thought about it.

So for those struggling, there are resources. For those that threw money at a prestigious university and now wants us to pay for their inability to use programs available, I just want to ask, "Did you try?" Your education is valuable, it is you. Yet so many go to ultra expensive universities so they can say they graduated from a prestigious university and expect to be hired because of that. I equate it to a doctor seeing you and believes the white lab coat makes him someone you must trust! I worked on a special project with a guy who had a "Named" degree. He did mention it a couple times. When we got into the project he was lost on how to proceed when it came to something he did not know. I showed him the process and he asked how come I knew it and he didn't? I told him that being Head of Safety on a military Base that had all facilities the same as a city, you had to learn so much about everything. And "Street Smarts" are so valuable. As I said about finding someone with experience over education if it meets your Vision and Goals, I never look down on someone who doesn't have a formal education, I work with and learn from them.

Bottom line; you may have gone to school with the intention to get prestige or maybe an honest education. Whatever, now you go to work, be part of a capitalistic society, and pay your bills. You can spend some time getting grants and scholarships to help, but please don't expect us taxpayers to pay your bill.

I hope this segment brought out avenues and concepts to get past the barriers and costs of the education system, I am a simple boy from Maine who was forced to look for things that I could use in my effort to prove to my mother that "I am not stupid!"

51

Why?:

When asked why I have to be first and best at what I do I only say that is what is in my DNA. Actually it isn't, because my DNA was so bruised as a child. I just wanted to scream from the roof tops "I AM NOT STUPID!" I guess doing that in itself would be stupid and bring attention to my deep insecurities, I have many. I am always trying to prove myself and based a lot of it on my childhood and my mother.

I have seen a few great psychiatrists and psychologists like Gina Simmons who pulled me out of the mental fire after Michael was killed at General Dynamics. I think she alluded to all the people's lives I have saved, or given them options they didn't have before could easily have been a multi pronged problem. I had to prove something to my mother, and sister. I didn't believe life was that important, why I swam out to save a girl from drowning, went into an area where I could be shot to drag a guy in, pulled a guy out of a jet aircraft intake, became a top motorcycle fatality investigator yet drove motorcycles knowing the hazards. And when shots were fired at us in Vietnam I stayed standing while others dove for cover and I shot the man who was going to shoot me. My first kill, can't remember any of the others but see the face of that first one every day. And the orphan boy I could not save. They all add up.

When I came out of my clinical depression I talked with another great professional and one I trust. We determined the inability of me to think a single thought and not having everything feed off a thought into scrambled mentality probably happened at a fairly young age. I had been depressed for decades. There were a lot of poor decisions I made. Looking back maybe I should have become a Medical Doctor, as one good example. But the worst thing I ever did was lose the trust of Peggy and almost lose her. There would be no surviving that, I would not live without her.

And during that time we were finding ourselves and me looking in the mirror asking myself first as to why I treated her so bad, and what was my real worth to anyone, we both learned an extremely important and emotional thing. We learned that if something is wrong it will occupy 90% of you. If you are always thinking of something, thinking you should have done something you didn't do, or are someplace you don't want to be, you are stuck. That 10% of your mind and being does not allow you to move.

I saw this in medical problems, social problems, life problems. If you believe you are terminally ill, your brain's 10% isn't enough. You worry about what you wanted to say to someone but didn't, it is hard to think of anything else. And if you are up against a barrier of any kind, it is hard to think of how to get past it with that 10%. For that reason, I am quick to embrace the philosophy of not worrying about things you cannot control. I could give you hundreds of examples but one comes to my mind often. What would have happened if I continued to think I was stupid? I could not control what others thought of me, so that word was no longer 90% of me. I could see past that barrier and see the opportunities.

One of my Veteran friends was in a rut and sinking deeper. We talked and his mind was tied to his situation. On top of that we both knew people that chose suicide as their only option. Like Jim laying in a pool of blood with one option, to die. I gave him another option. I took away the 90%. My friend concentrated on the 10% and it grew to where he saw possibilities! He saw what he could do, not ask why he could do nothing. About 8 months after we talked he took a job with the local VA. He found his time in the military could be used working with other former military members. He enjoys what he is doing and has been moving up within the system. I saw him a couple times while on travel and he seems happy. His nickname for me is "10%".

When asked "Why" as to what I did, what I achieved, why I can't settle for normal, I have said Altruism played a part. Under my high school yearbook picture where others wrote something funny or witty, I wrote the Shakespeare phrase, "To Thine Own Self Be True".

I really don't like conflict but many of my friends say that they are torn between being with me and avoiding me! So much has happened but when something happens I take care of it. I was told recently that I was a borderline narcissistic and that was what drove me to be better and first at everything. Don't let the bastard get you down.

So do I hate my mother and highly dislike my sister? My sister has a lot of my mother's traits and she can piss me off in a second with her blame game. When she calls me stupid I have to bite my tongue. But I find if I don't put myself in those situations, I can and do love my sister, I tell her that when we talk.

I studied Buddhism enough to know or at least understand the Wheel of Nirvana. And to believe you can't understand heat until you understand cold, same as you can't understand Hate until you understand Love. I thought and professed my hatred for my mother, maybe more disrespect than hate for her. And now I have the love of Peggy and her staying with me despite all my problems, especially Agent Orange and PTSD, it is more than I deserve but I deserve to appreciate and love it. I love her.

<h1 style="text-align:center">52</h1>

Mother:

Susan wanted to see Mom while we were up from Boston so I called ahead and we drove up to see her. She could not see us, her eyesight she let go, as she did her teeth. The last time I saw her she had blamed me for her losing her teeth and her curly hair. She was so nasty about it we took the girls and never went back. Susan wanted to see her grandmother, who was 92 years old.

Susan and I went into the Home and saw my mother. She was in a special room because she could not take care of herself at all. I said "Hi" to her but never touched her, Susan sat there and held her hand. Both Mom and Susan enjoyed that and Mom had to ask me, even then, if I was still married to the wrong girl. Susan did not understand. We stayed for a short while and Susan gave Mom a hug and I just said my goodbyes. When we left with Susan driving I casually asked her if she was glad to see her grandmother? I didn't mean to be as blunt as I was, however I told Susan that would be the last time she would see her grandmother. Susan was shocked and asked why I would say anything like that? I felt I knew and told her that she had just talked to her son and was now ready to die. Susan was upset.

All the years I had worked in a hospital, had responded to fatal or near fatal accidents and incidents, while interviewing witnesses had detected an unlawful comment and had stopped and legally administered the Miranda Act, and I am so glad it happened only once where a survivor at the scene asked me to administer Last Rights. I saw so much pain and so much resolve of those who let death take them, I could feel it. A very close couple to us went through hell as Cancer took over his body. One day he told his wife he was tired of fighting and let himself die two days later. My mother had waited to talk to her son and then let herself die. She was one month shy of age 93.

When I was dong my dissertation for my PhD I announced that I was not going to complete the PhD program because I knew if my mother ever called me "Doctor" it would be with malice. My sister and Susan talked me into completing the dissertation, which was the first published work of "Safety Within A Multicultural, Bilingual Workplace".

I still was mad at my mother, blaming her for many of the problems I had and had uncovered with professional help. When we got past my Clinical Depression we got out that it did not start with the Vietnam War, it most likely started when I was a child! Having one degree in Psychology I will be the first to denounce the "Blame it on your mother" syndrome, however we could see specific things that I grew up with, i.e. being called "Stupid" all the time and total support for my sister but none for me. It of course doesn't help that my sister still says I am stupid, a reason we don't see her much. I call her and we email and I tell her truthfully I love her, but I have some control over the conversation when not face to face.

Now I am not a "Road Warrior" traveling close to 300 days a year, and I don't have to put up with arrogant, narcissistic, assholes who think they know everything and believe they are above the law and can treat people like crap, I can breathe and think things through.

My thoughts are real and truthful. I have one issue I will never get past but the issue with my mother, no matter how nasty it was, I chose to move above it. I know all I did where others dared not to, putting myself in harms way, saving nine lives, etc. was my response to say emphatically "I AM NOT STUPID!"

I almost cry when I see kids going through what I did, being told they are stupid, not worth anything, a failure, not as good as their brother/sister, etc. because it has deep pain and severe damage is being done. I have talked to people who think the only way out is to take their own life, I have been there. I have literally talked a teenage girl off a high ledge. I talked a guy down, until a cop hit him along side his head with a long flashlight! He was spraying oven cleaner in his mouth and had a knife to his own throat. I just brought him down to where someone else could handle him.

I remember the young girl with pig tails and a fist print on her temple that died just minutes before our ambulance could get her to Raleigh Durham Hospital. I saw before she was taken in our ambulance how she went to her mother in hopes of lesser abuse, and that observation alone was the reason how they got her abusive murderer.

I remember the young photographer at the traffic accident scene that said the scene was to bloody for her to take the pictures. When I offered her to either take the pictures as I instructed her to or she would be out of a job, she told the world I was not a nice human being and I had no compassion! Yet she learned from me and found out what it was like being a professional. I never abused her or put her down in any way and she later said I was so different because I respected her where others didn't, and then proclaimed I was probably the most com-passionate person she had ever met. I can still see her smiling and saying she knew I was human when she heard after leaving a bloody scene I often stopped along the side of the road, away from any onlookers, and tossed my cookies. My sense of humor is still a little morbid as that was how we took the snake in our guts from seeing all this and made a worm of it. There are still people I know well that when I start to make a joke out of a tragic situation will say, "No Bruce, now is not the time, please!" I was at one bloody scene where an officer was bragging about how he had saved the enlisted guy's life by putting pressure on this guy's ear that was nearly cut off! I said, "Sir, you are an officer, all you had to do was order him to pull himself together!" When a guy died from an industrial accident, I was asked what I thought happened, and before I told him my analysis, i said, "It was just a dead end job".

There is no humor to the way I went through my young life. I just would not give up trying to prove stupidity was not a directed out-come. Many things I had done, like the letter to the head of VA to get disability for my PTSD, I discussed with my psychiatrist that I felt very torn because there are so many Veterans with problems like mine that will never get better because they don't have the resources or acquired talent to compose and send a letter as I did. He told me that many things like my experience with Transcendental Meditation and like the CD I gave him of spoken words to music that helped clear the mind. Because of my young years with Ida Hughes who taught me the mind was so much faster and I needed to tap into it to stop my stuttering, opened the door for me to process things before the "Fight or Flight" reaction stops everything. Why was I the one who pulled out the guy being sucked into the jet intake while others were frozen, and when I went out and saved the drowning girl while onlookers were frozen from reacting. And why did I step out into the courtyard and pull in a guy who had been shot in the back of his head while others yelled not to or were frozen? It would be easier to say it was because I am really crazy, but I don't think that is it at all. I now have to change my lifelong excuse, I must thank my mother.

You hear that God does not challenge you to fail, He will challenge you to succeed, He will not give you more than you can handle, etc. I am not an openly religious person, I despise the social hype many use church for, I worship by myself. I was asked once if I had only one religion I could honor, what would it be? I said many people think Buddhism is a religion but I know Buddha was not a God, he was an educator. And his beliefs that you must know and understand yourself on the road to Nirvana is my goal. To like myself, like others, make a difference, and be at peace, to me, is my goal. God is, of course a big part of that. My mother was just my excuse to do things under the premise I was to prove I wasn't stupid, but really I pushed myself to be someone that did things for others. My mother unknowingly pushed me to where I am today.

When airplanes were hijacked and the 9/11 aircraft that crashed because of the passengers overpowering the terrorists, a couple of the ladies Peggy worked with asked her if she was going to stop me from flying, and what did she think I would do if I was on a flight like that?

Peggy told them that I had to fly, and if something like that happened on a flight I was on, she simply told them that I would probably be the first one to get up, even knowing it would be my last act.

My psychiatrist I saw during the aftermath of the General Dynamics shooting said so many things that I believe I have led my life doing. When I told her what was asked me at Michael's funeral and my answer, I also stated I became a person who helps people, helps make them safe, and I said such a horrible thing when asked if I had a gun would I have shot Robert Mack before he shot Michael. Gina's response; "Thats your dark side, live with it!" When Jim English told national TV that he wishes whoever dragged him in, hadn't, I talked to Gina and she said he had only one option before I dragged him in, I gave him another option. Maybe that was my thinking, I gave people options they didn't have.

My friend I helped get a job at Cape Canaveral was supposed to understudy the Safety Manager for a year or more and take over his job. I contacted him near a year later and asked how he was liking the top job? His response was that he chose to stay at "grunt" level and not top management, because "We all can't do what you do!" I asked what he meant and he said many of the people we both worked with agreed I did one thing they could not do! "What?" and he said all had to think and sometimes double think their decisions where I made a decision and that was it, I didn't second guess my decision! I told him a simple secret, you develop a foundation of Knowledge, Education, Experience and Ethics. If the question or decision falls within that foundation and you make a decision, then there is no reason to question it, unless circumstances change or you admittedly are weak in that area. I believe my foundation covers a lot of things and I am constantly making it bigger and better. When I jumped in the save the drowning girl I immediately knew I had training as a Lifeguard and knew what I was doing, I didn't guess. Same as the Vietnamese firing at us, I knew my skills were adequate and although I killed a human being I believe I saved many lives in the truck that day. Ironically, I was forced to lie about the incident to protect my superior's ego, and when my coworker lied about what he did in the shooting, none of that mattered because I knew what I had done. If I thought about how much credit or publicity an act would bring, I would probably not have done the deed.

After the shooting and 14 of us were getting awards/rewards for what we did, I spoke up against it. I was the only one. I stated I was just doing what I was trained and paid to do, as did the others. I refused the Hawaii trip but relented when I was told my actions jeopardized the rewards for the others. And, of course, that trip was basically so I could have time with Peggy in Hawaii.

A young lady came to my office and said her friends had told her to come see me because she had just lost her job. She told me what her friends said and added, "What, do you have a job for me?" I listened, sort of interviewing her. She had a sharp tongue and a little pushy, but I decided to help her. I told her I would and told her she would be my guest at the next professional Society luncheon. I told her to send me her resume and what to wear to the meeting. She exploded and said loudly, "Are you telling me how to dress?" I calmly said yes. She got three job offers at that meeting. I continued to mentor her and when a high level job came on the market a year or so later she said she wanted to put in for it. I told her if I was the hiring person for that job, I wouldn't hire her! She exploded again! When she calmed down I said she didn't have the skills and experience in the area, but told her I would help her. When the job came open, she submitted her resume and I was the first reference for her. Later in the process she asked me if the Manager contacted me? "No". She said he contacted all her other references. I told her his boss contacted me. "Why?' I told her it had something to do with me being a PhD. She asked what I said but I would not tell her. After she got the job she asked again and I told her I had told the top man that if he hired her he was hiring one and a half people because I would never stop mentoring her! I showed my boss a letter she wrote me a while later, thanking me, and ending with the statement that I had helped so any people, "There will be standing room only at your funeral!"

So my mother put me down so far I didn't know when to stop rising to escape the literal abuse. I pray many who are living the life I led have the strength and opportunity to rise above it, and that they take some good people with them along the way. It seems funny to say that because it seems everything I have done to exception was because of a wrongdoing. Prior to the near fatal car accident I was an "A" or "B" student but after 7 months of recovery I not only was a failing student in both schoolwork and what I loved the most, sports, I was last in my class to barely graduate yet when I go back home I go as the most educated person ever to Graduate!

When I was asked to be one of the Charter Members of the first Air Force motorcycle Safety Training class, I was happy doing safety work, but my old boss volunteering me to be an Augmentee Driver, I would not have met such people as the Chairman of the Joint Chiefs of Staff, two Secretaries of the Air Force, the Prime Minister of Japan, etc. and because of my work with that I became the first person to retrain into Safety because of the highest ranking person in the Air Force! I also would not have had the opportunity to know an American hero, a Prisoner of War for over 6 years!

Because my first fatality investigation was my first official day at Safety and the person who died was a very close friend, Peggy and I toiled for a long time if I should pursue being a Safety person because of that first fatality, but it pushed me to be the best I could be. I saw early my weaknesses and tried to make them strengths, and I had three wonderful Mentors that helped me be a professional. When I was in the first few safety professionals who were awarded the Board of Certified Safety Professionals Award of Excellence, I was technically the second in the World, I asked the CEO of the Board what I had done to achieve this lofty award? She said, "You know what you did!" I guess Peggy knew it all along, "You have to be first and best at everything you do!" she also said I was borderline Narcissist!

When I became the top Weapons Mechanic on the Lead Crew that came into being and since I was recognized as such, I was sent to do the hard jobs and traveled a lot. Later in Safety I rose to the top and my last four assignments in the Air Force were "By Name" request and always to fix a problem. I traveled a lot and in doing so I wanted Peggy to see all of the world. She was in Spain for 4 years and Japan for 3, and because one day I said we should spend the little money left us from Dad's estate to travel as he had said when he visited us that he envied our travel. Maybe as a homage to that and maybe because Peggy and I are really a great couple when we travel, and definitely that we have seen so many other cultures we love coming back to ours, we travel and honor that time.

If my mother had not abused me growing up I might not have stuttered so much, and again the teacher would not have helped me cure that by using my brain before my mouth and using a lot of my brain usually untouched. That allowed me to do stuff like instead of standing with my hand to my face and pointing at the drowning girl, like everyone there was doing, I would not have been able to assess and tap into my skills to swim out and save her without a second thought. And be able to assess which parent was the abuser of the little girl. And have the wit about myself when being shot at to use my experience and shoot him before he shot us.

I traveled throughout the States speaking on Workplace Violence. I was a contributor to two books on that subject and was involved in writing about proper and safe worker termination processes. I talked on many safety subjects and when the investigation into the death of Sheri Sangji at the UCLA Laboratory fire December 29, 2008, I was the only outsider invited to be a part of the group brought together to see what could be done to prevent recurrence. All others, except one Government Official were from UCLA, I was not. One of the principle players from UCLA had sat in on one of my lectures and commented my understanding of safety concepts was needed in the group. My suggestion concerning hiring for experience and expertise instead of for the number of letters behind your name became part of their hiring guidelines. I'm proud of that.

I was always looking to strengthen my perceived weaknesses. One was I felt I could not think precise enough, memory was always a challenge, until I came out of my lifelong depression. I thought better, forgot less and chose to improve that, so I enrolled in the Memory Institute! The guy who presented it looked at the room full of students and asked each one of us to tell him our name and what we did. After he heard all this he told each to stay standing. Then he would point to a student and he would tell them their name and occupation and tell them to sit down! There were over 100 students in the room and he knew each and every one of them! Then he gave us a verbal list of 20 items delivered by his voice in 47 seconds. He passed out blank paper to each of us and told us to write down all 20 items in order! We did, then passed the paper to the person next to us. He then said the 20 items and we checked them off. When he asked who got all 20 right, four hands rose. He asked of those four, how many had attended the class previously? All four had. When he said "19" the guy next to me raised his hand, he was scoring my paper. So the instructor asked if I had attended before? "No" Had I attended any class like this before? "No". He asked again and then said that was remarkable and that I should see what the next number was. No hands until number 13! We talked and he said my system was better than most but I should learn two things; how to store information for recall, and how to use "Graphic Realization". That is putting a figure or cartoon or something "on a person's shoulder" so I would see it every time and remember their name, etc. I know there are skeptics, I also know how to turn this into an art.

When I was getting prepared to speak at a convention or in front of a group, I would look around the room and in sequence place a transition item on a fixed item. For instance, I was talking about Communication and the first transition was to discuss the telephone. So on the flagpole to the immediate left of the stage I put an old fashioned telephone cartoon like character on it in my mind. So when I started talking I used no notes and transitioned to each talking point as I looked around the room at my Graphic Realizations on objects like I had memorized the speech! When another speaker at the event asked me, "Do you have a photographic memory?" I would tell him that I have a trained memory. I equate that as my success with teaching and advancing in my profession.

I guess this is where I have to let go of not only the hatred but the constant need to be better and to prove I am not stupid. Mom is gone but I hung on too long, I have to move on. I didn't love my mother but now I have to say her early abuse was the driving force I needed to not accept what was given me but to move past it. I hate to think I am saying thank you to her, but maybe I am. It might show I have grown past it.

The altruistic meaning of this book is to reach out to those who feel they can't go forward or have the feeling they have gone as far as they can. I fought the stigma of not having money, having an abusive childhood and alcoholic parents. It was not a normal childhood, but it is reality of similar stories. If one of those living in that trap can see there are resources and avenues to move forward. Mine was the military, I know of others who were helped by teachers, mentors, coworkers, specialists, caring people, and God. Set a goal, maybe a small step or a dream, and reach for it. Build a foundation you don't have to second guess. Ask directions. Go over, under, or around those barriers. Do it with integrity and ethics. Be passionate.

I remember telling a good friend once that his barrier was himself! He was passionate to a fault, very outspoken, and usually right. But he was so persistent and pushy that soon he didn't have a problem, he became the problem. When he called or walked in the front door people didn't see him anymore as a man with a problem, they would say, "Here he comes again!" You can win the war without winning all battles.

The best and worst for last. Growing up I hardly ever used the word "love", it had little meaning and actually was something Peggy got upset with me for not telling her I loved her. I have since agreed with myself that it is often said with little love behind it, however, I am here today because of the love of and for Peggy. She has literally saved my life with her devoted and undying support and love for me. I have daughters, granddaughters, a grandson, and a great grandson and great granddaughter who I love unconditionally. I will continue to be there for Peggy and show her my undying love. I'll get her flowers when I feel like it, not when a greeting card company tells me I should. I will show her the world until we can't anymore. I truly love you Peggy.

And the one thing I cannot forget or forgive, I never got the chance to say "goodbye" to my father. I'll see you later, Dad.

9 798986 139920